A History of the Ancient Near East

ca. 3000–323 BC

Blackwell History of the Ancient World

This series provides a new narrative history of the ancient world, from the beginnings of civilization in the ancient Near East and Egypt to the fall of Constantinople. Written by experts in their fields, the books in the series offer authoritative accessible surveys for students and general readers alike.

Published

A History of the Ancient Near East ca. 3000–323 BC, third edition
Marc Van De Mieroop

A History of the Later Roman Empire, AD 284–621, second edition
Stephen Mitchell

A History of the Hellenistic World
R. Malcolm Errington

A History of the Ancient Near East ca. 3000–323 BC, second edition
Marc Van De Mieroop

A History of the Classical Greek World, second edition
P. J. Rhodes

A History of the Later Roman Empire, AD 284–621
Stephen Mitchell

A History of Byzantium, second edition
Timothy E. Gregory

A History of Ancient Egypt ca. 3000–323 BC
Marc Van De Mieroop

A History of the Archaic Greek World, second edition
Jonathan M. Hall

A History of Greece, ca. 1300 to 30 BC
Victor Parker

In Preparation

A History of the Roman Republic
John Rich

A History of the Roman Empire
Michael Peachin

A History of Babylon, 2200 BC–75 AD
Paul-Alain Beaulieu

A History of the Achaemenid Persian Empire
Maria Brosius

A History of the Ancient Near East

ca. 3000–323 BC

Third Edition

Marc Van De Mieroop

WILEY Blackwell

This third edition first published 2016
© 2016 John Wiley & Sons, Inc.

Edition history: Blackwell Publishing Ltd (1e, 2004 and 2e, 2007)

Registered Office
John Wiley & Sons Ltd, The Atrium, Southern Gate, Chichester, West Sussex, PO19 8SQ, UK

Editorial Offices
350 Main Street, Malden, MA 02148-5020, USA
9600 Garsington Road, Oxford, OX4 2DQ, UK
The Atrium, Southern Gate, Chichester, West Sussex, PO19 8SQ, UK

For details of our global editorial offices, for customer services, and for information about how to apply
for permission to reuse the copyright material in this book please see our website at
www.wiley.com/wiley-blackwell.

The right of Marc Van De Mieroop to be identified as the author of this work has been asserted in
accordance with the UK Copyright, Designs and Patents Act 1988.

Library of Congress Cataloging-in-Publication Data

Van De Mieroop, Marc.
   A history of the ancient Near East ca. 3000–323 BC / Marc Van De Mieroop. – Third edition.
       pages cm
   Includes bibliographical references and index.
   ISBN 978-1-118-71816-2 (paperback)
   1. Middle East–History–To 622.   I. Title.
   DS62.2.V34 2016
   939′.4–dc23   2015005041

A catalogue record for this book is available from the British Library.

Cover image: King Shalmaneser III meeting a Babylonian king, from pedestal of throne of Shalmaneser
III, 858–824 BC Assyrian king, 9th century BC from Nimrud. Photo © The Art Archive/Alamy.

Set in 10.5/12.5pt PlantinStd by Aptara Inc., New Delhi, India
Printed and bound in Malaysia by Vivar Printing Sdn Bhd

1   2016

Contents

Sept 12
2016

Illustrations

Charts

Maps

Debates

Boxes

Documents

Preface

In the year 334 BC, a young king from Macedon and his well-trained army crossed from Europe into Asia, confronted the vast empire of Persia, and conquered it in the course of a decade. Alexander's troops marched through an antique world that contained the remains of thousands of years of earlier history. Their previous encounter with Greece could not have prepared them for what they saw in the Near East and Egypt. They entered cities like Uruk that had existed for three millennia, and visited pyramids and temples that had stood for almost as many years. This was a world steeped in history, not a world in decline, waiting for fresh inspiration. The city-dwellers knew their traditions were so ancient that they claimed they dated from the beginning of time itself. People wrote in scripts that had been used for almost thirty centuries, they read and copied texts that were hundreds of years old. These were not idle claims, as for a long time their lands had indeed been home to the most advanced cultures in the world, well before Greece had developed its great classical civilization.

It is in the Near East and northeast Africa that many of the elements we associate with advanced civilization first originated, including agriculture, cities, states, writing, laws, and many more. Because this region lies at the juncture of three continents, practices and concepts from numerous and diverse people came together there, inspired and complemented one another, and were used by the inhabitants to manipulate their surroundings. They created their environment rather than reacting to it. This had happened over many centuries, indeed millennia, through processes that saw developments both smooth and abrupt, reversals of fortune, and false starts. Today we are naturally attracted to finding out how and why such things happened, and who was involved. Nineteenth- and early twentieth-century scholarship used to trace the roots of modern civilization in the ancient history of this region, but an approach of this kind is no longer acceptable as we now realize that history is not just a long and uninterrupted evolution from a single source. We can assert, however, that in the Near East and northeast Africa, we are able to study for the first time in history how humans lived, in circumstances that include many of the elements of our own culture. We can study this on the basis of a written record as well as from material remains, since the first literate societies in world history are found there. And this study acquires greater poignancy because we often see the indigenous creation of cultural factors here, rather than elements borrowed from elsewhere.

The Near East and Egypt encompass a vast area, stretching from the Black Sea to the Aswan dam, and from the Aegean Sea to the highlands of Iran, an area that was densely inhabited throughout its history. The diversity of cultures and histories in this entire stretch is immense, too vast to describe in a single book. Therefore I shall deal only with the Near East, that is, the regions of the Asian continent, and shall exclude Egypt from the discussion. This still leaves us to deal with an enormous collection of peoples, cultures, languages, and traditions. There is a certain unity in this diversity, however, that makes combined study desirable. In the variety we can see numerous similarities. Political and military circumstances at times brought many of these people together under a single system, and we can see almost constant processes of social and cultural interaction and exchange that connected the varied regions.

Near Eastern history should not be one of beginnings only, or of interest solely because it provides the earliest evidence on questions the historian can ask. Many other aspects are involved. It is a history of some three thousand years, a period somewhat longer than that which separates us from Homer. This long time span, with its countless people, can be studied through a continuous historical record that enables us to see changing circumstances and human reactions with a detail that exists nowhere else in the ancient world. The past has been described as a foreign country, and to study it is like traveling: we meet people who are much like us, but also distinctly different. As when we travel, our access is restricted and we do not get to see everything. We are nevertheless provided with an abundance of information for the ancient Near East, and that abundance enables us to see much more than for many other cultures of the past.

As visitors to a foreign country, we do not comprehend all we see, because we are not full participants in the lives and cultures we encounter. Hopefully, however, we learn to appreciate differences as responses to challenges and opportunities that are as human as our own. We learn that our habits of behavior and thinking are not the only ones that make sense. Historians are like travel guides: claiming greater familiarity with the foreign countries than their readers, they point out what they find interesting, and phrase their enthusiasm in ways they find logical. They hope to inform readers, while inviting them to explore further. That is the aim of this book, too: it provides an introduction to a rich and fascinating subject that can be examined in many ways, and from many different perspectives. It is *A History*, not *The History*. Since the material at hand is so abundant and diverse, a summary book like this one will necessarily present the author's personal view on the subject, and my interests and prejudices are clearly reflected in the topics I address and the interpretations I suggest. The intent is not to write a definitive history of this region and era of human history, but to inspire readers to travel ahead on their own through this ancient Near Eastern world.

This is the third edition of this book, written a decade after the first one appeared. Readers familiar with earlier versions will notice both minor and major changes in the text. Those are partly the result of new research, which continues despite the fact that tragic events in today's Middle East make it impossible to visit many parts of the region. Some of the changes are the result of my own reconsideration of things and my shifting interests, although I maintain the basic approach that places political history at the center of the narrative. Some were inspired by published reviews or remarks made by teachers who use the book in class. I have added one chapter at the end and have introduced a new feature called Debate in each chapter. Because a survey like this by nature uses assertion and ignores the discussions among scholars about almost every point, I provide sections in which I outline a number of approaches and scholarly stances on certain issues and provide bibliographical references. Those are still limited in number, but I hope will show students how researchers disagree and change views on certain topics.

I would like to thank the staff at Wiley Blackwell for its continued support for this book. I owe my greatest debt to a succession of groups of students at Columbia University, and for a while at the University of Oxford, who continue to force me to make sense of the material I study and who by their mere presence make it all worthwhile.

Marc Van De Mieroop
New York

Author's Note

I have tried to render the numerous names of places and persons in this book in a way that makes them as easily recognizable as possible. Thus, when a familiar English form exists, for example, Nebuchadnezzar instead of the more accurate Nabu-kudurri-usur, Aleppo instead of Halab, I use it. My colleagues will be aware that there is inconsistency in my practice, but they will know what the various renderings of such names are. For others, I hope it will facilitate reading this book. I have not attempted to represent some phonetic forms of the ancient Near Eastern languages, such as the emphatic s, pronounced ts, which is rendered as a simple s here. Long vowels are not especially indicated except when an entire term is in Akkadian.

I have tried to use terms in the various ancient languages of the Near East sparingly, but when I do, I follow the common practice in the discipline to render them in italics, except for those in Sumerian, which are in the regular font style.

In the translations of ancient texts, restorations of broken passages are not always indicated, in order to increase legibility of the text. When they are indicated, they appear between square brackets. When a word is partly inside the brackets, partly outside them, it indicates that part of it is still legible. Uncertain translations are in italics.

1

Introductory Concerns

1.1 What Is the Ancient Near East?

Few people use the phrase "Near East" today. Yet, it has survived in the study of ancient history in a scholarship that is rooted in the nineteenth century when the term identified the remains of the Ottoman empire on the eastern shores of the Mediterranean Sea. Today we say Middle East to designate this geographical area, but the two terms do not exactly overlap, and ancient historians and archaeologists continue to speak of the Near East. Already this habit gives a certain vagueness to what constitutes the ancient history of this area, and the geographical boundaries of the region can differ substantially from study to study. Some definitions, then, of what this book covers are in order.

In this survey of history, Near East designates the region from the eastern Mediterranean coast to central Iran, and from the Black Sea to the Red Sea. Egypt, whose ancient history intersects with that of the Near East at many times, is not included, except when its empire extended into Asia in the second half of the second millennium. The boundaries remain vague, because in essence we study a set of core areas, and the reach of each one of them shifted in different periods. Foremost in any study of the ancient Near East is Mesopotamia, a term we use to designate the area between the Tigris and Euphrates rivers in modern-day Iraq and northern Syria. It was home to many cultures and political formations, whose sequence we know well from an abundant documentation. At times Mesopotamian states extended far beyond their borders, drawing otherwise poorly known regions, such as the Arabian peninsula, into their orbit. The same is true for other core areas in central Anatolia, southwest Iran, and elsewhere. As historians, we rely on sources; their coverage, both in geographical terms and in what facets of life they document, fluctuates enormously over time. When they report on activity somewhere, that place becomes part of the Near East; when

A History of the Ancient Near East ca. 3000–323 BC, Third Edition. Marc Van De Mieroop.
© 2016 John Wiley & Sons, Inc. Published 2016 by John Wiley & Sons, Inc.

they do not, we have little to tell. The ancient history of the Near East is like a dark room in which the sources offer isolated points of light, some brighter than others. They shine especially clearly on certain places and periods, but leave much else concealed. It is the historian's task to try to make sense of the whole.

The chronological boundaries of ancient Near Eastern history are also ambiguous, and both the beginning and the end dates are flexible. If we consider history to rely on written sources, as tradition often does, the origins of writing in Babylonia around 3000 BC, must be seen as the start of history. Yet, script was just one of several innovations that had roots in earlier times, and the earliest texts contain no "historical" information that we can understand beyond the fact that people had the ability to write. Thus, most histories of the Near East start in so-called prehistory, oftentimes around 10,000, and describe the developments that took place before writing existed. During these seven thousand years, so many important changes happened in the lifestyles of humans that they deserve in-depth treatment, using archaeological sources and methodologies. There is not enough room in this book, which intends to discuss the historical periods thoroughly, to do full justice to all prehistoric developments. Therefore we will start in the late fourth millennium when several prehistoric processes culminated simultaneously, and also writing appeared, changing the nature of our source material. I will outline earlier developments only cursorily in this introduction.

History rarely knows clear-cut endings. Even when states are definitively destroyed, they leave an impact, the duration of which depends on whether one looks at political, economic, cultural, or other aspects of history. But the historian has to stop somewhere and the choice of when needs justification. Various dates are commonly used to end the ancient history of the Near East, most often either the fall of the last native Mesopotamian dynasty in 539 or Alexander of Macedon's defeat of Persia in 331. I have chosen Alexander as the last figure of my political history, because while the changes he instituted were probably not momentous for most of the people at that time, our access to the historical data is transformed starting in his reign. The gradual shift from indigenous to external classical sources necessitates a different historiographical approach. The arrival of Hellenism is a fitting borderline because the historian's access to events changes significantly.

Some twenty-seven centuries elapsed between 3000 and 331. Few historical disciplines engage with such a long time span, comparable to what is covered in surveys of European civilization that link Homeric Greece to the present day. While we can see clearly distinct periods in that western evolution and appreciate the pivotal changes that took place over time, it is harder to do so for ancient Near Eastern history. Our distance from the Near East, both in time and in spirit, sometimes leads to a view that blurs distinctions and reduces everything to one large static mass. On the other hand, one can take a diametrically opposed view and fragment this history into short, coherent, and manageable segments. Discontinuity then becomes the focus. The latter attitude lies at the basis of the standard periodization of Near Eastern history, which strings together a sequence of phases that are mostly named after royal dynasties. Each phase experienced its cycle of rise, prosperity, and decline, as if it were a biological entity, and in between fell the so-called Dark Ages, moments of historical silence.

I take an intermediate stance here, and while I maintain the traditional subdivisions into dynastic periods, I group them into larger units. We should not overemphasize continuities, but we can recognize basic patterns. In political terms, for example, power in the Near East was oftentimes fragmented and there were only relatively short-lived moments of centralization under rulers or dynasties whose territorial reach became increasingly wider. But these moments of centralization tend to draw our attention more, because they produced large numbers of written and archaeological sources. Taking the escalating growth of political forms into account, this history is divided into the ages of city-states, territorial states, and empires, each with their moments of greatness and disruption (if we equate power with greatness). The city-state was the primary political element from 3000 to approximately 1600, territorial states dominated the scene from that point on to the early first millennium, and empires characterized later history. Mesopotamian states usually demonstrate these stages of development most conclusively, but it is clear that they also occurred elsewhere in the Near East.

In the end, the availability and extent of the sources define the ancient Near East as a historical subject and subdivide its history. Extensive written and archaeological documentation appears in certain places at certain times, and those regions and moments form the core of the subject. The cultures of Mesopotamia dominate in this respect. They were often the leading civilizations of their time and had an impact over the entire Near East. When they influenced or controlled non-Mesopotamian regions, those areas become included in our research; when they did not, we often lose track of what happened outside Mesopotamia. Archaeological exploration in recent decades has made it increasingly apparent that other regions of the Near East experienced developments independent of Mesopotamia and that all cultural innovations cannot be credited to that area. Still, it remains difficult to write continuous histories of those regions without relying on a Mesopotamia-centered model. Mesopotamia provides the geographical and chronological unity to Near Eastern historiography. Its use of an age-old script, its preservation of religious practices, and its cultural continuity from the third to the first millennia allow us to look at its long history as a whole. The study of the other cultures in the region is mostly pegged to that of Mesopotamian culture, but we should not ignore their contributions to the history of the Near East.

1.2 The Sources

The presence of sources determines the confines of ancient Near Eastern history. Fortunately, they are incredibly abundant and varied in nature for the whole of this long history. Texts, the primary source for the historian, have survived in the hundreds of thousands – a recently published estimate speaks of more than one million. From early on, kings carved inscriptions on stone monuments, many of which were among the first archaeological finds made in Mesopotamia in

> ## Box 1.1   *What's in a name?*
>
> Just as the use of the term Near East is now uncommon outside the study of ancient history and archaeology, the exact meaning of many other geographical names is peculiar to those disciplines. Oftentimes usage is a matter of habit and it is rarely spelled out explicitly what names designate. They regularly derive from ancient sources, but their meaning was modified to indicate a somewhat different reality, oftentimes following British imperial terminology of the nineteenth century, when the study of the ancient Near East developed. One such term is Mesopotamia, a Greek label for the area encircled by the great bend of the Euphrates in Syria, but now applied to the entire region between the Tigris and Euphrates rivers and sometimes even beyond these boundaries. Two distinct zones make up Mesopotamia: Assyria in the north and Babylonia in the south. These are in origin political terms referring to ancient states that existed after 1450 BC, but they are often used purely as geographical designations at any time in history – I will use them in this way here. Many scholars utilize another political name, Sumer (or at times the non-existent Sumeria), to refer to the southern half of Babylonia in the fourth and third millennia. I do not follow that practice.
>
> Outside Mesopotamia, ancient Near Eastern histories often speak of the Levant, that is, where the sun rises from a European perspective, to designate the region along the eastern Mediterranean coast between Turkey and Egypt. To its north the Asiatic part of modern Turkey is usually referred to as Anatolia, a name derived from the Greek word for sunrise. Also the Roman phrase Asia Minor is used to refer to the same region. Country names, such as Iran, Syria, Egypt, and Israel often appear but their borders do not exactly coincide with those of the modern nation-states. The use of the term Iraq is rare, except for in British publications. Syria-Palestine and the adjective Syro-Palestinian is a purely geographical term. All this may sound confusing at first, but quite soon it is usually clear what the author has in mind.

modern times. More important, however, was the clay tablet, the medium of writing that developed in southern Mesopotamia and that all Near Eastern cultures adopted. It has amazing durability in the dry soil of the region, and texts from the receipt of a single sheep to the long *Epic of Gilgamesh* are plentiful. The survival of numerous documents of daily use distinguishes the ancient Near East from other ancient cultures. In Egypt, Greece, and Rome, similar things were written, but on parchment and papyrus, materials that have survived in unusual conditions only. The writings from the ancient Near East are rich not only in number but also in what they cover: the economy, royal building activity, military campaigns, government business, literature, science, and many other aspects of life are abundantly documented.

Archaeological material has become increasingly important as one of the historian's tools. Not only do excavations allow us to determine that the Hittites were present in northern Syria in the fourteenth century, for instance, but they also permit us to study the material conditions of their lives there. The Near East is covered with artificial mounds that were formed over the centuries by the debris of human occupation. Those are called *tell* in Arabic, *tepe* in Persian, and *hüyük* in Turkish, terms we find in the names of most archaeological sites. The possibilities for excavation are so great that we have only scratched the surface so far, despite more than 150 years of work. Major cities such as Uruk, Babylon, Nineveh, and Hattusa have been explored over many decades and have yielded numerous buildings, monuments, objects, and texts. But when one compares what has been uncovered with what remains hidden, it is clear that this is only a beginning. There remain thousands of unexplored sites, not all of which can be systematically investigated. Since dams, roads, and agricultural developments are constantly being built and threaten to annihilate ancient sites, rescue efforts often determine the selection of what is excavated.

We should not underestimate how much the ups and downs of archaeological exploration influence our outlook on Near Eastern history. Political circumstances in the modern Middle East especially have determined where one can excavate. Imperial competition between Great Britain and France in the mid-nineteenth century led their representatives to focus on the massive sites in northern Iraq, the region of Assyria. There they found the most impressive monuments to be displayed in national museums, which triggered the early interest in Assyrian history. Only later in the century, when concerns about origins peaked, did archaeologists explore the south of Iraq systematically, in search of the earlier Sumerians. More recent events have had a dramatic impact on archaeological research. The Iranian revolution of 1979, the Iraq wars of 1991 and 2003, the current civil war in Syria, and other conflicts have forced archaeologists to abandon projects, especially in the heartland of Mesopotamia. They have sought new terrain in regions previously considered peripheral, and thereby have highlighted developments there. As a consequence they forced us to reconsider the primacy and dominance of Mesopotamia in many aspects of history.

A final point needs to be made about the distribution and nature of the sources. In the ancient Near East, there is a direct correlation between political centralization of power, economic development, the construction of monumental architecture, and the increased production of written documents of all types. Thus the sources, both archaeological and textual, accentuate moments of political strength. History is by nature a positivistic science (meaning that we discuss what is preserved), and necessarily focuses on those moments for which the sources are most plentiful. In between appeared what we call the "Dark Ages." Still, there is almost a continuous coverage for the three millennia of ancient Near East history, and at times sources are very abundant. What is available for twenty-first century Babylonia, for example, surpasses in number and scope the written documentation from many later periods in history. The ancient Near East provides the first cultures in world history in which true and detailed historical research can take place. In this research we have to remain very aware of the nature of the sources, however. Since they derive almost exclusively from the institutions and individuals that held power, they focus on their activities and present their points of view. They always describe the successes of kings, for example, never their failures. They show the holders of power as the sole actors in societies, ignoring people and processes that opposed their actions or weakened their effectiveness. It is easy to be misled into seeing the history of the ancient Near East as a long sequence of glorious deeds of kings, whose holds on their societies was absolute. That was certainly not the case and throughout history policies failed, opposing trends operated, individuals and communities escaped the controls the official sources proclaim to have existed, and so on. Counter narratives existed, but we cannot recover them from explicit accounts. Instead we need to question those accounts we do have – to read between the lines – to balance out the picture.

1.3   Geography

The Near East is a vast landmass situated at the intersection of three continents: Africa, Asia, and Europe. Three tectonic plates meet there and their movements determine the geology of the region. The Arabian plate presses to the north underneath the Iranian plate, pushing it upwards, and is itself forced down. Where the two plates meet, there is a long depression stretching from the Mediterranean Sea to the Persian Gulf in which the Tigris and Euphrates rivers flow, turning a desert into highly fertile land wherever their waters reach. The African and Arabian plates meet at the western edge of the Near East and are separated by a narrow valley alongside the Amanus and Lebanon mountains, which run parallel to the Mediterranean coast. There is little room for coastal settlement except in the south, where the plain widens. The north and the east of the Near East are also dominated by high mountain ranges, the Taurus and Zagros, which contain the sources of all rivers in the region. The south of the region is a huge flat landmass, forming the Syrian and Arabian deserts. These become more mountainous the farther south one goes and they are almost entirely deprived of water.

Geological phenomena, earthquakes and volcanic eruptions, as well as the effects of wind, rain, and water have created a highly diverse area. Quite in contrast to the popular view of the Middle East as a flat monotonous expanse, the variation in natural environments is enormous, ranging from large marshes to vast arid deserts and from low-lying alluvial zones to high mountains. Also on a local scale great ecological variation exists in distinct microenvironments. Two examples demonstrate this. Babylonia, the area between the Persian Gulf and modern-day Baghdad, may seem an area with little diversity that relied on irrigation by the Euphrates and Tigris rivers for its survival. But that stretch contained very different ecological zones. The north was a desert plateau where agriculture was only possible in the narrow river valleys. Somewhat downstream the rivers entered a flat alluvium, but still had clearly defined channels, allowing for irrigation agriculture in square fields. South of the city of Babylon the rivers broke up into constantly shifting branches that ran almost on top of the land, and numerous man-made canals brought water into elongated fields. Finally, near the Persian Gulf vast marshes made agriculture impossible. In each of these zones distinct ecological niches were present in close proximity to one another, depending on access to water and other factors, each providing a variety of resources: fish and reeds in the marshes, fodder for herds of sheep in the northern steppe, and so on. The extent and location of these niches shifted due to natural factors and human activity, and the landscape underwent change over time. But natural diversity always characterized the area we summarily call Babylonia.

In the mountains of the Lebanon there was an even greater range of ecologies. The Beqa'a valley between the Lebanon and Anti-Lebanon ranges is some 100 kilometers long and 25 kilometers wide. On a map this small area looks uniform, but there are local differences. The high mountains cause plenty of rainfall on the western side; the area to the east is consequently dry. Springs, while numerous, are unevenly dispersed through the region and the Orontes River is not a good source for irrigation water. Wetlands alternate with very dry areas, zones of intensive horticulture with zones where only animal herders can survive. The valley is thus a collection of what has been called micro-ecologies, each enabling different lifestyles.

Within this vast area we have to recognize great variability in the natural environment. However, there are certain basic characteristics with important repercussions for the livelihood of the inhabitants. Agriculture, the prerequisite for the permanent settlement of large populations, is difficult. Rainfall is scarce almost everywhere because the high mountains in the west leave large parts of the Near East in the rain shadow. Agriculture that relies on rain, so-called dry farming, requires at least 200 mm of water annually. The 200 mm isohyet, that is, the line that connects those points of equal rainfall, runs in a great arch from the southern Levant to the Persian Gulf. The mountains and foothills receive more rain, the plains less to almost none at all. But the line on the map is misleading: annual variability is great and there is a large marginal zone which at times receives sufficient rain, at times does not. Rainfed agriculture is only guaranteed when one reaches the 400 mm isohyet. The effect on human settlement is drastic. South of the 400 mm isohyet, agriculture is possible only if there are rivers to provide irrigation water. The Tigris and Euphrates afford a lifeline to the Mesopotamian plain where rainfall is scarce and erratic. These two rivers and their tributaries, the Balikh, Habur, Greater and Lesser Zab, Diyala, Kerkheh, and Karun, originate in the mountains of Turkey and Iran where rainfall and snow feed them. As perennial rivers, their water can be tapped to irrigate the crops with careful management and using techniques we will discuss later in this chapter.

Long periods of drought could easily have occurred in the time span we study here. While we can assume that over the last 10,000 years the climate in the Near East has not substantially changed, it is certain that even marginal variations had serious consequences for the inhabitants and affected historical developments. Did the so-called Dark Ages result from a drying of the climate? It would have made rainfed agriculture impossible in zones that usually relied on it, and would have lowered the rivers to such an extent that irrigated areas were substantially reduced. Or should we focus on human factors in trying to explain such periods? We will see that explanations for decline and collapse are always complex and involve multiple factors. Climate probably played a role in many occasions, but

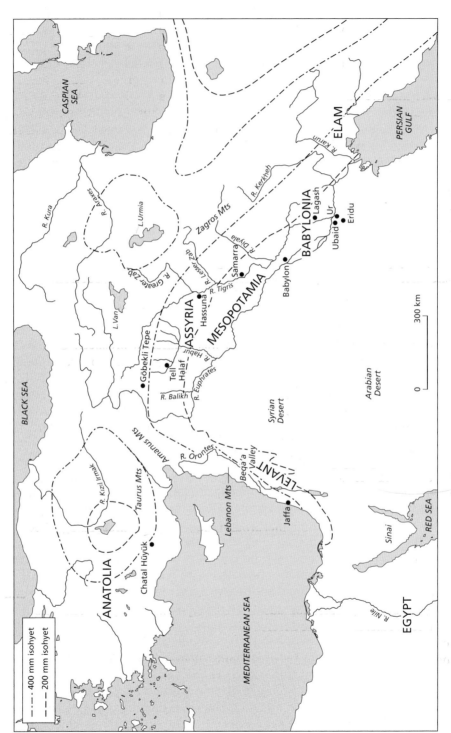

Map 1.1 The ancient Near East.

unfortunately insufficient details on the ancient climate are available to serve as a historical explanation for the drastic political and economic changes we observe.

A second important characteristic of geography involves boundaries. These were created by mountains, seas, and deserts, which could all be crossed, although in limited places and with special technology only. The Zagros and Taurus mountains were massive barriers to the states of Mesopotamia, and could be entered only through the river valleys. Military expansion was thus always restricted there, even by such mighty powers as Assyria. The mountain ranges in the Levant left a narrow corridor only for movement from northern Syria to Egypt, and control over a single valley could deny passage between the two. Mountains were also home to many groups that the states we will study were unable to govern. To the dwellers of the plains, the mountains thus often presented a fearful and inhospitable sight.

Seas formed a very different kind of boundary, the Mediterranean and the Persian Gulf being the most important. They did create a border, but once crossed, they provided access to distant regions. Thus the Persian Gulf and the marshes at its head made up the southern limit of Mesopotamia, but from the fifth millennium on, Mesopotamians sailed in primitive craft to regions along the Gulf coasts. In the late fourth millennium sailors may have reached Egypt that way, and in the third and early second millennia direct seaborne contacts with the Indus valley were common. The Mediterranean was a different prospect. Only a few harbors existed along its coast, none south of Jaffa. By the late third millennium, however, Aegeans sailed to the Syro-Palestinian coast, and in the second half of the second millennium shipping throughout the eastern Mediterranean was common. Around 1200, technological innovations enabled people from Syro-Palestinian harbors to travel long distances, and the entire Mediterranean came within their reach. First-millennium Phoenicians established colonies as far west as Spain and the Atlantic coast of North Africa.

More formidable as a border was the great desert stretching between Mesopotamia and the Levant. For millennia, people could only make their way along the Tigris or Euphrates river valleys and cross the northern Syrian steppe. With the domestication of the camel around the year 1000, direct passage became possible, although it remained infrequent. Even when small companies of people could cross directly through it, the lack of water still forced armies to take the roundabout route through the Levant and northern Syria to get from Egypt to Mesopotamia. The desert, like the mountains, was home to groups feared and hated by the settled people, nomads whose lifestyles were despised and who were impossible to rule. Even if the desert could be crossed, the states of the Near East could not overpower its inhabitants.

The permeability of boundaries not only allowed Near Easterners to move outward, but also enabled outsiders to enter the region. The area's position at the juncture of three continents is unique in the world. Populations from Africa, Europe, and Asia have moved into the region from early prehistory till today, causing interaction, exchange of technologies, and increasing pressures on the natural resources. This may explain why so many "revolutions" in the lifestyles of humans occurred there: the emergence of farming, of cities, and of empires. It is certain that population movements took place throughout ancient history, but studying them is difficult. While we can say with confidence that the Mongol tribesmen who invaded Iraq in the thirteenth century AD came from inner Asia, we are not so certain about the origins of the Hittites, for instance. Perhaps, as speakers of an Indo-European language, they came from a region north of India and arrived in Anatolia in the early second millennium. But the presumed Indo-European homeland north of India could be a pure phantom, and speakers of Indo-European languages could just as easily have resided in Anatolia from pre-history on, only entering the historical record in the early second millennium. The same is true for so many populations – Sumerians, Hurrians, Sea People, Israelites, and so on – who once were thought to have invaded parts of the Near East. To reprise the earlier metaphor, the Near East is one area of light in a world of prehistoric darkness. When people suddenly enter its spotlight it is often impossible to establish whether they came from far away or nearby – or if they had always been in the region where they first appear in the documentation.

1.4   Prehistoric Developments

We must undertake the study of the long cultural evolution of prehistory from a perspective that takes the entire Near East into account. Despite the great ecological diversity in the region, we see simultaneous developments in several places. The absolute chronology of events is still uncertain and debated, but we have a good idea about overall trends. Especially with the beginning of the Neolithic period around 9000, important cultural developments occurred that established the setting for the later historical civilizations.

The most crucial technological development was agriculture, which made it possible for large groups of people to remain in the same place year-round. The Near East was the first region in the world where agriculture was invented. The process took several millennia and involved the domestication of plants, primarily cereals, and of animals. The archaeological sites where we see these changes happen are usually located at the borders of different ecological zones, whose occupants took advantage of varied plant resources and hunted different animals. The natural variety described above may in fact have been one of the reasons why agriculture evolved so early in the Near East. People became so used to having access to a variety of food resources that they sought to guarantee supplies by interfering in the growing cycles of crops and animals. Moreover, by chance the wild resources available to them were more suitable for domestication than those elsewhere. Harvested wheat and barley can be stored much longer than most African plants, for example.

For millennia, humankind had lived by gathering food locally, and moved when the supply was exhausted. The hunting of animals probably complemented a diet that relied primarily on wild cereals, fruits, legumes, fish, shellfish, and whatever else the environment provided. Their lifestyle should not necessarily be considered as harsh and difficult. Ethnographic studies show that the life of early farmers was more arduous than that of hunter-gatherers, especially in the resource-rich areas of the Near East, where food could be readily collected without much effort. The question of why people moved toward agriculture thus remains difficult to answer, and the desire to live in larger communities may have been the main driving force. Some prehistoric sites show an amazing willingness to cooperate even before agriculture. The recently discovered site of Göbekli Tepe in southeast Anatolia contains monumental stone structures with images carved on them, which could only have been built by large groups of workers (figure 1.1). These must have come from various foraging communities in the region, who used the location to gather in what can be called religious ceremonies. Permanent settlement made such interactions easier.

Direct control of the food supply via cereal agriculture was achieved through a series of probably inadvertent steps from the eleventh to seventh millennia as humans became more practiced at sowing, husbandry, harvesting, and storage. Wild cereals have two characteristics that cause problems for human consumers – they have weak stems so that their seeds easily disperse and fall to the ground before they are harvested. Also, it is hard to get at their seeds, which are covered with strong husks in order to prevent premature germination. When harvesting, people would gather more seeds that had not fallen to the ground from plants with stronger stems, and they promoted the growth of such plants once their seeds were sown. More consciously, they may have selected grains with thinner husks for sowing, thereby propagating such species. Over many centuries humans genetically modified the cereals through selection and crossbreeding. The einkorn and emmer wheats that grew wild in the Near East mutated to develop into the modern bread and club wheats.

Selective hunting of wild animals also replaced previous indiscriminate killing. People culled wild herds to procure a proper age and gender balance, and protected them from natural predators. Sheep and goats were the most common domesticates, and among them preference was given to breeds that provided the most resources, such as sheep with thick wool coats. Over time, humans became responsible for all aspects of the animals' existence, whose behavior had now totally diverged from that of their wild progenitors and whose physical attributes had become very different as well. Sheep developed long hair that could be turned into thread for weaving. Domesticated dogs ate cereals, something their wild ancestors would never have done. The human body changed as well. For example, some people developed the enzymes needed to digest unprocessed animal milk.

Thus there was not a sudden change from hunting-gathering to farming, but rather a slow process during which people increased their reliance on the food they grew, but still supplemented their diets with wild resources. It is clear that the process was not irreversible. Sometimes populations had to return to a hunter-gatherer existence or increase their intake of wild resources when the domesticated supply did not meet their needs. We have to keep in mind that both lifestyles existed in the same geographical area: agriculture developed where wild resources were abundant.

Agriculture enabled people to stay in the same place for long periods of time. The various archaeological cultures we distinguish between the years 9000 and 5000 exhibit a greater permanence of residence and larger communities. The house is the attribute of sedentary life that is most recognizable in the archaeological record. In the Levant, houses were built of stone or with stone foundations; elsewhere in the Near East their walls were of piled mud, and later of mud brick. The settlements became increasingly large, which demonstrates the ability to feed greater numbers of people. A shift from round to rectangular houses took place in the ninth millennium, and it shows that larger groups of people cohabitated with some type of social hierarchy and a specialization in room use. In the earliest villages of the ninth millennium, people used clay storage bins to keep wild and domesticated cereals, but in the seventh millennium they developed fired pottery. Although perhaps not a major technological breakthrough, since it was merely an extension of earlier storage practices and work with clay, it facilitated cooking and enabled the safe storage of goods. Coincidentally, pottery provides the archaeologist with an extremely useful tool for dating excavated remains, in part because it was a constantly developing technology (see box 1.2).

By 7000, completely agricultural villages existed throughout the Near East, all of them located in areas with sufficient rainfall for farming. The focus of subsequent technological developments shifted at this time to the east, especially the region below the dry-farming area, that is, the plains of Mesopotamia. Shortly after 7000, farming communities developed in areas of northern Mesopotamia that had insufficient rainfall and needed to rely on irrigation. The technology of leading water from rivers and basins to crops had already been used much earlier in areas such as the Levant, but with the move of settlements into arid zones, irrigation became essential. There was a radical change in the farmers' interactions

---

Box 1.2   *The use of pottery in archaeological research*

Ceramic remains provide an important tool to the archaeologist. Pottery is ubiquitous in the archaeological record, the shards are almost indestructible, and styles of decoration as well as pot shapes change relatively rapidly over time, indicating the tastes of distinct groups of people. Just as in our day the shape and decoration of soda bottles develop over time and we can date a photograph by the bottle in a person's hand, so the changing styles of pottery in antiquity can be used as a way of dating sites and the archaeological levels within them. Consequently, prehistoric cultures are often named for the type of pottery that represents them: Hassuna, Samarra, Ubaid, and so on, whose pottery styles were first identified in the sites with those names (see figure 1.2). When several ceramic assemblages are found in a stratigraphic sequence, we can establish their relative chronology. All *tells* of the Near East are covered with potsherds that represent the periods of occupation. Thus even without excavation, the archaeologist can determine when a site was inhabited on the basis of pottery remains.

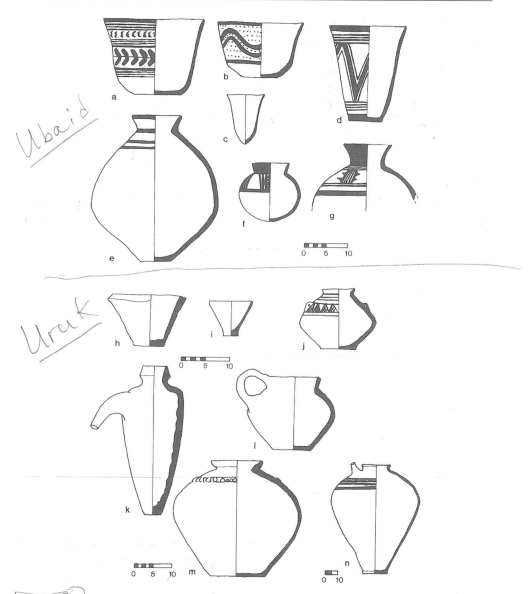

Figure 1.2 Pottery sequence. Pottery shapes and decorations can differ drastically between different archaeological cultures, standing out as markers of their identity. In the southern Mesopotamian sequence the painted Ubaid pottery (a–g) is very distinct from the sober Uruk vessels (h–n) that replaced it, but on the other hand, the later potters experimented with new shapes. Credit: S. Pollock, *Ancient Mesopotamia: The Eden that Never Was* (Cambridge: Cambridge University Press, 1999), p. 4. After Neely and Wright 1994, fig III.5c,f, III,4a,h, III,7d,f, III,8b,c; Safar et al. 1981, 74/8, 80/1, 9. Author originals courtesy of S. Pollock.

with natural crops. While previously they had promoted the growth of cereals that also existed in the wild, they now introduced them into areas where they were unnatural and depended fully on human support. The challenges they faced in Mesopotamia were great. Unlike the Nile in Egypt, which provides water in the late summer just when it is needed to prepare wet fields for planting seeds, the Tigris and Euphrates rivers rise in the late spring when too much water can destroy the almost full-grown plants. The rivers are at their lowest when the sowing season arrives, and farmers had to build canals and storage basins to control the water and allow it to enter the fields only when needed. The system did not have to be elaborate and small communities could manage it, but still there had to be an awareness of the cycles of the rivers and the crops, and planning and organization were required to irrigate using the Mesopotamian rivers.

Small irrigation systems first appeared in the foothills of the Zagros, and probably also near the marshes in southern Babylonia. The technology had to be further developed, however, before it could be extended into southern Mesopotamia, where the extreme flatness of the plain exposed fields to floods, especially from the Euphrates, which has almost no valley at all. The river, with its many branches and man-made canals, had to be carefully managed and farmers did not only have to lead water to the crops but also protect them from too much water. Any time a river branch overflowed, a natural levee developed from the deposit of silt left behind by the water losing its speed. While levees could be reinforced artificially and turned into dikes, sedimentation often caused riverbeds to be higher than the fields around them. There was no natural drainage of water deposited in the fields, and the hot climate led to evaporation and a high level of salt in the soil, arresting the growth of plants. Moreover, the water table rose after irrigation, damaging roots when it came too near the surface. Yet, over the millennia inhabitants of Babylonia developed the technology to irrigate increasingly larger areas. While irrigation agriculture became the characteristic feature of economic life in the region in later periods profiting from the high fertility of the soil, its potential alone did not encourage people to settle there. The remarkable abundance of resources in the marshes – reed for buildings and animal fodder, fish and other animals for food – also played a crucial role. The ecological diversity had a great appeal. Between 6000 and 5500, permanent settlement in the lower Mesopotamian plain became common and remained a constant feature.

Primarily on the basis of pottery styles, archaeologists delineate a sequence of Near Eastern cultures in the period from 7000 to 3800: Proto-Hassuna and Hassuna in the rainfed areas of northern Mesopotamia in the seventh millennium, and Samarra in the irrigated zone of the north in the late seventh millennium. A less-developed culture identified as Amuq B characterized the west of the Near East at the time. The sixth millennium saw a massive expansion of the north Mesopotamian Halaf culture that ranged over the entire rainfed zone abutting the Mesopotamian plain and extended into the Levant. At the same time southern Mesopotamia became permanently settled by people using a cultural assemblage we call Ubaid. Around 4500, this Ubaid culture replaced the Halaf in the north and in the Zagros Mountains.

Chart 1.1   Chronology of the prehistory of the Near East

date BC	Levant	Anatolia	N. Mesopotamia	S. Mesopotamia
9000	Proto-Neolithic (PPN A)	Göbekli Tepe		
8500	Aceramic Neolithic (PPN B-C)			
7000	Pottery Neolithic			
6500		Chatal Hüyük	Proto-Hassuna	
	Amuq B		Hassuna/Samarra	
6000	Halaf	Halaf	Halaf	Early Ubaid
5500				
5000				
4500	Ubaid	Ubaid	Ubaid	Late Ubaid
4000				Early Uruk
	Chalcolithic			
3500			Uruk	Late Uruk

The most remarkable aspects of these cultures are their wide geographical coverage and their long-distance contacts. Keeping in mind the fact that these were small communities without any organization beyond the village level, the spread of a cultural assemblage such as that of Halaf from the central Zagros to the Mediterranean coast is astonishing. There are limited remains and local differences are blurred, but aspects of Halaf's material culture are quite specific, such as the unique layout of its houses and terracotta figurines (figure 1.3). Moreover, we observe that luxury materials traveled enormous distances. For instance, obsidian was only naturally available in central Anatolia, but it was found in sites throughout the Near East. Archaeologists often think that the success of Chatal Hüyük, a large site in central Anatolia that existed from ca. 7200 to 6000, resulted from its trade in this volcanic stone. Less prestigious goods were obtained in distant regions as well. Ubaid pottery produced in southern Mesopotamia appeared along the Persian Gulf as far south as Oman, and scholars have interpreted this as the remains of fishing and pearl-diving expeditions.

Another characteristic of these early cultures is their longevity. The Halaf culture lasted almost a thousand years and gradually gave way to that of the southern Ubaid. The latter's durability over almost two millennia, and the high degree of cultural continuity it demonstrates, are startling. These factors seem to suggest that once communities had settled in lower Mesopotamia, they retained a stable and local development. They preserved the same material culture throughout their existence, only gradually becoming more extensive and complex.

Figure 1.3   Figurines of women from the Halaf culture. These terracotta figurines representing headless women whose breasts and thighs are exaggerated are typical for the Halaf culture, which spread across northern Mesopotamia and Syria. These figures are usually associated with fertility and childbirth. Louvre Museum, Paris. Left H: 8.3 cm, AO 21095; Right H: 6.3 cm, AO 21096. c. 6000–5100 BC. Credit: akg images/Erich Lessing.

Primary among the social developments were the rise of a hierarchy and the centralization of powers and functions, a result of the growth in size of communities. There are fundamental differences visible between the north and the south of Mesopotamia in this respect. In the southern Ubaid culture, some members of the communities had a distinct status, as is indicated by the larger size and the particular layout of the buildings they inhabited or supervised. The power of these newly developed elites seems to have derived from control over agricultural resources. Among the families that made up communities, one would emerge to administer the storage of harvests in a central location. This is already visible in the south, whereas the contemporary Halaf culture in the north exhibits a high degree of social homogeneity. When the Ubaid culture spread into Halaf territory after 5500, social differentiation arrived there as well. The new elites are visible to us in their claim to rare and exotic foreign goods. Possibly they were immigrants from the south who imposed a type of political authority over the weaker local families and controlled long-distance trade. Only late in the Ubaid period did they start to exercise the type of local agricultural dominance visible earlier in the south.

The physical focus of these centralized functions seems to have been a building that may already be called a temple. Starting in the mid-sixth millennium, the site of Eridu near the Persian Gulf shows a sequence of increasingly larger buildings on the same spot, culminating in a great temple of the late third millennium. Projecting the function of early historical temples back in time, it is likely that from the early Ubaid period onward, this building functioned both as a communal place of worship and as a center for the collection and distribution of agricultural goods. Some of Eridu's archaeological levels contained masses of fish bones, which seem to be the remains of offerings made to the deity. A social organization beyond the individual household was thus developing within communities, with all families of the settlement contributing to the temple cult. There also developed a hierarchy of settlements in the far south of Mesopotamia, a few measuring 10 to 15 hectares (25 to 37 acres) surrounded by smaller ones that were usually only 0.5 to 2 hectares (1.2 to 5 acres) in size. This demonstrates that individual communities became integrated into a wider cooperative territorial organization.

The prehistoric evolutions very summarily sketched here demonstrate that many of the cultural aspects of later Near Eastern history evolved over long periods. A culmination of these processes occurred in the fourth millennium, when the coalescence of several innovations led to the establishment of Mesopotamian civilization. We will discuss these events in more detail in the next chapter.

Debate 1.1 *Dating Near Eastern history*

Following the practice of almost every other history, this book uses absolute dates to indicate when events took place. These dates are set within the artificial construct of the Christian or Common Era, and since the entirety of ancient Near Eastern history took place before the start of that era, all are B(efore) C(hrist) or B(efore) C(ommon) E(ra), the higher numbers preceding the lower ones. That is merely a convention to enable us to comprehend the sequence of events and their distance in time, even if the era has an ideological basis without relevance to the ancient Near East. All dates in this book thus have to be read as BC, except when AD (*Anno Domini*; alternatively CE) is added explicitly.

The numbers give a false impression of certainty, and the absolute chronology of Near Eastern history is a vexing and controversial problem. The Mesopotamians were pretty good at documenting sequences of rulers, although sources can differ on the number of years a king ruled and other details. For absolute chronology the biggest difficulty is to establish a firm point in time to which the king lists can be attached. The tools employed derive from multiple disciplines (e.g., astronomy, archaeology, philology) and the scholarly debates are very technical. First-millennium chronology is secure because of several reliable data, including the king list in Greek compiled by the astronomer Ptolemy of Alexandria in the second century AD, which goes back to 747 BC, and the record of a solar eclipse that took place on June 15, 763, which allows us to anchor a long sequence of Assyrian eponyms (see chapter 6). But uncertainty emerges in the early centuries of that millennium and becomes worse for the second millennium and before. Scholars have reconstructed an accepted relative sequence, primarily based on Assyrian and Babylonian lists of kings, but that sequence cannot be absolutely dated with confidence. In 1912 AD one scholar thought he had discovered solid astronomical evidence in a record of the appearances and disappearances of the planet Venus during King Ammisaduqa's reign, reported in an astrological omen list preserved in a manuscript of the seventh century BC. The planet's behavior fits several moments in the early second millennium BC, and after scholars floated many suggestions three systems were considered the most likely: the long, middle, and short chronologies. They dated the reign of the most famous king of the period, Hammurabi of Babylon, in 1848–1806, 1792–1750, and 1728–1686 respectively, and the end of his dynasty in 1651, 1595, or 1531 (see Garelli et al. 1997: 225–40; Eder and Renger 2007: 8–9; and Pruzsinszky 2009: 23–30 for surveys of the scholarship). In the 1950s most scholars began to adhere to the middle chronology, which also determined the absolute dating for third millennium events and before.

The deceptive certainty has come under attack for some time now. Doubts about the reliability of the information in the *Venus tablet of Ammisaduqa*, written a thousand years after the events it describes, arose when the tablet was reedited (Reiner and Pingree 1975), and some have suggested it should be ignored altogether (Cryer 1995: 658), although there has been a recent defense of its merits (Mebert 2010). Spurred by concerns that the 1595 date for the fall of Babylon assumes a much too long Dark Age in the middle of the second millennium, a major reinvestigation of archaeological, textual, and astronomical evidence forcefully argued for an ultra-short chronology and placed the event in 1499 (Gasche et al. 1998). This has inspired an avalanche of new studies, incorporating such evidence as tree rings from Anatolian buildings, historical references in omens, the incidence of solar eclipses, and so on (see Pruzsinszky 2009 for a detailed survey of all evidence), but in the end there is no certainty. The Middle Chronology remains thus "too convenient to discard" (Roaf 2012: 171), advice I follow here to make it easier for readers of this book to consult other scholarship.[1]

[1] The absolute dates I use for Assyrian and Babylonian history come from a list Regine Pruzsinszky prepared for Gonzalo Rubio, ed., *A Handbook of Ancient Mesopotamia*, de Gruyter (in press).

Part I
City-States

2

Origins: The Uruk Phenomenon

3500	3000	2500	2000	1500	1000	500

4000–3500	Early Uruk period
3500–3100	Late Uruk period
3400–3100	Uruk IV level, Eanna precinct, Uruk
3100–3000	Uruk III level, Eanna precinct, Uruk

In the late fourth millennium the Near East reached a critical moment in its history. Several processes of prehistory culminated into numerous innovations of seminal importance for people's lives; these included cities, states, and writing, all of which reveal the existence of an urban society with a social hierarchy and specialized labor. The developments were a Near East-wide phenomenon and in many regions from Anatolia to western Iran we observe how the people started to live in larger communities that were economically and socially more complex than before. But it was in the very south of Mesopotamia near the Persian Gulf that after 3500 they grew to such an extent that we can identify the first true city. At the height of its development that city, Uruk, left its mark on the entire Near East.

An indication of the changes appeared in an everyday utensil, pottery. In the early fourth millennium throughout the Near East rough and undecorated wheel-made plates, bowls, and jars which seem to be purely utilitarian, replaced the carefully fashioned and decorated vessels of previous cultures (see figure 2.1 below).

A History of the Ancient Near East ca. 3000–323 BC, Third Edition. Marc Van De Mieroop.
© 2016 John Wiley & Sons, Inc. Published 2016 by John Wiley & Sons, Inc.

Figure 2.1 Stack of beveled-rim bowls. Characteristic for Uruk period pottery are the so-called beveled-rim bowls which were mass-produced in standard sizes and appear in every archaeological site of the period. Their exact function is unclear, but they may have been used to issue rations to temple dependents. These are from Susa in western Iran. Louvre Museum, Paris. Credit: © RMN-Grand Palais /Franck Raux.

Their appearance was the result of a change in society: more people living together needed more pots, and mass-production fulfilled the increased demand. What happened in the Uruk period, which lasted for the whole of the fourth millennium and was entirely the result of indigenous forces, was so radical that scholars used to refer to it as "the urban revolution," on a par with the industrial revolution of the nineteenth century AD. The term revolution might be somewhat of a misnomer for a process that occurred over one thousand years, but the changes affected most areas of life. They did not only comprise the origins of cities. Many other innovations in other aspects of society, the economy, technology, and culture were equally significant for humanity. Consequently, when studying the period anthropologists, for instance, focus on the development of the state and emphasize the relationship between settlements and their surroundings. Historians stress the origins of writing, which provides us with a whole new means of access to the people we study. Art historians focus on the appearance of monumental art, signifying a completely new relationship between art and society. That these innovations coincided was certainly not accidental. We will discuss them separately, however, to understand what happened more clearly.

2.1   The Origins of Cities

It is not easy to define in absolute terms what a city is. Intuitively we think of large numbers of inhabitants living in close proximity to one another and of monumental buildings, but these are relative concepts depending on historical circumstances. While today we consider a community of 30,000 people to be a small town, to classical Greeks, for example, it would have been a large city. Also, monuments by themselves do not make a city; they have to be part of environments that support them and benefit from them, with people associated with them living nearby. A fundamental characteristic of a city is that it does not exist in isolation. Not only does it cater to the needs of its own residents, but it is also important to the people who live in its surroundings in smaller settlements, towns and villages. These do not turn to the city for everyday needs, perhaps, but when they require special items and services they do rely on it. A city acts as a mediator between people, both those living inside its limits and those in permanent or seasonal settlements in the surroundings; it acts as a point of collection and redistribution of goods and provides central services. The city is a hub in its geographical setting, the focal point both for its own inhabitants and for the people living in the countryside. Conversely, a city needs its hinterland to survive.

Most historians believe that the first true city in world history appeared in the very south of Mesopotamia at Uruk, a massive settlement in the last quarter of the fourth millennium, perhaps ten times the size of any of its contemporaries. Some argue that there were precedents in the northern Mesopotamian plains earlier on in that millennium, but although these were large settlements indeed, they did not reach the truly urban proportions found in the south. Frustratingly, that area remains archaeologically poorly known. In one site only substantial Uruk period levels have been excavated, that is Uruk itself, and even there only monumental architecture has been exposed. But there is another source of information, which actually reveals the patterns toward urbanization much better than the excavation of a single site: settlement surveys. In this approach archaeologists walk over the countryside and gather pottery remains to determine where people lived and they date their presence on the basis of the pottery styles residents used. The technique allows archaeologists to calculate the sizes of settlements at various moments, and using size as an indicator of importance, it permits us to establish a hierarchy. The largest and central sites can be considered to be cities, smaller ones towns, and the smallest villages.

It is this method that reveals the growth of cities in Mesopotamia in the fourth millennium. In the Ubaid period, which lasted some two thousand years, the number of settlements gradually increased and they started to show a differentiation in their size. Some were small centers with subsidiary villages around them, which suggests the presence of local chiefs with authority over the nearby country-side. In the early fourth millennium, with the start of the Uruk period, the number and size of sites suddenly increased vastly all over the Near East. There were differences between the north and the south, however. In northern Mesopotamia densely inhabited central settlements appeared with a circle of smaller ones nearby around them. Over time these merged together into large settlements, at Tell Brak, for example, 130 hectares (320 acres) in size. These were dispersed over a wide area with vast open spaces between them. In contrast, southern Mesopotamian people settled throughout the countryside. In the early Uruk period the total number of inhabitants seems to have been almost equal in central and in southern Babylonia, but in central Babylonia they lived in three centers of 30 to 50 hectares (74 to 123 acres), while in the south one settlement alone dominated, with a size of some 70 hectares (173 acres): Uruk (see map 2.1). The rapid increase of settled population at that time cannot be explained with certainty. It seems too fast to have been the result of indigenous population growth alone, even if new agricultural conditions promoted demographic expansion. There may have been an increased sedentarization of semi-nomadic people previously unrecognizable in the archaeological record, or outsiders may have entered the region because of climatic changes or other reasons.

The first true city appeared in the Late Uruk period and in one region only, the south of Babylonia. After the middle of the fourth millennium the increase of permanently settled population in central Babylonia was minor and can be explained as the result of natural growth. In the south around the city of Uruk, however, there was an enormous escalation in the area occupied by permanent settlement. A large part of that increase took place in Uruk itself, now 250 hectares (620 acres) in size, which became a real urban center surrounded not only by just one level of secondary settlements, but by a hierarchy of them, towns, villages, and small villages. While population estimates are notoriously unreliable, scholars assume that Uruk inhabitants were still able to support themselves from the agricultural production of the fields surrounding the city that could be reached in a daily commute. But Uruk's dominant size in the entire region, far surpassing that of other settlements, indicates that it was a regional center and a true city. Its existence caused a restructuring of how people lived over a large area. The number of people who resided in its orbit was so great that they could not have come from Babylonia alone. Some seem to have migrated from western Iran and northern Mesopotamia to the south.

The massive increase in numbers of people living together naturally had repercussions on how society functioned. In early prehistoric communities there were few disparities in wealth and power between families, whose members were mostly occupied with agricultural tasks. But over time differences developed as we can see in the archaeological record from house sizes and the amount of goods deposited in graves. In urban societies with tens of thousands of inhabitants there was a complex hierarchy with elites in control of others and a specialization of economic activities. The remains excavated at Uruk show the reality of this. Two

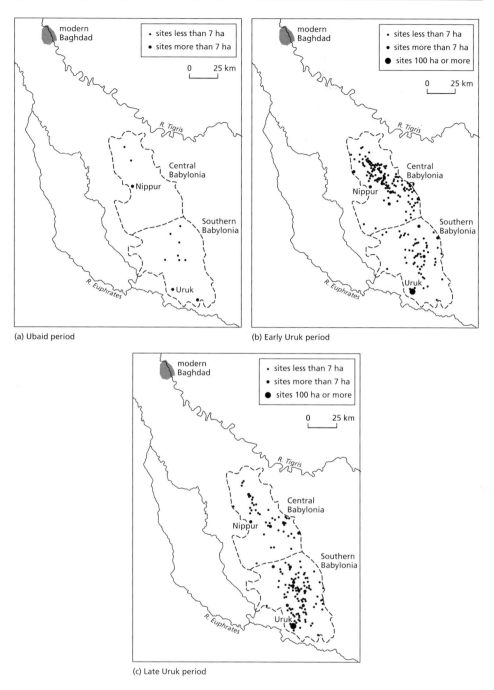

(a) Ubaid period

(b) Early Uruk period

(c) Late Uruk period

Map 2.1 Changing settlement patterns in Babylonia during the Ubaid and Uruk periods. After Susan Pollock, *Ancient Mesopotamia: The Eden That Never Was* (Cambridge: Cambridge University Press, 1999), pp. 56–8.

areas in its center contained fourth millennium materials near the surface, both with monumental architecture: a complex called Eanna, "House of Heaven," with a sequence of layers numbered as Eanna XIV (the earliest) to Eanna III (the latest) and associated with the goddess Inanna, and one where the cult of the sky god Anu took place. The structures of the Eanna complex were the most elaborate and were rebuilt several times in the Uruk IV period (we distinguish the earlier IVb from the later IVa levels). Within an area surrounded by a perimeter wall, several enormous buildings were in use simultaneously. These were not only large, in the order of 50 by 80 meters, but also decorated with a technique that was typical for the Late Uruk period. Within the walls were stuck clay cones colored white, black, and red, which formed mosaics in geometrical patterns on the surface. In one building these cones were of stone, a material more difficult to obtain in the region of Uruk than clay. The Anu – or White – temple was constructed on an artificial platform repeatedly raised in the Uruk period and in the end 13 meters high. At its base lay a 25 by 30 meter building made of limestone that had been brought in from the distant desert.

The architectural layout of both complexes shows that these were cult places and that access to parts of them was restricted. Their monumentality tells us much about society at Uruk. They could only have been built by a large labor-force that required organization and leadership. Archaeologists have calculated that for each complex some 15,000 laborers worked ten hours a day for five years.[1] Although religious sentiments may have partly inspired them to do so, some type of coercion was probably involved as well. While such enterprises could only succeed in large communities, they also strengthened the social ties between the people who were themselves involved or had relatives who were. They generated a common sense of purpose.

Agriculture remained the basis of the economy and would be so for the rest of ancient Near Eastern history, but building projects like these required that some people redirected their attention to other tasks and became specialized in them. Specialization of labor is one characteristic of an urban society and we can observe this in both the Uruk countryside and the city. Uruk was located just inland of the marshes at the head of the Persian Gulf. Its agriculture relied on irrigation water provided by the Euphrates, enabling abundant cultivation of cereals and orchard fruits, especially dates. In between the irrigated areas was the steppe, where animal husbandry of sheep and goats took place in addition to hunting. Nearby were the marshes, with a plentiful supply of fish and fowl, where water buffaloes were herded for their milk, and where reeds could be harvested for animal fodder. The different ecological niches encouraged labor specialization among producers: fishermen, farmers, gardeners, hunters, and herdsmen were more productive if they devoted most of their time to the care of the resources closely available to them. Certain technological developments may also have made specialization more desirable. Thus the invention of the seed-plow, an instrument that deposits seeds in the furrow while it is being plowed, made farming more difficult and required the hand of an expert.

The vast majority of the population remained active in agriculture, even those living within the city itself. But a segment of the urban society started to focus on non-agricultural tasks as a result of the city's new role as a center in its geographical surroundings. Within the productive sector, craftsmen became specialists. Already early in the Uruk period, the turn to undecorated utilitarian pottery was probably the result of specialized mass production. In early fourth-millennium level XII of the Eanna sequence at Uruk, a pottery style appears that is most characteristic of this process, the so-called beveled-rim bowl (figure 2.1). It is a rather shallow bowl, which was crudely made in a mold, hence in only a limited number of standard sizes. For some unknown reason many were discarded, often while still intact, and hundreds of thousands have been found all over the Near East. The beveled-rim bowl is one of the most telling diagnostic finds for identifying an Uruk period site. Its use will be discussed later. Of importance here is the fact that it was produced rapidly in large amounts, most likely by specialists in a central location.

A variety of documentation indicates that skilled artisans mass-produced other goods as well, while earlier on each family made them for private use. Certain images depict groups of women involved in the weaving of textiles, an activity we know from later third-millennium texts to have been vital in the economy and to have been centrally administered. A metal smelting workshop may have been excavated in a small area at Uruk. It contained a number of channels lined by a sequence of holes, ca. 50 centimeters (19.5 inches) deep, all showing burn marks and filled with ashes. This has been interpreted as the remains of a workshop where specialists scooped up molten metal from the channel and poured it into molds in the holes.

Objects themselves show that they were the work of skilled professionals. In the Late Uruk period, there first appeared a type of object that remained characteristic for Mesopotamia throughout its entire history: the cylinder seal. This was a small cylinder, usually no more than 3 centimeters (1.2 inches) high and 2 centimeters (0.79 inches) in diameter, of shell, bone, faience, or a variety of stones (e.g., carnelian, lapis lazuli, crystal), on which a scene was carved in mirror image. When rolled over a soft material – primarily the clay of bullae, tablets, or lumps attached to boxes, jars, or doorbolts – the scene would appear an indefinite number of times in relief, easily legible (see figure 4.4). The cylinder seal was an important administrative device and its use will be discussed later. The technological knowledge needed to carve it was far superior to that for stamp seals, which had appeared in the early Neolithic period. From the first appearance of cylinder seals, the carved scenes could be highly elaborate and refined, indicative of the work of specialist stonecutters. Similarly, the Late Uruk period shows the first monumental art, relief and statuary in the round, made with such a degree of mastery that only a professional could have produced them.

With this specialization of production the need for exchange became imperative and this is where Uruk gained its true status as a city, coordinating this for its surroundings. Agricultural producers exchanged their assorted produce

Figure 2.2   The Uruk vase. The carving on this ceremonial vessel shows how the leader of the city community provides the goddess Inanna with the produce of the land. Found within the Uruk temple complex, the vase represents that building's role in collecting the resources of the region for redistribution to the community. Iraq Museum, Baghdad. Credit: M. Van De Mieroop, *The Ancient Mesopotamian City* (Oxford: Oxford University Press), 1999, p. 32.

and obtained tools and luxury items this way, while craftspeople got their food through this system. It required some type of authority to organize this, and this authority had to rely on an ideological foundation shared by the participants in the system to make it acceptable for them to contribute part of their production in return for something else in the future. In Uruk period Mesopotamia, religion provided that ideology: the god of the city received goods and redistributed them to the people. The monumental temple, the house of the god and built by the community, was the central institution that made the system work. Its buildings presented an impressive sight and a visual focus for the surroundings of Uruk, which was located in an extremely flat region. They had a cultic role in that goods were offered to the god(s). One of the major works of art of the period, the Uruk vase (figure 2.2; see box 2.1), pictorially expresses the role of the Eanna temple complex in Uruk society: it collected the produce of the land as if it were an offering to the goddess. A human, distinguished from the others through his height and dress, acted as intermediary. We can most likely identify him with the head of the temple organization, perhaps referred to by the title "lord," EN in Sumerian.

Box 2.1   *The Uruk vase*

Found in a deposit of cult objects from Uruk III levels was an alabaster vase, circa 1 meter high, the surface of which is entirely carved with an elaborate scene (see figure 2.2). It depicts a procession of naked men carrying bowls, vessels, and baskets containing farm produce. Ears of grain and sheep and goats in the bottom register summarily represent the agriculture of the region. The high point of the relief's story is where a female figure faces the male human ruler, who is ornately dressed with an attendant carrying the train of his garment. At some later date the depiction of the man was cut from the scene, but we can reconstruct his appearance from contemporaneous representations on other objects. The symbols standing behind the woman identify her as the goddess Inanna: two so-called reed-ring bundles, which acted as doorposts in the reed homes of the time, were the basis of the writing of Inanna's name in cuneiform script. Animals and storage jars stand behind her symbols, as well as two small human figures on pedestals, probably statues. A woman has the symbol of Inanna behind her, while a man holds in his hands a stack of bowls and something like a box, which together form the shape of the cuneiform sign for "lord," EN in Sumerian. That sign is the most common in the tablets from the period and seems to indicate a high temple official. While not inscribed with a text, the Uruk vase relief can be read as describing the human ruler offering the region's produce to the goddess.

The temple's role in the collection and redistribution of goods created the need for an entirely new class of specialist – the administrator. The economy became so complex that accounting mechanisms were necessary to record goods coming into and going out of the central organization. This required the skills of people capable of working with the tools and techniques of a bureaucracy. Standard measures for amounts of dry and liquid goods, for land, for labor, and for time were in place, and writing, the technology to record for future consultation, had originated. In considering changes in the society, it is important to realize that all this bureaucratic activity was the domain of a specialized group of people.

The specialization of labor that characterized the establishment of urban life in southern Mesopotamia caused a fundamental restructuring of society. The process of social differentiation culminated in the existence of a stratified society in which professional occupation primarily determined one's rank in the hierarchy. The large majority of people still were farmers, fishermen, herders, and so on, living in communities with little social differentiation beyond that within the individual family. These communities were probably in a tributary relationship with the city and provided part of their income to it, but they remained otherwise socially free and owned the land they worked. Many of the city-residents (we are unable to determine what percentage, however) were part of the temple organization, whose members were wholly dependent on the former for their survival. They were organized along strictly hierarchical lines. Most indicative of the urban hier-archy is a text called the *Standard List of Professions* (document 2.1). It appeared first at the end of the Late Uruk period, thus amongst the first texts written, and was copied faithfully for some 1,500 years, the later versions being clearer to us than the earlier ones. The list provides in several columns the titles of officials and names of professions, ordered in a hierarchy starting with the highest rank. While the first entry is not entirely comprehensible to us, later Babylonians equated it with the Akkadian word for king, which was probably an anachronistic way of indicating that the highest official of the land was meant. The following entries in the *Standard List of Professions* contain a number with the element NAM2, which we think represents "leader," and with the sign GAL, which means "great." The titles include such terms as "leader of the city," or "of the plow," and "great one of the cattle pen," or "of the lambs." The list contains terms for priests, gardeners, cooks, smiths, jewelers, potters, and others. While not fully understood, it is clear that it provides an inventory of specialist professions within the cities.

At the top of the Uruk society, then, stood a man whose powers derived from his role in the temple. Scholars often call him a "priest-king." At the bottom of the social ladder of temple dependents were the people involved in production, both agricultural and otherwise. How extensive this group was remains impos-sible to determine, but through a projection from third-millennium conditions, we assume that the temple had a staff large enough to take care of all its needs. In the third millennium, dependent laborers received rations, fixed amounts of barley, oil, and cloth, as a reward for their services. It is likely that such a system already existed in the Late Uruk period. The Uruk IV tablets contain accounts of grain distributed to workmen, which seem to be precursors of later ration lists. The issuing of rations to numerous people may explain the abundance of the beveled-rim bowl in the archaeological record. These bowls, in a limited number of sizes, possibly functioned as containers for measuring out barley rations. The resemblance of the early cuneiform sign for ration (NINDA) and the beveled-rim bowl supports this suggestion. If correct, the first appearance of the beveled-rim bowl in the mid-fourth millennium would attest to a system of grain distribu-tion already in place at that time. A fundamental opposition existed in this early period between the temple dependents, who were provided for yet unfree, and the inhabitants of the countryside, free but uninsured against disasters such as bad harvests. The temple, located in the city, was a focal point for all, however, and through its collection of tribute drew the entire region together. A state, albeit small, had developed by the late fourth millennium where the city held organiza-tional controls.

2.2   The Development of Writing and Administration

Bureaucracy enabled the control of the regional economy in urban centers. By the end of the Uruk period, there existed a system of recordkeeping with texts, which was the basis of all subsequent administrative cuneiform writing used

Figure 2.3   Uruk III tablet. This account of cereals, written around 3100 BC, is still primarily a set of numbers that indicate amounts of wheat and barley using circles of various sizes. On the side shown here the accountant recorded the totals of disbursements made. 6.2 × 4.7 × 1.65 cm (2.44 × 1.85 × 0.65 in). Credit: © 2014 The Metropolitan Museum of Art/Art Resource/Scala, Florence.

for more than three thousand years afterwards. Uruk writing is called proto-cuneiform because the signs are drawn into the clay with thin lines rather than being impressed with wedges, as is the later cuneiform script. There is no need to see a conceptual difference between the earliest script and later developments, however. This is the first time in history that people developed a writing system, and the oldest evidence for real script comes from the city of Uruk itself. The earliest tablets appear in the Uruk IVa and III archaeological layers of the Eanna precinct (figure 2.3). These terms have become used to refer to stages in the development of the script itself, and as such are applied to texts found outside Uruk.

Accounts provide two sets of data: a record of quantities, and an identification of the person or office involved in the transaction as a participant or supervisor. Techniques other than writing can indicate the second element. Seals, for example, can imply a controller, and they were in use long before the Uruk IV period. From the seventh millennium on, stamp seals impressed on jars or on lumps of clay attached to containers identified the authority that guaranteed the contents. In the middle of the Uruk period the cylinder seal replaced the stamp seal. It enabled much speedier coverage because the seal could be rolled over the surface in one smooth movement. Numerous seals are attested with a large variety of pictorial imagery. Each seal belonged to an individual official or to an administrative office whose identity could be recognized through the design. The profusion of distinguishable seals demonstrates the presence of a class of officials in the city of Uruk who supervised transactions and guaranteed their legitimacy by attaching their mark of authority.

The seals did not disclose the quantity or actual contents involved in a transaction. Several techniques to record such information seem to have been tried out at the same time or in quick succession, and are documented in various sites throughout the Near East. At Uruk itself the archaeological stratigraphy is too confused to establish a sequence of techniques there. At the west Iranian site of Susa, however, we see, prior to the archaeological level corresponding to Uruk IV, a level where *bullae* first appeared, followed by one with numerical tablets. *Bullae* are hollow spheres of clay with seals rolled all over their surface, containing collections of small objects that we call tokens. The latter are stone and clay geometric objects, shaped as cones, spheres, disks, cylinders, and many other forms. These are thought to record the measure of a particular item (goods, animals, humans). The receipt of three units of barley, for example, could have been acknowledged by handing over three tokens representing one unit each. It is likely that larger tokens of the same form indicated a higher unit in a metrological system. They were kept together in the clay envelope, which was sealed to guarantee the contents through the authority of the sealer.

As consultation of such records was impossible without breaking them, the idea arose to impress marks on the outer surface. Simultaneously there appear *bullae* onto which impressions were made, most likely by the tokens inserted inside, and solid tablets with sets of numerical signs traced on them. The "numerical tablets" do not reveal to us what items are accounted for, but the metrological system and the shape of the numerals must have provided such information to the people using them. These recording devices were found at Uruk and other sites where Uruk influence extended. Only at Uruk itself and in Susiana in western Iran finally did records appear that removed this ambiguity: numbers were combined with one or two signs indicating what was involved, sheep, grain, textiles, etcetera. While the two regions shared the same system, immediately afterwards they developed distinct and independent systems of true writing. In the archaeological levels Uruk IVa and III, the proto-cuneiform script appeared; somewhat later the proto-Elamite appeared in Susiana.

Proto-Elamite remains undeciphered because subsequent scripts in the region are very different in character and do not show later forms of the signs used. The Uruk system is better understood because its practices were continued in later cuneiform script, which is well known. The script contained two types of signs to indicate numbers and words. The existence of a numerical sign system was fundamentally important, since 90 percent of the proto-cuneiform tablets were accounts. Numbers of goods, animals, humans, and time had to be recorded. The Uruk IV notations seem complicated to us because seven different systems

Chart 2.1   Examples of systems of weights and measures used in Uruk period accounts. Credit: Based on Hans J. Nissen, Peter Damerow, and Robert K. Englund, *Archaic Bookkeeping: Early Writing and Techniques of Economic Administration in the Ancient Near East* (Chicago and London: University of Chicago Press, 1993), pp. 28–9.

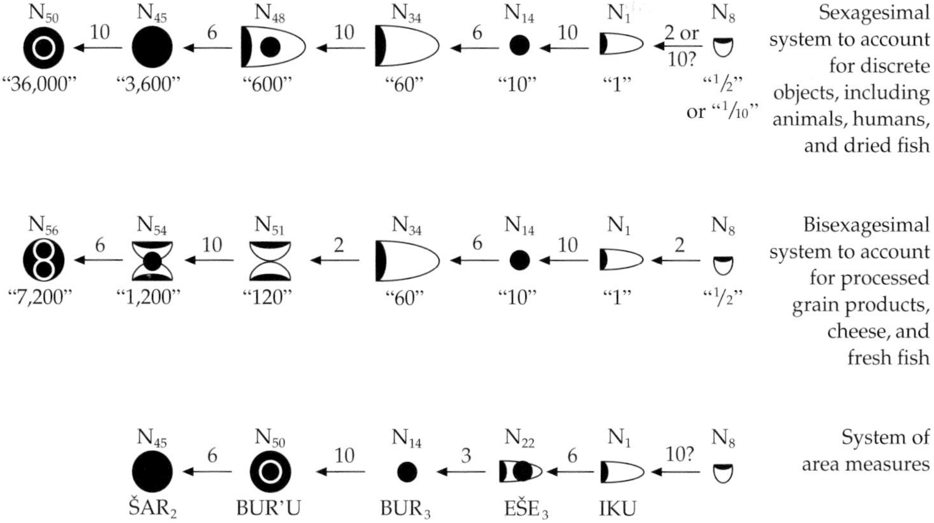

were in use simultaneously, each of which varied the physical shape of the numerals according to what was measured. For example, a sexagesimal system, relying on units with increments of six and ten, was used to account for animals, humans, and dried fish, among other things. A bisexagesimal system, which diverges from the previous one as its units also show increments of two, was used for processed grain products, cheese, and fresh fish. Volumes of grain or surfaces of fields were measured differently. The basic sequence of units varied, then, from system to system (see chart 2.1). Although the shape of the number signs could differ between systems, the same shapes are found in various systems but sometimes with different values. For example, ● indicates 10 when counting discrete objects, but 18 when the surface of a field was measured. In total, there were sixty different number signs.

A much larger group of signs, some 900, designated non-numerical concepts. Each sign stood for a word, a physical entity such as barley or a cow, or an action such as distribution or receipt. The origin of the sign shapes is a matter of controversy. The ideas that they were based on drawings of the objects they signify or that they were two-dimensional renderings of the shapes of tokens do not by themselves explain the forms of all signs. Various sources of inspiration were involved. Some of the outlines reflected the physical object represented or a part of it, such as an ox-head for an ox. Others were purely arbitrary in shape, such as a circle with a cross to indicate a sheep. New signs were created by combining several basic ones, slanting them, or cross-hatching parts of them. For example, the area of the mouth on a human head was marked with hatchings in order to indicate the word mouth, or the sign for water was added to that for head to indicate the verb "to drink." In order for the system to function, all users had to know the meaning of these signs and conventions must have existed to enable someone to recognize the writer's intent and to guide the creation of new signs.

Document 2.1   *Lexical lists*

From the very beginning of writing in Mesopotamia the tablets included a genre we call lexical texts. They provided long lists of words of the same categories, such as designations of professions, animals, objects, and so on. The lists remained a central part of writing until the end of the use of the cuneiform script, and in the first millennium included compendia with thousands of entries. They appeared not only in Babylonia, but in all areas where cuneiform was written from the third millennium on. At first monolingual Sumerian, they later added translations into other languages, especially Akkadian, and indicated how to pronounce the Sumerian terms. An important early example was a list of professional designations, *The Standard List of Professions*, which appeared from the Uruk IV period on and was faithfully copied into the Old Babylonian period, 1,500 years later. It provides a sequence of some 120 terms, which we think were organized to reflect a hierarchy beginning with the most important official. Because of the list's antiquity we cannot translate most of the words, however. The popularity of the list was enormous, even though many of the terms found in it were not used in contemporary documents. Manuscripts of it appeared in numerous Babylonian cities for the entire period from Uruk IV to the early second millennium. Outside Babylonia manuscripts appeared at Ebla in western Syria and at Susa in western Iran. In Ebla the list was used as the basis for another one that taught scribes how to pronounce Sumerian signs (the Ebla syllabary).

We read its first five lines as follows in Sumerian:

NAMEŠDA (written with the signs ŠITA.GIŠ.KU)
NÁM KAB
NÁM DI
NÁM NÁM
NÁM URU

The meanings of these terms are vague to us, as the words do not appear in context and no translation into another, better understood, language is provided. Yet, although the list was no longer copied after the Old Babylonian period, terms from it appear in later lexical texts when the scribes included a guide to pronunciation and an Akkadian translation. They wrote, for example for line 1:

eš-da ŠITA.GIŠ.KU *šar-ru.*

The last word is the Akkadian term for "king," and strongly suggests that the first Sumerian entry in the Uruk *Standard List of Professions* referred to the highest official in the urban society.

The word signs are the central concern of the second group of tablets found at Uruk, the lexical texts, which make up 10 percent of the Uruk corpus. They are lists of words designating cities, officials, animals, plants, and manufactured goods, always in the same sequence. Their function was to show scribes how to write signs, and many manuscripts are the work of students copying out parts of a list. Such texts remain part of the Mesopotamian corpus for the entirety of its history, later expanded to thousands of entries with translations into one or more languages. Lexical texts are a fundamental part of the Mesopotamian cultural tradition, reflecting an organization of the vocabulary for practical purposes. Yet, ideological concerns also informed the order given. First, the grouping of words in the same list indicates that a system of classification existed. Second, the ordering of words in a list may have been important: the interpretation that the *Standard List of Professions* reflects social hierarchy suggests that the ranks of officials and their relative importance had been systematized.

The proto-cuneiform signs show little connection to the spoken language, but there are indications that people speaking Sumerian developed them. They represented the Sumerian word for mother, AMA, for example, by the drawing of a star into a box-shaped sign. As the star could be read AM, it intimated the pronunciation of the entire sign. The phonetic value of signs permitted their use to indicate terms beyond the names of concrete objects. The rebus principle was employed to extend their range. For example, the sign for "reed" was used to indicate the verb "to return," as both words sounded alike in Sumerian, GI. The majority of Sumerian words were monosyllabic. Consequently, the signs to write them could also be used to render syllabically a longer word or a grammatical element. A person's name could be spelled out with several syllables. Cuneiform writing was never intended to give a full phonetic rendering of a text, however, even if it had the ability to do so. Throughout its history a single sign could record a word, such as "king," irrespective of the language of the text or the grammatical form of the word. It was only in the mid-third millennium that markers of the conjugation of Sumerian verbs were written down, and only in the early second millennium, when Sumerian was probably a dead language, was a consistent effort made to record all grammatical elements in a sentence. It is important to keep in mind that cuneiform is a script, not a language. Just as the Latin alphabet has the potential to record any language, cuneiform script could do the same, and a large number of ancient Near Eastern languages were written in it (see box 2.2). We can only determine the identity of the language based on the syllabic writing of words, or on grammatical elements. The script invented in the Late Uruk period had all the components of cuneiform writing. It developed further by reducing the number of signs, increasing the use of syllables, and changing the signs themselves, replacing curvy lines traced into the clay with increasingly rectilinear ones impressed onto it. A single line looks like a triangle because the scribe first pressed the head of the stylus into the clay and then pushed down its thin side to create a mark. This shape led to our modern designation of the script as cuneiform, that is, wedge-shaped writing.

Box 2.2 *Languages of the ancient Near East*

The Near East always had people speaking various languages living side by side. Not every vernacular found its way into the written record, and oftentimes only the names of people give us an idea of what language they spoke. All languages could be written in cuneiform script, which was always the dominant writing system in the region until the last few centuries of the first millennium BC. In that millennium alphabetic scripts began to be used throughout the Near East and slowly supplanted cuneiform.

The most extensively written languages of Mesopotamia were Sumerian and Akkadian. The first was a language without any known cognates, and with a unique grammar and vocabulary. It was spoken throughout the third millennium in the south of Mesopotamia. By the early second millennium, only bureaucrats and cult personnel still used it; the date of its disappearance as a spoken language remains uncertain. Akkadian was a Semitic language related to Hebrew, Arabic, and many other languages of the Near East, but of a somewhat different grammatical structure. Its verbal system classifies it as an "east Semitic" language. Akkadian was written and spoken from the mid-third millennium to the late first over a wide geographical region. There were two main dialects: Assyrian in the north of Mesopotamia, Babylonian in the south. Both dialects show lexical and grammatical variations over time and according to the genre of the texts. We use the terms Old, Middle, and Neo-Babylonian and Old, Middle, and Neo-Assyrian for chronological phases, and Standard Babylonian to refer to a literary dialect found both in the south and the north. Earlier versions of Akkadian were used prior to the second millennium. We speak of Old Akkadian for the dialects found in texts from the Akkad and Ur III dynasties. The traces of the Semitic language found in texts predating these periods are more difficult to identify, and the term proto-Akkadian is used to refer to it. Babylonian was the language of culture and diplomacy throughout the Near East during the latter half of the second millennium. It was used from Anatolia to Egypt, from the Levant to the Zagros Mountains, always written in cuneiform on clay tablets. It existed in parallel to native languages and scripts, such as Ugaritic, a west Semitic language recorded in an alphabetic script in western Syria.

In the mid-third millennium, various other Semitic dialects were written down in cuneiform script, the one from Ebla being the best known. The language shows grammatical affinities with later west Semitic languages, but also with the Akkadian of Babylonia at the time. A commonly spoken west Semitic language in the early second millennium was Amorite, found from western Syria to southern Babylonia. No texts completely written in that language are preserved, however, and it is primarily known from the names of people. The same is true for the first-millennium west Semitic language Aramaic, which had a great vernacular spread. It was mainly recorded in an alphabetic script on perishable materials and relatively few remains are known. Only a couple of Aramaic texts in cuneiform have survived.

During the second millennium, the Hittites of central Anatolia used a large variety of languages, several of which were written in cuneiform. Those included Hittite, an Indo-European language, and Hurrian, linguistically related only to Urartian, a language used in first-millennium eastern Anatolia. Hurrian was in use in northern Syria from the mid-third millennium on, and was very important in that area until the late second millennium, but few texts written in that language are preserved.

Finally, Elamite was written from the third through the first millennium in southwestern Iran. It was linguistically distinct from the other Near Eastern languages and evolved over time. In certain periods Akkadian supplanted it as the language of administration in western Iran. Elamite was still written by the Persians in the fifth century, but these rulers used other languages across their vast empire, including Old Persian written in an especially developed simplified form of cuneiform.

In order for accounting to function properly, a fully developed metrology had to exist as well. In the Late Uruk period, a complete system of weights and measures appeared that laid the foundation for all later Mesopotamian systems. The basic units were inspired by natural phenomena and ordered with a mixture of the sexagesimal and decimal systems that characterized the numerals. In the recording of time, a year consisted of twelve months of thirty days each, and an additional month was added intermittently to adjust the cycle to the solar year. In weights, the load a man could carry, a talent, was subdivided into sixty minas, each of which contained sixty shekels. Lengths used the forearm as the basic unit, subdivided into thirty fingers. Six forearms made up a reed. A set of equivalences was established at this time in order to facilitate the exchange of goods measured in different ways. These equivalences remained essentially the same for the entirety of Mesopotamian history: one shekel of silver = one gur of grain = six minas of wool = twelve silas of sesame oil.

There was thus not an evolution of precursors to writing, from *bullae* with tokens to tablets with signs impressed on them, as is very often suggested. These presumed stages coincided and must be seen as different and competing attempts at conceptualizing the surroundings. The most successful and consequential of these attempts ended up being the cuneiform writing system. It provided a new way to signify the physical world surrounding its users, and organized that world as a logical system that could be expressed through writing. The development of writing was a conceptual breakthrough, not merely an administrative one.

The tools of bureaucracy – script, seals, measures, and weights – all continued to develop in later Near Eastern history based on the foundations laid in the Uruk period. To a great extent, these elements define the ancient Near East: cuneiform writing on clay tablets, the cylinder seal, and the mixture of decimal and sexagesimal units in numerals. While there were local variations and changes over time, the continuation of the elements that we first observe in the Late Uruk period shows how important that period was for the formation of Near Eastern culture.

2.3   The "Uruk Expansion"

The developments just described all happened in the far south of Mesopotamia in the area around the city of Uruk. We are unable to determine whether

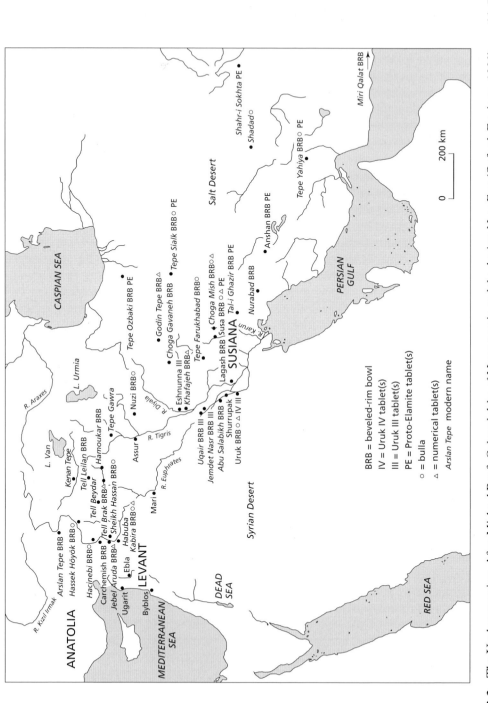

Map 2.2 The Uruk expansion. After Michael Roaf, *Cultural Atlas of Mesopotamia and the Ancient Near East* (Oxford: Equinox, 1990), pp. 64–5.

similar processes took place independently in other parts of southern Mesopotamia because of an overall lack of excavation of Uruk period levels there. Nevertheless, the sheer size of Uruk, roughly 250 hectares (620 acres), suggests that it was an unusual center whose complexity led to the use of writing and the organization of a city-state. Ironically, much more archaeological information for the Uruk period comes from regions outside southern Mesopotamia, especially western Iran, northern Syria, and southern Turkey. In the mid-fourth millennium, local developments there became fundamentally influenced by southern Mesopotamia. A variety of interactions between local populations and people from the Uruk region is attested, and some of the difficult questions are to determine why these interactions took place and to what extent local or foreign impulses caused change.

Just to the east of lower Mesopotamia is the area of southwest Iran, itself an alluvial plain below the Zagros Mountains, that is often called Susiana after the large site of Susa at its center. Although geographically similar to southern Mesopotamia and close by, travel between the two regions is difficult as marshes separate them. The nearest access route is in the foothills of the Zagros, going around the marshes. The difficulties of communication might explain why the cultures of the two areas remained distinct until the fourth millennium. Probably due to indigenous forces in the early fourth millennium, a large center emerged at Susa, but at the time of the Late Uruk period, Susa's material culture became entirely influenced by southern Mesopotamia. We find typical Late Uruk pottery in great quantity and the precursors of proto-cuneiform writing: *bullae* with tokens, numerical tablets, and tablets with numbers and one or two word signs. Seemingly inspired by Uruk, Susa had become a city in its own right, commanding resources from the entire Susiana region. Moreover, Susa extended its cultural influence over a wide area in Iran, as is shown by the appearance of the beveled-rim bowl in sites all over the country. Examples have been excavated in the Zagros Mountains (e.g., Godin Tepe, Choga Gavaneh), in northern (e.g., Tepe Ozbaki, Tepe Sialk), central (e.g., Tepe Yahiya), and southern Iran (e.g., Nurabad). They were even found on the coast of modern Pakistan (Miri Qalat). Some of these locations were more than a thousand kilometers from Susa, which we assume was the transit point for Uruk influences, as the contacts between these sites and Susa survived after the Uruk expansion had ceased.

The situation in the north was different. In northern Iraq, Syria, and southern Turkey, elements of the Uruk culture appeared starting in the mid-fourth millennium, but the degree to which these affected local cultures varied. Southern influence had waned after the Ubaid period and the local cultures attested are subsumed under the name Late Chalcolithic (see chart 1.1). In the first half of the millennium large centers with monumental architecture arose in the region, commanding the resources of their immediate surroundings as the result of local developments toward centralized power. Some scholars call these cities, but their growth stalled in the mid-fourth millennium, while Uruk in the south increased massively in size and complexity. The new southern city established close links with the north, although its influence varied between different sites.

In some places settlements of urban proportions appeared on virgin soil with a cultural assemblage imported wholesale from southern Mesopotamia, such as Habuba Kabira on the Middle Euphrates, which was a densely inhabited and fortified city. Most scholars think that southern immigrants founded these cities as colonies.

In other places Uruk people established themselves into existing settlements, creating enclaves for themselves. Their interaction with the local populations introduced innovations within the context of native traditions. For instance, at Tell Brak southern pottery, including the beveled-rim bowl, became dominant and people used painted cone mosaics, sealed *bullae* and numerical notation tablets, all items inspired by southern influences. But they did not fully replace local products. In still other places, the Uruk presence was restricted to a few buildings. But even there the influences on the local populations could be drastic. At Arslan Tepe in southern Turkey, for example, local elites seem to have imitated southern practices and constructed a massive monumental building. Finally, there were ancient settlements, such as Kenan Tepe in Turkey, where Uruk influence was completely absent.

The Uruk cultural elements that appeared in this region are building plans and decoration, pottery (especially the beveled-rim bowl), and precursors of writing, *bullae* with tokens and numerical tablets. Proto-cuneiform writing, found in Uruk IVa levels in the south, did not make its way into the north, so contacts must have ceased just before this development. These material elements are less important than the social change the Uruk expansion caused. Urban centers suddenly arose with the concomitant social hierarchy and economic organization. It remains unclear what was most important in this process, indigenous evolution or foreign influence. Local trends toward larger settlements and a hierarchy of settlements predated the Uruk expansion. Uruk influence may thus have accelerated a process that had its roots in the local cultures. On the other hand, the massive foreign influence observed in a city like Habuba Kabira clearly shows southern inspiration.

Aspects of Uruk culture penetrated beyond the spheres where its impact was direct. The beveled-rim bowl is found at several sites near the north Syrian coast, for instance. Most intriguing is the possibility that Uruk influenced early Egypt, where in the late fourth millennium a number of cultural characteristics similar to those of Mesopotamia appeared: niched mud brick architecture, decorative clay cones, some pottery styles, cylinder seals, and certain artistic motifs. That these elements appear in central Egypt and not in the north suggests that the contacts were made through travel via the Persian Gulf and the Red Sea rather than overland across Syria.

The most difficult challenge remains to explain why this expansion took place. For what reason did the young city-state or states of southern Mesopotamia decide to send out people to distant places in order to settle there, bringing along their cultural baggage? Most scholars suggest that Uruk people wanted access to resources rare or absent at home, and they stress that Babylonia lacks wood, stone, and metals. That deficiency is exaggerated, however, and materials were

locally available to compensate for it. It seems more appropriate to take the fundamental demographic and ideological changes that occurred in Uruk-times southern Mesopotamia into account. States had developed with a new type of ideology and a new social structure. Certain people held positions of importance
never seen before and had influence over the lives of many. The newly emergent
elites may have wished access to exotic materials, whose possession distinguished
them from the rest of the people. Many luxury goods were only available outside
Mesopotamia: semi-precious stones, gold, silver, and so on. The settlements to
the east and north could have been colonies of southerners, assuring access to
these resources through interaction with local populations. Moreover, the conviction that a god had influence beyond the city limits may have contributed to
an expansionist ideology. Not only the immediate surroundings but also distant
regions may have been considered as dependent on the city-god. Such ideological elements, while impossible to ascertain in the documentation, should not be
entirely ignored in our interpretation of the Uruk expansion.

2.4   Uruk's Aftermath

The end of the Uruk period came with fundamental changes at home and abroad.
Those outside southern Mesopotamia are the clearest to us, as we see a sudden discontinuation of contacts. Habuba Kabira, the fully southern installation
in Syria, disappeared for unknown reasons. In places where local cultures had
adopted Uruk practices, indigenous traditions reemerged. Village life and social
organization became the norm again in northern Mesopotamia and Syria. In
Susiana immigrants from the Zagros Mountains seem to have taken over the center at Susa. Instead of political fragmentation, as in the north, the region became
a state equivalent to what we find in southern Mesopotamia. We call it the proto-
Elamite state because it seems to have been the precursor of later political entities
in the area. Proto-Elamite culture maintained some Uruk traditions, but adapted
them as local ones. It developed a distinct script, which differed from the contemporaneous Uruk script and was in use over a wide area of Iran for some two
hundred years. Tablets inscribed with the proto-Elamite script were excavated as
far as 1,200 kilometers from Susa. The Uruk-inspired centralization of power in
the region of Susa led thus to a competing state there, which has been blamed for
cutting off southern Mesopotamia's access to the Iranian plateau and areas farther
east. The timing of the collapse of the Uruk system is indicated by the discontinuation of accounting practices in the north and the independent development of
a script in Susiana. The precursors of proto-cuneiform tablets are found everywhere, but not the Uruk IV-type tablets. The latter are found only at Uruk at the
very end of the period (in archaeological level IVa), and it seems thus that contacts
with outlying areas were cut off just before.

What happened in Uruk itself is harder to discern. The monumental buildings
that dominated the Eanna complex were razed and the entire area was leveled. On
top, in level III, a new set of buildings was constructed wherein were found many

tablets, more elaborate than those in Uruk IV. Small numbers of closely related tablets were found at Jemdet Nasr and Uqair in northern Babylonia. Archaeologically, this period is called Jemdet Nasr after the site where its cultural assemblage was first discovered. The city of Uruk continued to be substantial in size, but other Babylonian centers developed as well, as people moved into them from the countryside, possibly as the result of social upheavals or invasions. The far-flung contacts of the earlier centuries ceased, but the Jemdet Nasr culture penetrated more profoundly into nearby regions, such as the Diyala River valley, which had been marginal before then. Moreover, direct contact with the Persian Gulf area is attested. There was thus a reorganization of society in southern Mesopotamia into more and similar-scale centers with more profound influence in areas nearby. The bases for further political development in the region were in place.

Debate 2.1   *Why cities?*

What inspired people to move in large numbers to live packed together into small spaces with lots of noise, dirt, and disease? Ancient cities were deathtraps with such high mortality rates that many scholars believe that they could not maintain their population levels without constant immigration. If in the Uruk period people from all over Babylonia, if not farther away, indeed relocated to Uruk and its surroundings, there must have been something that encouraged them to do so – unless we accept that it was an accidental outcome of many people doing the same thing (Ur 2014).

Modern scholars tend not to ask the question in these terms, but focus instead on the processes that gave rise to urban societies, which were also the first states in world history (see Rothman 2004 and Ur 2014 for surveys). The short book by Robert McC. Adams, *The Evolution of Urban Society* (1966), in which he compared early Mesopotamia to Mexico in the first millennium AD, was groundbreaking. He saw cities develop as the result of ecological diversity, which encouraged the specialization of agricultural production and made exchange necessary. Environmental variety is even more accentuated in very recent research that shows how the earliest cities in Babylonia were inserted in a marshy countryside and extensively relied on its resources (Pournelle 2013). Specialization of labor in agriculture, manufacture, and administration led to people becoming more closely attached to their professional peers than their family members and to a truly urban society, which was very different from the earlier village communities.

While other scholars recognize the importance of the environment, they focus on different elements, however, as major motors toward urbanism. Some see a universal development of bureaucratic regulation and emphasize the proliferation of tools of administration (Wright and Johnson 1975). Others see long-distance exchange as fundamental and stress Uruk's interactions with distant areas. Control over the access to wood, semi-precious stones, etcetera gave urban elites their legitimacy (Algaze 2005). The most recent book-length study uses a more local perspective and sees the increased productivity of specialized labor and the need for exchange as well as the presence of an excellent infrastructure for it in the waterways as fundamental (Algaze 2008). Most scholars think that a small segment of society only, the elite, benefited from the new conditions. Some portray the city as a means of dominating and exploiting the people (Pollock 1999). But not all agree; it has also been suggested that Uruk society was very egalitarian and attempted to distribute wealth as democratically as possible (Charvát 2002). Were rations a social service for all or a means to tie laborers to their employers?

There are also voices that caution us not to see urban society as the necessary result of increased social complexity. There were always people who lived outside the reach of urban institutions and the latter did not seek to make things more complex, but rather simpler (Yoffee 2005). It is remarkable, however, how in the source material available to us throughout Mesopotamian history people saw the city as the standard center of political, economic, and religious activity. We do not see an alternative to it or nostalgia for non-urban life.

To return to the question of why people would have preferred to live in cities, we may draw a parallel with later history. During the Industrial Revolution in the nineteenth century AD, life in English cities was truly miserable, as the writings of Friedrich Engels and Charles Dickens eloquently show. Yet, people flocked to them because there were more opportunities for work there than in the countryside. Perhaps the situation had been similar in fourth-millennium-BC Babylonia.

NOTE

1   Algaze 2013: 78–9.

3

Competing City-States: The Early Dynastic Period

3000	2500	2000	1500	1000	500

ca. 2800	Archaic Ur
ca. 2500	Tablets from Fara and Abu Salabikh
ca. 2500–2350	Lagash–Umma border conflict
ca. 2400	Uru'inimgina of Lagash
ca. 2400–2350	Bau-temple archive at Girsu
ca. 2350	Ebla archives

At the end of the Uruk period, around the year 3100, Babylonia's far-reaching cultural influence over the Near East waned and people throughout the region reverted to local traditions and stopped writing to record transactions. In southern Mesopotamia, however, written sources vastly increased in number, enabling us to study political and cultural developments in much greater detail than before. They show that a network of city-states, constantly interacting and competing with one another, characterized the political situation there. After several centuries, cultural contacts between Babylonia and the rest of the Near East reemerged, which allows us to broaden the geographical focus of historical study once more and shows that elsewhere, too, small states formed the predominant political organization.

Babylonia thus becomes our focus of attention in the 550-year era that is usually referred to as the "Early Dynastic period." This period is often subdivided into

A History of the Ancient Near East ca. 3000–323 BC, Third Edition. Marc Van De Mieroop.
© 2016 John Wiley & Sons, Inc. Published 2016 by John Wiley & Sons, Inc.

Early Dynastic I (ca. 2900–2750), II (ca. 2750–2600), IIIa (ca. 2600–2450), and IIIb (ca. 2450–2350), but these are archaeological distinctions based on stylistic changes in the material remains that have little historical value. The period should be regarded as a unit in political terms, displaying the same basic characteristics for its entire duration.

3.1   The Written Sources and Their Historical Uses

The written sources for the study of this period cover a variety of genres. Administrative documents continue to dominate in number, but we also have political narratives written for some rulers of the period, and later literary tales about others. Administrative archives appear in different sites in increasingly large quantities. The information they contain becomes more wide-ranging, and we understand the texts themselves better because they reflect the spoken language more closely through writing out phonetic and grammatical elements. At Ur, some 280 tablets were excavated dating to around 2800. The administrative tablets from Fara (ancient Shuruppak; ca. 1,000 tablets) and Abu Salabikh (ancient name uncertain; ca. 500 tablets) date to around 2500 and were mixed together with lexical material. The largest number of texts comes from the very end of the period, with Girsu yielding some 1,500 tablets. For most of the Early Dynastic period the inhabitants of Babylonia alone seem to have used writing and it was only later on that the technology appeared in Syria, where archives were excavated at Mari (ca. 40 tablets), at Nabada (modern Tell Beydar; ca. 250 tablets), and especially in the west at Ebla (ca. 3,600 tablets), all dating to around 2350.

For the study of political history a new type of text, the royal inscription, provides the most useful information. At first it was a simple writing of a royal name and title on a votive object, indicating what individual dedicated it, for instance, "Mebaragesi, king of Kish," on a stone vessel dating to around 2650. Soon royal inscriptions included short statements, such as that the ruler commissioned the building of a temple, and over time they became lengthier, giving accounts of military feats associated with the event commemorated. The genre culminated in the first millennium with long and detailed year-by-year reports of campaigns and descriptions of buildings constructed. These records provide important data on the activities of the ruler both as builder and as warrior. From the Early Dynastic period, a handful of texts each were found in the Babylonian sites of Adab, Kish, Nippur, Umma, Ur, and Uruk. Mari on the Euphrates is the only Syrian city where royal inscriptions were excavated. But the largest group by far comes from the southern state of Lagash, where nine members of the local dynasty left a total of 120 of them. These give an explicit description of the wars between that state and its neighbor, Umma, clearly biased toward the Lagashite point of view since its kings wrote the inscriptions. This group of texts allows us for the first time in Near Eastern history to narrate an event based on contemporary sources.

In later Mesopotamian literature from the late third and early second millennia several compositions deal with kings from the Early Dynastic period. They are often quite detailed and thus feature prominently in modern historical reconstructions, but their reliability as historical sources is suspect. Most influential among these has been the so-called *Sumerian King List*, which includes a long sequence of city-dynasties and kings of the Early Dynastic period (see box 3.1 and figure 3.1). The earlier portions record fantastically long reigns – 3,600 years, for example – and royal names such as Dog, Scorpion, and Gazelle, and are clearly

Box 3.1   *The Sumerian King List*

Among the later Mesopotamian texts that deal with the Early Dynastic period, the *Sumerian King List* has been the most influential in modern historical reconstructions. The text is known from one manuscript of the twenty-first century and seventeen from the nineteenth and eighteenth centuries, including from two sites outside Babylonia: Susa in western Iran and Shehna in northern Syria. It depicts a world in which kingship "descended from heaven" and was passed on from city to city whose local dynasties held temporary hegemony over the entire region. The number of dynasties included increased over time. A typical segment reads as follows:

> At Ur, Mesannepada was king; he ruled 80 years; Meski'agnuna, son of Mesannepada, was king; he ruled 36 years; Elulu ruled 25 years; Balulu ruled 36 years; four kings ruled 177 years. Ur was defeated in battle and its kingship was taken to Awan.[1]

Chronologically, the text in its latest edition addresses the period from the moment kingship first appeared, before the flood, to the end of the reign of Sin-magir of the Isin dynasty (1817). In the segment that covers the Early Dynastic period, the city-states mentioned are primarily located in Babylonia, giving special prominence to Ur, Uruk, and Kish. Also included are three non-Babylonian cities, Awan in the east, Hamazi in the north, and Mari in the west. From other evidence we know that some of the kings listed consecutively ruled concurrently. The text enumerates them sequentially because the main ideological elements expressed in this text are that there is only one divinely legitimized ruler at a time, and that hegemonic kingship circulated among a restricted number of cities. Incorporated in it were dynastic lists of kings from different cities and the number of years they ruled. The accuracy of the later parts can be checked against information from dated economic documents. The earlier parts of the *Sumerian King List* are legendary, however, assigning impossibly long reigns of 3,600 years, for instance, to mythological figures such as Dumuzi, who was known as the husband of the goddess Inanna and was probably purely fictional. In its final version, kings of the Isin dynasty used the text to legitimize their claim to supreme power in Babylonia, even though they did not politically control the entire area covered by the King List.

[1] Translation after Glassner 2004: 120–1.

Figure 3.1   The Weld-Blundell prism inscribed with the Sumerian King List. This is the most complete manuscript of the Sumerian King List known to us, perhaps from Larsa in Babylonia. Each of its four sides has two columns that list a sequence of cities in which kingship was held and the rulers of the dynasties with the number of years they ruled. The list begins with rulers from before the flood and ends with Sin-magir of the Isin dynasty (r. 1827–1817) and was probably written in that king's final year or soon thereafter. Ashmolean Museum, Oxford. Baked clay; four equal sides, each about 20 cm (7.9 in) high and 9 cm (3.5 in) wide. Credit: Ashmolean Museum, University of Oxford/Bridgeman Images.

unreliable. Although later sections seem more realistic and can sometimes be confirmed from other sources, the overall work was undoubtedly a later construct to legitimize the political situation then. Consequently, the list loses much of its value as a historical source, although its concept of city-dynasties remains our primary means of structuring Early Dynastic history. Other Sumerian literary texts, again known from much later manuscripts only, tell stories about three kings of the city of Uruk (Enmerkar, Lugalbanda, and Gilgamesh), and involve far-flung military adventures and local conflicts. These texts are more important for the view they provide on the Sumerians' sense of the past than as sources on the Early Dynastic period.

A study of Early Dynastic Babylonia should be based first on the textual remains of the period itself, and by 2400 certain places provide us with a mixture of writings that enable us to investigate questions from various angles simultaneously. From the state of Lagash, for instance, we have royal inscriptions relating military and political events, and a large number of administrative documents that record the activities of an important public institution. These allow us to reconstruct the royal administration and compare the official rhetoric to records of actual day-to-day affairs. One problem is that some of the words found in these sources are only understood because they appear in more extensive later documentation. We have to allow for the possibility that their sense became different over time owing to new circumstances, and we cannot simply apply a meaning of the twenty-first century to explain a term used in a record from the twenty-fifth. For example, the title énsi, well known later as a provincial governor in the service of the king, appears in the Early Dynastic period to refer to a ruler who acts autonomously. Changes in the political situation and other circumstances had an effect on the meaning of such terms.

The increasing number of written sources and the subjects they discuss is a great asset to the historian, but we have to be conscious of a major bias in them. They are the products only of the leaders of state organizations – kings, temple administrators, and so on – and they reveal their interests alone. This is true as well for the works of visual arts produced at this time. Not only is their purview centered on the city-states, mostly ignoring what lay outside them, but also they may express more the ambitions of their authors than reality. Kings may have wished that they had crushed an opponent's army rather than have done so. This bias of the written documentation remains a challenge throughout the entire history of the Near East, but is especially acute in this early period when the voices of non-state actors are fully absent.

3.2   Political Developments in Southern Mesopotamia

The basic element of the political organization of Babylonia in the Early Dynastic period was the city-state: an urban center that directly controlled a hinterland with a radius of some 15 kilometers (10 miles), where people lived in villages.

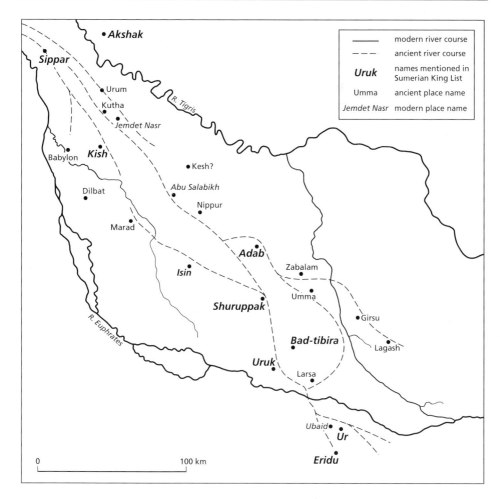

Map 3.1   The city-states of Babylonia in the Early Dynastic period. After Joan Oates, *Babylon* (London: Thames and Hudson, 1986), p. 13.

Because agriculture in the region was wholly dependent on irrigation water for its crops, settlements had to be near rivers, primarily the multiple branches of the Euphrates, or canals dug alongside them. Throughout Babylonia about thirty-five city-states existed, more or less evenly spread through the region (map 3.1). Some of them contained several urban centers, most importantly Lagash, which incorporated three cities, Girsu, Lagash, and Nina. The steppe lay between the cultivated and permanently inhabited zones and was used for seasonal animal herding and hunting. These areas and their inhabitants were only indirectly controlled by the urban powers.

In the early third millennium Babylonia saw a general population growth, possibly accelerated by immigration or the settling down of semi-nomadic groups.

Throughout the region there was a general increase in the number of cities, their size, and the density of their population. Each one of them constituted a small state with a political hierarchy under a single ruler. These city-states at first were located at sufficient distance from one another so as to be separated by steppe and land that was not part of their agricultural zones. But the continued increase in the population necessitated an extension of the cultivated areas, so the borders of the city-states, especially in the south, became contiguous or even overlapped. A drying of the climate may have aggravated this process, as it caused a lowering of the sea level and a retrenchment of the rivers into fewer branches. The disappearance of interstitial zones had important repercussions both within the states themselves and throughout the region. Among the changes were a secularization of power within the city-states and its centralization in regional terms.

A fundamental element in Mesopotamian ideology was the concept that each city was the dwelling of a particular god or goddess. People thought that cities had been constructed in primordial times as residences for the gods, who acted as their patron deities. Thus Ur was the house of Nanna, Uruk of Inanna, Nippur of Enlil, etcetera. This concept was linked to the role of the temple, or god's household (see below), in cities. The temple's function as collector and distributor of agricultural resources was founded in the ideology that the god received them as gifts and redistributed them to the people. Thus the head of the temple administration served as leader in the city, and from the Uruk period on the primary ideological support for the city-ruler was his function in the temple household. The temple was, in fact, the dominant institution in the early city and the largest structure within its walls, sometimes built on an earthen platform towering over the other buildings. The gods were imagined as living in a world parallel to that of humans, so each god had a household, a spouse, children, and servants. The dependent deities also had smaller temples and shrines in the cities, sized according to their status, and every city had a multitude of temples.

With the expansion of the city-states' zones of influence, competition for the remaining open areas grew and soon led to intercity wars over agricultural land. A leader's military rather than his cultic role became of primary importance in such situations. In the later Sumerian stories looking back on this period, the people granted a war leader authority on a temporary basis in moments of crisis. The popular assembly elected a physically strong man as war leader and that body controlled his movements. Modern historians often call this practice evidence of a "primitive democracy" that unraveled into a dynastic system under which rule was passed on from father to son over several generations. The dynastic ideal of war leader was not compatible with that of chief temple administrator chosen by the gods for his managerial competence. They had different bases of authority, one deriving from prominence in warfare, the other from a perception of divine favor. We associate the new military class with the palace and kingship. In the Early Dynastic period, we see the first appearance of a new type of monumental building, the palace, identifiable as such by its residential plan. Moreover, documents of the time mention a new central institution, the é-gal, literally the "great house," which in later periods clearly refers to the royal household. This is distinct from the é, "house," of the city-god, the temple. These two sources of authority need not be regarded as inherently antagonistic to each other, but merging them into one was not a simple task.

The evidence from Lagash, the best-documented state of the period, shows how the two bases of power became harmonized. Around 2450, its ruler Eanna-tum set up a large flat stone stele carved with an inscription and visual images on both sides to commemorate a victory in his war against Umma. Its modern name is "Stele of the Vultures" (figure 3.2). One side shows the patron deity Ningirsu capturing enemies in a net and subduing them with his mace. On the other side the king leads his troops in battle. God and king are like two sides of the same coin: together they succeed but they are distinct. The last independent ruler of

(a)   (b)

Figure 3.2   Stele of the Vultures, front and back. Excavated at Girsu, the stele shows an episode in the war between Umma and Lagash visually and describes it in the text. On one side, the king of Lagash, Eannatum, appears leading his troops on foot and by chariot, on the other the large figure of Lagash's god Ningirsu is portrayed holding a net filled with the bodies of enemies. The name "stele of the vultures" derives from a small scene of vultures hovering over the human troops. Louvre Museum Paris, ca. 2450 BC. Limestone; H. 180 cm; W. 130 cm; Th. 11 cm (70.8 × 51.2 × 4.3 in). Credit: (a) akg images/Erich Lessing; (b) © RMN-Grand Palais/Hervé Lewandowski.

Lagash seems to have erased this distinction, however. He was a usurper called Uru'inimgina. Early in his reign he proclaimed a reorganization of the state, ostensibly removing control over the agricultural land from himself and his family and granting it to the city-god Ningirsu and his family. Moreover, he abolished several duties and taxes and canceled certain obligations of indebted families. At the same time, we see a fundamental change in the administration of the best-documented institution in the state of Lagash. What had been called the é-mí, the household of the wife (of the city-ruler), was renamed é-Bau, the household of the goddess Bau, Ningirsu's wife. But, first Uru'inimgina himself and later his wife appeared as chief administrators, although the estate's holdings allegedly belonged to Bau. The name-change of the institution coincided with a substantial increase in its activities, doubling the number of its dependents and agricultural areas through a transfer of resources from other temples. These moves seem to indicate an attempt to merge the various households of the city under the ruler's family. As king and war leader, Uru'inimgina ostensibly transferred the ownership of land and estates to the city-god and his family, while in practice he and his family members took control of the gods' estates. The king ruled by divine favor, but he had total command over the gods' earthly possessions, so any prior distinction between secular and divine authority had disappeared. This idea found its fullest expression in the subsequent period under the Akkad dynasty. As we will see, its fourth king, Naram-Sin, declared himself a god and when he depicted a military victory on his stele (figure 4.1), he merged the two sides of the "Stele of the Vultures" into one: as god king Naram-Sin led his troops in battle.

The increased competition over land among city-states is most explicit in a series of inscriptions found in the southern state of Lagash (see document 3.1). Over a period of 150 years, from about 2500 to 2350, kings there wrote accounts of a border conflict with their northern neighbor Umma. They described the war in terms of a dispute between Ningirsu, patron deity of Lagash, and Shara, god of Umma, over a field called Gu'edena, that means "edge of the plain." The kings portrayed themselves as deputies acting on behalf of the gods. On the Stele of the Vultures, Eannatum even described himself as the giant son of Ningirsu, who engendered him to fight for his cause. According to the Lagash accounts, the chief god Enlil in the distant past had demarcated the border between the two states running through the Gu'edena. The inscriptions acknowledge that historically a king of Kish called Mesalim, who would have lived around 2600, had performed the act. Thus already at that early time the two city-states had competing claims and sought recourse to outside arbitration. The sequence of events is difficult to establish, as only the Lagashite point of view is documented. Whenever the state was strong, it tried to enforce its claims over the land, whether justified or not. Successive kings stated that Umma had illegally occupied the land and that the army of Lagash repeatedly pushed back the enemy. Yet the conflict persisted over several centuries, which shows how inconclusive these battles were as well as the importance of the agricultural area to both states. We may assume that other states similarly attempted to extend their farming zones by annexing the fields of neighbors.

Document 3.1   *The Umma–Lagash border conflict*

The war between the southern city-states of Umma and Lagash over an agricultural area that they both claimed is the best-documented event of the Early Dynastic period. Over a period of 150 years five rulers of Lagash and one of Umma devoted royal inscriptions to it, including large monuments like the Stele of the Vultures (figure 3.2). They placed their own participation within the historical context of the entire war. Enmetena in this inscription, for example, states that the original border was set in the time of Mesalim, king of Kish, around 2600. King Ush of Umma first violated the border shortly after 2500 and the god of Lagash, Ningirsu, drove him back. (Akurgal, not mentioned, was king of Lagash at that time.) He then recounts how his uncle, Eannatum, reestablished the border when Enakale ruled Umma. In a passage not quoted here, he states that his father, Enanatum, waged war with Ur-lumma, a war Enmetena continued. The final opponent was Il, who had usurped Umma's throne around 2425. Remarkably, this type of historical depth disappears from Assyrian and Babylonian royal inscriptions later on.

Excerpts of the account by King Enmetena

Enlil, king of the lands, father of the gods, upon his firm command drew the border between Ningirsu and Shara.[1] Mesalim, king of Kish, at the command of the god Ishtaran, measured the field and placed a stele. Ush, ruler of Umma, acted arrogantly. He ripped out the stele and marched unto the plain of Lagash. Ningirsu, the hero of Enlil, at the latter's command did battle with Umma. Upon Enlil's command he cast the great battle-net upon it. Its great burial mound was set up for him in the plain. Eannatum, ruler of Lagash, the uncle of Enmetena ruler of Lagash, with Enakale, ruler of Umma, drew the border. He extended the channel of the Inun-canal into the Gu'edena, giving up 2,105 nindan (ca. 12.5 kilometers or 7.8 miles) of the field of Ningirsu to the side of Umma. As a field without an owner he established it. At the canal he inscribed a stele, and the stele of Mesalim he returned to its place. He did not cross into the steppe of Umma. . . .

At that time Il, who was the head of the temple of Zabalam, made a retreat from Girsu to Umma. Il received the rulership of Umma there. Into the boundary channel of Ningirsu and the boundary channel of Nanshe, the levee of Ningirsu – being at the edge of the Tigris and on the boundary of Girsu – the Namnundakigara of Enlil, Enki, and Ninhursag, its water was diverted. Of the barley of Lagash he repaid only 3,600 gur$_7$. When Enmetena, ruler of Lagash, because of these channels sent men to Il, Il the ruler of Umma, the one who steals fields, said in a hostile way: "The boundary channel of Ningirsu and the boundary channel of Nanshe are mine. From the Antasura to the Edingalabzu I will shift the levee," he said. But Enlil and Ninhursag did not give that to him. Enmetena, ruler of Lagash, named by Ningirsu, at the just command of Enlil, at the just command of Ningirsu, at the just command of Nanshe, constructed that channel from the Tigris to the Inun-canal. He built the foundation of the Namnundakigara in stone. For the lord who loves him, Ningirsu, for the lady who loves him, Nanshe, he restored it. Enmetena, ruler of Lagash, given the scepter by Enlil, given wisdom by Enki, chosen in the heart of Nanshe, chief administrator of Ningirsu, the one who grasps the commands of the gods, may his personal god Shuturul stand before Ningirsu and Nanshe forever for the life of Enmetena. If the man of Umma, in order to carry off the fields crosses the boundary channel of Ningirsu and the boundary channel of Nanshe, be he a man from Umma or a foreigner, may Enlil destroy him, may Ningirsu after casting his great battle-net, place his hands and feet upon him. May the people of his own city, after rising up against him, kill him in the midst of his city!

Translation after Cooper 1986: 54–7.
[1] i.e., between Lagash and Umma.

Not all interactions between states were hostile, however. The royal houses communicated with one another as equals and had diplomatic relations. The exchange of gifts strengthened these ties. In a hoard of precious items found at Mari, there was a bead inscribed with the name of Mesannepada, king of Ur: the group of objects was likely given by one king to the other. The ruler's wife at Lagash, Baranamtara, is known to have exchanged presents with her counterpart at Adab, and this was probably common practice.

Although the city-state characterized the political situation of the period, various processes of the centralization of power into larger territorial units were at work, due both to hostile and peaceful interactions between states. Wars between neighbors could lead to territorial occupations. Around 2400, for example, a king of Uruk, Lugalkiginedudu, claimed kingship over Ur, a city 50 kilometers (31 miles) to the south. The process of conquest and unification culminated at the end of the Early Dynastic period when the king of Umma, Lugalzagesi, conquered Ur and Uruk and then defeated Uru'inimgina of Lagash, thus governing the entire south of Babylonia. True, he may have overstated his accomplishment in his own inscriptions, in which he claimed control from the Upper to the Lower Sea, that is the Mediterranean to the Persian Gulf. But certainly the extent of his power reached beyond the traditional borders of a single city-state.

Political alliances whose participants agreed to accept the authority of an outsider are documented from ca. 2600 on. One example of such a regional superstructure can be inferred from the title "King of Kish." When the god Enlil demarcated the border between Umma and Lagash, it was Mesalim, "King of Kish," who measured it out and set up a boundary marker. That Mesalim had some sort of power in Lagash is borne out by a ceremonial mace-head inscribed with his name found there; but the text ends by mentioning that Lugalsha'engur was the city-ruler (Sumerian énsi) of Lagash at the time. Similarly, an inscription of Mesalim from the central Babylonian city of Adab acknowledges the existence of its local ruler, one Ninkisalsi. The title "King of Kish" appears repeatedly in the royal inscriptions of the late Early Dynastic period, and cannot be considered to indicate only kings who controlled the northern Babylonian city of Kish. Eannatum of Lagash, for instance, after defeating a number of southern cities was granted kingship of Kish by the goddess Inanna. Why did the kingship of Kish carry this prestige? It is highly unlikely that the title conferred full control over Babylonia and that the other city-rulers whose inscriptions we read were merely dependents of a dynasty in Kish. The king of Kish's power seems to have derived from some kind of political understanding in the region. Backed by military might (remember that Eannatum became king of Kish only after defeating several neighbors), he had an authority that was regionally accepted.

Another such political agreement is attested in the administrative texts from Shuruppak, dating to around 2500. Records of soldiers from Ur, Adab, Nippur, Lagash, and Umma were kept in this small city. Those men are said to be "stationed at KI.EN.GI,"[1] a term that a few centuries later came to mean Sumer, the southern half of Babylonia, but which at this time probably referred to a single locality. The same group of texts also makes reference to a coalition in a place called Unken, the Sumerian word for "assembly," made up of Lagash, Umma, and Adab. These arrangements were ephemeral: the last two were upset by the border conflict between Umma and Lagash. They probably were a result of the struggles characteristic of the period: cities concluded various alliances in order to stand up to enemies.

Yet, there was a shared understanding that all the city-states belonged to a common religious system that joined them together in war and peace. This is already attested around 3000, when multiple cities had just developed, and not surprisingly the oldest urban center, Uruk, played a prominent role in it. The existence of collective cult practices centered on Uruk is suggested by a group of seal impressions on tablets and lumps of clay, which display symbols that render the names of several other cities. Seal impressions on tablets from the Jemdet Nasr period (3100–2900) show a fixed sequence of city-symbols, including those of Ur, Larsa, Zabalam, Urum, Arina, and probably Kesh. It is likely that the tablets reported contributions made to the goddess Inanna of Uruk, and that the inhabitants of various cities supported her cult. In the slightly later Early Dynastic I levels at Ur, a large number of sealings were found, giving somewhat different combinations of city symbols and often combined with the rosette symbol of Inanna. These had been mostly used to lock doors, indicating that a storeroom in Ur had been set aside to contain materials for her cult.

At some moment in the Early Dynastic period the focus of the unified cult shifted to the city of Nippur in the center of Babylonia. The divine families of individual cities were joined together in a common Babylonian pantheon that, by the late Early Dynastic period, was headed by Enlil, patron of Nippur. He had supreme power in the divine world, and demarcated, for example, the border between Umma and Lagash as we saw before. Enlil's city, Nippur, attained a unique status that was to last until the eighteenth century. In the late third millennium all Babylonian cities were to provide support for its cult, and in the early second millennium political control over it gave a king the right to claim sovereign rule. Somehow the priests of this militarily unimportant city had the authority to grant a special status to one of many competitors. They seem to have had this power already in Early Dynastic times, when kings of Adab, Kish, Lagash, Umma, and Uruk left short inscriptions at Nippur, suggesting that they sought to curry favor with its priesthood.

This sense of unity was not restricted to speakers of a single language. We can state with certainty that at least two languages were spoken in Babylonia during the Early Dynastic period: Sumerian and a Semitic language sometimes referred to as proto-Akkadian. The two languages were very different in character, but they shared some vocabulary and Sumerian grammar influenced Akkadian, which indicates that the same people used them simultaneously. It is not easy to determine someone's spoken language in a multilingual ancient society. All literate Babylonians in this period (or Near Easterners for that matter) shared the same scribal culture, which will be described below. Although they could record their own vernaculars, all of them mostly wrote Sumerian. A text written in Sumerian is thus not evidence that the author's mother tongue was Sumerian. The scribes of Abu Salabikh, around the year 2500, bore Semitic names but wrote almost exclusively in Sumerian. Indeed, the names of people are probably a better indicator of the language they spoke. In the ancient Near East, people's names were often short sentences and so give an indication of their familiarity with a language. For instance, the Sumerian name Aba-a'a-gin means "Who is like the father?" We tend to take the language of name-giving – Sumerian, Akkadian, and later Amorite, Aramaic, etcetera – as evidence of the language spoken at home. So we see in Early Dynastic society a mixture of Sumerian and Semitic names, the former predominant in the south of Babylonia, the latter in the north. This distinction did not lead to ethnic conflict, as has sometimes been argued. Members of the two linguistic groups lived side-by-side. Politically, Early Dynastic Babylonia was divided; culturally it was not.

3.3   The Wider Near East

Early Dynastic Babylonia did not exist in a void (map 3.2). Countries that the Babylonians considered to be foreign and with which they had diverse relations surrounded it. The political situation in the rest of the Near East needs to be pieced together primarily from archaeological data as people there did not write until late in the period when texts appear in a few Syrian sites. By then Babylonian documents start to refer to the outside world as well. This is an unfortunate situation in that it leads to too great an emphasis on contacts with Babylonia and a focus on the south. With the end of the Uruk expansion in the late fourth millennium, contacts between Babylonia and the surrounding world changed radically. In the early third millennium, local traditions reemerged in full strength in the north and the east, and the Near East shows a great deal of cultural variety. Whatever southern influence there had been vanished. Simultaneously, certain nearby regions became more closely drawn into the Babylonian orbit, including one that had been outside the Uruk sphere, the Persian Gulf.

   The Gulf gave access to Omani copper mines, which were crucial to the newly developed bronze technology. Babylonian interest in the region was thus not unexpected. Texts start referring to a land of "Dilmun" as an important trading partner and a source for wood and copper. Dilmun had been attested only once in texts from the Uruk IV period, but throughout the Early Dynastic references to it

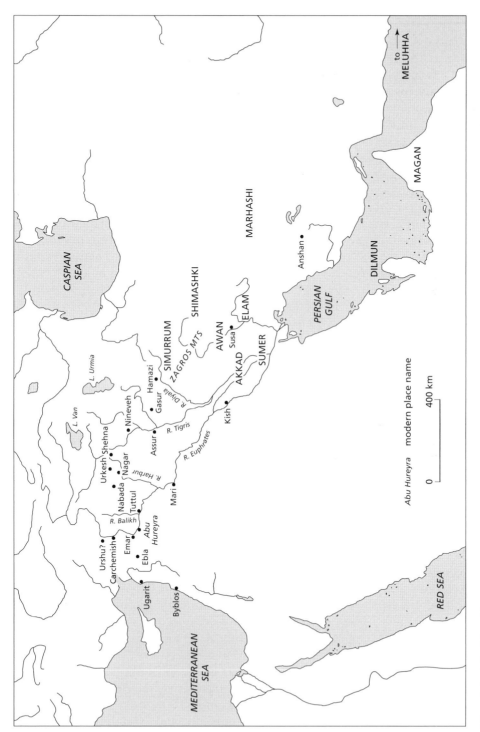

Map 3.2 The Near East ca. 2400.

became more numerous. Its location is uncertain: for this period northeast Arabia or the island of Bahrain are the most likely candidates. In either case, Dilmun itself was not the producer of timber and copper, but rather acted as a mercantile center, trading goods obtained farther away. Archaeological material from eastern Arabia and Oman shows a great deal of contact with Babylonia. Many pottery vessels were Mesopotamian imports, but they were found within archaeological contexts that are not at all Mesopotamian in character. In Oman, for instance, many circular tombs with stones piled over them were constructed in this period, an entirely un-Mesopotamian practice. So we see here a kind of interaction different from that attested in the Uruk period: at that time the Babylonians seem to have traded through colonies, while in the Early Dynastic period they did so without a permanent presence in the region.

The countries to the east of Babylonia had been incorporated in the Uruk expansion and Uruk IV culture had heavily influenced Susa, the main urban center there. This suddenly changed with the beginning of the third millennium, and a local culture we call proto-Elamite appeared, more closely related to eastern Iran. Some 400 kilometers (250 miles) to the southeast of Susa another center, Anshan (present Tal-i Malyan), became prominent and expanded substantially in size. Susa dominated the lowlands to the west of the Zagros Mountains, Anshan the highlands of the southern mountain range. It is unlikely that a territorial state including both cities and the territories in between had developed this early, yet mid-third-millennium texts from Babylonia start referring to a land of Elam. This was probably a loosely joined coalition of polities, some of which also appeared independently in Mesopotamian texts. Late Early Dynastic rulers from Lagash campaigned against Elam, probably for access to trade routes that reached places far afield. For instance, carnelian beads made in the Indus valley and lapis lazuli from Afghanistan appear in archaeological contexts in Babylonia at this time. Babylonia seems to be on the receiving end, importing luxury goods its new elites demanded. In return most likely textiles and other easily transportable manufactured goods were exported. The material culture of Iran does not demonstrate strong Babylonian influence, which suggests that there was no permanent presence of Babylonian traders.

Throughout northern Iraq and Syria east of the Euphrates River, a new material culture appeared at the beginning of the third millennium, which we term by its pottery style, Ninevite 5. Its remains are usually found at sites on important overland routes, and it seems that the people with this culture were in control of trade. Areas farther west show a variety of material cultures, suggesting the absence of any regional entity. These societies were not urbanized, at least in comparison with Babylonia. Several settlements that later developed into important centers originated at this time, but truly urban characteristics were absent until about 2600. Only then did walled cities and dense habitation reappear. While southern influence may have been a catalyst in this late urban development, it was an indigenous process and there were clear differences from the south.

The agricultural regime of northern Mesopotamia and Syria differed from that in Babylonia in that it relied on rainfall rather than irrigation for growing cereal crops. Yields per hectare were lower than when irrigation was used, however, so larger areas were cultivated to feed the same number of people, though with less intense labor. Consequently, cities in the north tended to be smaller than those in the south, and more of the population lived in outlying villages. Another difference was in the role of the palace in northern society. Unlike in the south, where the temple was the foremost institution in early cities, secular authority was preeminent in the north and the palace dominated the cityscape.

Northern cities were the cores of small states incorporating the surrounding countryside where villagers farmed. Settlement in these states was more spread out than in the south and the hinterlands were larger, but with their focus on the central city these were still, in essence, city-states. We know many of them by name: for example, Nagar, Shehna, and Urkesh in the Habur region, Mari, Tuttul, Emar, and Carchemish along the Euphrates, Assur and Hamazi in the east, and Ebla, Ugarit, and Byblos in the west. These states were in contact with one another through diplomatic and commercial means. The subject of trade dominates the palace documents found at Ebla, which suggests widespread diplomatic contact. Kings and other foreign state representatives commonly visited Ebla, they concluded diplomatic marriages, and regularly exchanged gifts. Warfare was also part of these contacts. Ebla had a long-lasting conflict with Mari on the Euphrates, probably for control over trade to Babylonia, and for some time had to pay a heavy tribute until Ebla's last ruler of the period, Ish'ar-Damu, reversed the situation. Some of these centers – Mari, Nagar, and Ebla – seem to have become able to impose their will on surrounding states, but the details of their military actions remain unknown. Alongside the centralization of secular power, a sense of religious unity also developed, as rulers from various cities took oaths in the temple of Dagan at Tuttul on the Euphrates. The latter city may thus have had a regional prestige comparable to that of Nippur in Babylonia.

Another similarity between Babylonia and the region to its north is that both had multilingual societies. Most people spoke Semitic dialects, but we also find evidence of Hurrian, a language that is neither Semitic nor related to Sumerian. Personal names again are the prime marker of this linguistic multiplicity. Hurrians were probably predominant in the north of Syria, where a Hurrian state of Urkesh and Nawar later arose, but people with Hurrian names appeared soon after the Early Dynastic period as far south as Nippur in Babylonia. Also people with Semitic names lived throughout Syria and northern Mesopotamia. This linguistic heterogeneity did not lie at the basis of any social or ethnic conflict to our knowledge.

The political organization of the north – a much larger area than Babylonia – was thus essentially similar to that in the south. Urban centers were the seats of power and dominated the surrounding countryside, even if the northern states were geographically larger. There was a difference in the ideological basis of power, however: in the north it was secular rather than religious. The city of Kish in the far north of Babylonia functioned as an intermediate point between these two worlds. It maintained close contacts with both the southern and the Syrian states and may have had a political organization that was based more on secular than on religious power. It is perhaps unsurprising, then, that a man from Kish, Sargon, was to upset the entire system.

3.4 Early Dynastic Society

For the study of social history in the Early Dynastic period we must rely primarily on administrative documents. Characteristic for the period – and for the entire third millennium – was the organization of society into "households." Those were entities whose members resided together, including various generations of a family as well as dependents such as servants. Households originated in economically independent kinship groups, but the concept was expanded as the structure for large institutions centered round gods and kings. Thus the Sumerian word for palace was é-gal, "great household," that for temple, é and the name of a god, for instance "household of the god Ningirsu." All important tablet archives derive from these units and portray a world with the household at its center, leaving other activity undocumented. Each household can be regarded as an autonomous and self-sufficient unit: it owned land, livestock, tools, and fishing boats, and included farmers, shepherds, fishermen, and people to produce and prepare food and to manufacture goods. Larger households incorporated several departments with distinct tasks, which were often themselves designated by the term é. In the late Early Dynastic period, individual members of the elites also had their own households. In Lagash, for instance, the queen had one, called the women's household (in Sumerian é-mí), which she ran independently. Her property was smaller than that of the king, but it was self-sufficient and it seems that women administered the queen's household. We cannot document this for the Early Dynastic period, but in the later Ur III period its officials were mostly women.

Internally, the personnel of each household was hierarchically organized. Male and female workers (Sumerian gurush and géme) were at the bottom of this hierarchy and were by far the most numerous of its members. While they were not unfree, in the sense of slaves, they were dependent laborers. They could live with their families or in institutional lodgings provided by the organization for which they worked. They were rewarded with rations: standard amounts of barley, accounted for on a monthly basis, and of oil and wool, accounted for annually (see document 3.2). The persons receiving these goods were mainly active men and women, but they also included children and old people. It is clear that rations constituted the support given to all the household's dependents, whether they were productive or not. The amounts were calculated according to the sex and status of the worker: a man regularly received double the amount of grain given to a woman, supervisors received more than their subordinates, specialized craftsmen more than unskilled laborers, and so on. This pattern whereby the household provided for its dependents by issuing them basic necessities of food and clothing remained a fundamental characteristic of Near Eastern society throughout the third millennium. Since the goods given did not constitute a complete diet, we have to conclude that these people had access to other foods through channels

---

Document 3.2 *Extract from a ration list*

Many administrative accounts list the rations issued to temple dependents in great detail. They provide the names of the recipients or identify them by gender and age, and list the amounts of barley issued to them. These texts often end with a summary of the totals and identify the official responsible for the disbursement. For example:

In total: 1 man at 50 liters
1 man at 40 liters
5 men at 15 liters each
23 men at 10 liters each
They are males
56 female laborers at 20 liters each
72 female laborers at 15 liters each
34 women at 10 liters each

A grand total of 192 people, including young ones and adults, received barley.
   The barley was 2,935 liters. Barley rations. The female laborers and children are the property of the goddess Bau.
   Shasha, the wife of Uru'inimgina, king of Lagash.
   In the month of the eating of malt for Nanshe, did Eniggal, the inspector, distribute this from the granary of Bau. It is the ninth distribution of year 4.

Translation after Selz 1989: 93–4.

---

outside the ration system. Vegetables and fish were probably homegrown or gathered by family members; or perhaps workers exchanged part of their rations for those foods.

The majority of workers provided repetitive manual labor. Women were especially engaged as millers and weavers. Milling at this time was a backbreaking chore which required that grain be rubbed back and forth over a stone slab with a smaller hand-held stone. The women were supposed to produce set quotas of flour or cloth on a daily basis. The amounts produced depended on the quality of the final product, which varied enormously. From later Ur III period texts we know that the quotas were high: one woman had to produce 10 liters of regular flour or 20 liters of coarse flour per day. Weaving quotas could easily be as high as 2 square meters (21.5 square feet) a day. Those were heavy tasks and they could lead to physical injuries, as the skeletons of women excavated at the seventh millennium Neolithic site of Abu Hureyra in Syria illustrate: their knees, wrists, and lower backs showed signs of arthritis while their toes were deformed from constantly tucking them under the foot in a position needed when milling.[2] While the Early Dynastic accounts are for women as groups, it is likely that they worked individually at home, simultaneously taking care of children. These tasks were primarily cottage industries.

Belonging to a great household also provided a means of survival to the weak in society, however. Widows and children unable to feed themselves entered temple households, where they received basic support. Households not only existed in the cities but also in the countryside, where rural communities, composed of large families that owned land in common, survived outside institutional control. Their presence in the Early Dynastic society – but also the decline of their importance – is clear from a group of about fifty land-sale documents. When a piece of agricultural land was sold, it usually went from multiple sellers to a single buyer. The sellers had unequal levels of claim to the land. Those most closely associated to it received the highest recompense, others somewhat less, and large groups of people were given symbolic gifts, such as meals, at the time of the transaction. Originally the land was thus probably communally owned. But all of the recorded buyers were single actors, members of the elite who were able to acquire individual ownership of rights, possibly at times by force. These elites were probably all members of the institutional households, who took advantage of their status to obtain personal property.

Several institutional households coexisted within each city-state: some belonged to gods, others to secular authorities. Among the temples there was a hierarchy reflecting that of the gods in the local pantheon. For instance, in Lagash the household of the city-god Ningirsu was larger than that of his divine wife Bau; and hers was in turn larger than those of their sons Shulshagana and Igalima. It is remarkable how encompassing the control of these institutions could be; the records from Shuruppak, for instance, show highly centralized control of the economy. Barley accounts register amounts that could provide 10,000 people daily rations for a full year, and grain silos excavated at the site show that such quantities could be stored together. The agricultural areas attached to institutional households were similarly enormous. However, since all our textual documentation from southern Babylonia derives from temples, it used to be thought that temples were completely dominant in Early Dynastic society. Because the temple of the goddess Bau there is our primary source of texts, Lagash was once described as a temple-state, where the gods owned all land and property. Today, most scholars reject this idea, acknowledging the fact that other sectors of society were important participants in economic life but simply remain undocumented.

The far-reaching nature of central administration is even clearer in the case of Ebla in northwest Syria. All our documentation there was excavated in a palace archive and demonstrates how this institution controlled widespread economic activity. It administered multiple units including the king's household and entities referred to with a term that in Babylonia meant "village." Whether the use of the word indicates that village communities coincided with administrative units, or were turned into administrative units with the advent of centralized power, is unclear. We can say, however, that agriculture in Ebla's territory remained the responsibility of villages under royal supervision, unlike in Babylonia where much of it was directly undertaken by institutional labor forces.

The ability of certain individuals to draw unequal shares of resources to themselves is best shown in the archaeological record. The so-called Royal Cemetery at Ur clearly reveals the existence of a small group of people who could command great amounts of luxury items to be buried with them. Sixteen of the roughly two thousand graves excavated had elaborate chambers of stone and brick. Extremely valuable grave goods were placed in them: golden helmets, daggers, inlaid musical instruments, and so on (figure 3.3). Most telling of the power of the buried is the fact that some of them were accompanied by human attendants, killed or willing to die at their master's or mistress's funeral. We do not know who exactly was honored with such elaborate burials, whether they were members of the palace or temple elites. This in itself demonstrates how power structures gaining legitimacy on various ideological bases coexisted in the late Early Dynastic period, and that the full definition of social and political hierarchies was still wanting then.

3.5   Scribal Culture

During the Early Dynastic period in Babylonia, the recently invented technology of writing evolved both in its ability to render spoken languages and in the extent of information it provided. The system changed in several ways. First, scribes started to impress the signs into the clay of the tablet using a bevel-tipped reed rather than tracing them. When the tip of the stylus was pushed into the clay, it formed a small triangle and a thin line, creating thus the wedge shape we now call cuneiform. Signs became increasingly schematic and standardized, and it was possible to impress them rapidly with a limited number of strokes. By the end of the period few of the signs any longer resembled the pictorial elements on which they were originally based.

The use of signs rendering syllables also expanded, indicating more and more elements of the spoken language. Nevertheless, signs that represented entire words and required the reader to supply grammatical elements remained dominant. While indications of verbal conjugation, for instance, were absent in the proto-cuneiform texts from Uruk, the expression of such elements became increasingly explicit, although there was never an obligation in the cuneiform writing system to express them all. The growing use of syllabic signs made it possible to write languages other than Sumerian; scribes could write out personal names in Semitic dialects and in Hurrian, they inserted Semitic prepositions in the text, and so on.

They also standardized the layout of tablets, dividing them into one or more vertical columns of boxes to be read from top to bottom, mostly containing one word only, with or without grammatical elements. The sequence of the signs reflected the pronunciation of words better, although even in the latest Early Dynastic texts they were sometimes still scrambled. These developments made texts more comprehensible to their readers in antiquity, and to us today. Administrative records became more explicit, indicating, for example, whether a specific person issued or received goods. Royal inscriptions expanded from simple marks of ownership to lengthy narratives. Writing thus acquired an expanded function and increased its ability to inform someone of new knowledge, while information was preserved for future generations. A king who left a votive object in a temple could indicate on it that he had given it, so that later visitors would acknowledge his act.

These developments took place in Babylonia where there was a continuous use of writing from the Uruk period onward. Outside the region even the people who had been exposed to Uruk writing or to the Proto-Elamite script of Elam had abandoned the technology. It was only late in the Early Dynastic period that inhabitants of several cities in Syria took it up again, clearly under Babylonian influence. The increased use of syllabic signs there facilitated the adaptation of the script for different language groups. The Syrian scribes imported Babylonian tablet shapes, sign forms, and their readings, and although they used primarily Sumerian word signs to write out their texts, it is clear that they pronounced them in the languages they spoke. At Ebla they regularly inserted Semitic grammatical elements between words.

The archaic texts from Uruk already show that writing was not restricted to economic transactions, even though these texts continue to dominate the corpus numerically. Lexical lists, words in a set sequence, provide the earliest systematic evidence of speculative and associative thought. They include lists of god-names, professions, animals, birds, metals, woods, city-names, and so on. In the Early Dynastic period this genre flourished and shows the acceptance of the same traditions over a wide geographical area. Most remarkable is the faithfulness with which these texts were copied in every city where they are found. Lists from Abu Salabikh are duplicated with only minor variants in Ebla, some 900 kilometers (560 miles) away. There are other literary texts from the period, usually short compositions including incantations, hymns, and wisdom literature, that is, catalogs of proverbs or proverbs set in an artificial dialogue where a father gives advice to his son. These are difficult to understand because the writing system was still very terse. The same compositions are often found at different sites (those of Shuruppak and Abu Salabikh especially show much overlap), which demonstrates that a common source inspired the various scribal schools. While most of the material is in Sumerian, there is a proto-Akkadian hymn to Shamash, which was found both at Ebla and Abu Salabikh.

In the middle of the third millennium, we thus see a cultural *koine* in the literate Near East. The intellectual center was Babylonia, where the scribal practices and most literary texts were first produced. After urban cultures developed in Syria and northern Mesopotamia they adopted the technique anew from Babylonia, and certain cities probably acted as intermediaries in this process. Northern Babylonian Kish was very important, as was Mari on the Middle Euphrates. Some texts at Ebla state that "the young scribes came up from Mari," which suggests that the city provided training to Syrian scribes. People from western Syria read the same texts as those of southern Iraq. They employed the same scribal practices, shaped their clay tablets similarly, wrote the same cuneiform signs, organized them in the same way on the tablets, and so on. Politically they were separate, however, living in independent city-states. The states in the south were relatively small in territorial extent, while those in the north and in western Syria had a wider expanse. The states competed through military and other means, and rulers routinely gained supremacy over their neighbors or concluded ephemeral alliances with them. These actions laid the groundwork for Sargon of Akkad, who initiated a new period in Near Eastern history by pursuing a policy of conquest to the extreme.

Debate 3.1   *What happened in the Royal Cemetery at Ur?*

In the 1920s the British archaeologist Leonard Woolley, excavating in the southern city of Ur, discovered in the center of town a cemetery which had been in use for 500 years and contained some 2,000 graves. The earliest burials belonged to the Early Dynastic period and dated to around 2600 to 2450, at a time when Ur was one of the independent city-states of Babylonia. A small number of the graves took the excavators aback: they contained vast amounts of wealth and, even more surprising, seven of them showed evidence of human sacrifice. Woolley immediately announced his find as the Royal Cemetery of Ur in such popular publications as the *Illustrated London News* and it drew as much attention as the discovery of Tutankhamun's tomb in Egypt had done a few years before.

Woolley did not hesitate to call his tombs royal, but they contained remarkably few inscriptions, all of them very brief, and none of the names recorded in them were known as royal elsewhere. So the occupants could have derived their powers from other sources, temples perhaps (Moorey 1977). Some scholars have argued at length that these people were royals (Marchesi 2004), but doubts remain. We know very little about them.

More startling, however, is how they could have acquired such distinctive burials. After all, Ur did not control a vast territory at this time and even if it was the sea harbor of Babylonia, the city was not exceptionally rich it seems. Yet, the grave goods were made of very expensive imported precious materials – gold, silver, lapis lazuli, carnelian, and others – and they were so finely crafted that their manufacture must have required numerous days of highly skilled work. Moreover, how were these people able to demand that other humans died to serve them in the afterlife? Up to seventy-four men and women were deposited in a single grave as musicians, attendants, and bodyguards. Woolley believed they died willingly, committing suicide by drinking poison in a ceremony accompanied by music (Woolley 1982: 74–6). If this were true, how could they have been convinced to accept their fate? It is possible that they were essentially brainwashed to believe they contributed to the well-being of society and that rituals involving banquets – often depicted on objects discovered in the tombs – enticed them into this (Pollock 2007).

Recent reexamination of a few skeletons suggests, however, a more chilling alternative. The people were killed with a blow of a pointed ax to the back of their heads. Afterwards the bodies were heated, embalmed with mercury, and dressed (Baadsgaard et al. 2011). Then they were laid out neatly as if they formed musical groups, lines of guardsmen, etcetera (Vidale 2011). It is still possible that people voluntarily submitted to this fate, but also that the occasions were displays of cruelty to scare citizens into submission (Dickson 2006). It could also be that people captured in war were the victims.

Why would anyone have thought this necessary? The burials could have been ritual occasions that hoped to create public support for the institution of dynastic rule and show that the death of one king or queen did not affect the office (Cohen 2005). The fact that it happened relatively early in the history of the state in Babylonia may indicate that the sources of political power were still uncertain at this time and needed confirmation. The practice ended around 2450 and never reemerged in the region. Perhaps when kings felt more confident they no longer needed to call attention to their power over the lives and deaths of others.

NOTES

1   Capital letters are used to render the name KI.EN.GI as we are not certain about how to read it.
2   Molleson 1994.

4

Political Centralization in the Late Third Millennium

3000	2500	2000	1500	1000	500

2288   Accession of Sargon of Akkad

2211–2175 Naram-Sin of Akkad

ca. 2100   Gudea of Lagash and Puzur-Inshushinak of Awan

2110   Start of the Ur III period

2003   Fall of Ur

Successive periods of centralization of power under two city-dynasties charac-terized the last centuries of the third millennium: one from Akkad in northern Babylonia in the twenty-third and twenty-second centuries, the other from Ur in the far south in the twenty-first century. They not only exercised direct control over southern Mesopotamia, but their armies exerted great influence over large parts of the wider Near East. There is a substantial increase in the available sources, which modern historians also understand much better, and this enables a more detailed reconstruction of these periods than those before. The two states shared a number of characteristics: they were both created through military actions in Babylonia proper and in the surrounding regions; they pursued policies of centralization in political, administrative, and ideological terms; and they collapsed through a combination of internal opposition and external forces. They differed in the extent of their reach and their internal cohesion, however.

A History of the Ancient Near East ca. 3000–323 BC, Third Edition. Marc Van De Mieroop.
© 2016 John Wiley & Sons, Inc. Published 2016 by John Wiley & Sons, Inc.

4.1 The Kings of Akkad

The Sumerian King List portrayed the dynasty of Akkad[1] in the same way as it did for the dynasties that came before it: a list of city-rulers who held universal kingship, which had been transferred to the city of Akkad (for a list of kings, see Section 1 in the King Lists at the end of the book). The nature of its rule was very different from what preceded, however, and temporarily Akkad ended the system of city-states that had characterized Babylonia until then. The processes of political centralization in Babylonia and the spread of Babylonian influences throughout the Near East evident in the Early Dynastic period attained an unprecedented climax. Moreover, never before had Babylonian armies systematically campaigned that far, nor had the political dominance of one city ever been so great. The focal point of the developments was northern Babylonia. The creator of the dynasty, Sargon, seems to have been a commoner who rose to prominence in the city of Kish. He probably usurped power there, taking the programmatic Akkadian throne-name Sharru-kin, which means "the king is legitimate." His two successors still bore the title "King of Kish," but Sargon moved the center of his rule to Akkad, either an entirely new city, as later sources state, or a place previously of little importance. Although its location is unknown, it certainly was in the very north of Babylonia, perhaps underneath modern Baghdad. This geographical position reflects the dual interests of the dynasty: full dominance of the Babylonian heartland and an extensive presence throughout the Near East.

Akkad attained its prominence through military might. It was written of Sargon that "daily 5,400 men ate at his presence,"[2] which may refer to the existence of a standing army that would have had superiority over the armies of conscripts his opponents fielded. Military activity is the sole subject of his own inscriptions. The south of Babylonia, where the city-states of the late Early Dynastic period had been partly united, was one area where he campaigned actively. Lugalzagesi, who ruled Uruk, Umma, and several other southern cities, acted as the focus of opposition to Sargon, and the latter claimed that he captured "fifty governors . . . and the king of Uruk,"[3] a victory that clinched his control over the entire region.

A new system of government had to be developed: the formerly independent city-states needed to be integrated within a larger structure in every respect, politically, economically, and ideologically. Politically, the original city-rulers mostly remained in place, only now acting as governors for the king of Akkad, despite Sargon's claim that these were Akkadian officials. Thus kings Meskigal of Adab, Lugalzagesi of Uruk, and perhaps Uru'inimgina of Lagash are still attested under the first Sargonic rulers. The Sumerian title énsi, which in the Early Dynastic period designated independent city-rulers, now became used throughout Babylonia to indicate governors. This system did not work well, however. Sentiments of independence could be rallied around native governors, and over the entire period Akkad's kings had to deal with rebellions, as described later in this chapter.

Still, the court actively pursued centralizing policies. It developed a new system of taxation in which part of the income of each region was siphoned off and sent to the capital or used to support the state bureaucracy locally. In the reign of

Box 4.1   *The year name*

One aspect of the administrative centralization of the Akkad state was the introduction of an annual dating system that would be applied throughout Babylonia, although not at the expense of other systems used for local records. One of the earlier existing systems was chosen, which we call the year name. Each year was identified with a name referring to a major event from the year prior or early in the year itself. For instance, Sargon's destruction of Mari was used to name the following year. This system remained in use in Babylonia until about 1500, and provides us with a list of what the rulers themselves saw as important events. The names usually mention military campaigns, the building or restoration of temples or city-walls, the digging of canals, the appointments of high priests or priestesses, or the donation of cult objects. The dates appear primarily on economic records (not on letters). In order to remember the proper order of years, official lists of year names were drawn up from the Ur III period on. While we have not fully recovered the sequence of names for the entire period, long stretches are certain. These provide an extremely useful insight into the chronological order of events, and allow us to date the numerous administrative documents preserved.

Under the Kassite dynasty in Babylonia in the second half of the second millennium, a system numbered by the regnal year of each king replaced year names. The first official year started with the first New Year's Day of his reign. The period between the death of the former king and that day was indicated as the accession year. This system stayed in use until the Seleucid period.

Naram-Sin a standardization of accounting is visible in certain levels of the administration in order to facilitate central control. For those aspects of the economy that concerned the crown, scribes had to use a standard system of measures and weights. Thus we see the introduction of the "Akkadian gur" of ca. 300 liters to measure barley. The shape and layout of the accounting tablets and the formation of the cuneiform signs were centrally prescribed. In order to have a consistent method of dating in centrally controlled accounts, year names were used throughout the state (see box 4.1).

The local scribes, who were forced to adopt new techniques of accounting, also had to adjust to a new language. Akkad was a northern Babylonian city situated in the region where people spoke a Semitic language rather than the Sumerian of the south. The language, in fact, came to be known as the language of Akkad, hence our term "Akkadian." The existing cuneiform script, however, had been developed as a vehicle for Sumerian, rooted in an entirely different language family. Akkadian required more flexibility and accuracy in the indication of grammatical forms, which could be obtained through the increased use of syllabic signs. The royal inscriptions of the Sargonic kings were mostly written in Akkadian, either by itself or, less often, with a Sumerian translation. Few of these texts are known in a Sumerian version alone. Sumerian remained commonly written in areas of

Babylonia with a long tradition of the language, however. The royal administration only demanded the use of Akkadian and of centralized accounting practices for the records it needed to consult. Those had to be uniform; local affairs were left to traditional ways.

The royal house drew many economic resources to itself, and the Akkadian kings probably confiscated the estates previously owned by the city-rulers. Yet even this was seemingly insufficient for their needs. The Obelisk of King Manish-tushu, one of the major monuments of the period, is a 1.5 meter high (59 inches) diorite pillar onto which was carved a text recording his purchase of eight large fields in northern Babylonia, totaling almost 3.5 square kilometers (865 acres). Although the price paid was not unusually low, it is almost certain that Manish-tushu forced the sale on the owners in order to be able to parcel out the land to his own supporters. The creation of agricultural estates granted by the king to privileged people was a novelty the Sargonic kings introduced. They seized the land needed from local owners, which certainly led to resentment and opposition to Akkadian rule.

In ideological terms also, the dynasty tried to unite Babylonia, and sought to connect the cultic system of the region, with its shared pantheon, to the royal family. For instance, Sargon installed his daughter as high priestess of the moon god Nanna at Ur, where she was made the god's wife. For that function she received a purely Sumerian name, Enheduanna, "priestess, ornament of heaven." Thus an Akkadian princess resided in one of the main Sumerian centers of the south and she actively participated in the religious and cultural life there. The authorship of several literary compositions in the Sumerian language is credited to her (making her the first identifiable author in world literature), including a set of hymns to temples located in thirty-five cities throughout Babylonia. The compilation of those hymns into one series shows how the various cults of the region were considered to belong to an integrated system. For some five centuries afterwards, the control of the high priesthood of Nanna at Ur remained an indication of political prominence in Babylonia. Any ruler who could claim authority over Ur installed his daughter there, giving her access to the temple's considerable economic assets. Naram-Sin expanded this policy by placing several of his daughters as high priestesses of prominent cults in other Babylonian cities, a clear attempt to gain a solid foothold throughout the region. He also explained his own deification (see below) as the result of a decision made by the gods of various cities all over his state.

Akkad's kings did not exert power over Babylonia alone, however. Some Early Dynastic kings had declared that they campaigned in different areas of the Near East, but none even remotely measured up to what the Sargonic kings accomplished. To determine the regional extent and nature of their influence, we have to turn to royal inscriptions and year names. Many Akkadian royal inscriptions are preserved and military matters dominate their contents. They were originally inscribed on statues that the kings set up in the courtyard of the temple at Nippur, continuing the Early Dynastic tradition that gave this city regional prominence.

We no longer have the statues themselves, but scribes in the early second millennium copied out the texts in which the first five Akkadian kings boasted about their military exploits, and some of these copies have survived. The statements of Sargon and Naram-Sin stand out, because of their wide geographical range: they were certainly the greatest military men of the time. Yet, as Naram-Sin had to repeat many of his grandfather's campaigns, it seems these often amounted to no more than raids.

The kings focused their military attention on the regions of western Iran and northern Syria. In the east they encountered a number of states, such as Elam, Parahshum, and Simurrum, whose location we cannot always exactly pinpoint. In the north they entered the upper Euphrates area, reaching the city of Tuttul at the confluence with the Balikh River, the cult center of Dagan that acted as a central focus of northern and western Syria. Mari and Ebla, the most prominent political centers of the region up till then, they destroyed. These places, which had been so close to northern Babylonia in cultural terms during the Early Dynastic period, were now considered to be major enemies.

The accounts mention many places even more remote, such as the cedar forests in Lebanon, the headwaters of the Tigris and Euphrates rivers in central Turkey, Marhashi, east of Elam, and areas across the "Lower Sea," that is, the Persian Gulf. Akkad's kings claim to have reached these in far-flung forays to procure rare goods, such as hard stone, wood, and silver, and booty from these areas poured into Babylonia. Several stone vessels excavated at Ur and Nippur were inscribed with the statement that they were booty from Magan (Oman), for instance. It seems unlikely, however, that Akkad established firm control over these areas. Rather, the raids aimed at securing access to trade routes. Ships from overseas areas, such as Dilmun (Bahrain), Magan, and Meluhha (the Indus valley) are said to have moored in Akkad's harbor. So when Naram-Sin claims that he conquered Magan, it seems more likely that he used his military might to guarantee the supply of its resources.

Local circumstances determined to a great extent how Akkad maintained influence over this wide region. We observe a variety of interactions. After Rimush established full control over Susa in western Iran, for instance, the language of bureaucracy there became Akkadian and local officials bore Sumerian titles, such as governor (énsi) or general (shagina), which imply a full dependence on Akkad. Yet, the rulers of Susa retained some degree of authority. Naram-Sin concluded a treaty with an unnamed ruler or high official of Susa, a document written in the Elamite language but in Babylonian cuneiform. The agreement specified no submission to Akkad, only a promise by the Elamite to follow Naram-Sin's lead in international affairs: "The enemy of Naram-Sin is my enemy. The friend of Naram-Sin is my friend." The autonomy of Elam should not be underestimated.

In Syria, the Akkadians set up footholds in certain existing centers, indicated by the presence of military garrisons or trade representatives there. At Nagar (modern Tell Brak), they constructed a monumental building with bricks stamped with the name of Naram-Sin. Its character – military or administrative – cannot be

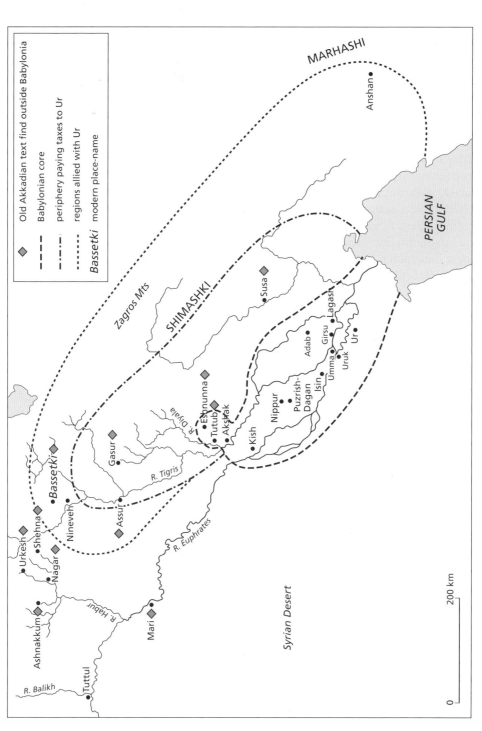

Map 4.1 The Old Akkadian and Ur Ur III states. After Piotr Steinkeller, "The Administrative and Economic Organization of the Ur III State: The Core and the Periphery," in McGuire Gibson and R. D. Biggs, eds., *The Organization of Power: Aspects of Bureaucracy in the Ancient Near East* (Chicago: The Oriental Institute, 1987), p. 38.

established, however. At Nineveh, King Manishtushu is said to have built a temple devoted to Ishtar, which suggests that he wanted to promote the cult of a goddess who was of special importance to his dynasty.

The question remains how thorough Akkadian presence in the periphery was. Throughout the Near East, documents in the Akkadian administrative style appear: in the Diyala region (probably part of the Akkadian core); at Susa in Elam; Gasur and Assur in Assyria; Mari on the Middle Euphrates and in northern Syria at several sites, Nagar, Urkesh (modern Tell Mozan), Shehna (modern Tell Leilan), and Ashnakkum (modern Tell Chagar Bazar). The records using Akkadian style are not necessarily evidence of an Akkadian royal administration, however: just as in the late Early Dynastic period, this may merely show the spread of southern scribal practices. Widespread territorial control of the region seems unlikely. The Old Akkadian kings probably established points through which they could channel their commercial interests, such as Nagar, and possibly used the threat of military action to obtain what they wanted.

More distant areas were tied to Akkad through diplomatic means, including marriages. We find sealings of Naram-Sin's daughter, Taram-Agade, in the north Syrian city of Urkesh, and it is likely that she was living there as the wife of the local ruler. A princess of the eastern state of Marhashi was, conversely, married to Sharkalisharri or his son. Such marriages indicate that the Old Akkadian state did not exist in a political void, but was surrounded by states with which it had to negotiate on a level of equality. Unfortunately, the latter are only known to us through Akkadian eyes, so we cannot evaluate their extent or powers with any degree of certainty.

Akkad's far-reaching influence had a great effect on how the kings perceived themselves and presented themselves to their subjects. Already under Sargon the traditional title "King of Kish" came to mean "king of the world," using the similarity of the name of the city of Kish and the Akkadian term for "the entire inhabited world," *kishshatum*. Naram-Sin took such self-glorification to an extreme. First, he introduced a new title, "king of the four quarters of the universe." His military successes led him to proclaim an even more exalted status. After crushing a major rebellion in Babylonia, he took the unprecedented step of making himself a god. A unique inscription found in northern Iraq, but not necessarily put there in Naram-Sin's days, claims that the citizens of the capital requested this from the major deities of the state. As a newly founded city Akkad needed its own patron deity, and Naram-Sin had shown he could fulfill that role when he had protected the city against numerous rebels:

> Naram-Sin, the strong one, king of Akkad: when the four quarters of the universe together were hostile to him, he remained victorious in nine battles in a single year because of the love Ishtar bore for him, and he took captive those kings who had risen against him. Because he had been able to preserve his city in the time of crisis, (the inhabitants of) his city asked from Ishtar in Eanna, from Enlil in Nippur, from Dagan in Tuttul, from Ninhursaga in Kesh, from Enki in Eridu, from Sin in Ur, from Shamash in Sippar, and from Nergal in Kutha, that he be the god of their city Akkad, and they built a temple for him in the midst of Akkad.[4]

Henceforth his name appeared in texts preceded by the cuneiform sign derived from the image of a star; it indicated that what followed was the name of a god.

Conceptually, this placed him in a very different realm from previous rulers. Earlier kings had been granted a cult after death, but Naram-Sin received one while he was still alive. The court initiated a process of royal glorification through other means as well. Perhaps the most visible of these efforts was in the arts. Stylistic changes originating in the reign of Sargon culminated in amazing refinement, naturalism, and spontaneity during Naram-Sin's reign. Most impressive is his victory stele, a 2 meter high (79 inches) stone carved in bas-relief depicting the king leading his troops in battle in the mountains. Naram-Sin dominates the composition in a pose of grandeur, and is much larger than those surrounding him. Wearing the insignia of royalty – bow, arrow, and battleaxe – he is also crowned with the symbol of divinity, the horned helmet (figure 4.1). Court sponsorship led to technological and stylistic excellence in other areas of the arts as well. Sculpture in the round now showed enormous refinement. The copper Bassetki statue (bearing the text regarding Naram-Sin's deification), for example, shows great naturalism in the representation of the human body. It presents a technological breakthrough too, as it was made with the lost wax technique, a technique long credited to the classical Greeks. The stylistic elegance of these sculptures is also visible in the minor arts. Seals of royal family members and of many others in the Akkadian administration are remarkable works of art. Even the script of the time displays a high level of elegance in the writing of cuneiform signs. The impression one obtains from the material remains of this period is one of skill, attention to detail, and artistic talent.

Old Akkadian hegemony was unstable, however. Both in Babylonia and in the wider Near East, it met resistance, a problem exacerbated by outside pressures on the state. Opposition to Akkad in Babylonia was a permanent feature of the period and may have been the main cause of its failure. Rebellions were violently suppressed; in several of his inscriptions Rimush claimed to have killed or displaced tens of thousands of men from southern cities. Even allowing for exaggeration, these were very drastic measures. The most elaborate description of an uprising derives from the reign of Naram-Sin, when he confronted two coalitions of Babylonian cities: a northern one under Iphur-Kish, king of Kish, and a southern one under Amar-girid, king of Uruk. That even the region of Kish near the capital participated in the opposition to Akkad is a sign that the idea of centralized rule was intolerable everywhere. The battles are described as taking place in the open field and between two well-organized armies with numerous men. The ability of the rebels to mount such military opposition indicates that local structures had continued to exist even after decades of Akkadian rule. Naram-Sin claimed victory in a quick succession of battles, and it was probably after this that he proclaimed himself a god. The threat to his rule had been serious. It is probably not without irony that Naram-Sin stated that the gods of the very same rebellious cities were asked to grant him divine status.

Opposition to Akkad in other areas of the Near East exacerbated these Babylonian problems. Since our knowledge of the Akkadian presence in different places is

Figure 4.1 The stele of Naram-Sin. The scene shows Naram-Sin as a god (identified as such by the horned crown) leading his troops in battle against a mountain people called the Lullubi in the accompanying brief inscription. The portrayal is much more dynamic than in the earlier Stele of the Vultures. The king crushes enemies beneath his foot and one of them is shown falling naked into the netherworld. When he took the stele to Susa in the twelfth century, King Shutruk-Nahhunte carved his own inscription on the mountainside. Louvre Museum, Paris. Spicular limestone, H. 2 m (79 in); W. 1.5 m (59 in). Credit: akg images/Erich Lessing.

haphazard at best, and the nature of that presence varied in the first place, it is hard to determine when and how it was successfully rejected. At Susa in Elam the local governor, Epir-mupi, appeared with the title "the strong one," an epithet usually reserved for kings. Ititi of Assur raided Gasur, an act that probably would have been impossible if the Akkadian ruler had firmly controlled both cities. Since we do not really know how direct dominion over these regions had been, we cannot determine whether this represents a serious weakening of Akkadian rule.

Akkad was frequently on the defensive, in fact, against military threats from groups within or adjacent to its zone of influence. A major opponent had always been the Iranian state of Marhashi, which lay to the east of Susa. In Sharkalisharri's reign it seems to have overrun Elam, and together the states fought a battle against Akkad near Akshak at the confluence of the Diyala and Tigris rivers, a site very close to the capital. The most severe threat came from mountain people in the east, the Gutians, whose homeland most likely was in the Zagros. In Sharkalisharri's time they appeared in increasing numbers in Babylonia as settlers, which necessitated the appointment of a Gutian interpreter in Adab. While they primarily seem to have entered Babylonia in the process of migration, their arrival there was not always peaceful. Sharkalisharri fought them in an unknown location, and we have at least one letter where they are accused of cattle rustling.

The combination of internal and external pressures led to a rapid collapse of Akkad's rule during Sharkalisharri's reign. The entire Near East reverted to a system of independent states, some of them now governed by new populations. In Babylonia, the Gutians took over several city-states and may have been the strongest power in the region. Gutian rulers even presented themselves as heirs to the Akkad dynasty. One of them, Erridu-pizir, set up statues at Nippur in imitation of the Akkadian kings and claimed their title "king of the four quarters of the universe," added to that of "king of Gutium." They did not supplant Akkad, however, as several independent city-rulers existed alongside them. Best known to us is the state of Lagash, where a local dynasty left numerous archaeological and textual remains. The statues and inscriptions of one of them, Gudea, rank among the masterpieces of third-millennium Mesopotamian art and literature (figure 4.2). In the city of Akkad itself, the dynasty of Sargon continued to rule. The situation was so confused that the *Sumerian King List* exclaimed: "Who was king? Who was not king?"

Outside Babylonia, the disappearance of Akkadian influence permitted the development of several new states. In the north of Syria, people speaking the Hurrian language created a small kingdom named "Urkesh and Nawar" after two of its main cities located quite close to each other in northern Syria. At Mari, a "dynasty of generals" (Akkadian *shakkanakku*) had perhaps already come into being in the reign of Manishtushu, and ruled the city as an independent state for the next 300 years. Susa became the capital of a state called Awan, a political entity that may already have existed in the Early Dynastic period, stretching from the central Zagros to the area south of Susa. When Akkad lost its power, however, a new king there called Puzur-Inshushinak embarked on a major program of military conquest. He unified the entire southwest of Iran and also occupied parts of northern Babylonia and the Diyala valley, while the Gutians held sway in the south. It is perhaps at this time that a new indigenous script came into use in western Iran. Although Puzur-Inshushinak commissioned several inscriptions in Akkadian cuneiform, there are also a few written in a script we call linear Elamite, vaguely related to Proto-Elamite and not yet deciphered. Together with a small number of short inscriptions on objects such as silver vases they are evidence of the development of a local script that disappeared together with Puzur-Inshushinak. He became the target of military campaigns by Gudea of Lagash and the first

Figure 4.2   Gudea statue. This statue showing the ruler of Lagash seated is one of the smaller examples of a group of some fifteen excavated at his capital, Girsu, and the only one where the king's image is fully preserved. The inscription on the skirt states that he built temples for Nanshe and Ningirsu, and gives the statue's name "Ningizzida gave life to Gudea, the builder of the house." It was customary in Mesopotamia for each statue to have its individual name. Louvre Museum, Paris. Diorite; H. 46 cm; W. 33 cm; D. 22.50 cm (18 × 13 × 9 in), AO 3293, AO 4108. Credit: akg images/Album/Oronoz.

Ur III ruler, Ur-Namma, who managed to destroy his state and occupy Susa. But, Puzur-Inshushinak may have laid the basis for political centralization in the region later on.

The century of Akkadian rule and influence over the entire Near East was an important first in the region's history. Never before had armies campaigned so consistently across such a wide area, and the Mesopotamians never forgot this. Sargon and Naram-Sin became the paradigms of powerful rulers and were the subjects of numerous detailed stories, created and preserved for almost two

---

Document 4.1   *Later traditions about the kings of Akkad*

Sargon and Naram-Sin in particular were remembered throughout Mesopotamian history in numerous texts that granted them increasingly far-flung military successes until they ruled almost the entire world. These texts also included elements of criticism, however, from early on for Naram-Sin, though only in the first millennium for Sargon. An example of a later tradition on Sargon is found in a chronicle of the first millennium that discusses several early kings:

Sargon, king of Akkad, rose to power in the era of Ishtar. He had no rival or equal, spread his splendor over all the lands, and crossed the sea in the east. In his eleventh year, he conquered the western land to its farthest point, and brought it under his sole authority. He set up his statues in the west, and he sent their booty across the sea by rafts. His courtiers he made reside at intervals of five double miles and he governed all lands at once. He went to Kazalla and reduced it to a ruin, destroying it to the last spot on which a bird could perch. Afterwards, in his old age, all the lands rebelled against him and laid siege to him in Akkad. But Sargon came out to fight, and defeated them, he overthrew them, and overpowered their large army. Later, Subartu rose up in full force and made him take up his arms. Sargon set out an ambush, defeated it, overthrew it, overpowered its large army, and sent its possessions to Akkad. He dug up earth from the clay-pit of Babylon, and made a counterpart of Babylon next to Akkad. Because of this transgression the great lord Marduk became angry and wiped out his people with a famine. From east to west they rebelled against him, and he (Marduk) afflicted him with insomnia.

Translation after Glassner 2004: 268-271.

---

millennia. Fact and fiction were combined in tales that accorded them increasingly greater achievements (see document 4.1). These literary creations, while providing us with an abundance of information, also pose great challenges to the modern historian (see debate 4.1). How do we recognize historical facts in the accounts we have? How much did later Mesopotamians or other inhabitants of the Near East add to the images of these rulers for their own purposes? If we do not include information from the later stories in our historical reconstruction, although they are much more detailed and explicit than the texts produced during the actual reigns of these kings, we seem to ignore important data. Yet some of those very details may be entirely fabulous, or embroidered with anachronisms, and might produce only stories of how those early kings were perceived in later times. To keep the two types of sources fully separate is impossible; historians will always fill in gaps in the contemporary record based on an awareness of the later stories. But we can work to remain conscious of anachronisms and "improvements" these later stories included. And we can use them to study their creators, people as distant in time as the Assyrians of the seventh century, and try to understand why the Old Akkadian rulers left such a deep impression on them.

Not all later accounts presented the Akkad kings in a positive light. For a long time Sargon was seen only as a heroic warrior, until the mid-first millennium when accusations of arrogance appear. Naram-Sin had already been faulted for his insolence in the late third millennium. He was said to have destroyed the Enlil temple at Nippur, for which he was punished with the loss of his state. So the Mesopotamians also saw the negative aspects of these outbursts of military power and the self-aggrandizement these kings expressed in their texts and art.

4.2   The Third Dynasty of Ur

The period of fragmentation of power after Akkad's hegemony was short-lived. Although the chronology is confused – the *Sumerian King List* records thirty-two otherwise mostly unknown rulers – probably only some fifty years separated the death of King Sharkalisharri from the start of Babylonian reunification, which began with the expulsion of the Gutians. King Utu-hegal of Uruk relates how he chased them from southern Babylonia and returned kingship to Sumer. His brother and successor, Ur-Namma, imposed the rule of a new dynasty over the entirety of Babylonia, using the city of Ur as his capital. Ur-Namma continued Utu-hegal's work: he forced into submission autonomous rulers and those dependent on the Gutians, but the details are vague. Neither his inscriptions nor his year names devote attention to battles in Babylonia. Was there little opposition, or did he not want to describe how he won supremacy? In any event, by the end of his reign he could claim a new title, "King of Sumer and Akkad," referring to the entirety of Babylonia. The expulsion of the Gutians did not stop at the domestic borders, however. Ur-Namma campaigned in the Diyala region against them, and this brought him into conflict with Puzur-Inshushinak of Awan, who had unified a wide area of western Iran. Soon Ur occupied his capital city of Susa.

Around 2100 Ur-Namma started the Third Dynasty of Ur (or Ur III dynasty), a succession of five rulers from the same family (for a list of kings, see Section 2 of the King Lists at the end of the book). According to the *Sumerian King List*, it was the third time that Ur held kingship, hence our modern designation. For about seventy years, this dynasty governed Babylonia and adjacent regions to the east, using an elaborate bureaucracy that produced a vast number of written documents. Virtually no period of ancient Near Eastern history presents the historian with such an abundance and variety of documentation. Indeed, even in all of the ancient histories of Greece and Rome, there are few periods where a similar profusion of textual material is found. And since the succession of year names is well-known from the start of Shulgi's reign to the end of Ibbi-Sin's, we can reconstruct the basic sequence of political events for some ninety years. The royal court also produced inscriptions commemorating military campaigns and building activity and its scribes composed a series of hymns honoring the kings, which refer to some of their important acts (see document 4.2).

Most plentiful are the archival texts from this period. Close to 100,000 of them are now published and thousands more are known to exist in museums and other collections. They range from the simple receipt of one sheep to the calculation of the harvest of 38 million liters of cereals. They document many aspects of

Document 4.2 *Hymns to kings of the Ur III dynasty*

With the Ur III dynasty appeared a new form of royal celebration in literary form, the composition of hymns that sang the king's praises. His accomplishments were wide-ranging, including especially skills in warfare, but also as an athlete, a virile sexual partner, a scholar, and a just ruler. The hymns connected the king to the pantheon, claiming that the gods protected and promoted him, and sometimes declared that he was related to mythical heroes of the past, such as Gilgamesh. The genre was popular until the late Old Babylonian dynasty, and used the Sumerian language. The compositions are mostly known from manuscripts schoolboys wrote in the early second millennium, when they formed an important part of scribal training. King Shulgi of the Ur III period had the largest number of such hymns devoted to him, probably because of his long reign of forty-eight years. The extract here praises his skills as a student as well as a warrior, using metaphorical language.

I am a king, offspring begotten by a king and born by a queen. I, Shulgi the noble, have been blessed with a favorable destiny right from the womb. When I was small, I was at the academy, where I learned the scribal art from the tablets of Sumer and Akkad. None of the nobles could write on clay as I could. There where people regularly went for tutelage in the scribal art, I qualified fully in subtraction, addition, reckoning and accounting. The fair goddess Nanibgal, the goddess Nisaba, provided me amply with knowledge and comprehension. I am an experienced scribe who does not neglect a thing.

When I sprang up, muscular as a cheetah, galloping like a thoroughbred ass at full gallop, the favor of the god An brought me joy; to my delight the god Enlil spoke favorably about me, and they gave me the scepter because of my righteousness. I place my foot on the neck of the foreign lands; the fame of my weapons is established as far as the south, and my victory is established in the highlands. When I set off for battle and strife to a place that the god Enlil has commanded me, I go ahead of the main body of my troops and I clear the terrain for my scouts. I have a positive passion for weapons. Not only do I carry lance and spear, I also know how to handle slingstones with a sling. The clay bullets, the treacherous pellets that I shoot, fly around like a violent rainstorm. In my rage I do not let them miss.

Translation: Jeremy Black et al., http://etcsl.orinst.ox.ac.uk/cgi-bin/etcsl.cgi?text=t.2.4.2.02#.

economic life, including agriculture in all its aspects, manufacture, trade, taxation, and the sale of goods, and they derive from many cities in the state. The largest groups are from Ur, Umma, Girsu, Puzrish-Dagan, Nippur, Garshana, and Iri-Sagrig (the exact location of the last two places is unknown) in the southern half of Babylonia. But smaller finds were made throughout Sumer and Akkad. Ironically, this abundance presents a great challenge. Confronted with this mass of documents, scholars had to develop approaches that enable them to look at groups of texts rather than individual documents. This task is complicated by the fact that looters excavated most of them and that they were dispersed into innumerable collections through the antiquities market. More serious is the impression that is created by the mass of texts, namely, that it is complete in its coverage of economic activity. That is not the case. The record is extremely biased, produced almost exclusively by the state, and it illuminates that area of society, leaving other aspects, such as private business activity, nearly in the dark. While these documents mostly provide information on the economic life of the period, political figures appear in them as well: when kings, queens, high officials, and foreign dignitaries are mentioned we get a better idea of when and where they were active, how they were related, and other aspects of the lives of the state's elites.

Remarkable is the lack of interest in this period by later Mesopotamians when compared to how long they remembered Akkad's kings and the amount of tales they created about them. In the first centuries of the second millennium, Ur III rulers were known primarily through the school curriculum. Students at that time copied out hymns, royal correspondence, and some inscriptions, but few new compositions were created around the Ur III kings. The failure of Ur, rather than its success, was the focus of these new literary texts. Soon after its collapse several laments were composed describing the destructions of Ur, Nippur, and other southern cities. These did not narrate the ruin of the Ur III state for its historical interest, but were probably intended more to justify the presence of new dynasties, which could claim to have restored order after great calamities. In later centuries, only a handful of references to the Ur III kings appear. Those are almost totally restricted to omens giving vague remarks about kings' deaths, like one that states that Amar-Suen died from "a bite of his shoe," a reference we fail to understand. These kings did not leave the impression on the Mesopotamian consciousness that the Akkadian ones did.

The Ur III state was indeed of a different character than its predecessor: geographically more restricted in size, but internally more centralized. The state itself had two distinct parts: the heartland of Sumer and Akkad, and a militarily controlled zone to the east in between the Tigris River and the Zagros Mountains. Outside lay the rest of the Near East with which Ur maintained diplomatic contacts or where its armies raided. The system was developed primarily during the forty-eight year reign of King Shulgi, who restructured the heartland of the state and conquered the adjacent zones to the east starting in his twentieth regnal year. It was not put in place overnight – nor did it stay unchanged over time – but in its general outlines it worked as follows.

The heartland was the traditional area of Babylonia including the lower Diyala valley. It was divided up into about twenty provinces, in essence the territories of the formerly independent city-states. Governors administered these on the king's behalf and were identified with the Sumerian term énsi, which in Early Dynastic days had designated the sovereign ruler of the city-state. The men often were from prominent local families, and the office of governor regularly passed from father to son. Other family members held high positions in the province. Part of the king's strategy was thus to keep these families on his side, something he may also have pursued through marriage. Shulgi, for instance, is known to have married at least nine women, each of whom may have been from various important local families. The governors primarily controlled the temple estates, which were especially extensive in the south. They were responsible for the maintenance of the canal system and acted as the highest judges in the province. While representing the king, a wide range of powers was concentrated in their hands.

A military administration headed by generals (Sumerian shagina) paralleled the civil one of governors, although their zones of authority did not always fully coincide with the provinces. The province of Umma, for instance, had one governor and several generals, each in charge of a separate district. The generals were not native to the region where they were stationed or descendants of prominent old families, but the king chose them from groups of men who had made their careers in royal service. Many of them had Akkadian or foreign (Hurrian, Elamite, Amorite) names, the latter seemingly recent arrivals in Babylonia. They were personally tied to the king, often marrying women of the royal family, and they received their income from royal agricultural estates and other properties.

The central administration established a system of taxation that collected a substantial part of the provinces' resources. This system was given the Sumerian label bala, which basically meant "exchange." It was a massive fund to which all provinces had to contribute and from which they withdrew goods, enabling the state to use resources from all over its territory. The amount and composition of each province's contributions depended on its economic potential and the nature of its productive sector. For instance, Girsu provided grain, which it grew in abundance, while its neighbor Umma also contributed manufactured goods in wood, reeds, and leather. Many of the taxes were consumed locally by crown dependents, but some were sent to specialized collection points from which they were distributed when and wherever the goods were needed. Each province's contribution was calculated in advance on the basis of its agricultural and manufacturing potential. In the case of cereals, for example, officials measured the size of the agricultural area, and estimated the likely harvest. On the basis of that figure, they determined the amount to be contributed to the state. At the year's end, actual contributions were compared to what had been demanded and often a positive or negative balance was carried over to the next year. Also, contributions of the periphery, especially in the form of livestock, were added to the bala-fund (see below). Provinces were able to withdraw from the fund for their needs, thereby getting access to their neighbors' resources. State administrators carefully accounted for all these movements of goods.

Under the Ur III dynasty, Sumer and Akkad flourished economically, partly as the result of royal works. The archaeological record shows that there was a high level of urbanization at this time and that population density was higher than ever before. The degree to which wealth was available is also indicated by the extensive building activities of kings throughout the state. In their year names the kings often commemorated that they dug irrigation canals to expand the available agricultural zones. They needed a great labor force for these works and its organization perhaps best shows how far-reaching the influence of the crown in economic life was. Hundreds of able-bodied men and many women (called gurush and géme respectively in Sumerian) were conscripted to provide labor to the state, and that labor was also part of the bala-fund. Two classes of workers can be distinguished:

those who worked for the state year-round, and those who were only asked to do so part of the year. Service was predominantly paid for in rations – barley, oil, and wool – the amounts of which depended on the laborer's status. They were usually assigned specific tasks, such as weaving or the cutting of reed, but when needed in times of high demand they could be transferred to agricultural duties, for harvesting or canal maintenance. It seems that the people whose labor was only requisitioned part-time hired themselves out to the state at other times. Since the state's assets were so enormous, including fields, fishing grounds, manufacturing workshops, and so on, the demand for manpower was very high. The Garshana archive, from an unknown location in the Umma province, documents how large groups of women could be engaged as unskilled laborers in construction projects, in this case the building of a princess's estate in the countryside. They were hired to carry bricks from their place of manufacture to the building site. The Ur III state was not a totalitarian regime whose inhabitants were fully subjected to the bureaucracy, so labor had to be recruited by offering sufficient compensation. Many texts record the issuing of rations, which had to be taken from the state's central resources. Most recipients complemented those with homegrown or otherwise acquired vegetables and other foods. Some, however, received their entire food supplies from the state. The archive from a small city whose exact location we do not know, Iri-Sagrig, includes records of distributions of soup, meat, fish, bread, sweets, and beer to royal messengers and officials.

This depth of organization was applied throughout the heartland of the Ur III state, which included the region of the Mesopotamian alluvium where irrigation agriculture was practiced. Ur ruled the territories to its east through means different than those employed in the heartland. Already Ur-Namma had campaigned in the area between the Tigris and the Zagros Mountains, and by the end of Shulgi's reign Ur fully controlled the area there from Susa in the south to the Mosul plain in the north. The Ur III kings imposed a military government over this region. They put in place a system of direct exploitation that was headed by generals (shagina), who could be moved at will from one center to another. The royal chancellor (sukkal-mah) represented the interests of the crown and supervised the system from the capital out. He charged the generals with collecting tribute calculated in exact numbers of cattle, sheep, and goats to be procured by the military establishment. How the soldiers acquired the animals is not reported, but most likely they requisitioned them from the local populations. Large numbers of animals were taken to Babylonia where they were gathered in a place near Nippur called Puzrish-Dagan, which Shulgi founded especially for this purpose in his thirty-eighth year. There they entered the bala taxation system and could be issued as food for the court or for offerings in the numerous temples. Many animals were kept for their wool. The numbers of animals involved, both from the eastern territories and from Babylonia proper, were staggering: records demonstrate that up to two hundred sheep and goats and fifteen head of cattle could pass through Puzrish-Dagan on a single day. The eastern periphery was thus exploited for its resources of animals, which entered the economy of the heartland.

Beyond these eastern dominions were large regions considered to be hostile and frequently the targets of military campaigns. Royal inscriptions mention a variety of peoples and places raided for booty and captives. Some of the states encountered there had already existed in the time of Akkad and remained formidable opponents. The Ur III kings used diplomacy to appease their rulers: three of the five kings of Ur sent their daughters to marry Iranian princes. In the end the policy failed: eastern states such as Shimashki remained hostile, and eventually played an important role in the overthrow of the Ur III state. In the Persian Gulf, Ur maintained the trade contacts that had existed since the Old Akkadian period. Already Ur-Namma claimed to have restored trade with Magan, and throughout the Ur III period we find administrative documents that mention that region. Merchants' records indicate that woven cloth, abundantly produced in Babylonia, was sent there to be exchanged for copper and stones, such as diorite. Ur's contacts with the east and south were thus for the purpose of obtaining mineral resources, through trade, diplomacy, and military raids.

The Ur III kings approached the regions to the north and west differently. They established diplomatic relations with the states there and made no attempts toward military control. Ur-Namma arranged for the marriage of a Mari princess to his son Shulgi, perhaps in the hope that this state on the Middle Euphrates would act as a buffer and intermediary with regions farther north. Syrian states maintained friendly relations with Ur, but contacts were rare. The archaeological record shows that urbanism declined in Syria in the late third millennium. In the region along the Habur River cities almost fully disappeared while elsewhere they became smaller. Some scholars have suggested that this was due to climate change, but this is disputed. The raids of Akkad kings may have caused an economic downturn, and only those cities that controlled trade routes continued to maintain contacts with Babylonia. In the Ur III sources from Babylonia we find references to people from the Syrian cities Tuttul, Ebla, and Urshu, and messengers from the Mediterranean harbor of Byblos also appear. There is no indication of any single city dominating Syria politically or militarily. These events seem to have allowed semi-nomadic people to gain greater influence and probably their numbers expanded with people who abandoned urban life.

Akkad's military interactions with Syria had thus been replaced by diplomacy under Ur. Even if the Ur III rulers proclaimed themselves "kings of the four quarters of the universe," their military reach was geographically smaller than that of the Old Akkadian rulers. Yet the Ur III state's internal coherence was greater. Several reforms were instituted in Babylonia in order to facilitate the functioning of the state. The bala taxation system was a major organization that enabled the collection and distribution of resources throughout Sumer and Akkad. The state's involvement in the local economies was enormous, and its employment of men and women extensive. An elaborate bureaucracy was needed to account for all movements of its assets, which is why there is such an abundance of administrative records. The scribes who wrote them had to be trained to use proper accounting techniques and formulae. We see a uniformity of the writing system in official documents throughout the Ur III state, and it is likely that schools were

Figure 4.3   Dish inscribed with the name of the high priestess of the god Nanna. This dish was excavated at Ur and contains a brief inscription that identifies the owner or donor as "Enmahgalanna, the priestess of (the moon god) Nanna." Beside it is an unusual pictogram of the crescent moon and the cuneiform sign EN, "priestess." From other texts we know that Enmahgalanna was the daughter of King Amar-Suen. British Museum, London. 19 cm (7.5 in) base, 24.30 cm (9.5 in) exterior rim, H. 3.50 cm (1.4 in). Credit: © The Trustees of the British Museum.

established to teach this. The system of weights and measures was simplified, and Shulgi may have attempted to introduce a standard calendar throughout the land. While each city continued to use its own sequence of month names, a calendar appeared in his reign that was used at Puzrish-Dagan and elsewhere for royal business. It was never imposed on the entire region, however, not even for central accounts, which shows that local practices had great resilience. Only in the next century, when the region was once more politically fragmented, did one calendar, the Nippur one, become used throughout Babylonia.

The kings did pursue an active policy to unify the land in ideological terms as well. They placed their children as high priests and priestesses in the major cults, and they built and restored temples all over the kingdom (figure 4.3). Before his twentieth year of rule, Shulgi was deified and his successors assumed this status when they came to the throne. They were regarded as gods of the entire land, rather than of individual cities, and cults for them existed throughout the state. Temples and statues of the kings as gods were built in various cities, thus providing a focus of centralization through the cult as well. Many officials used cylinder seals to certify the business they undertook, and those usually contained an inscription providing the owner's name and his or her title (see figure 4.4). It is important that they always referred to their status as "servant of the king," indicating that their authority ultimately derived from him. Moreover, people gave their children names referring to the king as god, and officials were encouraged to change their names to include a reference to the king. Names such as "Shulgi is my god" were

Figure 4.4 Cylinder seal, with its impression, used by King Ibbi-Sin's official, Ilum-bani. This is one of the typical cylinder seals from an Ur III official, which shows the owner of the seal being introduced to a seated deity by an interceding goddess. The inscription also has a very standard text for the period. It praises King Ibbi-Sin as king of Ur and of the four quarters of the universe, and states that Ilum-bani a nubanda-official was his servant. This suggests that this was the seal he used for official business. The Metropolitan Museum of Art, New York, Gift of Martin and Sarah Cherkasky, 1988 (1988.380.2). Hematite; H. 2.8 cm, Diam. 1.7 cm ($1\frac{1}{8} \times \frac{11}{16}$ in). Credit: © 2014 The Metropolitan Museum of Art/Art Resource/Scala, Florence.

common. The ideology of the centralized state thus permeated down to the level of the entire citizenry.

We can doubt, however, that in practice this royal ideal was achieved. The local economies and hierarchies survived quite independently, even if they had to pay taxes and homage to the king at Ur. This is most clearly demonstrated by the aftermath of the Ur III state's collapse. Babylonia did not experience a period of decline at that time, but regions that had been part of the unified state reverted to their local habits without evidence of disruption. This would not have been possible had their economies become specialized and interdependent components of a single system. We have to remember the bias of the documentation: almost all the texts derive from the state bureaucracy and describe the state's activities. It would thus be easy to see the Ur III state as a highly authoritarian one, documenting and directing all the movements of its dependents. But within this abundance of state records we see traces of economic activity that was not controlled by it. People often simultaneously provided services to the state and interacted economically with others on their own behalf. We also see that regional variations in many respects had survived: in the south the state administered its extensive holdings through the temple-estates that had existed for many centuries, while in the north it relied more on individual agents who may have contracted other business on the side. Other traditions survived through this period, and the multiplicity of local systems must not be forgotten.

The end of Ur's hegemony was sudden and (as usual) we do not fully understand what happened or what the main causes were. Both internal and external factors played a role. Within Babylonia itself, the former city-states and their local governors had always nursed feelings of independence. Early in the reign of Ur's last king, Ibbi-Sin, provinces stopped contributing their taxes, and by his ninth year the whole bala system had disappeared. Scribes no longer dated their accounts with Ur III year names in Puzrish-Dagan, Garshana, and Iri-Sagrig after Ibbi-Sin's year 3, at Umma after year 5, and at Girsu after year 6, which indicates that these cities had broken off ties with Ur. In Ibbi-Sin's eighth year, a man called Ishbi-Erra set up an independent dynasty at Isin, near Nippur, the religious center of Babylonia, and soon he annexed that city. Simultaneously, a famine may have struck the region of Ur. The king's correspondence, known only from later copies and perhaps fictional, includes letters in which Ibbi-Sin implored Ishbi-Erra to acquire grain in the north at whatever price was necessary. At Ur grain seems to have risen fifteen times in price and it could no longer be used as animal fodder. How much of that was due to the lack of good harvests and how much to the refusal of the provinces to pay their taxes is unclear. The idea that climate change, floods, or droughts contributed to the problems seems contradicted by the fact that certain spheres of the economy performed well at this time. Ur had a workshop that produced precious goods for the temples and palace, and accounts from Ibbi-Sin's fifteenth year indicate that some 18 kilograms of gold and 75 kilograms of silver were used that year. The state's coffers were still well stocked and despite his much-reduced powers Ibbi-Sin remained king for twenty-five years.

The decisive blow to Ur came from outside Babylonia. The ruler of Shimashki, which had been Ur's major opponent in the east, seized Susa and Elam when Ibbi-Sin's authority waned in his third year. Two decades later he turned against Babylonia itself. He captured the capital Ur and deported King Ibbi-Sin to Susa. For some seven years the Elamites occupied the city, until Ishbi-Erra of Isin chased them out. Ishbi-Erra and his successors claimed to be the heirs of the kings of Ur, but they could not control the same geographical area. More and more independent city-states emerged throughout Babylonia, a situation that we will discuss in the next chapter. The spotlight on Babylonia in the twenty-first century is so bright that the rest of the Near East is often ignored in historical reconstructions. Regions often can be studied only when they were in Ur's orbit. But states in the east, such as Shimashki in Iran, escaped the control of Ur. And these external forces took advantage of the internal opposition to Ur's centralized rule to put an end to that state.

At the height of its powers the royal court of Ur sponsored literary creativity, which to a large extent was self-serving as the texts included many hymns of praise to the kings (see document 4.2). It is also likely that much Sumerian literature regarding heroes such as Gilgamesh was composed at this time, and the Ur III kings claimed that they were related to them (e.g., Shulgi alleged he was the brother of Gilgamesh). But almost no manuscripts from the Ur III period of that literature survive. We know of it from copies students made during their training in the early second millennium. Hymns of praise of the Ur III kings were part of the curriculum, and scribes learned of the greatness of the dynasty at a young age.

At the same time, however, they copied out literature that focused on Ur's failures. Two types of texts especially dealt with that topic. Most explicit was a group of poems we call "city laments." They described how the gods became displeased with the leading Ur III cities Ur, Nippur, Eridu, and Uruk, abandoned them, and left them to the Elamites to destroy. The *Lament over the destruction of Sumer and Ur* narrates how they carried off King Ibbi-Sin in chains to Elam. A second type of text that students copied out purported to be part of the correspondence Ur's kings maintained with officials. These identified as the state's main enemy a group of people called Amorites, the subject of other literature of the time that depicts them as the negation of civilized life. The role of the Amorites in Near Eastern history is a difficult question (see debate 5.1), and there is little evidence from the Ur III period that confirms the picture the royal correspondence draws. Yet, in the early second millennium they were assigned much of the blame for Ur's collapse.

After the Old Babylonian period memories of Ur III seem to have become vague. Unlike for the Akkad dynasty its military successes were ignored and in omens Ibbi-Sin became the model of a ruler whose reign ended in disaster. The end of the dynasty was of more interest than its successes. As the *Lament over the destruction of Sumer and Ur* states: "Ur was indeed given kingship, but it was not given an eternal reign."

Debate 4.1   *Can we trust later Mesopotamian accounts about the dynasty of Akkad?*

The dynasty of Akkad was never forgotten in ancient Mesopotamia: in the Persian period, close to 2,000 years after his death, a statue of King Sargon still received offerings as if he were a god. He and several of his successors, but especially Naram-Sin, were the subjects of a long tradition of legends, which over time ascribed greater and greater feats to them (Westenholz 1997). Not only Babylonians, but also Assyrians, Hittites, and even Egyptians, read about them. New texts continue to be discovered, including an account of Sargon's heroic abilities written by Assyrians in the nineteenth century and recently found in their Anatolian colony at Kanesh (Günbatti 1997). The meaning of that text is much debated: some say it is a parody (e.g., Foster 2005: 71–5), others that it should be taken seriously (e.g., Dercksen 2005). In the mid-first millennium Sargon was depicted as living on the edge of the world with the sole survivor of the flood, Utnapishtim, and a description of his "empire" has it stretch from Crete in the Mediterranean to Oman and from Anatolia to Egypt (Van De Mieroop 1999a: 59–76).

How reliable is this information and how useful is it for our understanding of the Akkad dynasty? Some scholars take a maximalist approach and argue that we would be foolish to ignore what these stories tell us. Their authors lived much closer to the events than we do and they must have had access to information now lost (Hallo 1998 and

2001; see also there for the terms maximalist and minimalist). Of course, we need to ignore the exaggerations, but there is a "historical kernel" to be discovered through critical examination of the legends combined with other sources (Potts 2001). What can serve as external evidence, however, that helps verify the statements made in the legends? Regularly there seems to be circular reasoning. For example, omen literature sometimes claims to describe signs that appeared when something happened to an Akkad king, such as when Naram-Sin conquered the city of Apishal, probably in northwest Syria. Some scholars have stated that historical allusions in omens are the only reliable information the Mesopotamians provided us (Finkelstein 1963). But these references clearly derive from the same background as the legends on the kings (see Liverani 1993a for a survey of the literature up to then).

Much more critical minimalist attitudes appear as well, and some argue that there is no indication that actual events inspired any literary creations in Mesopotamia (Cooper 2001). It is more important to study the context in which an account was written than the historical details it pretends to give, as all histories are part of their own mental world (Beckman 2005). Thus, scholars have tried to connect legends about the kings of Akkad to later moments in Mesopotamian history. For example, when around 1950 the Isin ruler Ishme-Dagan planned to restore the Ekur temple at Nippur, a lobby in his court developed a tale of Naram-Sin's mistreatment of the sanctuary to urge the king to restore it to its pre-Akkad glory (Liverani 1993a). The problem with such an analysis is that we often do not know when exactly a particular work of literature was composed. We study manuscripts that may reproduce or edit stories that existed for centuries before. So it is more appropriate to ask why anyone would have written out a story about Akkad's kings at the time the manuscripts are dated (Van De Mieroop 1999a). The legends are not sources on the kings they describe but on the people who thought those tales to be of sufficient interest to read them.

NOTES

1 There are various designations for the state, most commonly Old Akkadian or Sargonic. The name of the dynastic seat, Akkad, is sometimes anglicized as Agade or Accad.
2 Frayne 1993: 31.
3 Frayne 1993: 16.
4 Translation after Farber 1983.

5

The Near East in the Early Second Millennium

3000	2500	2000	1500	1000	500

2019	Ishbi-Erra founds dynasty at Isin
ca. 1970–1719	*Karum*-Kanesh
1898	Beginning of open warfare between Isin and Larsa
1835	Kudur-Mabuk dynasty established at Larsa
ca. 1800–1762	Mari archives
1793	Rim-Sin of Larsa conquers Isin
1763	Hammurabi of Babylon conquers southern Babylonia
1762	Hammurabi sacks Eshnunna
1761	Hammurabi conquers Mari

In the four centuries between the years 2000 to 1600 similar political and social structures existed throughout the Near East. Numerous states were spread over the landscape from western Iran to the Mediterranean coast, and their rulers, all military men, vying for power, joined in ever-shifting and ephemeral alliances. A passage from a letter excavated at Mari and written in the early eighteenth century sums up the situation aptly:

> No king is truly powerful on his own. Ten to fifteen kings follow Hammurabi of Babylon, Rim-Sin of Larsa, Ibal-pi-El of Eshnunna or Amut-pi-El of Qatna; but twenty kings follow Yarim-Lim of Yamkhad.[1]

A History of the Ancient Near East ca. 3000–323 BC, Third Edition. Marc Van De Mieroop.
© 2016 John Wiley & Sons, Inc. Published 2016 by John Wiley & Sons, Inc.

A handful of powerful rulers from southern Babylonia to western Syria had carved up the Near East by forcing smaller kings to be their vassals. Abundant diplomatic correspondence, especially from the palace of Mari strategically located on the border between Babylonia and Syria, gives an unparalleled detail on the political and military situation of the time. It shows that warfare was almost constant and that kings repeatedly formed and broke alliances, betrayed one another, and turned against former friends without any qualms. It seems that they trusted no one, not even in their own court, and their survival depended not only on military leadership but also on diplomatic skill. After 1800, some succeeded in establishing dominance over larger territories, most famously Hammurabi of Babylon; but these unifications were only short-lived. There is no clear chronological division between the moments of political fragmentation and those of centralization. Here we will explore the former, which still exemplifies the basic political structure of the Near East in its early history, the prevalent city-state. In the next chapter we will examine the moments of centralization. A purely chronological sequence of the narrative is not possible by this arrangement.

With the start of the second millennium our grasp on Near Eastern history becomes very wide-ranging in geographical terms. Writing in cuneiform became a common skill known from southwestern Iran to central Anatolia and western Syria. Babylonia clearly continued to be the source of most of the scribal traditions. Its language, which can now be identified as a separate dialect of Akkadian, was used almost everywhere by native speakers of other languages (Amorite, Hurrian, Elamite), who also adopted the southern writing style and spellings. The most prominent exception to this appears in a central Anatolian colony of merchants from Assur, who wrote a distinct dialect of Akkadian, Old Assyrian. They used different forms of the cuneiform signs, and read them often unconventionally. This is all the more remarkable since the official texts found in their hometown were Babylonian in character. Sumerian flourished as a language of culture, but almost exclusively in Babylonia.

There is a great variety in the origin of the texts available to us, as they derive both from institutional and private contexts. The primary source varies regionally, however. In Babylonia the recovered cuneiform records are predominantly from private contexts, in great contrast to the Ur III period, when they had almost all come from central archives. It is remarkable how widespread literacy had become in the region; even in small villages there were people who could read and write. Also in the Assyrian colonies in Anatolia we find only private records, but elsewhere in the Near East it is the palaces and other royal institutions that provide almost all the texts in the early second millennium (see box 5.1). Especially in northern Syria, royal chancelleries trained in Babylonian practices left the writings we have. One genre of writing that flourished in these centuries is that of the letter, and we have remains of the correspondence of businessmen in Babylonia and Assur, members of royal courts, officials, generals, ambassadors, and so on. Mostly they wrote to each other about business matters, but once in a while we get a glimpse of other concerns – health, love, rivalries … The letters provide us with

Box 5.1   *The Mari letters*

French excavations since the 1930s at the site of Mari in Syria have unearthed a large royal palace of the nineteenth and eighteenth centuries, in which some 20,000 tablets were found. Many of these are letters written between the palace and its court representatives, both domestic and foreign. Because of Mari's location between Babylonia and Syria, and between the agricultural areas of the Euphrates valley and the steppe used by semi-nomadic tribes, they inform us about a vast array of political and military affairs throughout the Near East, and about the interactions between settled and pastoral people. The letters were carefully drafted documents in which the scribes often summarized the original queries or orders before they gave a reply. They were composed in full Babylonian manner: the language, writing style, and tablet shapes were of southern derivation although the majority of people at Mari, and at other courts with which Mari was in contact, spoke a west Semitic language rather than Akkadian. Influences from the vernaculars can be identified in the letters from various regions. When Hammurabi conquered Mari in 1761, his scribes made inventories of the palace archives, and identified and removed letters involving Babylonian affairs, which were probably taken off to the capital. This indicates how important he considered these diplomatic archives to be.

The court at Mari was not the only one to have such archives. Palaces excavated at Qattara (Tell Rimah), Shushara (Shemshara), Shubat-Enlil (Tell Leilan), and others have yielded smaller, yet similar, diplomatic archives. They show how the entirety of Syria and Mesopotamia formed an integrated system of kingdoms whose rulers had to remain informed in order to survive.

a more intimate view of the people we study, a perspective not available before this period.

5.1   Nomads and Sedentary People

All our texts and archaeological remains derive from cities and other permanent settlements. Throughout the Near East, cities flourished in this period, and areas such as northern Syria, which had experienced a decline of cities in the late third millennium, again became fully urbanized by the nineteenth century. Very important in the political and social life of the Near East, however, were people whose livelihood was not tied to the cereal agriculture that supported the urban centers. These were semi-nomadic pastoralists who spent part of the year moving around with their flocks in search of pasture in the steppe, the other part in villages near the rivers. Such people were a lasting feature in the Near East, but in certain periods they became more visible in the urban record because they interacted more closely with city residents, competing for political power. Different designations were given to them, always from the point of view of the people in the cities who wrote the texts. In the late third and early second millennia they seem to have been grouped together under the name Amorites, which coincided with the term for the "west," in Akkadian Amurru. The expression Amorite did not refer to a well-defined ethnic or tribal group, but its use was flexible and referred primarily to people who were considered to have a semi-nomadic background and roots in the west. The question of who the Amorites were and what their role in Near Eastern societies of the early second millennium was, is much disputed (see debate 5.1). Here we will focus on their pastoralist lifestyle.

The life of pastoralists revolved around their flocks. Throughout the Near East millions of sheep and goats were herded for what is called their renewable resources: especially wool and hair and, when dead, skins, bones, horns, and tendons. Although people ate meat as well, it was a luxury, so relatively few animals were slaughtered. The natural environment with its dry summers made it necessary to move flocks around to different pastures. In the summer, they stayed near the fertile river valleys, close to cities and villages, while in the winter, the steppe had enough vegetation to graze the animals there. The patterns of movement were well planned and groups used the same winter pastures year after year. Pastoralists thus led a hybrid life – sedentary in villages in the summer, nomadic in the steppe in the winter – and modern scholarship uses the term semi-nomadic to refer to them.

The interactions between nomads and sedentary people took place on several levels. The two groups were economically complementary, one producing animal products, the other agricultural and craft goods, and exchange was to the benefit of both. They had to make arrangements to ensure that the animals did not destroy cereal crops by grazing or trampling them, but farmers also made fallow fields available to flocks for grazing which encouraged plant growth and provided natural fertilization. Because of this interaction, cities and states could enforce some control over the pastoralists. Depending on the proximity of the pastoralists' villages and grazing grounds to the centers of power, they were more or less subjected to political domination, military and labor levies, and taxation.

Whenever pastoralists moved into the orbit of settled societies, they entered the realm of the written documentation that we study. In the early second millennium, we are provided with a uniquely informative record from the palace archives of Mari on the Middle Euphrates. That city controlled a long stretch of the Euphrates valley, which incorporated villages of pastoralists who used the Syrian steppe for winter pasture. The social organization of the semi-nomadic pastoralists was tribal. People claimed descent from a common ancestor, real or fictional, but those affiliations were loose: sometimes tribes absorbed others and some people changed tribes. Tribes were flexible social units. Those that lived around Mari were divided into two major branches: "of the left," that is, the north when facing the rising sun, the Sim'alites, and "of the right," that is, the south, the Yaminites. The latter lived the closest to the city and we know their subdivisions better. They included, for example, Amnanu and Yakhruru, groups that were attested in Babylonia as well. So these designators had a long history by the early second millennium, and tribes over a wide geographical area could claim common descent. Tribal names were given to settled and non-settled people alike, a practice that shows the hybridity of the pastoralist lifestyle.

In the interactions between Mari and pastoral groups, the palace had the most control over those whose villages were near the agricultural zones. Their inhabitants were subjected to censuses, they had to provide labor and military service, and headmen were responsible for the group's interactions with the palace. More distant tribes, such as the Sutians, escaped this control and often Mari's relationship with them is portrayed in very negative terms. They were constantly accused of being robbers and murderers, an image that derived partly from the common prejudices settled people had against non-settled ones. On the other hand, we should not fully dismiss the accounts as bigoted: competition over scarce resources between farmers and pastoralists could be fierce and violent.

Ethnographic research shows that sedentarization by pastoral nomads usually took place among the richest and poorest of the group. Very successful herders could not continue to expand the size of their herds as they would become unmanageable, so they started to invest some of their wealth in land, and settled down to take care of it. The poorest had too few animals to support themselves and tried to gain employment among settled people, including as mercenaries in armies. At the turn of the third to the second millennium, we see a major increase in the presence of people designated as Amorites in cities throughout the Near East, and during the first four centuries of the second millennium many people claimed to be of Amorite descent. Amorites had been present in the Near East from the mid-third millennium on, as is documented in texts from Shuruppak and the Old Akkadian dynasty. In Ur III texts they appeared in increasing numbers: we can recognize them either because they are explicitly identified as Amorite, or because their names are in the Amorite language, a Semitic idiom distinct from Akkadian. While they were active in all levels of society, including as generals in the army, early second millennium tradition placed much blame for the collapse of the Ur III state on the Amorites. The literature of the time included very negative portrayals. A poem called *Marriage of Martu* states, for example:

> (The Amorite,) he is dressed in sheep's skins;
> He lives in tents in wind and rain;
> He doesn't offer sacrifices.
> Armed [vagabond] in the steppe,
> he digs up truffles and is restless.
> He eats raw meat,
> lives his life without a home,
> and, when he dies, he is not buried according to proper rituals.[2]

Amorite life was thus the total opposite of the civilized urban one.

Upon the disappearance of the Ur III state and the political fragmentation that followed in Babylonia, starting in the mid-twentieth century some of the new dynasties claimed Amorite ancestry. They mentioned this with pride in contrast to the negative depiction of Amorites in literature. After 1800, Hammurabi of Babylon, who came to rule a large urbanized territory, still referred to himself as "king of the Amorites," and under his fourth successor, Ammisaduqa, a list of ancestors of the dynasty explicitly recognized that they were Amorite. The same names appeared in a list of ancestors of King Shamshi-Adad found at Assur and there was thus perhaps a set of common ancestors that all Amorites acknowledged. There was no stigma attached to being Amorite.

From the fragmentary and sometimes contradictory information this picture emerges. Semi-nomadic pastoral groups existed throughout the Near East from the beginning of agriculture there; pastoralism and farming were complementary activities and originated at the same time. In the mid-third millennium the name Amorite became common to refer to pastoralists, and some individuals among them rose in the political hierarchies of the existing city-states, often through a military career. When centralized power in Babylonia fell apart in the early second millennium, men with Amorite names were able to seize the throne in several city-states. Possibly because of the competition between old and new lineages of authority, between urban Sumerians and Akkadians and non-urban Amorites, these backgrounds were emphasized. The clear acknowledgment of dynastic roots outside cities in ancestral lists may indicate that the concept of the city-state as the center of all power was waning, and that the idea of a larger territory as a political unit started to develop. The presence of Amorites throughout the Near East, however, did not translate into the creation of a new cultural ideal. In Babylonia, Amorites fully adopted the existing culture, including the use of Sumerian and Akkadian for their literature; nowhere did the Amorite language become the official language in the written record.

5.2 Babylonia

The end of Ur's hegemony over Sumer and Akkad did not lead to an immediate fragmentation of political power there. Early in the reign of Ibbi-Sin, the last king of the Ur III dynasty, Ishbi-Erra had established a dynasty in Isin, and took over control of much of Babylonia. When the Elamites captured Ur, it was Ishbi-Erra who liberated the city, and his successors adopted the title "King of Ur" as their own. Even so, decentralizing forces were strong, and an increasing number of local dynasties arose in the twentieth and nineteenth centuries. Most prominent were the royal families at Isin and Larsa in the south, and Babylon in the north, but cities such as Uruk, Kish, and Sippar at times had their own kings. In the region to the east of the Tigris, independent dynasties established themselves at Eshnunna and Assur, while Elam remained outside the Babylonian political orbit. Rulers claimed the right to issue year names, and the presence of tablets dated with the names of particular city-dynasties allows us to identify what areas they controlled and when. By the early nineteenth century, competition escalated into open conflict and resulted in what seems to us incessant warfare. Nevertheless, the states of Babylonia acknowledged that they were part of a common system, one that centered round Nippur as religious capital. Political control over that city, which shifted several times, gave a king the right to call himself "King of Sumer and Akkad." A calendar of month names from Nippur was used as the official one throughout the region, and the blessing of Nippur's priesthood provided a king with a special status. Another tradition that survived and shows that the cities regarded themselves as partners in a common system was the appointment of the high priestess at Ur. From the time of Sargon of Akkad, the daughter of the dominant ruler of the region had held that position. In the early second millennium, high priestesses were installed by the city-dynasty that ruled at Ur, but the incumbent was not immediately replaced when political control changed. For instance, the daughter of the Isin king Ishme-Dagan remained in office after Gungunum of Larsa had conquered Ur, and cults of the deceased priestesses survived long after the authority of their hometown dynasties. The conviction that the Babylonian city-states were part of a single system enabled the local rulers to adhere to an ideology that there was only one kingship in Babylonia, which passed from one city to another. Whoever the Nippur priesthood acknowledged was king of Sumer and Akkad, even if in reality his powers were limited. It is in this context that we have to see the message of the *Sumerian King List*, a document that promoted the idea that there was only one king at a time.

Isin and Larsa were the main actors on the political scene in southern Babylonia. At first the Isin dynasty was heir to the much-reduced Ur III state (for a list of kings, see Section 3 of the King Lists at the end of the book). The Nippur priesthood acknowledged its kings, who maintained control over most southern cities, including Ur, and undertook public works in several of them. For a century the region was at peace. Later in the twentieth century, however, a rival dynasty established itself at Larsa (for a list of kings, see Section 4 of the King Lists at the end of the book), soon taking full control over the south and east of Babylonia, while Isin's power was reduced to central Babylonia. In 1898 Abisare, king of Larsa, openly attacked his Isin colleague, which enabled other cities to reject Isin's supremacy. At this time the region had the greatest number of rival dynasties in the period, several of which could claim the support of the Nippur priesthood in turn.

Centralizing forces were at work as well, however, and the initiative came from the city of Larsa. After a period of internal instability, with a series of short-lived rulers often of different families, a family from the area east of the Tigris, the so-called Kudur-Mabuk dynasty, seized the throne of Larsa. The father Kudur-Mabuk set up base in the easternmost city of central Babylonia, Mashkan-shapir. He placed his son Warad-Sin (ruled 1834–1823) on Larsa's throne, but meddled in local affairs. When Warad-Sin died, his brother Rim-Sin succeeded him and had the longest reign recorded in Mesopotamian history, sixty years (1822–1763). His life vividly illustrates the political and military vicissitudes of the time, which we can reconstruct from a variety of sources including year names, economic records, and letters. Upon his accession, the territory Rim-Sin's family controlled was a 230 kilometer long (145 miles) stretch of eastern Babylonia from

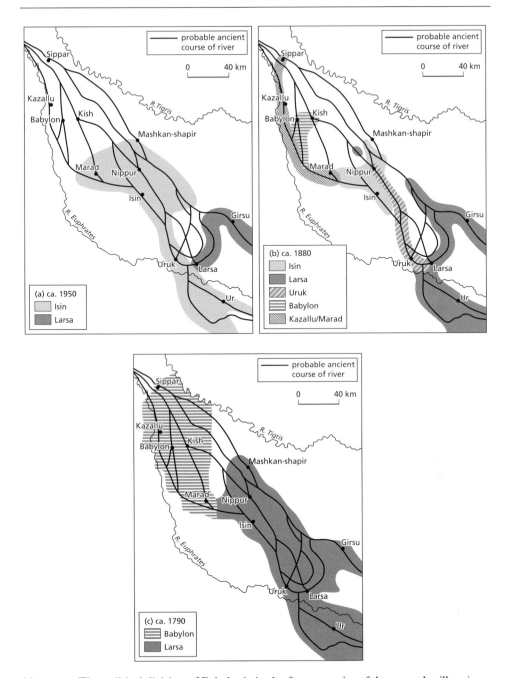

Map 5.1   The political division of Babylonia in the first centuries of the second millennium. After Michael Roaf, *Cultural Atlas of Mesopotamia and the Ancient Near East* (Oxford: Equinox, 1990), p. 109.

Nippur and Mashkan-shapir in the north to the Persian Gulf in the south, where it extended westward to include Larsa and Ur. The states of Babylon, Isin, and Uruk bordered it from north to south. The death of Kudur-Mabuk shortly before Rim-Sin's eighth year may have placed the entire area in the latter's charge, and soon he asserted himself militarily. In his thirteenth year (1810), Rim-Sin defeated a coalition of forces led by Uruk, Isin, and Babylon, and he captured villages near Uruk. After further military successes near Larsa and a reconquest of Nippur, which he had lost to Isin in his ninth year, he destroyed Uruk in 1800.

When Rim-Sin defeated Isin in 1793, his thirtieth year, Larsa's only remaining rival in Babylonia was the state of Babylon, where Hammurabi inherited the throne the next year. Rim-Sin spent the following thirty years consolidating his grasp over the south by concentrating administrative functions in the capital, and he seems to have reduced the economic independence of the earlier city-states. Hammurabi waited until Rim-Sin was an old man to initiate his swift conquest of all his neighbors, including Larsa, which he captured in 1763. He left Rim-Sin's organization in place, however, and continued to rely on men from Larsa to supervise the administration of southern Babylonia. Rim-Sin thus laid the groundwork for Hammurabi's centralized state, to be discussed in the next chapter.

Despite political fragmentation and extensive conflict, there are no indications of an economic decline of Babylonia in the first three centuries of the second millennium. Urbanization remained dense, and documents from an increasingly large number of cities show high levels of economic activity. Even the city of Ur flourished, despite being deprived of the regional system that had supported it before. Fundamental changes in the administration of the economy took place, however. In the twenty-first century, state bureaucracy had supervised virtually everything and had employed large segments of the population as a labor force, which it supported with rations. In the early second millennium there occurred what we could call a partial "privatization" of the economy through a gradual and probably unplanned process. The large institutions, palaces and temples, still held very extensive resources. They owned large tracts of land and other properties and were great consumers of goods and services. At the start of the second millennium, there was a continuation of Ur III practices, albeit on a local scale as political power had fragmented. For example, we have an archive from a craft workshop attached to the palace at Isin that was responsible for the manufacture of goods in wood, reed, leather, and wool for the royal household. Royal administrators supervised the workshop, but the craftsmen it employed spent part of their time working for others as well. Other institutions started to contract out work and services. Instead of having their lands farmed by dependent staff, they gave the use of fields to tenant farmers who were expected to hand in a share of the harvest and keep the rest for their own needs. Herds of sheep and goats were assigned to shepherds, who were obliged to deliver set amounts of wool and hair and to increase the herd by a fixed number of animals. Excess production was to the producers' benefit, but they had to make up a deficit from their own share. When the institutions required labor they hired people, paying them salaries for the time of employment only, rather than year-round rations. Gradually, more tasks were undertaken by people outside the institutions, and earlier offices, such as that of the temple brewer, became sinecures broken down into parts as small as half a day a year. These were traded as they guaranteed a small percentage of the institution's income for the period the office was held.

Independent contractors also took on administrative tasks. Instead of employing and supporting large bureaucratic staffs, the institutions asked private entrepreneurs to act as intermediaries between themselves and the citizenry, collecting dues, issuing payments, and organizing the collection and distribution of resources. In addition, the entrepreneurs converted those collections, paid in perishable produce and of limited use to the pared-down institutions, into easily storable silver. Our sources do not record how they did so, but most likely they sold them to organizations and individuals for silver. As reward for their services the entrepreneurs kept a share of the assets transferred. The privatization of the administration was well suited to the new political circumstances. In Ur III times, bureaucrats had owed their appointment to the king, and a change in dynasty would lead to a disruption of administrative practices. The private businessmen who were contracted for their services did not owe political allegiance to any dynasty, and were left alone to function in politically uncertain times.

Ultimately the effects of this system of economic organization and management on Babylonian society were disastrous, however. The contributions required from producers seem to have been high and, in a region like Babylonia where stretches of bad harvests were not uncommon, people were often unable to meet the demands. They could only ask for credit from the businessmen who collected their dues. Moreover, when they could not even survive until the next harvest on the amounts set aside for their own needs, they turned to these same men for emergency loans. These were high-interest loans: tradition and royal proclamations allowed for a 20 percent interest on silver loans and a 33 percent rate on grain loans. The rates were collected whatever the duration of the loan, and since such loans were usually short term, their repayment with the full rate of interest after only a month or less placed an enormous burden on the debtors. The records found in the houses of businessmen include a great number of loan contracts, and show that the level of indebtedness was high. That there was a debt crisis is clear from repeated edicts in which kings claimed to restore order by annulling outstanding consumer loans. References to such acts are especially clear in the official statements of the kings of Isin, Larsa, and Babylon. Only one of the original edicts, issued by Ammisaduqa of Babylon (ruled 1646–1626), is sufficiently well preserved for us to understand its detail. In it he abolished all debts producers had taken on for their survival or to pay for outstanding dues, but not those of businessmen who sought capital for commercial enterprises (document 5.1). It was the palace that absorbed the loss, but it did so because of the tradition that a king needed to maintain order and justice in the land – and because, after all, a large indebted population would no longer form a stable tax base, but would exist only to enrich a competing class of private businessmen.

Document 5.1 *Extract from the edict of King Ammisaduqa of Babylon*

Kings of early second-millennium Babylonia drastically intervened in the economies of their states by abolishing the outstanding debts of producers at irregular intervals. They called this restoring order in the land and saw it as part of their duty as guardians of the people. All the texts are poorly preserved, except for the Edict of King Ammisaduqa, which still remains enigmatic in many parts.

§ 1: The tablet [of the decree that the land was ordered] to hear when the king established justice for the land.

§ 2: The debts of farming agents, shepherds, animal carcass disposers of the provinces, and other crown tributaries – the ... of their firm agreements and the promissory notes ... of their payments are herewith remitted. The collecting officer may not sue the crown tributary's household for payment.

§ 4: Whoever has given barley or silver to an Akkadian or an Amorite as an interest bearing loan or as fees, and had a document drawn up – because the king has established justice in the land, his document is voided; he may not collect the barley or silver on the basis of his document.

§ 8: An Akkadian or an Amorite who has received barley, silver, or (other) goods, either as merchandise for a commercial journey, or as a joint enterprise for the production of profit, his document is not voided; he must repay in accordance with the stipulations of his document.

Translation after Pritchard 1969: 526–7.

5.3 Assyria and the East

Throughout the Near East the political situation at this time paralleled what we saw in Babylonia. From western Iran to the Mediterranean coast local dynasties headed small states that often competed for power. The study of their histories is much facilitated by the fact that many places have yielded their own textual record, but the evidence is still very partial and its focus of attention varies from place to place. In the early second millennium, the material from the region of Assyria stands out for its full emphasis on international trade, which merchants from the city of Assur conducted. Located on the Tigris in the very south of Assyria, Assur was the central point of a network that traded tin from the east, textiles from Babylonia, and silver and gold from Anatolia. We know the system from some 22,500 tablets left by Assyrian merchants in a colony at the edge of the central Anatolian city Kanesh, about 1,200 kilometers from Assur (figure 5.1). The colony, while under the control of the local ruler, functioned as a self-governing entity, and Assyrian texts refer to it as *Karum*-Kanesh, the port of Kanesh.

The colony's fortunes depended on local events in Anatolia, poorly known to us. Archaeology has distinguished several periods of occupation. Almost all of the

(a)   (b)

Figure 5.1   Old Assyrian cuneiform tablet and its envelope. The text is a legal deposition in which one merchant claims that another has stolen personal valuables as well as two containers with business records, which it lists in detail. The case is impressed with two different seals rolled on front and back. The brief text written on it identifies the owners of the seals who witnessed the trial. The Metropolitan Museum of Art, New York. Gift of Mr. and Mrs. J. J. Klejman, 1966 (66.245.5a and b). Tablet 16.9 × 7.3 cm (6$^5/_8$ × 2$^7/_8$ in.); case 18.5 × 9 cm (7$^5/_{16}$ × 3$^9/_{16}$ in). Credit: © 2014 The Metropolitan Museum of Art/Art Resource/Scala, Florence.

tablets come from houses in level II, dated between ca. 1970 and 1834, when the settlement was destroyed. It was soon reoccupied in level Ib, which lasted until ca. 1719, but substantially fewer tablets from that period are preserved. About 90 percent of the dated textual material derives from the period from 1895 to 1865, and it provides an extremely detailed view on the activities of Assyrian traders at that time.

Assur acted almost solely as a transit point in the trade. It imported tin from unknown sources in Iran or beyond (Afghanistan and perhaps even western China) and textiles from Babylonia. The tin was needed for the production of bronze, which required one measure of tin for every ten measures of copper. The Babylonian textiles must have been of very high quality and made from fine wool; the texts contain terms for them we do not fully understand, but they seem to have included carpets and covers as well as cloaks and tunics. Since people wove textiles in every part of the Near East, those involved in this trade must have been extremely well-made and in high demand. We know that women in Assur wove additional textiles, but the Babylonian ones seem to have been the best. There is no direct documentation on how the tin and textiles came to Assur or on how they were paid for.

The connections with Anatolia are very well known, however. Donkey caravans were organized in Assur, each animal loaded with some 70 kilograms (150 pounds) of tin and thirty textiles. Groups of traders shared the expenses by investing their own resources or those assigned to them by others: they paid for the animals, the merchandise, the personnel to accompany the caravan, and the various taxes and expenses incurred during the trip. The voyage to Kanesh easily lasted fifty days, and was impossible for four months in winter when weather prevented passage through the Taurus Mountains. When the caravans arrived in Kanesh, most of the donkeys were sold and the merchandise was exchanged for silver and gold, which was then taken back to Assur. Assyrian merchants, who were usually brothers or sons of those in Assur and permanent residents of Anatolia, distributed the imported goods throughout Anatolia using a network of smaller trade settlements. They also collected the bullion to be readied for the next caravan. Although firm estimates of the volume of trade are difficult to make, on the basis of extant evidence it has been calculated that annually 4,000 textiles and 10 tons of tin, that is about 150 donkey loads, were imported in Kanesh. Private entrepreneurs were at the heart of all this activity, and the palace was not directly concerned. Since family firms undertook the trade, women also were actively involved in it. They often remained home in Assur while their husbands, fathers, or brothers went off to Anatolia, and they were in constant contact by letter about the business. The women were responsible for the textiles that were used in the exchange and had to arrange for weaving in Assur, if they did not do it themselves. The men often criticized the quality of the products sent to them, and, conversely, women complained about the lack of resources given to them or even that they did not have enough to eat. The domestic situation sometimes led to difficulties in the marriage. Men often stayed away for many years and married local Anatolian women while their wives in Assur felt abandoned and ignored (document 5.2).

Document 5.2   *Old Assyrian correspondence: Examples of letters written by and to women*

Many correspondents are represented in the thousands of letters found at Kanesh, and they include a substantial number of women. As most businesses were family affairs, all members were involved and women often wrote to their husbands, fathers, and brothers to inform them of what happened in Assur, where they stayed while the men left for Kanesh. By far the majority of their writings involve business matters, but there are clear indications that they felt abandoned and insufficiently appreciated for the work they did. Some examples follow.

Tell Pushuken; Lamassi[1] says:

Kulumaya is bringing nine textiles to you, Iddin-Sin three. Ela has refused to take care of textiles, while Iddin-Sin has refused to take care of five (more).
Why do you keep on writing to me: "The textiles that you send me are always of bad quality!" Who is the man who lives in your house and criticizes the textiles that are brought to him? I, on the other hand, keep on striving to produce and send you textiles so that on every trip your business gains ten shekels of silver.

Translation after Michel 2001: 430 no. 302.

Tell Innaya; Taram-Kubi[2] says:

You wrote to me as follows: "Keep the bracelets and rings that you have; they will be needed to buy you food." It is true that you send me half a pound of gold through Ili-bani, but where are the bracelets that you have left behind? When you left, you didn't leave me one shekel of silver. You cleaned out the house and took everything with you.
Since you left, a [terrible] famine has hit the city (of Assur). You did not leave me one liter of barley. I need to keep on buying barley for our food. [several unclear lines] Where is the extravagance that you keep on writing about? We have nothing to eat. (Do you think) we can afford indulgence? Everything I had available I scraped together and sent to you. Now I live in an empty house and the seasons are changing. Make sure that you send me the value of my textiles in silver, so that I can at least buy ten measures of barley.
With respect to the tablet with the witness list that Assur-imitti, son of Kura, obtained: he has caused a lot of trouble to the business and has seized servants as guarantee. Then your representatives have settled the affair. I had to pay two-thirds of a pound of silver so that he will not lodge a complaint until you arrive. Why do you keep on listening to slander, and write me irritating letters?

Translation after Michel 2001: 466 no. 344.

Puzur-Assur says; Tell Nuhshatum:

Your father has written to me about you so that I would marry you. I have sent my servants and a letter to your father about you so that he would let you come. I am asking you, the moment you read my letter, ask your father (for permission) and come here with my servants. I am alone. I have no one who serves me or who sets my table. If you would not come with my servants I would marry a young girl from Wahshushana. Pay attention. You and my servants, don't delay and come!

Translation after Michel 2001: 507–8 no. 397.

[1] Wife of Pushuken.
[2] Wife of Innaya.

The profit margins in this trade were high: tin cost at least double in Anatolia what it cost in Assur, and textiles tripled their value. A merchant could easily make a 50 to 100 percent profit on a shipment. That was the reward for a high-risk enterprise. The trade functioned within a political setting where it could not rely on one power alone for its protection and support. The caravans to and from Anatolia, Babylonia, and Iran traveled through territories of many independent, and sometimes hostile, rulers. Assur was no more powerful than its neighbors, but it could negotiate trade agreements. Only four treaties are known today, all partially preserved. Assur demanded that its merchants were fairly judged if they got into legal trouble, that their property was protected, and that local Anatolians did not directly deal with Babylonians. It was very important that Assur kept the monopoly over the trade and in the twentieth century Assur's King Ilushuma proclaimed that Babylonian merchants who traveled from the Persian Gulf to Assur were exempt from taxes. Although we hear a lot about war at this time, it seems that commercial interests kept states from blocking traders.

The two most powerful states to the southeast of Assur were Eshnunna in the Diyala region and Elam in southwest Iran. Their histories can be pieced together only in the barest outlines because of our lack of chronological data on the lengths of reigns and sometimes even the correct sequence of kings. These states did follow similar patterns of behavior on the international scene, however. Eshnunna (present-day Tell Asmar) had become independent from Ur early in Ibbi-Sin's reign. The local governor proclaimed himself ruler, but kingship of the state was said to belong to the city-god, Tishpak. After the first independent ruler, Shu-ilija, who alone deified himself and took the title king (Sumerian lugal), the rulers of the state merely used the title "governor (Sumerian énsi) of the god Tishpak" for more than a century. It was only in the early nineteenth century that the rulers again took on the title king. Similar behavior is visible in other places where Ur had politically dominated. At Assur, the local independent rulers became "governors (Sumerian énsi) of the god Assur," and at Elam the highest title was "grand regent" (Sumerian sukkal-mah), the title that had previously been held by the region's foremost Ur III official. Eshnunna's final acceptance of the title king may have been the result of Isin's loss of control over Nippur. If in Babylonia it had become unclear who was the true king, perhaps its neighbors felt more at ease in claiming the title themselves. It is at this time that Eshnunna expanded its control over the Diyala valley as far as its confluence with the Tigris, incorporating such previously independent cities as Nerebtum (modern Ishcali), Shaduppum (modern Tell Harmal), and Dur-Rimush (location unknown). Ipiq-Adad's sons Naram-Sin and Dadusha continued his expansionist policy, which brought Eshnunna into the maelstrom that characterized Mesopotamia in the early eighteenth century, becoming one of the most powerful players in the region (for a list of kings of Eshnunna, see Section 5 of the King Lists at the end of the book).

Eshnunna competed with the other states in its surroundings and mixed war and diplomacy to gain prominence. For example, its King Dadusha joined forces with Shamshi-Adad of the kingdom of Upper Mesopotamia in 1781 in order to conquer the region between the two Zab rivers, and commemorated the campaign in a victory stele, where he stated that he handed the lands over to Shamshi-Adad (figure 5.2). Somewhat later the latter turned against his ally and seized some of Eshnunna's territory, but when Shamshi-Adad died the roles were reversed and Eshnunna captured cities close to Assur. By then it was the strongest state of the region.

Crossing along the northern border of the still-isolationist state of Babylon, Eshnunna entered the Euphrates valley and reached Mari. When Shamshi-Adad's son Yasmah-Addu had governed there, relations had been hostile. With the establishment of a new king at Mari, Zimri-Lim, Ibal-pi'el II of Eshnunna sought to conclude an alliance, which Zimri-Lim rejected. In a letter to his envoy to Aleppo he stated:

> When you find yourself in the presence of Yarim-Lim (king of Aleppo) speak to him as follows about Eshnunna: "The king of Eshnunna keeps on sending me messages with respect to an alliance. A first time he sent me a messenger and I sent him back at the border. A second time he sent me a messenger and I sent him back at the border. Then a high official came and I sent him back at the border, stating: 'How could I conclude an alliance with Eshnunna without the consent of Yarim-Lim?'"[3]

A war between the two states broke out and Eshnunna forced Mari into submission. Three years later, however, Elam's ruler allied himself with Mari, Babylon, and probably also Larsa, and attacked and pillaged Eshnunna in 1766. He appointed a puppet ruler over it, but soon a native Eshnunnan king named Silli-Sin replaced him. Silli-Sin helped Hammurabi of Babylon in his destruction of the Elamite state, but in 1762 Hammurabi turned against his former ally and sacked Eshnunna. He did not incorporate the Diyala region into his state, but prevented it from having a strong ruler. The state's subsequent history is unclear.

Elam was a crucial player in all the events described above, but its exact role remains vague since indigenous sources from this period are rare. These centuries show it to have been more closely involved in Mesopotamia than at any other time of its history. Elam incorporated both the lowlands surrounding Susa and the Zagros highlands around Anshan, a duality reflected in the ruler's title "King of Anshan and Susa." The sukkal-mah, "grand regent," who continued to use a title from the Ur III period but now as an independent ruler, headed the political

Figure 5.2 The stele of Dadusha. This stone stele, found by accident in 1983 when digging a well near Eshnunna and damaged in the center, shows the king's conquest of Qabara and the defeat of its ruler Bunu-Eshtar. The long inscription (220 lines divided over 17 columns) describes some of the scenes on the relief. For example, it states the city walls shown are those of Qabara. Iraq Museum, Baghdad. H. 180 cm, W. 37 cm, D. 18.5 cm (71 × 14.5 × 7 in). Credit: Drawing by Frans van Koppen, in Mark W. Chavalas, ed., *The Ancient Near East: Historical Sources in Translation* (Oxford: Blackwell 2006), p. 100.

organization. Next to him functioned officials with such titles as sukkal of Susa and of Elam, often the son of the sister of the ruling sukkal-mah. When the latter died, at times his nephew succeeded him, but we are uncertain that this was the normal rule of succession.

Soon after Elam had gained independence from Ur, it turned against its former master and its troops seized the capital and took King Ibbi-Sin prisoner. The armies of Isin shortly thereafter liberated Ur and subsequently prevented Elam from having much influence in Babylonia. A century later, however, when other Babylonian cities asserted independence at the expense of Isin, they often sought foreign aid and drew Elam into their shifting alliances and conflicts. Several kings of Larsa conquered Elamite cities, and Elam allied itself with Uruk, Isin, and others in the local Babylonian wars. It is possible that the last two Larsa rulers, Warad-Sin and Rim-Sin, were of Elamite descent: they were sons of Kudur-Mabuk and grandsons of Simti-Silhak, both rulers of tribes from an area east of the Tigris. Their relationship to the state of Elam is unknown, but it is possible that they may have acted on its behalf in Babylonian conflicts, making the already complicated political and military picture even more complex.

Until the disappearance of Eshnunna as a major power, Elam kept a distance from affairs in the north of Babylonia and Mesopotamia in general, even if everyone acknowledged its importance. The removal of Eshnunna by a coalition of Babylon, Mari, and Elam brought the latter in direct contact with Mesopotamian states. Now its influence was remarkable and very wide-ranging. The ruler of Qatna in western Syria, for example, offered submission to Elam in order to gain support in his conflict with Aleppo. The sukkal-mah received correspondence from Hammurabi of Babylon, Zimri-Lim of Mari, and others. They all declared themselves to be his "sons" rather than his "brothers," the usual term when they corresponded with one another. To them he was "the great king of Elam." His armies placed rulers on thrones as far away as Shubat-Enlil in northern Syria. Elam's strength derived from the size of its state and the manpower it could summon. Contributing to its prominence was also the fact that it controlled the flow of Iranian tin to the west after the end of *Karum*-Kanesh. This crucial ingredient for bronze production reached the Mediterranean from Elam via Mari. Elam was also in close contact with Dilmun in the Persian Gulf, so it may have monopolized access to other foreign resources and routes as well. Its success was ephemeral, however. Hammurabi of Babylon concluded an alliance with Mari and Aleppo against Elam, and in his twenty-ninth year (1764) defeated it. While Elam was not incorporated into the Babylonian state, its influence ended and our knowledge of it ceases.

5.4   Mari and the West

Ambassadors to the king at Mari submitted reports on the final days of Larsa, Eshnunna, and Elam to their master, which enable us to study these events in great detail. Because of Mari's location and its role as intermediary between southern

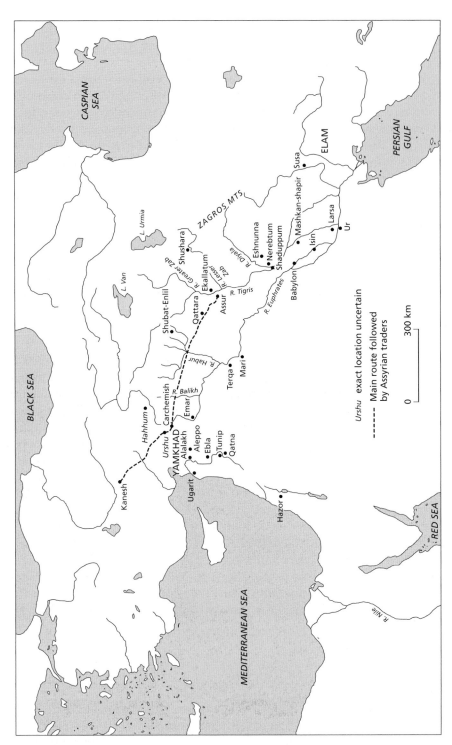

Map 5.2   The Near East in the early second millennium.

Mesopotamia and Syria, its archives also shed abundant light on affairs in the west where numerous states fell into the orbit of Mari's representatives. Cities as distant as Hazor in modern Israel are mentioned. The western area of the Near East made up a single, politically integrated system of small states. The royal houses of its petty kingdoms were often related by blood and intermarriage, and the king of Mari visited cities as far away as Ugarit on the Mediterranean coast. The histories of a few states will serve to demonstrate that the pattern of competition, coalition, and hegemony described for the eastern part of the Near East was also found in the west. Here I will describe the histories of Mari and Yamkhad, the two most powerful states in the region, but half a dozen others could be written just as well.

Mari had been independent from the Ur III state, albeit in close diplomatic contact with it. Nevertheless, the collapse of Ur coincided with a downward turn in Mari's fortunes: although its dynasty of rulers who held the title "general" (Akkadian *shakkanakku*) remained in power for another century, the city's importance greatly diminished. Finally the dynasty ended, for reasons unknown, and the city may even have been abandoned. By the mid-nineteenth century, however, a new dynasty was in place, and Mari began its most prosperous century (for a list of kings, see Section 6 of the King Lists at the end of the book). The new dynasty had its origin in northwestern Syria among the Sim'alite branch of the Amorites, who had conquered various cities in the Middle Euphrates valley before settling at Mari. The first ruler we can study was Yahdun-Lim who, despite his western roots, introduced Babylonian language and writing style as a chancellery standard, including the practice of using year names. He established Mari as the dominant state on the Middle Euphrates, stretching as far north as the Balikh confluence, and pursued the Yaminites as far west as the Lebanon Mountains. Development works in the region, such as the building of irrigation systems and fortresses, consolidated his grasp. The expansion into the Habur River region brought him into conflict with the newly emergent Kingdom of Upper Mesopotamia, however, and he fought several battles against Shamshi-Adad. Yahdun-Lim was assassinated in a palace conspiracy, and his son, Sumu-Yaman, did not survive long thereafter. Two or three years later in 1795, Shamshi-Adad conquered Mari and integrated it into his large state (discussed in the next chapter). Shamshi-Adad placed his younger son Yasmah-Addu on Mari's throne in order to keep an eye on the western states and on the Amorite tribes.

The rule of Yasmah-Addu lasted some twenty years and ended suddenly when his father died in 1775. Shamshi-Adad's kingdom fell apart, the pieces picked over by ambitious men. At Mari that man was Zimri-Lim. Although he often declared himself to be the son of Yahdun-Lim, it is clear that he was not, and may at best have been his grandson or nephew. When he took power, Mari once again acted fully in its own interests. Zimri-Lim reestablished strong ties with Babylon and especially with Aleppo, whose princess Shiptu he married. His state encompassed the Euphrates valley from just south of Mari to the border with Aleppo and the lower Habur valley. Farther north he exercised control through vassals and he made sure that independent rulers were on his side. Mari flourished: Zimri-Lim's palace is one of the greatest architectural monuments of the early second millennium known to us and was famous for its opulence in its own time (figure 5.3). The kingdom was respected by its competitors in the region and kept the nomadic tribes at bay. While Zimri-Lim was a faithful ally of Hammurabi of Babylon, his prestige and wealth must ultimately have pushed the latter to turn against him. In his thirty-second year (1761), Hammurabi defeated Zimri-Lim and conquered Mari. Two years later, his anger incited by unknown causes, Hammurabi razed the palace and the city-walls and incorporated the Euphrates valley up to Mari into his state. Mari lost its preeminent status and the center of power for the Middle Euphrates shifted some 100 kilometers (60 miles) north to Terqa.

The city of Aleppo was the capital of the state of Yamkhad (for a list of rulers, see Section 7 of the King Lists at the end of the book). Strategically located on the trade route from the Euphrates valley to the Mediterranean Sea, it seems to have come to prominence only in the early second millennium, perhaps after Ebla's decline. Since Aleppo has been continuously occupied from that time until today, excavations there are difficult and no written sources from this period are known from the city itself. But the Mari archives shed light on Aleppo's history at the time. They show that it was a major cult center of the storm god Addu, whose temple was excavated on the city's citadel. In political history, the Mari texts reveal that Yamkhad's most stubborn opponent in the west was Qatna, a city of central Syria located to its south, which received support from Shamshi-Adad of the Kingdom of Upper Mesopotamia. The first two known rulers of Yamkhad, Sumu'epuh and Yarim-Lim, became involved in wars with Shamshi-Adad, which sucked them and their successors into the volatile politics of the south. The death of Shamshi-Adad created the space for Yarim-Lim of Yamkhad to expand down the Euphrates valley as far as Mari, whose king, Zimri-Lim, was his son-in-law. Yarim-Lim's prominence in the west is clear from the Mari letter quoted at the beginning of this chapter in which twenty kings are said to follow him, more than any other ruler at the time.

When Hammurabi of Babylon picked off his neighbors one by one, Yamkhad, like Mari, at first provided him with support. But then Babylon turned against its old allies and conquered Mari. Yamkhad remained simply too far for Babylonian troops to reach, so the two major states were not in direct conflict. Subsequently, southern sources stop dealing with matters concerning Yamkhad. Around this time, however, texts from the smaller city of Alalakh to the west of Yamkhad indicate that Abba'el of Aleppo had placed his brother on the throne there. Yamkhad remained the dominant force of northwest Syria and controlled a large number of vassals and allies in cities like Carchemish, Urshu, Hashshu, Ugarit, Emar, Ebla, and Tunip. It presented thus the main obstacle to Hittite military expansion from Anatolia into Syria during the second half of the seventeenth century. The Hittite King Hattusili I reports in his annals how he attacked and destroyed several vassals of Yamkhad over the years, such as Alalakh, Carchemish, and Hashshu. He did not seem to engage Yamkhad itself, however. That task was left to his son, Mursili I, who captured and destroyed the city on his way to Babylon in 1595, thereby ending the political situation that had characterized the Near East for four centuries.

Debate 5.1   *Who were the Amorites?*

Near Eastern writings from the early second millennium contain numerous references to people we call Amorites in English. What the term exactly means and who these people were is one of the most contested questions in the history of the period. Miscellaneous ancient data are usually combined when scholars talk of Amorites. No individual ever called himself an Amorite; it was a term used by others. The texts regularly state that someone is a Martu (or Mardu) in Sumerian or Amurru in Akkadian or use either name to refer to a group of people: the *Edict of King Ammisaduqa*, for example, speaks of Akkadians and Amorites. The ancients also distinguished an Amorite language, but no complete sentence in it has survived in writing. Modern scholars recognize Amorite language when analyzing the grammar of people's names, a large number of which appear in texts from cities from all over the Near East in the early second millennium. References from Mari are especially numerous, including some of the names of its kings, such as Yahdun-Lim, which means, "He pleases Lim," that is, a god often invoked in Amorite personal names. The terms Martu and Amurru were also used throughout Mesopotamian history to indicate the west, and in the second half of the second millennium there was a Kingdom of Amurru in western Syria. Moreover, the Hebrew Bible speaks of a pre-Israelite population, Emori, which is rendered as Amorite in English. The later people most certainly had no direct connection to those of the early second millennium, and to avoid confusion some scholars prefer to use the term Amorrite for the earlier references (Fleming 2004; see Whiting 1995 for all these usages). While scholars recognize that the divergent references cannot all indicate the same people, most of them think there existed an identifiable group of Amorites in the late third and early second millennia. What characterized them, however?

Until the mid-twentieth century it was common to see the Amorites as one of a sequence of waves of Semitic nomads who invaded the Mesopotamian agricultural zones from a desert region somewhere to its west. The Akkadians did so before them, the Arameans and Arabs later on (e.g., Moscati 1960: 30, 204–5). An in-depth analysis of the Mari evidence replaced this model with one where Amorites as semi-nomadic pastoralists constantly tried to settle down in agricultural zones, a move resisted and resented by sedentary populations (Kupper 1957). Many scholars still see the Amorites as pastoralist people from the west of the Near East who infiltrated settled society and seized power in the early second millennium (e.g., Charpin and Ziegler 2003; Jahn 2007). In their opinion, these immigrants were so successful politically that we should call the early second millennium "the Amorite era" (e.g., Charpin 2004, adopted by Milano 2012: fig. XXVII and Frahm 2013: 135). The Amorites would have introduced radical changes in the political and social structures of Babylonia and the Near East in general.

Studies of the interactions between sedentary and nomadic people in the Middle East throughout its history reject the idea that there was a constant desire of the latter to settle down. The groups were complementary, each providing different resources, and they shared the same spaces, albeit for different purposes. The so-called nomads were pastoralists who were present in Middle Eastern societies from the beginning of agriculture into the modern era (Briant 1982). Other scholars find little evidence of a fundamental impact of the Amorites on Babylonian life and politics. There is no clear involvement of the Amorites in the overthrow of the Ur III state, no indication of Amorite infiltration or invasion, nor even evidence that the people called Amorite were living to the west of Babylonia. Instead, already in the Ur III period Amorites were well-integrated in all parts of Babylonian society. The term did not refer to a distinct ethnic group (Michalowski 2011).

It is a mistake to collect all types of references to Amorites (as a group, as individuals, in the language of people's names) and regard them as indicating the same, clearly identifiable, group, irrespective of when and where and in what context they appear. "Amorite" regularly suggested a pastoralist lifestyle, but many Amorites were urban residents. Various people in the Near East claimed Amorite roots, but what that exactly meant is unclear to us. Sometimes the term was used in a very negative way (in the *Marriage of Martu*, for example), sometimes it distinguished one group of people from another (in the *Edict of King Ammisaduqa*, for example), and other meanings existed as well. Amorite is one of several so-called "ethnic" terms we find throughout ancient Near Eastern history, whose sense depended on the context in which they were used. Other such terms are Gutian, Kassite, Aramean, Sutean, and many more. They appear in the record in multiple contexts and we cannot see them as simple and clear-cut categorizations of people within Near Eastern societies. Their use was flexible and depended on circumstances we today can rarely recognize.

NOTES

1   Translation by Jack Sasson in Sasson, ed., 1995: 906.
2   Translation after Bottéro & Kramer 1989: 434.
3   Translation after Durand 1997–2000, volume 1: 441–2.

6

The Growth of Territorial States in the Early Second Millennium

3000	2500	2000	1500	1000	500

1807	Shamshi-Adad seizes power in Assur
ca. 1795	Yasmah-Addu placed on throne of Mari
1792	Hammurabi inherits throne of Babylon
1775	Death of Shamshi-Adad
ca. 1740	Samsuiluna loses control over southern Babylonia
ca. 1650	Creation of the Old Hittite state
1595	Hittite King Mursili sacks Babylon

Within the hurly-burly of competing dynasties that characterized the first half of the second millennium, a small number of highly accomplished rulers stand out. For short periods of time, these men were able to extend their political control over a wide geographical area, creating short-lived territorial states. These states were not radically different in nature from others of the period, only more successful in competing with their neighbors. They were the result of an individual's military successes and disintegrated soon after their founders' deaths. First, Shamshi-Adad unified northern Mesopotamia, then Hammurabi Babylonia, and later Hattusili I Central Anatolia (map 6.1). Despite the ephemeral nature of their states, the changes these men initiated laid the foundations for the system of territorial states in later centuries.

Since these events overlapped with the developments discussed in the previous chapter, the available historical sources are largely the same. In Babylonia and

A History of the Ancient Near East ca. 3000–323 BC, Third Edition. Marc Van De Mieroop.
© 2016 John Wiley & Sons, Inc. Published 2016 by John Wiley & Sons, Inc.

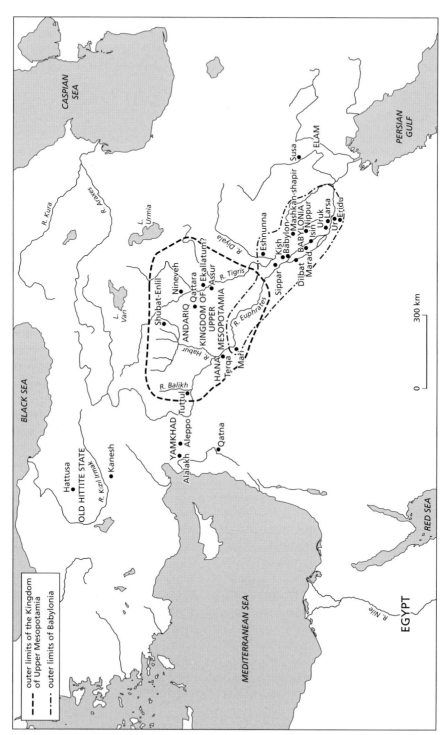

Map 6.1 Territorial states of the early second millennium.

Upper Mesopotamia, the most explicit records do not derive from the capitals but from other cities the territorial rulers conquered and controlled. Conversely, in the case of the Old Hittite state, almost all our information comes from the capital Hattusa, but the texts are dated centuries later and can only claim to be copies of original royal annals. Their information thus has to be checked carefully against sources contemporary to the events they describe.

6.1   Shamshi-Adad and the Kingdom of Upper Mesopotamia

The early history of King Shamshi-Adad is vague to us. We cannot even establish when and where he first ascended any particular Mesopotamian throne. Most likely around 1830 he inherited rule from his father, Ila-kabkabu, in Ekallatum, a city still unlocated but certainly in the vicinity of Assur. There he governed for about ten years, until he had to flee to Babylon when Naram-Sin of Eshnunna conquered Ekallatum. Seven years later Shamshi-Adad took advantage of Naram-Sin's death to return from exile, and three years later he conquered Assur as well. There he integrated his ancestors into the list of city-rulers, and is said to have been king for thirty-three years (for a list of early Assyrian rulers, see Section 18 of the King Lists at the end of the book). This allows us to date his accession to Assur's throne to 1807.

At that time he was still only a minor player in the region. Soon, however, he extended his influence westward into northern Syria, where he clashed with Yahdun-Lim of Mari. Shamshi-Adad took control over the northern Habur valley and annexed kingdoms such as the land of Apum whose capital, Shehna, he turned into his own royal seat and renamed Shubat-Enlil. The mighty kingdom of Mari to his south became easy prey when Yahdun-Lim was assassinated, and probably in 1792 Shamshi-Adad captured its capital. He ruled now an area from Assur on the Tigris in the east to Tuttul on the Balikh in the west. The entire region to the north of Babylonia was incorporated in his state, which we will here call the "Kingdom of Upper Mesopotamia" (figure 6.1).

Shamshi-Adad was very tolerant of existing practices in the various states he had united. At Assur he took on the customary royal title there, "governor of the god Assur," and in Nineveh he restored the Ishtar temple said to have been built by Manishtushu five centuries before. Certain cities, such as Qattara, retained their former rulers, who now became his vassals. Local administrative procedures survived, although officials used seals that indicated that they were in the service of Shamshi-Adad. Perhaps his administration imposed one crucial change – the dating of documents with Assur's eponym system to indicate the years (see box 6.1). Under Shamshi-Adad's rule it came into use in such varied places as Mari, Tuttul, Shubat-Enlil, and Terqa. This "Assyrian" system of dating thus became official practice for the Kingdom of Upper Mesopotamia.

Having to control this large kingdom, Shamshi-Adad, who resided in Shubat-Enlil, placed his two sons in strategic locations. The eldest, Ishme-Dagan, ascended the throne at Ekallatum, the ancestral home, while the younger,

Figure 6.1 Fragmentary stele, probably of Shamshi-Adad. The fragmentary stele is carved on both sides and contains an inscription that records the victory over the city of Qabara, also commemorated in the stele of Dadusha (figure 5.2). It is likely that Shamshi-Adad commissioned the monument and that he is the man depicted as hitting an enemy with his ax. Louvre, Paris, AO2776. Diorite, H. 49 cm; W. 55 cm (19.3 × 21.6 in). Credit: akg images/Album/Prisma.

Yasmah-Addu, was instated at Mari. The southeastern and southwestern frontiers were thus given direct attention. In the east the Kingdom of Upper Mesopotamia bordered on Eshnunna and states at the foothills of the Zagros, in the west it bordered Yamkhad and the Syrian steppe controlled by semi-nomadic groups. The two sons in turn were given supervision of a number of districts with governors to represent them: Ishme-Dagan looked after those between the Tigris and the Zagros, Yasmah-Addu those along the Euphrates, lower Balikh, and Habur rivers. Shamshi-Adad directly governed the region of Shubat-Enlil, while military governors were in charge of cities to its south. Ishme-Dagan clearly had more authority than his younger brother, and often scolded Yasmah-Addu for his inaction. The father kept ultimate authority, however, sending numerous letters to his sons. Those to Mari accused Yasmah-Addu of being a lazy weakling. He stated repeatedly:

> How long do we have to guide you in every matter? Are you a child, and not an adult? Don't you have a beard on your chin? When are you going to take charge of your house? Don't you see that your brother is leading vast armies? So, you too, take charge of your palace, your house![2]

Box 6.1   *The eponym dating system*

Unlike Babylonia, where years were identified with names based on important events of the previous years, in northern Mesopotamia a dating system existed where each year was named after an individual. The Akkadian term used to refer to such an individual was *limmu*, meaning something like rotation, which we translate with the Greek word indicating a rotating office, "eponym." The dating system probably originated in the city of Assur, and it remained the official system in Assyria to the end of the Assyrian empire in the seventh century (see document 12.2). The individuals who became the eponyms were originally selected by lot, but in the first millennium a fixed rotation of officers headed by the king constituted the *limmu*. The office in the first millennium was of a cultic nature.

In the early second millennium, the office of eponym in Assur had an administrative character, and seemingly was more involved with trade than was the king. The earliest known attestations of year eponyms are at Kanesh. They became used in other Assyrian colonies in Anatolia corresponding in time to the later occupation of that site. The dating practice is attested throughout northern Mesopotamia,[1] and its spread was undoubtedly due to Shamshi-Adad's unification of the north: we see that in some places like Mari, eponyms replaced year names under his occupation alone. When his state fell apart, several cities continued to use eponyms and adhered to a shared system throughout the region. Thus, while they were politically independent, they chose to coordinate their dating systems to facilitate interactions.

In order to keep track of the sequence of years, eponym lists were drawn up, sometimes also adding succinct statements about events. These are securely reconstructed from the tenth through seventh centuries. For the second millennium the situation is not always clear, but new discoveries continue to improve our knowledge. Recently published eponym lists from Kanesh have been especially important for the chronology of the early millennium. We now know the nearly complete sequence of eponyms from ca. 1972 to 1718.

The meddling in local affairs by great leaders was not unusual, and this micromanaging was part of the ideal of kingship of the time, as I will show in the discussion of Hammurabi of Babylon. That their subjects did not always appreciate it is clear from an episode in which Shamshi-Adad arranged for the marriage of Yasmah-Addu to Beltum, the princess of Qatna, a crucial ally in his conflict with Yamkhad. The king of Qatna wanted his daughter to have a prominent role at Mari, but Yasmah-Addu already had a leading wife, the daughter of Yahdun-Lim. So Yasmah-Addu preferred to keep Beltum in a secondary position outside his palace, among the lower-ranking women. Shamshi-Adad sternly reprimanded him and forced his son to keep her at his side. The hierarchy of power in the kingdom was unmistakable.

Shamshi-Adad's state disappeared suddenly and under unclear circumstances. When he was old, his two major neighbors Yamkhad and Eshnunna attacked simultaneously, and he died in battle or of natural causes in 1775. Local powers quickly reasserted themselves. Zimri-Lim, an Amorite upstart, chased Yasmah-Addu from Mari, while Ishme-Dagan lost control over his father's kingdom except for Ekallatum and Assur. Northern Syria became a patchwork of small independent states, while in the south Eshnunna picked up the pieces nearby. Some of the histories of the new states can still be written because Mari kept a close watch on developments, but also because some of the local kings maintained court bureaucracies and actively communicated with one another by letter. The politically divided region was open to attacks from Eshnunna, Elam, and Babylon, whose kings could make or break local rulers. Political intrigues and military conflicts were numerous and complicated. Zimri-Lim of Mari was the most powerful ruler of the area but too geographically marginal to control everything that happened. While local dynasties existed throughout Upper Mesopotamia, some kings, such as the ruler of Andariq, exercised strong influence over their neighbors, sometimes imposing rulers on their thrones. The palaces in these cities continued to dominate the economy and maintained a centralized administration. By 1720, northern Mesopotamia became unable to sustain this lifestyle, however. Many cities were abandoned for reasons we can only suspect. Possibly a mixture of popular opposition to the court's domination and changes in rainfall patterns led to a shift to a semi-nomadic life in villages and in the steppe. With the end of the palaces, the historical record disappeared.

6.2 Hammurabi's Babylon

During the last decades of Shamshi-Adad's life, a man who would become one of the most famous kings of Mesopotamian history occupied the throne at Babylon: Hammurabi. Babylon had existed for several centuries, known from the Old Akkadian period on, and Hammurabi's predecessors had managed gradually to create a state incorporating previously independent northern cities, such as Sippar, Kish, Dilbat, and Marad. But it was hemmed in by the more prominent states of Eshnunna, Larsa, and the Kingdom of Upper Mesopotamia. When Hammurabi became king in 1792, Rim-Sin had just unified the entirety of southern Babylonia while Shamshi-Adad reigned supreme in the north. Hammurabi may at first have even owed allegiance to Shamshi-Adad: a contract drawn up at Sippar in 1782 contains oaths to both kings, which points to Shamshi-Adad's authority there. Hammurabi ushered in what we now call the "Old Babylonian period," the beginning of Babylon's political dominance over southern Mesopotamia for the next 1,500 years (for a list of Old Babylonian kings, see Section 8 of the King Lists at the end of the book).

In these extremely volatile times, the young king could not avoid being drawn into regional conflicts. His early year names mention campaigns against all of his powerful neighbors, but the results of those were ambiguous. Most of Hammurabi's attention seems to have been devoted to the internal development of his state, mainly digging canals and fortifying cities. When he decided to act on a wide scale, his military movements were swift and devastating, and he used his considerable diplomatic skills with great effect as well. At first using troops from allies such as Mari, he turned against those who earlier helped him once he was strong enough. The diplomatic correspondence from Mari shows how he first used diplomacy, then military action, to reach his goals (see document 6.1). In just five years, from 1766 to 1761, Hammurabi established his full dominance over southern Mesopotamia, after the death of Shamshi-Adad and when Rim-Sin was an old man. He defeated Elam, Larsa, Eshnunna, and Mari in quick succession, and incorporated Larsa and the Middle Euphrates area up to Mari into the Babylonian state. Eshnunna he left without a leader, while he blocked Elam's ability to exercise any influence over Mesopotamia. The only area of concern remained northern Mesopotamia, where Hammurabi campaigned twice in later years without fully establishing control. There is no doubt, however, that he was the strongest king in Mesopotamia. After these events, he could proclaim himself "the king who made the four quarters of the earth obedient."[3]

Document 6.1   *Letters to Zimri-Lim of Mari regarding Hammurabi and Eshnunna*

As a colleague and oftentimes ally of Hammurabi of Babylon, Zimri-Lim of Mari wanted to remain informed about the latter's interactions with other states. He knew well that alliances were ephemeral and that all leading kings of the time sought to strengthen their positions by seeking outside support. Here are two examples of letters Yarim-Addu, who was stationed in Babylon, sent to his master about Hammurabi's search for a treaty with Silli-Sin of Eshnunna, a king whom Zimri-Lim also courted for an alliance. Yarim-Addu reports that Silli-Sin was reluctant to accept Hammurabi's offer and that Hammurabi had started direct talks with Elam in a possible move against Eshnunna. We know that in the end Hammurabi succeeded in forming his alliance and that he married Silli-Sin's daughter. But soon afterwards he marched against Eshnunna and defeated it in 1762.

Tell my Lord (Zimri-Lim); Yarim-Addu, your servant, says:
I have written to my Lord about the instructions regarding the man of Eshnunna that Hammurabi issued to [ ]. When Hammurabi was in Borsippa messengers of the man of Eshnunna came to him, but he did not see them. Only on the second day they met with him. After having them wait a night, he gave an answer to their news. He gave instructions to [Sin-], son of Kakkaruqqum and Mar[duk-mushallim, son of], and he sent them along. They took with them the small tablet (i.e., draft treaty), and they will make the man of Eshnunna accept it. [ ] will go and Hammurabi will accept it. After they will have accepted the small tablet, Hammurabi will send a large tablet, that is a treaty tablet, to the man of Eshnunna, and he will make him swear to it. The man of Eshnunna will send the large tablet, the treaty tablet, back to Hammurabi and they will establish an alliance. The alliance between Hammurabi and the man of Eshnunna is concluded or will be so very soon, that is certain. At this moment the answer to the diplomatic mission of Sin-[ ]

and Marduk-mushallim has not yet arrived from Eshnunna. I cannot report on it for my lord. After this letter I will write to my lord all the news that reaches me from Eshnunna.

The letter continues with news about Larsa and Andariq.

Translation after Charpin 1988, volume 1, part 2: 179–82.

Tell my Lord (Zimri-Lim); Yarim-Addu, your servant, says:
I have written earlier to my Lord that the words of Hammurabi were secret. Hammurabi has renewed frank conversations with the ruler of Elam as he did before. Elamite messengers who have come from the ruler of Elam to Hammurabi are staying at the entrance of his palace right now. After the ruler of Elam had given them his instructions they were escorted from Susa to Der of the god Ishtaran. The man of Der received them and has sent them under escort to Malgium, and the man of Malgium was supposed to give them an escort to Babylon. But the army of Eshnunna barred their way and they were unable to enter (the territory). Hammurabi heard that the army of Eshnunna blocked the roads. He no longer sends regular missions to Elam via Malgium and Der, as he did before. But there are open areas in the land Eshnunna and his couriers go to the ruler of Elam through these areas. The message from the ruler of Elam has not yet reached him.

The letter continues with news about Malgium and about Ishme-Dagan of the Kingdom of Upper Mesopotamia.

Finally, regarding the small treaty tablet that Hammurabi previously sent to the king of Eshnunna, Silli-Sin. Silli-Sin continues to answer with a refusal and he has not concluded a treaty with Hammurabi.

Translation after Charpin 1988, volume 1, part 2: 182–4.

His inscriptions make clear, however, that the core of his state was Babylonia. Many of the earlier city-states there and their cults received the benefit of Hammurabi's rule. It is in this region that we can study his style of government: as ruler he concerned himself with the smallest detail. Due to extensive later rebuilding and the recent rise of the water table, the city of Babylon itself is virtually unknown archaeologically for this period, and only a handful of tablets from it have survived. Our information derives primarily from other cities, where royal agents represented Babylon's interests. In Larsa, for instance, these men were Sin-iddinam and Shamash-hazir, and some two hundred letters the king wrote to them are preserved. These treat matters of seemingly little importance, for example:

> To Shamash-hazir say, thus speaks Hammurabi: "From the fields that belong to the palace give one that measures one hectare (2.47 acres) near the gate of Larsa, a fallow field that is of good quality and lies near water, to Sin-imguranni the seal-cutter."[4]

This concern perhaps does not fit our image of a great ruler, but well reflects the ideology of kingship at the time. The king was a shepherd and a farmer. He had to take care of his people, providing them with fields for their sustenance and making these fields fertile through irrigation projects. The people expected such a level of concern from him.

The same ideology was expressed repeatedly in the introduction and conclusion of his most famous monument, Hammurabi's law code. He stated there:

> I am indeed the shepherd who brings peace, whose scepter is just. My benevolent shade was spread over my city, I held the people of the lands of Sumer and Akkad safely on my lap.

The function of the law code itself has been much discussed, but there is now consensus that the modern designation of it is wrong: it is not a code of law but a monument presenting Hammurabi as an exemplary king of justice (see debate 6.1). The text is best known to us from a black basalt stele almost fully covered with an inscription (see figure 6.2). Framed between a prologue and epilogue are listed some three hundred statements, all structured on the same pattern: "if . . . , then . . ." For example, "If a man commits a robbery and is caught, that man will be killed" (§ 22). While dealing with many areas of life, the entries do not, by far, cover all possible crimes, and there are even some contradictions. Moreover, the many legal documents of the period, including records of law cases, never make reference to the code. Instead of a list of legal precepts, the entire monument is a vivid expression of Hammurabi as a king who provides justice in his land. He said himself:

> May any wronged man who has a case come before my statue as king of justice, and may he have my inscribed stele read aloud to him. May he hear my precious words and may my stele clarify his case for him. May he examine his lawsuit and may he calm his (troubled) heart. May he say: "Hammurabi . . . provided just ways for the land."[5]

To prove his ability to guarantee justice, Hammurabi listed these three hundred or so cases, and urged future kings to study and follow his example.

Notwithstanding this, the code's contents provide insights into Babylonian society at the time. It demonstrates a social hierarchy with a tripartite structure of free man (Akkadian *awilum*), dependent (*mushkenum*), and slave (*wardum*). Punishments varied according to the status of the victim and the perpetrator of a crime: injuring a free man led to a harsher penalty than injuring a dependent. But these terms were not absolute, often defining someone's position in relationship to another. A high court official was still a "slave" to the king. The status of the intermediate group of dependents (*mushkenum*) is most difficult to define. The term could indicate a relationship to the palace or to another person, but we do not understand exactly what was the basis or degree of dependence. The structure of society had changed from the third millennium, partly through the process of "privatization" described in the previous chapter. Full-time palace dependents were rare and contract labor provided most services. Hence the dependent class of

Figure 6.2   The stele of Hammurabi. The 2.25 meter (7.2 foot) high basalt monolith is fully inscribed with a cuneiform text, except for a small scene representing the king in front of the god of justice, Shamash. The empty space on the bottom was the work of a later king who erased part of the text. The signs are carved in horizontal bands using archaizing monumental script. The stele was taken to Susa in the twelfth century where it was excavated and now it stands in the Louvre Museum in Paris. Louvre, Paris, Sb 8. Basalt. H. 2.25 m; W. 0.65 m (88.6 × 25.6 in). Credit: © RMN-Grand Palais/Franck Raux.

Hammurabi's code was often in a situation where it owed obligations to private citizens. The use of entrepreneurs to take care of palace business was a characteristic of the period, and their credit transactions led to the social disturbances described in chapter 5. Loan contracts continue to be numerous in private archives. Hammurabi and several of his successors are known to have decreed the annulment of debts several times, but the need to repeat such acts indicates their failure to rectify the situation.

By the end of his reign, Hammurabi had fundamentally altered the political landscape of Mesopotamia. Babylonia was the single great power, surrounded by weak remnants of formerly great rivals: Elam, Eshnunna, and Assur. Only in

western Syria states such as Yamkhad were unaffected by his actions. His unification of Babylonia was short-lived, however. Less than ten years after his death
his son, Samsuiluna, faced major rebellions, especially in the south. There a man
calling himself Rim-Sin after Larsa's last ruler was declared king of Larsa, Ur,
Nippur, and other cities, while simultaneously a Rim-Anum became king at Uruk.
It took Samsuiluna more than two years to defeat these and other rebels with what
seem to have been ruthless military actions, although as in the past diplomacy also
played a role – Rim-Anum switched sides to support Babylon. But Samsuiluna's
grasp on Babylonia gradually slipped away. Texts dated with his year names disappeared from southern cities by his tenth or eleventh year. By his thirtieth year,
Nippur and other middle Babylonian cities ceased to be under Babylon's control.
The problems were not purely political, however. Archaeology shows that previously flourishing cities like Ur and Nippur were mostly abandoned. Segments
of the population, such as the priesthood of Uruk, migrated to northern Babylonian cities. It is difficult to determine exactly what happened. Babylon's
response to rebellions may have been so ferocious that the southern urban infrastructure was irreparably damaged, watercourses perhaps deflected, and agricultural fields turned into steppe. It is also possible that the policies of Hammurabi
and his predecessor in the region, Rim-Sin, ultimately had a negative result. They
had integrated the local economies of southern Babylonia into a system under
which districts became interdependent. When the center required for the coor-
dination of production weakened the exchanges of goods stopped, leading to an
economic decline of all the regions. A vaguely known "Sealand dynasty" emerged
in southern Babylonia and took over the control of several cities there, but economic and cultural activity was minimal, as far as we know, and by 1712 the region
had already entered a Dark Age.

Northern Babylonia continued to flourish, however. Hammurabi had five successors who ruled uncontested for 155 years over the area that he had originally
inherited as a young king, in addition to the Euphrates river valley up to Mari.
Samsuiluna led military campaigns to the north and perhaps annexed the new
northern state of Hana that had arisen around Terqa after Mari's end. In 1728
his troops even reached the Upper Habur and sacked Shamshi-Adad's old capital
Shubat-Enlil, now again called Shehna. New opponents appeared on the scene,
which indicates that the political situation was unsettled. A previously unattested
group of people called Kassites became a target of Babylon's military activity. In
the sixteenth century they would become rulers of Babylon.

The rapid abandonment of southern and central Babylonian cities under Samsuiluna in the mid-eighteenth century had as an unintended side effect the preservation of most of the manuscripts of Sumerian literary texts now known to us.
Young men who were schooled as scribes in private houses (figure 6.3) copied
these out or excerpted them, and in Ur and Nippur the remnants of their work
have been excavated. Normally the tablets containing their exercises would have
been recycled and their clay reused, but when scribal activity stopped, the last
works were left behind. We can study the school curriculum on the basis of these
exercises, including mathematics, surveying, and music. Most elaborate was the

Figure 6.3   Quiet Street at Ur. When Leonard Woolley excavated areas with private residences in Ur, he discovered a house filled with evidence of schooling in a street he named Quiet Street after a street in Bath, England. The house was very small and administrative tablets found in it reveal that priests connected to the temple of Ur resided in it. But they also taught scribal skills to neighborhood children. Credit: Courtesy of Penn Museum, image number 8838.

training in cuneiform writing and the Sumerian language. Rote learning was the norm. At first the students had to practice making single strokes with the stylus. This led to learning cuneiform signs and their readings. They memorized the signs by shape or by the sound of their pronunciation, and the order of learning was based on their increasing complexity. Then the students moved on to copying lists of Sumerian words. The lexical corpus, already known from the late Uruk period tablets, was thus a central part of the curriculum. Some major revisions occurred in this period. The lexical lists focused on the elements that made up words and the first Akkadian translations of Sumerian words started to appear. Grammar was taught similarly by repeating the paradigms of nouns and verbs in different forms.

The students learned syntax by writing out actual Sumerian compositions, chosen for their grammatical complexity. Thus the study of certain Ur III royal hymns was introduced at this time. Finally, the training culminated with the copying out of passages from the classics of Sumerian literature. A wide variety of literary genres are represented: myths, hymns, proverbs, literary letters, and others. The student exercises are often the only manuscripts we have of these texts, whose original date of composition is unknown. The court's patronage is clear: many of the compositions were intended to glorify the living king or his distant ancestors. That message is most obvious in the royal hymns and the accounts of legendary rulers. The courts of the early second millennium continued the Ur III tradition of glorifying the king with hymnic songs. They portrayed him in super-human terms and thus perpetuated the ideology that saw him as a divinity. Similar ideas were expressed in a cycle of stories concerning the legendary rulers of Uruk: Enmerkar, Lugalbanda, and Gilgamesh. Part-human, part-divine, they were con-sidered to be the ancestors of the Ur III kings and the creation of the tales in that court seems likely. Their popularity in the early second millennium suggests that the ideals of kingship displayed there were still alive.

Royal hymns dedicated to such early second-millennium kings as Rim-Sin demonstrate the ability of some scribes to compose intricate texts in the Sumer-ian language, which probably was no longer spoken at the time. It is likely that other genres of literature were also composed during these centuries, while earl-ier compositions were recorded in a fixed form. The intensity of scribal activ-ity in the Sumerian language may have resulted from the fact that the language was under threat: oral preservation was no longer guaranteed, so written versions with explicit indication of all the grammatical elements were needed. The pri-mary writers of the extant manuscripts were boys trained to compose contracts and administrative accounts made up almost entirely of stock phrases. Their edu-cation went beyond the skills they would need on a daily basis. They were trained in the private houses of learned men, who each worked with a group of boys assisted by a student helper. The teachers were probably affiliated with the tem-ples and, when Sumerian texts needed to be composed for such occasions as a royal visit, they most likely were the authors.

Also in northern Babylonia literate people studied Sumerian literature. The majority of compositions found there are of a liturgical nature and often written out more syllabically than in the south. Scribal skills were not necessarily inferior, however. Models from Babylonia inspired the numerous letters written through-out the Near East. The courts were important patrons of scribes, and schooling may have been centralized in the palaces rather than in private houses of tem-ple affiliates. The situation in Babylon itself is not known, as we do not have access to archaeological remains of the period. Nevertheless, literature in the Babylonian language, as well as in Sumerian, continued to be composed. Some of the royal inscriptions of Samsuiluna, including bilingual Sumarian–Akkadian examples, are of a high literary quality. This was also the first significant period of literary composition in the Akkadian language. Certain texts that have a long history in Mesopotamia, such as the *Epic of Gilgamesh* or the *Flood Story*, are first attested in Old Babylonian times, and many Akkadian hymns and incantations of this period are known. Their mood reflected the political situation of the times: uncertainty and violence are dominant themes. The writers of these texts were not spared the difficulties that confronted the inhabitants of the Old Babylonian state.

At this time we find the first extensive written documentation of a science for which Babylonia was famous in the ancient word: mathematics. From the beginning of writing the administrators of Babylonia showed their mathematical abilities when measuring fields, harvests, numbers of bricks, volumes of earth, and many other things that were of importance to bureaucrats. The tools to calculate these had to be taught but, as with literature, the skills displayed in the school texts show a much higher level than was needed in daily practice. At first the students repeatedly copied out standard lists of capacity, weight, area and length, division and multiplication. Their most challenging tasks were formulated as word problems, but these were not really of great practical value even if their wording related to actual accounting tasks. For instance, the exercise provided the size of a grain pile and asked how one could calculate the contents, or it gave the circumference and the slope of a heap of grain in order to calculate its height:

> A heap. The circumference is 30. In 1 cubit the slope is 0;15. What is the height? You: Double 0;15, the slope. You will see 0;30. Take the reciprocal of 0;30. You will see 2. Multiply 0;30 the circumference, by 2. You will see 1, : the height. <This is> the method.[6]

The knowledge of mathematics displayed in such texts is very sophisticated, and based on algebraic logic. For example, the Babylonians had calculated the square root of 2 accurately, and applied it in geometric calculations (see figure 6.4). They were aware of the principles underlying the Pythagorean theorem that in a right-angled triangle the square of the hypotenuse is equal to the sums of the squares of the other sides. The basis of most of these calculations was information provided in tables, listing numbers in their sexagesimal notation and their reciprocals (that is, 60 divided by that number), and their creation is one of the many accomplishments of the Babylonian schools.

The political supremacy of Babylon shifted the religious focus of the region to that city. Kings Hammurabi and Samsuiluna favored Babylon's patron deity Marduk. He was integrated in the Sumerian pantheon of Nippur by making him the son of Ea, himself the god of Eridu in the extreme south. While Marduk's cult predominated only in the region surrounding Babylon at that time, a few centuries later it would become the primary cult of Babylonia. The popularity of northern Babylonian deities increased and people throughout Babylonia adopted them as their personal gods. Thus in the centuries of the Old Babylonian dynasty, many of the cultural elements characteristic of the Near East in the second half of the second millennium were developed, and the political, religious, and cultural focus of Babylonia shifted permanently to its northern part.

The end of this period is something of a mystery. Each one of Hammurabi's successors ruled for more than two decades, a situation that is usually indicative of political stability. They kept northern Babylonia unified for 155 years, longer than the entire Ur III period, for example. The written evidence from the region shows a continuation of administrative and economic practices, and there are no indications of a weakening of the Old Babylonian state. Yet it existed in a void, surrounded by sparsely inhabited regions. The only political powers equal to it were located at a great distance in northwestern Syria (Yamkhad) and in Anatolia

Figure 6.4 Old Babylonian mathematical tablet. On this round school tablet is a picture of a square with the diagonals drawn in. On one side of the square is written the number 30, along one of the diagonals is the number 1,24,51,10 and below it is 42,25,35. In the Babylonian sexagesimal system the bottom number equals 30 times the one on top. A square with sides 30 long has diagonals of the length 42,25,35. The number above it 1,24,51,10 closely approximates the square root of 2, which shows that the Babylonians were aware of the principles underlying the later Pythagorean theorem. Credit: Courtesy The Yale Babylonian Collection (YBC 7289).

(Old Hittite Kingdom). Conflict between those states ultimately affected Babylon. In 1595, King Mursili of the Hittites, after a campaign in northern Syria, led his troops down the Euphrates River, seemingly without much resistance. He sacked the city of Babylon, ending its famous dynasty, and left the region leaderless.

6.3 The Old Hittite Kingdom

Central Anatolia became a pivotal player in the history of the Near East at this time. The appearance of a Hittite army in the heartland of Mesopotamia was the result of a relatively short process of centralization of power and the creation of an entity we now call the Old Hittite Kingdom. Anatolia's earlier history is mostly shrouded in mystery: there are no written sources until the Old Kingdom period, and our information for those early centuries of the second millennium derives solely from the colonies of Assyrian merchants in the region. These sources depict a network of small kingdoms, often in conflict with one another, and with populations that used varied languages. Many of the languages survived into later centuries: Hattic, Luwian, Palaic, Hurrian, and what is now called Hittite. In the native tradition the latter was called Nesili, the language of Nesa, which was the indigenous name for Kanesh, where the main Assyrian merchant colony was located. Nesili became the official written language of the Hittite state, even if it may not have been spoken by most of its subjects. Several of the Anatolian languages in the second millennium, most notably Hittite, were Indo-European. Under the influence of an outdated idea that there was an Indo-European homeland somewhere north of India, much attention in scholarship has been devoted to finding out when and where the Indo-Europeans entered Anatolia and to finding evidence for an invasion. This search is futile, however. There is no reason to assume that speakers of Indo-European languages were not always present in Anatolia, nor can we say that they would have been a clearly identifiable group by the second millennium. We can only observe that when the textual sources inform us of the languages used in Anatolia, some people spoke Indo-European ones, others not.

The fact that Hittite was considered to be the language of Nesa, that is, Kanesh, provides a connection between the period of the Old Assyrian colonies and later Hittite history. Another link is the find of a dagger on the citadel of that city, inscribed with the name Anitta, who is identified as the ruler. The inscription was written in the Old Assyrian script and language, which seems to indicate that the Assyrian merchants imported the technology of writing at that time. Anitta was the central character of one of the earliest records of the Hittites, the so-called "Anitta text." It described how he and his father, Pitkhana, kings of the unlocated city of Kussara, conquered various central Anatolian cities, including Nesa, which may then have become the new capital. They unified the entire valley of the Kızıl Irmak River (called Halys in classical antiquity) up to its mouth on the Black Sea. Such military operations may have caused the end of the Assyrian trade network. While the kingdom of Anitta collapsed soon after his death, the preservation of his memory in later records suggests that he was regarded as the ancestor of the later Hittite royal house.

The history of the Old Hittite Kingdom is written using sources that are very different from those available for the rest of the Near East. The palace archives of the later Hittite state contained a set of texts that relate military campaigns of these early rulers or deal with succession problems (see document 6.2). For example, King Hattusili's campaigns are described in annals, which, if indeed from his reign, would be the oldest such texts from the Near East. But the manuscripts we have were mostly written in the fourteenth and thirteenth centuries, and it is unclear whether they are actual copies of older texts or later compositions set in ancient times for current political purposes. They often provide vivid descriptions of events, but their historical accuracy is hard to establish. The records relating to succession problems are to be seen as very biased as they were intended to portray the ruler under whom they were written as the legitimate successor. The Hittite habit of providing surveys of earlier reigns is a boon to the historian, but can be a trap where we repeat fictional accounts.

Document 6.2   *An account of early Hittite history: Extract from the Edict of Telipinu*

The writings of the Hittites stand out in the record of the second-millennium Near East in that they provide narratives of earlier political and military developments in a clear chronological framework. These often appear at the start of legal documents such as treaties, where they clarify the nature of the previous relations between the states, or in this edict of King Telipinu, who ruled around 1500. He hoped to solve the problems of royal succession and demonstrated the need for change by relating how violence had characterized the kingdom's earlier history. All preserved manuscripts date to the thirteenth century, and although most scholars assume that there is a degree of truth in the account, there is no guarantee that the portrayal was not heavily redacted to make a point relevant to the later period of Hittite history.

Afterwards Hattusili was king, and his sons, brothers, in-laws, family members, and troops were all united. Wherever he went on campaign he controlled the enemy land with force. He destroyed the lands one after the other, took away their power, and made them the borders of the sea. When he came back from campaign, however, each of his sons went somewhere to a country, and in his hand the great cities prospered. But, when later the princes' servants became corrupt, they began to devour the properties, conspired constantly against their masters, and began to shed their blood.

When Mursili was king in Hattusa, his sons, brothers, in-laws, family members, and troops were all united. He controlled the enemy land with force, took away their power, and made them the borders of the sea. He went to the city Aleppo, destroyed Aleppo, and took the deportees from Aleppo and its goods to Hattusa. Afterwards he went to Babylon and destroyed Babylon. He also fought the Hurrian [troops]. He took the deportees from Babylon and its goods to Hattusa. Hantili was cupbearer and he had Harapshili, Mursili's sister, as wife. Zidanta stole up to Hantili and they committed an evil deed: they killed Mursili and shed his blood.

Translation after Hallo 1997–2002, volume 1: 194–5.

Based on these sources, we can make a tentative reconstruction of Old Hittite history. A ruler called Hattusili created the Hittite state in the early or mid-seventeenth century (for a list of kings, see Section 9 of the King Lists at the end of the book). Heir to the throne of Kussara, he rapidly defeated his competitors in central Anatolia. Among his conquests was Hattusa, located in the center of the region in a strategic and well-protected site thanks to its position on a hilltop. He made Hattusa his capital, and possibly changed his name to coincide with that of the city (we know that the city name existed before his reign). The city was in the center of Anatolia, but not at the heart of the Hittite state, which primarily extended south into Syria. Its northern location exposed it to attacks from groups from the Black Sea shores, especially a people called Kaskeans, who at times sacked it. Although some later rulers temporarily established capitals farther south, Hattusa remained the political and religious center of the Hittite state until the very end of that state's existence.

Hattusili initiated a policy of southward expansion. As Anatolia is divided into river valleys with a limited agricultural area, the need to obtain access to large cereal fields may have driven the search for control over northern Syria. Hattusili repeatedly invaded the kingdom of Yamkhad, which by then controlled all of northwest Syria, and sacked several of its cities, including Alalakh. Aleppo, the capital of Yamkhad, remained independent, however. Hattusili also campaigned in southwestern Anatolia and had, by the end of his reign, created a large state. Internally, however, that state was in disarray. Hattusili's sons rebelled late in his life, and even the nephew he had chosen as his successor turned against him. Thus, on his deathbed, Hattusili appointed his grandson, Mursili, as heir. The new king's reign is poorly known, but the laconic sources mention two extremely important acts: the destructions of Aleppo and of Babylon. His military operations were not followed by an occupation, however. By annihilating Aleppo, Mursili upset the balance of power in northwest Syria and created space for other entities to develop. The conquest of Babylon is only mentioned in later Hittite and Babylonian sources, and nothing is known about it except that it took place. We can only speculate how and why Mursili led his troops so far south in what is sure to have been merely a raid. The result was a power vacuum in Babylonia as well.

The situation that had characterized Mesopotamia and Syria for two centuries was thus totally reversed. No longer did a set of strong rulers dominate the scene, and the entire region was reduced to political fragmentation. Neither did the Hittites themselves benefit from this situation: upon his return home, Mursili's brother-in-law, Hantili, assassinated him and seized the throne. When Hantili in turn was murdered, various parties contested the succession to the Hittite throne, and internal instability prevented the Hittites from maintaining control over anything beyond the heartland of their state. The Hittite state would not reemerge as a significant player on the international scene until the fourteenth century.

The Hittite scribal tradition was not an offspring of the Old Assyrian one, despite the fact that this was the earliest in Anatolia, but Babylonian practices were at its roots. Many of the early texts were bilingual, using Hittite and Akkadian. The Hittite language was written in cuneiform script inspired by the Babylonian forms and readings of signs, and the penetration of these practices into Anatolia must be seen as an extension of their influence throughout the Near East. Babylonia was thus the center of literate culture for all courts of the Near East, even if they spoke different languages.

The nature of the Hittite sources leads to an almost total ignorance about the workings of the Old Hittite state. No administrative archives from this period are known, so the organization of the economy, for instance, is a mystery. Much has been made in scholarship of the references to a gathering of warriors and officials in Hattusili's succession edict. This is thought to refer to an assembly of noblemen, who elected one from their ranks as king. Sometimes Indo-European practices are assumed here, since they are considered to be more democratic than those elsewhere in the Near East. But such conclusions are not founded in evidence, and most likely the Old Hittite court functioned in ways similar to the others of the time. The Hittite state is thus very poorly known beyond its military successes. On that front it had a radical impact on the Near East by its removal of Aleppo and Babylon. But neither the Hittites nor any other older powers immediately filled the void that was left behind.

6.4   The "Dark Age"

By 1590 the Near East looked very different from what it had been four generations earlier. A system of flourishing states, ruled by courts in close contact with one another, spreading from the Mediterranean coast to the Persian Gulf, had been fully wiped out. Some royal houses still functioned in cities such as Babylon, Terqa, and Hattusa, and the Sealand dynasty continued to rule southern Babylonia, but these were pale reflections of the past. Throughout the Near East, urbanism was at an all-time low since the year 3000. Many cities, such as Mari, had been destroyed as a result of military action. Others were abandoned for reasons unknown: changes in the river courses or rainfall patterns, social and political upheavals may all have played a role. The situation had the usual consequence for the historian: a lack of centralized power led to a discontinuation of administrative and scribal practices as the levels of economic and cultural activities decreased. Texts were only sparingly written and we have thus no data with which to work. We enter into a "Dark Age." The length of this age is controversial. Depending on whether scholars see continuity or discontinuity between the first and the second halves of the second millennium, their perception of the time span of historical silence will be shorter or longer. In my opinion it lasted for about one century. Some crucial changes took place in this hiatus, which would lead to a very different situation in later centuries.

The political ascendancy of new population groups, the Kassites in the south and the Hurrians in the north, seems to have been the most important development in the sixteenth century. Both groups had been present in the Near East before, but only in this "Dark Age" were they able to assert clear political control. Kassites had lived in the north of Babylonia from the eighteenth century on, recognizable by their names, which reveal a clearly distinct language from the other inhabitants in the region. There are many indicators that they had a tribal social organization, and they were most closely associated with the area where steppe and agricultural zones border one another. But as with earlier semi-nomadic groups, Gutians and Amorites, some Kassites were fully integrated social members of the agricultural and urban economy from the moment we encounter them. The Hana dynasty, which had emerged at Terqa upstream from Mari, included a ruler with a Kassite name. The Middle Euphrates region may thus have been the first area where the Kassites gained political control over cities. After Babylon was sacked in 1595, it was left leaderless, but within the next decades a Kassite dynasty had taken over control there. By 1475 it had incorporated southern Babylonia. It is only in the fourteenth century, however, that we can really study its history.

In northern Syria and Mesopotamia, there is evidence that people with Hurrian names had been present since the mid-third millennium. States with Hurrian rulers are attested from the end of the Old Akkadian period on. In the late third millennium, there was a nebulous state called "Urkesh and Nawar," after two cities in the northern Habur basin, ruled by a man named Atal-shen. Several of the early second-millennium states known to us had Hurrian rulers, and at certain places a substantial percentage of the population bore Hurrian names. They were spread out over a wide zone, from the Zagros Mountains to the Mediterranean. When the Kingdom of Upper Mesopotamia fell apart, groups of Hurrian speakers may have entered its territory from the mountains to its east. These immigrants probably brought some cultural elements we usually associate with Indo-Europeans, even if Hurrian itself is not an Indo-European language. Later Hurrians honored the Indian gods Mithra, Varuna, and the divine pair Nasatya. There has been much speculation as to whether the Hurrians themselves were subjected to an Indo-European military upper class: some rulers of Mittani, the Hurrian state of northern Syria in the later second millennium, bore names that were Indo-European and their charioteers were designated with the word *mariyannu*, a term that might include the Vedic word for "young man." The evidence is inconclusive as to the character of the military class, however, and it seems best to regard its members as men trained for warfare, especially as charioteers. In that aspect the Hurrians were very successful. They became formidable opponents, invading the Hittite kingdom several times. Their moves southward may have pushed people from Syria-Palestine into Egypt, where they formed the so-called Hyksos dynasties of the early sixteenth century. The Hurrians certainly became the most prominent population group in a vast area by the time the historical sources resume. Not only did they have their own territorial state by the early fifteenth century, called Mittani, but they were also dominant among the Hittites and in Kizzuwatna (Cilicia in southwest Anatolia), while several rulers of the Syro-Palestinian city-states had Hurrian names.

While Kassites and Hurrians became politically dominant during the "Dark Age," culturally they barely made an impression across the Near Eastern scene. Although many personal names were Kassite, and Babylonian texts indicate the existence of a Kassite vocabulary, no single text or sentence is known in the Kassite language. Some twenty Kassite names of gods are attested, but only for the divine couple that guarded the dynastic family do we know anything concerning a cult and the building of a special temple. The speakers of Kassite were fully assimilated into Babylonian culture.

The Hurrian tradition was older as far as we know and interacted with a variety of cultures that were not as dominant as that of Babylonia. We do have a number of Hurrian language texts, a few from the Mittani state itself, and a few from the Hittite state. The latter's multicultural environment permitted the survival of Hurrian myths and rituals. Still, in comparison with their political importance, the cultural impact Hurrians made in Near Eastern history was not that significant.

The Hurrians may have been responsible, however, for a major technological innovation that took place during the "Dark Age": the use of the horse and chariot. In the second half of the second millennium, all Near Eastern armies fielded chariotries while previously only infantries had fought, with asses or donkeys as draft-animals. A long Hittite-language manual for the training of chariot horses from the fourteenth century starts with the statement, "Thus speaks Kikkuli, the horse-trainer, from the land of Mittani," and the text contains a lot of Hurrian vocabulary as well as words related to an ancient Indic dialect. The instructions are very detailed, for example, "when the horses become restless and begin to sweat, (the trainer) removes their halters and blankets. Then he puts on their reins and they are led out of the stable. They are bathed in warm water."[7] Horses were clearly considered very precious at the time, and the Hurrians may have been responsible for the spread of horsemanship throughout the Near East.

At this time another technological change may have taken place, related to seafaring. After 1500 we observe a shift of attention of the people of the Near East from east to west: islands and countries across the Mediterranean Sea became incorporated in the Near Eastern world-view. Cyprus and the Aegean became regular trading partners, while trade contacts with Egypt intensified. A maritime trading system developed by which the countries along the eastern Mediterranean shores were tied together, visited by ships that circled the sea picking up items at all stops and exchanging them for others. Although the lands of Mesopotamia were too distant from the sea to participate directly in this system, they benefited from it. Tin, for example, which had been imported from the east until this time, now probably came from western sources. While contacts with Aegean islands such as Crete were already attested in the Mari archives, the mass of goods that entered the Near East from the west was much greater in the second half of the second millennium than ever before. It seems likely that innovations in boat construction and navigational techniques had something to do with this, but the details of those changes or who initiated them are unclear.

Our uncertainties about the events and historical developments of the sixteenth and early fifteenth centuries are great. That some radical changes took place is undeniable, however. The Near Eastern world that arose out of the "Dark Age" was in many respects a totally new one.

Debate 6.1   *What is the code of Hammurabi?*

Possibly the most famous text of Babylonian history is Hammurabi's inscription on the stone stele now in the Louvre museum, which was excavated in Susa in 1901 and published a year later. With its more than 3,500 lines it is the longest preserved text from early Mesopotamia, and the fact that its elegantly carved cuneiform signs cover most of the surface of a tall black stone stele adds to its appeal. By far the largest part of the inscription is a list of laws mostly phrased on the pattern, "if ..., then ...," a format called casuistic in Near Eastern scholarship, that is, one specific case after another. Originally there were between 275 and 300 paragraphs; a number of them were erased when the stele was taken to Susa in the twelfth century.

When first published, scholars interpreted the list as a code of legally binding and enforceable rules, comparable to such European codes as the *Code Napoleon*. It was seen as a document whose prescripts reflected legal opinion of the time, and which could be interpreted in the same way as Roman law (Driver and Miles 1952–5). Legal historians collected and categorized actual documents of the Old Babylonian period according to concepts they based on their reading of the laws (Kohler and Peiser 1904–23). But in 1960 a scholar pointed out that the format of the legal pronouncements was exactly the same as that used in medical and omen texts (Kraus 1960). This inspired a total reevaluation that focused on the scientific nature of the text and its function as a monument proclaiming Hammurabi's role as a "King of Justice," words he repeatedly used in the epilogue (Bottéro 1992: 156–84). Scholars emphasized the text's shortcomings. None of the numerous legal records and letters of the period make reference to the consultation of a code (Veenhof 1997–2000), although some stress that there may be a few exceptions (Roth 1997: 4–7; Stol 2004: 656). Also disturbing is the fact that important areas of Babylonian life, such as animal husbandry, are not addressed at all in the text (Bottéro 1992: 161).

While most historians now accept that the code of Hammurabi is not a code, they portray it in different ways. To some it is a scholarly treatise on the subject of law (Westbrook 1989), while to others it is a piece of royal propaganda to justify the king's rule to the court elites (Wells 2005: 201). The fact that the monument with the laws stood in a place where people could consult it is important – even if they were unable to read, they were aware of the fact that Hammurabi guaranteed justice in his kingdom. The mere existence of the laws was a message to the people (Bahrani 2007). Hammurabi declared to his subjects that there was a coherent system of law and he showed this by enumerating examples of just decisions: if someone is caught during a robbery, he will be killed; if a man breaks another man's bone, they will break his bone; and so on. They could count on it that justice would be done if anything happened to them.

NOTES

1   Shubat-Enlil, Qattara, Ashnakkum (present Chagar Bazar), Tuttul (present Tell Bi'a), Mari, Terqa, and Qala'at al-Hadi and Tell Taya (ancient names unknown).
2   Durand 1997–2000, volume 1: 138.
3   Frayne 1990: 341.
4   Translation after Kraus 1968: no. 1.
5   For a recent translation of Hammurabi's law code, see Roth 1997: 71–142.
6   Translation from Robson 1999: 224.
7   Translation by Gary Beckman in Aruz, Benzel, & Evans 2008: 158.

Part II
Territorial States

7

The Club of the Great Powers

3000	2500	2000	1500	1000	500

ca. 1365–1335   Amarna archive

1274   Battle of Qadesh

During the centuries from 1500 to 1200 the Near East became united in an international system that involved the entire region from western Iran to the Aegean Sea and from Anatolia to Nubia. A number of large territorial states interacted with one another as equals and rivals. Located between them, especially in the Syro-Palestinian area, were smaller states that owed allegiance to their more powerful neighbors, and which were often used as proxies in their competition. The system spanned beyond the confines of the Near East as defined in this book: it incorporated the Aegean world and Egypt, which at this time had its largest territorial expansion and was actively involved in the Near East to its north and Nubia to its south. Over these three hundred years the major states involved changed in some places, but there was a remarkable consistency in the division of power over the entire area. The great kingdoms were Kassite Babylonia, Hittite Anatolia, Egypt, and, in northern Mesopotamia and Syria, first the Mittani state, followed in the mid-fourteenth century by Assyria. On their eastern fringe was located the powerful kingdom of Elam, and in the Aegean region to the west Mycenae, whose political organization is more difficult to describe. In their midst were the states of Syria and Palestine, mostly city-states in extent and organization, and always dependent on one of the great powers. The histories of all of these great and small states can be written separately, and I will do so for those of the Near East in subsequent chapters. But the fact that they all participated in a common system without one of them dominating all the others makes this an unusual period of ancient history. Because its characteristics spread across political and cultural borders, scholars often refer to the period with the archaeological designation the Late Bronze Age. While it was not the archaeological conditions that unified this world, the term is useful because it suggests the existence of a common system throughout the Near East and eastern Mediterranean. It is this system that I will explore first.

The historian's task is greatly facilitated by an abundance of sources available for all but a few of the states involved. Except for the Aegean and some Syro-Palestinian states, all have yielded a wide variety of textual data. Royal inscriptions, legal and administrative documents, and literary texts appear almost everywhere. Moreover, since the courts were in contact with one another, their chancelleries contained diplomatic correspondence and international treaties. The centralized character of each of the states led to a high level of scribal production. Writing existed in the Aegean world as well, the so-called Mycenaean Linear B, but its use was limited to economic documents, and although these do provide historical information, it is not of the same detail as what appears elsewhere. Also the archaeological information is very rich throughout the entire region, as building activity and artistic creation were prolific as a result of the wealth of the states. We are presented with a multitude of sources, both in number and variety, which derive not from a single participant in the system but from many of them simultaneously. Our view on the period is thus not filtered through the eyes of only one of the actors.

The greatest difficulty confronting us is the uncertainty about chronology (see debate 7.1). While we may feel cautiously confident about the sequence of rulers and lengths of reigns in certain states, information about other kings and kingdoms remains vague. Thus, even writing the history of the Mittani state, for example, poses great difficulties, as we cannot date events based on evidence from the state itself. We have to rely on synchronisms with Egypt and Hatti to find out approximately when and how long a Mittani king ruled. When his name appears in a text of one of those states, we have some idea when he was active. Yet, the chronologies of all states are not as firm as one would wish, and even when contacts are attested, we are sometimes at a loss to fit events together, despite the close interactions. Consequently, the dates assigned here are often tentative (see chart 7.1).

7.1   The Political System

From 1500 to 1200 all the regions of the Near East and the eastern Mediterranean went through a cycle of creation, florescence, and fall of centralized states. There were at least five zones where political unification took place, followed by a period of prosperity that ended in a rather sudden collapse. In four of those zones the entire period can be studied as the history of one state: the Middle

Chart 7.1 Comparative chronology of the major states of the second half of the second millennium

Date	*Mittani*	*Babylonia*	*Assyria*	*Hatti*	*Egypt*
1500	Parrattarna				Amenhotep I
1450					Tuthmose III
1400	Artatama I				
		Kadashman-Enlil I			Amenhotep III
1350	Tushratta		Assur-uballit I		Akhenaten
		Burnaburiash II			
	Shattiwaza			Suppiluliuma I	
		Kurigalzu II			
1300				Mursili II	
			Adad-nirari I		
	Elam			Muwatalli II	
		Kadashman-Enlil II	Shalmanseser I		Ramesses II
1250	Untash-Napirisha			Hattusili III	
		Kashtiliashu IV	Tukulti-Ninurta I	Tudhaliya IV	
1200				Suppiluliuma II	Merneptah
	Shutruk-Nahhunte				
1150	Kutir-Nahhunte				Ramesses III
	Shilhak-lnshushinak				
			Assur-resha-ishi I		
		Nebuchadnezzar I			
1100			Tiglath-pileser I		
1050					

Elamite Kingdom in western Iran, Kassite Babylonia in southern Mesopotamia, the Hittite New Kingdom in Anatolia (a state its contemporaries called Hatti), and New Kingdom Egypt in North Africa. In northern Mesopotamia two distinct states dominated in succession, Mittani and Assyria. The latter was originally a province of the Mittani state, gained independence, and then replaced its original master as the regional power. A similar cycle of political unification and disintegration probably took place in western Anatolia and the Aegean, but the situation is murkier there, due to the absence of relevant textual sources (see map 7.1).

The simultaneity of these cycles all over the region cannot be pure coincidence. The proximity of the states and the close interactions between them, as attested in numerous sources, force us to look beyond their individual histories to explain the waxing and waning of their fortunes. The end of this period has been intensively investigated and its causes much debated. The beginning, however, has mostly been portrayed as the accidental coalescence of individual histories into a regional system and the result of interactions between courts that had established themselves independently. Local circumstances certainly were to a great extent responsible for what happened in the different areas, but also the rise of the individual states may be better understood when seen in a regional context. Just as the disappearance of the system that tied them together precipitated the end of these states, the growth of the system conditioned their rise. Since much of this took place in the so-called Dark Age, the development of the regional system is hard to study in detail. But by placing local histories within a wider context, we

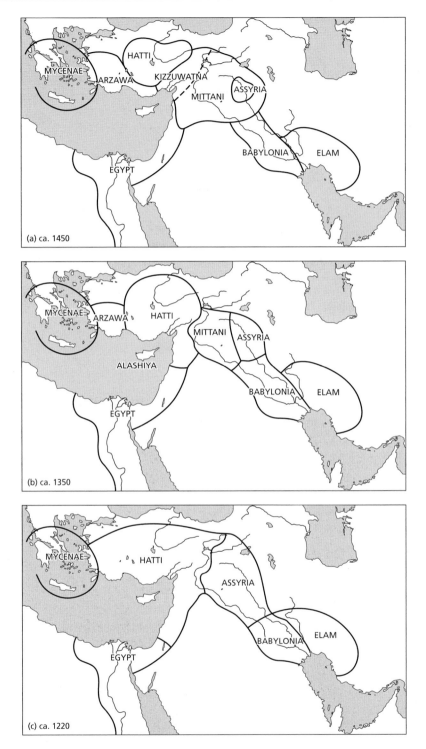

Map 7.1 The political systems of the Near East in the second half of the second millennium. After Mario Liverani, *Prestige and Interest* (Padua: Sargon, 1990), pp. 299–300.

can account better for the developments in individual states than by looking at the internal circumstances alone.

In the sixteenth century the entire Near East was politically fragmented: nowhere do we see strong states, and as a result textual documentation is extremely scarce. Only in Egypt do we have a grasp on the situation, but even there our understanding is limited. From the mid-seventeenth century on, the country had been divided into a number of principalities, several of which were ruled by foreigners called Hyksos. In the Near East, the great states had disappeared and competing dynasties ruled everywhere. The near-total absence of textual remains suggests that their economies were underdeveloped and their political control weak. Mesopotamia, Anatolia, and Syria-Palestine saw a sharp reduction of inhabited zones and an increase of semi-nomadic groups. The urban centers had become fewer in number, and were isolated in a surrounding with little permanent settlement.

The situation of political and economic decline was gradually reversed starting in the late sixteenth and the fifteenth centuries: out of the landscape of small and weak states developed an unprecedented system of territorial states with more or less equivalent power. Many, if not all, of the states involved attained a size and cohesion never known before in their histories. The best-known examples are Egypt, Babylonia, and Assyria. The Mesopotamian states became truly territorial. Babylonia and Assyria in the second half of the second millennium were regional entities, ruled from one political center by dynasties that considered themselves to govern a country, not one or more cities as had been the case before. The territories included several cities and their hinterlands, knit together by a degree of economic integration unseen earlier on. Ideologically, the idea that the city was at the heart of cultural and political life still survived, but the political and economic autonomy of cities had disappeared. Egypt, which had been a territorial state from its inception in the early third millennium, at this time developed into a large empire extending into foreign lands, stretching from Nubia in modern-day Sudan to northern Syria.

Also in the other regions of the Near East, territorial states developed where there had been a multitude of small states before the mid-second millennium. Northern Syria in the early second millennium had been politically divided between states such as Qatna, Yamkhad, Tuttul, and Apum. All those had suffered decline in the sixteenth century, and when the new state of Mittani arose in the fifteenth century, it was a territorial one that imposed its hegemony over the entire region. New Kingdom Hatti similarly instituted a political integration of Central Anatolia and northwest Syria. The cohesion of the Middle Elamite state and the differences from what preceded it are difficult to evaluate, as is true for the Aegean world. In the latter case, the mention of western states in Hittite texts (Arzawa and Ahhiyawa), and the homogeneity of material culture in the centuries after 1500, suggest a substantive political change compared to earlier times.

The only exception to this general trend toward larger political units was the Syro-Palestinian area: here the basic system of small states centered round a single city continued to exist. Numerous examples are known, such as Jerusalem,

Damascus, Byblos, and Ugarit. Qualitatively, we see no difference from the situation in the first part of the second millennium, even if the earlier picture is much less clear. Perhaps this exception to the rule underlines how fundamental the changes elsewhere were. The Syro-Palestinian region was sandwiched between competing territorial states: first Egypt and Mittani, later Egypt and Hatti, with Assyria lurking in the background. It acted as a buffer between these great states and as a place where they could interact competitively, both directly and by proxy. They did exert political influence and turned local rulers into vassals, but the region did not develop into a territorial state itself, nor did it become firmly integrated within the territories of one of its powerful neighbors. The surrounding states were strong enough to prevent that from happening. The difference between great and small states was clear in the formal interactions between their courts. Only the rulers of the territorial states regarded themselves as equals and addressed each other as "brothers," while those of the Syro-Palestinian states were of a lower rank and were "servants." Thus the latter were forced to pledge allegiance to one of the neighboring overlords, switching that allegiance to the stronger power as needed. The level of integration within these larger state-systems depended on the proximity to the political center and on the policies of the sovereigns. Egypt's control of Syria, for example, was a lot more hands-off than Hatti's. But the latter also used a flexible approach: it directly administered important regions such as that of Carchemish in northern Syria, while in Amurru farther south, for instance, it permitted a local king to govern as vassal. We cannot say that any of the Syro-Palestinian states ever became fully integrated in the territories of their dominant neighbors. They continued to exist as separate political entities, distinct from the suzerains in the great states, who at the same time prevented them from uniting with their neighbors.

We can seek explanations for these sociopolitical developments within the histories of the individual regions, and indeed the growth of territorial states during the first half of the second millennium has been studied in the previous chapter. But the presence of an overarching system in which all consciously participated must have reinforced the local processes toward greater political centralization. This becomes more likely if we consider how closely these states interacted with one another, both in friendly and hostile ways, and how they shared a social and ideological structure.

7.2 Political Interactions: Diplomacy and Trade

All participants in this system knew what their place was in the political hierarchy and how to interact with others. They behaved as if they lived in a large village where communications were close and people were related to each other. In order to maintain the system, they were in constant contact with one another, sending envoys back and forth with oral and written messages. All courts had a chancellery where scribes wrote in Babylonian, the international language of diplomacy. By far our best evidence for this practice comes from Egypt, where in the fourteenth century King Akhenaten moved the capital to the new city of Akhetaten (modern Amarna). In its ruins were found the remnants of his and his father's international correspondence, written on clay tablets. They are usually referred to as the Amarna letters (see box 7.1). Vassals in Syria-Palestine wrote most of the 350 letters to their Egyptian master, but around forty letters were from or to the kings Egypt's ruler considered to be his equals, the "Great Kings." Those were the rulers of Babylonia, Assyria, Mittani, Hatti, Alashiya (on Cyprus), and Arzawa (in southwest Anatolia). The last two were probably included because of their control of resources needed by all kings – in the case of Alashiya, copper. The letters from Arzawa were written in the Hittite language rather than Babylonian, which shows that its court was not yet fully integrated in the system. That the Egyptian archive was not unique is clear from small finds in Syro-Palestinian cities of similar diplomatic letters contemporaneous to the Amarna

---

Box 7.1   *The Amarna letters*

In the late nineteenth century AD, peasants found a group of cuneiform tablets at the modern-day site of Amarna, where in the fourteenth century BC King Akhenaten had built Egypt's new capital, Akhetaten. These contained the diplomatic correspondence between the kings of Egypt and their equals and vassals in the Near East, a total of 350 letters written in the reigns of Amenhotep III, Akhenaten, and two successors, probably Smenkhkara and Tutankhamun. Most of them were addressed to the king or high court officials by rulers of small states in the Syro-Palestinian area, and detailed their interactions with their overlord. They called themselves servants of the king of Egypt, and sought to ingratiate themselves by making their neighbors look like untrustworthy vassals. The letters show that Egypt had divided the region into three administrative districts and controlled it with a relatively small military presence. The region involved stretched from the south of Palestine to central Syria, with the state of Amurru as the northernmost Egyptian dependency. The language of the letters is Babylonian, but influences of the local Semitic languages are visible in the vocabulary and grammar.

A group of about forty letters was between the Egyptian king and his colleagues in the other great states of the time: Babylonia, Assyria, Mittani, Hatti, Alashiya, and Arzawa. These kings saw themselves as equals and addressed each other as brothers. They discussed diplomatic matters, especially the exchange of precious goods and of royal women, which reinforced the ties between them. While most of the letters were written in Babylonian, there were two in Hittite and one each in Hurrian and Assyrian.

The Amarna letters cover a short period of at most thirty years from ca. 1365 to 1335, but it is certain that this type of correspondence was maintained throughout the period at several locations. The state archives of the Hittite capital, Hattusa, have revealed similar letters, and a few examples were found elsewhere. All the courts must have had the same type of international exchanges. The use of the Babylonian language and writing material shows how the culture from that region continued to dominate in the Near East.

ones. International correspondence from the thirteenth century between kings of Egypt, Hatti, Assyria, and Babylonia has also been found, albeit in smaller numbers. The palace at Ugarit, one of the states subject to Hatti, had such texts as well, and isolated finds from other palaces throughout the Near East show that all courts were involved in this diplomacy.

The authors of the letters portrayed the world they lived in as an extended household: kings of equal status called one another brother; those of lower rank called themselves servants (see document 7.1). Each state's status was demarcated, but, since the political situation sometimes changed quickly, friction arose. When Assyria gained political and military prominence, King Assur-uballit I sent two letters to the king of Egypt as if he were an equal. This enraged Burnaburiash II, king of Babylon, who complained to his Egyptian colleague: "With regard to my Assyrian vassals, it was not I who sent them to you. Why did they go to your country without proper authority? If you are loyal to me, they will not negotiate any business. Send them to me empty-handed!"[1] Such quarrels were unavoidable as status was very important and the political reality changed faster than the willingness to acknowledge newcomers.

Document 7.1   *Examples of Amarna letters*

The Amarna letters provide unparalleled insight into the diplomatic relations of the ancient Near East in the second half of the second millennium. Probably left behind when the Egyptian capital moved from Akhetaten the cuneiform tablets show how the correspondence from rulers considered to be equals – those of Mittani, Babylonia, etcetera – had a very different tone and contents than the letters vassals wrote. The equals called Egypt's king a brother and discussed matters of diplomacy, while the lower ranked rulers called him master and brought up political issues relevant to their region.

1   Between equals: Letter from Tushratta of Mittani to Amenhotep III of Egypt

Tell Nimmureya, king of Egypt, my brother, my son-in-law, whom I love and who loves me; Tushratta, king of Mittani, who loves you, your father-in-law, says: All is well with me. May all be well with you. May all be well with your house, with my daughter Tadu-Heba, and with your wife, whom you love. May all be very, very well with your wives, your sons, your leading men, your chariots, your horses, your troops, your country, and whatever else belongs to you.

Shaushga of Nineveh, lady of all lands, said: "I wish to go to Egypt, the land that I love, and then come back." Now I send her and she is on the way.

Now, in the time of my father, she went . . . to this country. And as she stayed there and they honored her earlier, may my brother now honor her ten times more than before. May my brother honor her and let her come back at his pleasure.

May Shaushga, the lady of heaven, protect my brother and me for 100,000 years, and may our lady give us great joy. Let us act as friends.

Is Shaushga not my goddess and my brother's goddess?

Translation after Moran 1992: 61–62, no. 23.

2   From a vassal: Letter from Rib-Adda, king of Byblos, to the king of Egypt

Tell the king, my lord, my Sun; Rib-Adda, your servant, says: I fall at the feet of my lord seven and seven times. Let the king, my lord, know that Pu-bahla, the son of Abdi-Ashirta, has taken the city Ullassa by force. Ardata, Wahliya, Ampi, Shigata, all these cities are theirs. Let the king thus send help to Sumur, until he gives thought to his land. Who are the sons of Abdi-Ashirta, the servant and the dog? Are they the king of the Kassites or the king of Mittani, so that they can take the king's land for themselves? In the past they would take cities of your mayors, and you did nothing. Now they have driven out your governor and have taken his cities for themselves. They have seized Ullassa. If you will do nothing under these circumstances, they will certainly seize Sumur and kill the governor and the garrison. What can I do? I cannot go to Sumur. The cities Ampi, Shigata, Ullassa, and Erwada are hostile. Should they know that I am in Sumur, there would be these cities with ships, and the sons of Abdi-Ashirta in the countryside. They would attack me and I could not get out. Byblos would be joined to the *habiru*.[1] They have gone to Ibirta and an agreement has been made with the *habiru*.

Translation after Moran 1992: 177, no. 104.

[1] Semi-nomadic social outcasts; see chapter 8.

In one sense we see here a continuation of early second-millennium practices in which the royal houses of the Near East corresponded with each other. A major difference, however, is that the Great Kings never discussed political issues explicitly. Allusions to them appear, but these men were primarily interested in the diplomatic exchange of messengers, goods, and women. The opposite was true in the letters of vassals to their overlords. They focused on the everyday political situation in their neighborhoods, and often accused others of being unreliable vassals to the king. These accusations were strategic maneuvers in the competition over land and the control of routes. Their declarations of loyalty and the denunciations of their neighbors have to be regarded as hyperbole and rhetoric. Vassals tried to avoid or delay the payment of taxes and tribute, and drew attention away from that topic by pointing out the disloyalty of others. In contrast they claimed to be politically trustworthy, even if they did not obey all of the pharaoh's orders. In the period of the Amarna letters, Hatti did indeed threaten Egypt's widespread influence over the Syro-Palestinian area and sought to pick off its northern vassals one by one. The Hittites often carried out this policy by proxy using client kings, and what appear as petty local squabbles were, in fact, contests between the great states. Bickering is characteristic even of letters between equals: the Great Kings complained about the lack of respect others had for them. The Hittite King Hattusili III, for example, wondered aloud why his Babylonian "brother" no longer sent messengers. Was he so weak that he could not force safe passage through the lands in between? Did evil tongues in his court set him up against Hattusili? Since the exchange of gifts was a major aspect of maintaining good relations, their quality and quantity were often discussed. The kings were not shy about complaining and expressing their displeasure.

Relations between states had to be codified, especially when they involved the great kingdoms and their vassals. This was accomplished through treaties between their rulers. These were agreements between two men, not between two states, and had to be renewed whenever a new ruler came to the throne. The treaties that have been preserved all involve the Hittite state or Alalakh, but references in other texts suggest that they were common throughout the Near East. Two types existed: between equal powers, and between a Great King and his vassal. The first was probably only drawn up after a serious conflict or for special purposes. The examples are thus few. Hattusili III of Hatti and Ramesses II of Egypt concluded the most famous treaty of the period in 1259, fifteen years after their two armies had clashed in a major battle near the Syrian city of Qadesh. The agreement strove for full equality and brotherhood between the two, reflecting the idea of family found in the diplomatic correspondence. They promised not to attack each other, to help the other when attacked, and to extradite people who fled their respective territories. The only divergence between the two versions of the treaty we have, one for the Hittites, the other for the Egyptians, related to the question of succession to the throne. Since Hattusili had himself usurped kingship in Hatti, he was worried that his son would not be accepted, and he inserted a clause in the treaty that the Egyptian king should secure his succession. The extradition of people fleeing states was one of the main concerns of all these agreements. Three of the treaties between equal partners were entirely devoted to this subject, a reflection of the social situation of the time, as I will discuss below.

The treaties of subservience known from this period were all concluded with the Hittite king. The details of the arrangements varied, but they all contained some essential elements: the vassals in Anatolia and northern Syria had to contribute taxes and military contingents, and they had to yield their right to independent foreign relations. They could not engage in war with other Hittite vassals, nor contact other great rulers. They had to return fugitives. Loyalty to the Hittite king was the principal obligation and they swore this before numerous gods, from both the Hittite and vassal states. These treaties legitimized the relations between the rulers of the region, which were maintained through the exchange of messengers.

Diplomatic marriages further confirmed the close treaty relations and were often the concern of the letters sent by the Great Kings. Much of the Amarna correspondence between Babylon and Egypt dealt with this subject. The kings of Egypt were very eager to bring foreign women into their palace and demanded women of royal blood. They had a rule, however, that no Egyptian princess could marry a foreigner, leading to a great deal of frustration among the other kings. The latter usually did send their daughters to Egypt, however, as the bride price included the much-desired gold in which Egypt held a monopoly. Non-Egyptian kings used princesses extensively to strengthen political alliances. The kings of

Hatti, for example, often gave their daughters in marriage to vassals after a treaty had been signed.

These marriages could seriously affect the internal histories of states. The Babylonian King Burnaburiash II (ruled 1359–1333) had married Muballitat-Sherua, the daughter of the Assyrian Assur-uballit I (ruled 1353–1318). When their son and successor, Kara-hardash, was murdered in a Babylonian uprising, Assur-uballit intervened militarily, deposed the rebel king, and replaced him with Kurigalzu II. The bizarre episode of the recently widowed queen of Egypt shows a similar unhappiness with the idea that the offspring of a foreign king would rule. All our information comes from Hittite sources, and the identity of the Egyptian queen is debated. Most likely she was the young widow of King Tutankhamun, who asked the Hittite King Suppiluliuma for one of his sons to become her husband. After verification of the request, which he originally received with great skepticism, Suppiluliuma sent his son Zannanza from Hatti to Egypt, but he was murdered during the voyage. An alliance with Hatti was clearly not in the interest of some factions at the Egyptian court, who subsequently placed one of their own on the throne. The peculiarity of this episode in Hittite–Egyptian relations cannot be underestimated. First, the Egyptians were always eager to marry foreign princesses, but never allowed one of their own royal women to marry a foreigner. Second, in this instance the male traveled to the foreign court, not the other way around, as was customary. This was a complete gender reversal: a female ruler invited a male prince to become her spouse at her palace, instead of the usual request for a foreign princess to become the spouse of the Egyptian king.

Naturally, these marriages strengthened the idea that the rulers of the Near East all belonged to the same community. This concept was crucial in the way they perceived their interactions, but all knew that in reality it was merely a fiction, as circumstances were very different from those in a village. For example, when Kadashman-Enlil of Babylon wrote to Amenhotep III of Egypt to invite him to the opening of his new palace as if he were a close neighbor, the latter could not attend. The voyage would have required several months' travel each way! But the invitation had to be extended as one would invite a neighbor in the village. The distances between the courts were very great, and often led to questions about the fate of messengers and princesses. When Babylon's king protested to Egypt that he did not know whether or not his sister was still alive, the Egyptian pointed out that he should not complain. No messenger qualified to ascertain who among his consorts was the Babylonian princess had ever come to Egypt: "The men whom you sent are nobodies . . . There has been no one among them who knows her, who was an intimate of your father, and who could identify her."[2] So, the idea that they all lived in a village was a deliberate fiction.

The most frequent topic of discussion in the letters among equals was the exchange of gifts, another way in which the cohesion between these states was maintained. The transactions had a dual function. On the one hand, they enabled rulers to obtain luxury goods not locally available; on the other hand, they reinforced a system of mutual respect, prestige, and brotherhood. The two functions cannot be separated. The exchanges operated according to a set of (unwritten) rules. The idea of reciprocity dominated: someone's gift should be repaid with one of almost equal value, although the return did not have to be immediate. On certain occasions, such as on the accession of a new king to the throne, gifts were expected. Hattusili III of Hatti complained, for instance, to the king of Assyria: "When I assumed kingship, you did not send a messenger to me. It is the custom that when kings assume kingship, the kings, his equals in rank, send him appropriate gifts of greeting, clothing befitting kingship, and fine oil for his anointing. But you did not do this today."[3] Gifts were also sent when treaties were concluded or when a military victory was celebrated. These exchanges tied the rulers together in a common system.

On the other hand, the system created a circulation of precious and highly desired goods throughout the region. In a non-commercial way, the courts could obtain products that were absent at home. Gold was of special interest to all as a rare and exotic luxury. Only the king of Egypt could send it, as he alone had goldmines in his territory. The others sent Egypt horses, copper, craft goods, and so on, with the understanding that they would receive gold in return. Between other rulers similar exchanges took place. For example, Alashiya had great amounts of copper and Babylonia was the source for lapis lazuli, which came from Afghanistan. The gifts often included manufactured objects, fancy textiles, or fine oils. Everyone maintained the fiction that these were presents, although they knew that access to rare goods was the intent. Thus some seemingly irrational practices appear: the king of Alashiya, for instance, sent a small amount of ivory along with a large shipment of copper and wood to Egypt – the land where ivory was abundant. He did so in order to indicate clearly to his colleague that he hoped to receive ivory in return. In general the rulers had no qualms about discussing the quality and quantity of these goods. They mentioned this frankly in the Amarna letters, and complaints about the stinginess of the Egyptian king were common. For example, the king of Babylon wrote: "You have sent me as my greeting gift, the only thing in six years, thirty pounds of gold that looked like silver,"[4] while the Mittani ruler whined: "In my brother's country, gold is as plentiful as dirt."[5] Not only were the kings themselves involved in this exchange system of precious goods, but their wives also kept similar contacts with women of equal status in other courts.

The royal gift exchange focused on luxury items for a tiny elite. It was a small part of an extensive trade network that enabled the spread of materials and manufactured goods throughout the Near East. This activity is not well documented in the textual record, but archaeological finds show its extent and how it tied distant regions together. For example, cylinder seals carved in Babylonia were excavated in the mainland Greek city of Thebes. Seaborne trade in the eastern Mediterranean was intense and integrated the islands and coastal regions into a coherent system. Ships traveled in a counterclockwise direction, hugging the coastline as much as possible. The merchants picked up new cargo in every harbor in exchange for some of their stock on board. The ships were loaded with a mixture of goods and products from the entire region. This is best shown in a shipwreck found off the coast of southern Anatolia at Uluburun and dating to the

Figure 7.1 Excavation of copper ingots from the Uluburun shipwreck. When the Uluburun ship sank off the south coast of Anatolia it was loaded with ten tons of copper ingots neatly stacked to avoid sliding in bad weather. Still found in their original order during excavation, their so-called oxhide shape made it easier to carry them on the shoulder. They were part of a varied cargo that originated in all the regions of the eastern Mediterranean. Since Cyprus was the main source of copper in the area, the ship probably acquired them there shortly before it sank. Credit: © Institute of Nautical Archaeology.

late fourteenth century (see figure 7.1). Its main cargo was ten tons of Cypriot copper and one ton of tin of unknown origin, both poured into easily portable ingots. The amounts found reflect the proper ratio of ten to one required for bronze production. These metals were most likely picked up in Cyprus, southern Anatolia, and western Syria and intended for the various harbors along the sea route. There the merchants acquired local goods: the ship contained logs of ebony, which the Egyptians must have obtained in tropical Africa, and cedar logs from Lebanon. Ivory tusks and hippopotamus teeth also came from Egypt, while murex shells, prized for their dye, could have been obtained in various locations in North Africa and on the Syrian and Lebanese coast. In addition to these raw materials, the ship contained manufactured goods, such as Canaanite jewelry, Cypriot pottery, beads of gold, faience, agate, glass, and so on, all from different sources. There was even a jeweler's hoard on board with scraps of gold, silver, and electrum, a scarab with the name of the Egyptian Queen Nefertiti, and cylinder seals from Babylonia, Assyria, and Syria. The mixture of goods was so heterogeneous that it is impossible to identify the origin of the ship. Its cargo was truly international.

The trade also included goods that have not survived in the archaeological record. Wine and oil from the Aegean and Syria were exported to Egypt, as we can determine from the jars in which they were shipped. Drugs, perfumes, and incense were transported over great distances, often in vessels and jars with distinctive shapes to identify their contents. The maritime system was connected as well to the riverine and overland trade routes. Moreover, sailors from the Mycenaean world probably ventured as far west as Spain to obtain goods such as silver and tin. The eastern Mediterranean seaborne cycle must be seen as the nexus of a network that extended far beyond its shores.

Certain places acted as hubs in this system. Ugarit is a prime example, a city on the Syrian coast, which had its own dynasty but was vassal first to Egypt, then to Hatti. It was located on the crossroad of routes from Mesopotamia, Central Anatolia, and Egypt, and it had a good sea harbor. Trade at Ugarit was most likely undertaken by private entrepreneurs, both from the city itself and from other states. Merchants from Cyprus, Egypt, Anatolia, and northern Syria resided there, and texts in a multitude of languages (Ugaritic, Babylonian, Hittite, Hurrian, Cypro-Minoan) were found in the houses. They document contacts with other Syrian harbors, with Cyprus and Crete, as well as with inland cities such as Carchemish and Emar. Its archaeological record also contained many foreign goods. Not only did the city act as a transit point, it was also the site of manufacturing. A workshop for the production of bronze was found in its harbor district, and Ugarit was the source of purple textiles famed throughout the region. The states tried to regulate trade to a certain extent and to use it in their rivalries. For example, in his treaty with Shaushga-muwa of the northern Syrian state Amurru, Tudhaliya IV of Hatti (ruled 1237–1209) stated: "Your merchant shall not go to Assyria, and you shall not allow his merchant into your land. He shall not pass through your land. But if he comes into your land, seize him and send him off to My Majesty."[6] It seems unlikely, however, that trade embargoes were customary in this period, since all states of the region depended on this exchange for access to the foreign goods their elites desired.

Trade and diplomacy were thus intrinsically tied in this era: the trade of highly valued goods and materials cemented relations between the kings of the great states. This was portrayed as an exchange of gifts between friends, but was also the only means courts had to obtain prestige items they lacked at home. Royal gift exchange was only part of a much wider system of trade interactions between the different regions. Merchants traveled by land and by sea to circulate goods from all parts of this world across political boundaries. While this exchange still pertained to the elites of these societies, the presence of foreign goods everywhere raised the awareness that other people and cultures existed.

7.3   Regional Competition: Warfare

At the same time that the great states of the region traded and exchanged diplomatic messages with each other, they were in a constant situation of rivalry, and sought to extend their territorial influences at their neighbors' expense. The official rhetoric of both Egyptians and Hittites in royal inscriptions and annals was very much focused on warfare, and the careers of many kings can be sketched as a list of military campaigns. Elsewhere the focus on warfare developed later: in Assyria the practice of detailing campaigns started only around 1300, while in Babylonia it never replaced attention to building activity. That military conflicts also took place there can be gathered from other sources, however. The wars were fought in two ways: either by picking off the other's vassals, or by direct confrontation. The former was the preferred way for many years in the Syro-Palestinian area. At first Egypt and Mittani competed over the region; after 1340, it was Egypt and Hatti. Although Egyptian pharaohs claimed to have campaigned far and wide in the Levant, even up to the Euphrates River, they mostly confronted only the armies of small states. This is how, by 1400, they were able to extend control as far north as the city of Ugarit, whose king became an Egyptian vassal. The Amarna letters show how the Hittites tried to draw some of these vassals to their side. Syrian rulers incessantly complained to the pharaoh that neighboring kings acted as Hittite agents and urged them to turn against their Egyptian overlord. Even if much of this may have been an excuse for non-payment of taxes, the gradual expansion of the Hittite sphere of influence in northwestern Syria without major battles cannot be denied. By 1300, the Hittites had extended their system of vassal states as far south as Qadesh, making cities like Ugarit fully dependent on them.

In other regions of the Near East, a lack of large buffer zones between the great states led to more direct conflicts. Assyria and Babylonia had several border wars, but there were no attempts to annex or annihilate the other. The only great state that lost its independence in this period was that of Mittani. At first preeminent in northern Syria, it was greatly reduced in size and power by the Hittites under Suppiluliuma I (ruled 1344–1322), who turned its king into a vassal but allowed the state to survive. In the early thirteenth century, the Hittites and Egyptians broke their rules of competition-by-proxy when their armies clashed directly, most famously at Qadesh in 1274. The Egyptians presented this battle as a major confrontation between two enormous armies. Ramesses II claimed that Muwatalli fielded some 47,500 men against him (probably an exaggeration), and that both kings personally led their troops. The direct war resulted from Hatti's successful encroachment on Egyptian-controlled territory, which only the royal army itself could confront. Egypt lost the engagement, and subsequently Ramesses II limited his control to southern Palestine, where he fortified a firm boundary. It seems thus that warfare, while sustained but low-level, was not intended to destroy the system that characterized the region, but rather to readjust the power relations between the various states that continued to tolerate and respect each other's existence. It was not until late in the period, in the late thirteenth century, that this system began to fall apart and the rules of competition, and aims of warfare, were changed. We will discuss that in a later chapter.

The "small kings" of the Syro-Palestinian area were as actively involved in warfare as their superiors. At first they resisted the raids and annexation by their mighty neighbors, but once defeated they fought one another in local disputes when the sovereign powers' attention was engaged elsewhere, as the Amarna letters illustrate. The constant skirmishes required all states to devote substantial resources to their military, and the army consequently took on a leading role in these societies. The technology of warfare had fundamentally changed since the early second millennium. All the armies now had horse-drawn chariots that enabled warriors to advance rapidly against the enemy and shoot arrows (figure 7.2). The equipment was expensive, but clearly so effective that everyone adopted it. Charioteers and fighters had to be trained and acquired a special status. They became the military elites, and in Mittani society, for example, they

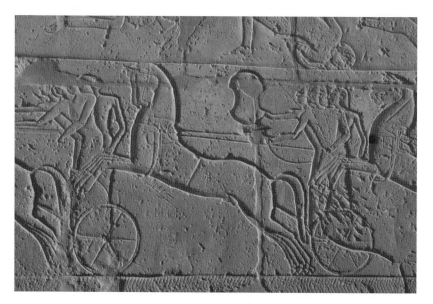

Figure 7.2 Representation of a chariot, Thebes, Egypt. A few centuries into the Late Bronze Age all armies had a chariotry, which formed one of the most important fighting forces. The scene here shows a detail of the battle of Qadesh between the Hittites and the Egyptians. Various chariots are on their way to the battlefront. Two horses pull each one of them and three men stand on the chariot, a driver, a shield bearer, and a warrior. Ramesseum, Thebes, Egypt. Credit: akg images/Album/Prisma.

were like an aristocracy. In all states men who had made their careers in the military became politically prominent. While we cannot say that the preceding or succeeding phases in the history of the region were more peaceful, the second half of the second millennium does stand out because of the great geographical distances regularly covered by the armies, and because no single power dominated the rest. Militarism was the order of the day.

7.4   Shared Ideologies and Social Organizations

The rulers of the Near Eastern states were well aware that they all belonged to a common system that encompassed the entire region. This is clear from the way they interacted with each other in diplomatic and military terms. They also shared an ideology about the social structures within their states and the role of the majority of the people living in them. While the political organization of the states varied, an enormous discrepancy in access to wealth and power between the numerically small elites and the mass of the populations characterized all of them. An international elite class emerged, whose participants had more in common with their colleagues in the other states than with the lower classes at home. The elites engaged in an unprecedented accumulation and display of wealth, and simultaneously distanced themselves from the rest of the people by living in separate cities or city-quarters. Everywhere in the region this was a period of great building activity and artistic production, an era that produced some of the most impressive monuments of ancient history. Egypt presents perhaps the most telling example of this. With the exception of the great pyramids, virtually every one of Egypt's most famous tombs and temples dates to this time. Its royal tombs were filled with gigantic treasures: the funerary goods from the tomb of Tutankhamun were, after all, only for a minor king. Elsewhere in the region the same was true, even in the small Syro-Palestinian kingdoms. Recent excavations at Qatna in central Syria, for example, have revealed a mausoleum below the palace. A ramp led to a set of chambers 12 meters underground, which contained the bones of at least nineteen to twenty-three men and women. These received large amounts of luxury items in gold, ivory, semi-precious stones and other materials, as well as containers with food and drink, which show that a cult of the dead existed (figure 7.3). Also the remains of Mycenaean Greece include several monumental fortresses and lavish burials.

   A common characteristic throughout the region is that public buildings, including palaces and temples, were often situated in clearly delineated and protected areas of the cities, or even that entire cities served as royal residences. Hattusa was perched on a well-defended rock and its palace on a high citadel within it (figure 7.4). The palaces of Mycenaean kings, such as those at Mycenae and Tiryns, stood on hilltops reinforced by cyclopean walls. The Qatna palace area towered over the lower city on a natural cliff whose sides were artificially cut into vertical blocks. In Assur the walled inner city, where all palaces and temples were located, was clearly distinct from the residential area. The desire of the ruling elites

Figure 7.4 City gate at Hattusa. One of the entrances of the Upper City of Hattusa was the so-called lion gate, named after the protective animals carved into the huge monolithic blocks of stone that lined the passageway. Originally two rectangular towers stood beside them and heavy wooden gates regulated access to the city. Credit: The Art Archive/Collection Dagli Orti.

to separate themselves from the rest of the population was taken to its logical conclusion by building new capital cities. We see the construction of entirely new cities in almost every state at this time: Al-Untash-Napirisha in Elam, Dur-Kurigalzu in Babylonia, Kar-Tukulti-Ninurta in Assyria, Akhetaten and Per-Ramesse in Egypt. The names of these cities themselves show how they were connected to the person: except for Akhetaten, all incorporate a specific ruler's name. The name Akhetaten referred to the god Aten, who was the king's personal deity. These were not cities for the people, but residences for king and court. The ability to construct them, all of them gigantic in size, demonstrates the wealth of resources that were available to kings. Psychologically, it points toward a desire to distance the ruling elites from the people. These cities also reflect the power struggles that went on among and between the elites. It is likely that in these places new bureaucracies were created, employing men who were fully dependent on the king rather than on their familial ties for their social status. But the old families could fight back: Akhetaten was abandoned upon the death of its founder, while Al-Untash-Napirisha and Kar-Tukulti-Ninurta lost their primacy when their founders died, but lingered on for centuries.

These cities, palaces, and temples were all extensively decorated. The need for conspicuous display inpired the requests for gold so often made in the Amarna letters. The rulers may have tried to outdo one another, attempting to impress the emissaries and visitors from other countries. What has sometimes been called an "international" style developed in several of the arts of the time. The high culture in the different states was a hybrid of local traditions mixed with foreign influences. Perhaps the elites strove for a fashionable lifestyle that was shared amongst themselves, and that distinguished them more from their own populations than from their counterparts elsewhere. These cultural borrowings were certainly not limited to materials we can recognize in the archaeological record today, but must have involved ephemeral things such as clothing, foods, perfumes, drugs, and so on. Could they have included language? Just as the European elites in the eighteenth century AD conversed in French, the Near Eastern elites of the fourteenth century may have shown off their knowledge of Babylonian, not because they were erudite but to demonstrate their social identity. We know well that the scribes attached to the palaces used the language for international correspondence with various levels of competence, but we may be looking at their skills too much in a purely utilitarian way. Amongst the tablets excavated at Hattusa, Emar, Ugarit, and Akhetaten were several examples of Babylonian literature. A fragment of the *Epic of Gilgamesh* was found at Megiddo in Palestine, and it seems certain that the numerous palaces of the region will yield further evidence that the Akkadian language was not just used for wholly practical purposes. We cannot determine who enjoyed reading or listening to these texts; their presence suggests, however, that a certain class in these societies thought it useful to use a foreign language and its literature (see document 7.2).

The textual documentation shows the existence of a strict social hierarchy, one that involved two sectors of society: the palace dependents and the free population in village communities. We cannot talk, then, of a single hierarchy based solely on wealth or access to the means of production. The palace dependents were not "free," they did not own their own land, but if we take wealth as an indicator of social status, they were often much better off than the free people. It is in the palace sector that we see the greatest degree of social stratification. On the bottom of the hierarchy were serfs working the agricultural estates. Since status depended on the services one provided for the palace, the more specialized skills bestowed a higher status. Thus specialist craftsmen, scribes, cult personnel, and administrators all had their particular positions.

For a long time, military elites topped this hierarchy: specialist charioteers in these societies were highly prized and well rewarded for their services. In the Syro-Palestinian area they were designated with the term *mariyannu*, which became a generic term for an elite social status. The rewards given to palace dependents were issued in various forms: rations for the lower levels, payments and the usufruct of fields for the higher ones. As service was expected in return, the use of these fields was granted on an individual basis, not to families. Later in the period, military elites tried to make tenancies heritable and paid for this in silver rather than with services.

Document 7.2   *Babylonian literature in the Greater Near East*

The elites of the Near East in the late second millennium shared a literary tradition that was fundamentally inspired by Babylonia. Throughout the palaces of the time were kept cuneiform tablets with compositions in the Babylonian language. The content was sometimes adapted to local tastes, however. The following example derives from a collection of counsels given by a man with a Babylonian name, Shupe-Ameli, to his son. The composition was found in variant versions in Emar and Ugarit in Syria, and in Hattusa, the Hittite capital, where a partial Hittite translation had been added. No version of it is known from Babylonia proper, but the text fully fits within the cultural tradition of the region, where this genre of literature originated in the third millennium.

Do not open your heart to a woman you care for,
Seal it up, even if she wrestles or attacks.
Keep your present in a strong room,
let your wife not know what's in your purse.
Those who came before us established this,
our fathers only divided income with the gods.
They drove in a peg, made firm a ring and attached clay (i.e., they sealed off the door).
Keep your seal on a ring.
Surround the ring, and guard your house.
May your seal be the only access to your assets.
Whatever you see, leave it.
Only when you need it, spend it.

Translation after Foster 2005: 418.

The free people, however, were not entirely outside government control: they were also obliged to pay taxes or provide corvée labor when requested. But they owned their fields, often as a community rather than as individuals, where they scratched a poor living from the soil. The palace gave them some support: in the irrigation societies of Mesopotamia and Egypt, they maintained the canal system, while other infrastructures were probably kept up elsewhere. The extent of the free sectors of the various societies is hard to establish and varied from state to state. In terms of social stratification, its members, together with the agricultural palace serfs, were at the bottom. Much of their labor and the harvests they produced were usurped by those higher up, as the elites' wealth had to be created somewhere. To some extent the wealth came from foreign conquests – in the case of Egypt, especially from Nubia with its goldmines – but the mass of producers in each of these states must have carried a heavy burden. The rulers no longer felt the obligation to restore social balances wholesale, as they had done in the early part of the millennium, and the level of indebted servitude increased substantially. Individuals and families had little respite from this system, and consequently many fled their communities and sought refuge outside the grasp of the states. They joined groups in inaccessible regions, such as mountains or deserts, and crossed political boundaries to escape their former masters. This development explains why the return of refugees was so important in the international treaties of the period, as states could not afford to lose the manpower. In the end, this social erosion may have been one of the main causes the entire system collapsed, as I will discuss in a later chapter.

Debate 7.1 *Synchronizing histories in the Late Bronze Age eastern Mediterranean*

If establishing the chronology of a single region is already complex (see debate 1.1), integrating the data from all the cultures of the eastern Mediterranean in the second half of the second millennium into a coherent system is an even greater problem. It is a necessity, however, as international relations epitomize the period and can only be understood properly if we know what happened simultaneously in the histories of the different participants. Were the absolute chronologies of all cultures secure all problems would be solved, but the situation is the opposite: information from various sources and cultures gives solutions that seem incompatible. Numerous research projects and conferences have addressed the issues involved (e.g., Bietak 2000–7), and opinions remain much divided. The discussions can be very technical and often use opaque terminology (e.g., short chronology, modified short chronology), and regularly leave non-experts mystified.

Evidence from textual sources derives almost exclusively from Assyria, Babylonia, and Egypt, where ancient king lists provide sequences that can be connected to more secure first millennium dates. No such information exists for important states like Hatti and Mittani, which did not survive after 1200. Fortunately we can establish synchronisms between various histories on the basis of diplomatic correspondence and treaties. We know, for example, that the reigns of Burnaburiash II of Babylon and Akhenaten of Egypt overlapped because they wrote Amarna letters to each other. We know that Ramesses II fought Muwatalli II of Hatti in the battle of Qadesh and that he concluded a peace treaty with the latter's second successor, Hattusili III, fifteen years later. Other such synchronisms exist. Scholars who base themselves on textual evidence tend to support a low chronology (see Kitchen 2007 for a survey).

Scientists have much to contribute to the debate and can rely on data that seem more firm, such as radiocarbon (^{14}C), dendrochronology (dating wood by the shape of its tree rings), and ice cores from Iceland. A major natural event occurred in the Aegean in the second millennium: the eruption of the volcanic island Thera (modern Santorini), which caused a tsunami destroying coastal sites and emitted huge quantities of ash into the air that left traces in the Icelandic ice cores. The event should be datable in absolute terms, and provide archaeologists with a firm point to anchor their pottery sequences, which are especially elaborated for the Aegean world. The finds at Thera show that the eruption happened during the so-called Late Minoan IA archaeological period and because the Aegean exported many vessels to the Levant and Egypt it should provide chronological information for other cultures as well. Many complications exist (see Wiener 2007 for a survey), but this evidence supports a long chronology as the eruption seems to have taken place in the late seventeenth century, a hundred years earlier than the short chronology that textual information suggests would allow (Manning 1999; Manning et al. 2006).

The debate appears to be at an impasse (Wiener 2003). Whenever someone suggests changing a piece of the puzzle it affects the entire structure, which can necessitate very different historical reconstructions. For example, if we accept the ultra-short chronology for Mesopotamia that places the fall of Babylon in 1499 (Gasche et al. 1998), the Hittite raid that caused it as well as the sack of Aleppo must have taken place at the same time as Egypt's military actions in northern Syria. How does the rise of the Mittani state fit that scenario? On the other extreme, if the Thera eruption took place in Egypt's early New Kingdom period and thus pulls the date of the start of that era up to 1650 (Bietak 2003), how can we explain the later synchronisms with Babylonia and Assyria?

NOTES

1   Translation after Moran 1992: no. 9.
2   Moran 1992: no. 1.
3   Beckman 1999: 149.
4   Moran 1992: no. 3.
5   Moran 1992: no. 19.
6   Beckman 1999: 106.

8

The Western States of the Late Second Millennium

3000	2500	2000	1500	1000	500

ca. 1500	Parrattarna of Mittani rules northern Syria and northern Mesopotamia
1344–1322	Reign of Suppiluliuma of Hatti
ca. 1325	Aziru of Amurru switches allegiance from Egypt to Hatti
1267	Hattusili III usurps Hittite throne
1259	Peace treaty between Hattusili III and Ramesses II of Egypt

The states that made up the international system of the Near East in the Late Bronze Age all had discrete histories, which we can reconstruct with varying detail on the basis of their own sources. One significant feature of this period is the fact so many places provide us with independent historical information at the same time, a situation unprecedented in the history of the ancient Near East. Although foreign relations crucially affected what happened everywhere, internal factors continued to shape local histories; we have to remember that each was situated in a distinctive ecological environment and was made up of different populations, who often spoke a multitude of languages, and had diverse cultural and religious preferences. In the next two chapters we will step back from the international character of the time to look at these distinct histories, although they all involve a lot of international affairs: here we will focus on the states in the western part of the Near East, while the next chapter will deal with those in the east.

A History of the Ancient Near East ca. 3000–323 BC, Third Edition. Marc Van De Mieroop.
© 2016 John Wiley & Sons, Inc. Published 2016 by John Wiley & Sons, Inc.

8.1   Mittani

The political history of Mittani is much more difficult to write than that of its great neighbors because of the near total absence of official texts from the state itself. Egyptian, Hittite, and Assyrian sources are our primary guide, which we can complement with mostly legal and administrative documents from vassal territories. Very few texts from the core of the state are known; they include a handful of records of legal transactions sworn before the king. But no royal archives have been found so far. The state was known under various designations: the native term was Maittani, later Mittani, a name we also find in texts from Palestinian cities and the Hittites. Simultaneously, Hanigalbat was in use in Mittanian writings, and in texts from Assyria, Babylonia, and Hatti. The Hittites also referred to the state as the "land of the Hurrians," while Egyptians used Nahrina as well. This variation in terminology seems to depend on whether one referred to the state as a polity (Mittani, Hanigalbat), to the perceived ethnicity of its inhabitants (Hurrians), or to its location on the Euphrates River (Nahrina).

The center of the Mittani state was the north Syrian area between the Tigris and the Euphrates, some 400 kilometers (250 miles) from east to west. At the height of its power it incorporated territories beyond these limits, to the east of the Tigris and on the south coast of Anatolia. In the south it had influence along the Middle Euphrates valley and perhaps bordered Babylonia directly. We cannot determine at present how far north it reached. Its capital was Washukanni, a city that has not been identified archaeologically, but most likely it was situated in northern Syria near the sources of the Habur River. A secondary capital called Taidu was located farther east at the modern site of Tell al-Hamidiya.

Another difficulty in the study of Mittani's history is uncertainty about chronology. The exact lengths of the reigns of all its rulers are unknown because no ancient king list is preserved (for a list of kings, see Section 10 of the King Lists at the end of the book). We also cannot establish when exactly we first encounter the state. The earliest references to it are in the accounts of eighteenth-dynasty Egyptian rulers, but their campaigns can be associated with various Mittanian kings. So there is no firm chronological point that anchors Mittani history into that of Egypt. In particular, the early history of the state is a mystery. We know that northern Syria in the eighteenth century was made up of small kingdoms, while around 1500 there was a Mittanian ruler with broad regional powers. How and exactly when his state developed is uncertain, but the power vacuum left after the Hittite destruction of Aleppo around 1600 probably made the creation of a new entity possible. It is clear that by the first half of the fifteenth century the Mittanian king, Parrattarna, had control as suzerain over an area including Kizzuwatna (Cilicia in southwest Anatolia) in the west, Nuzi across the Tigris in the east, and Terqa on the Euphrates in the south. His state was the most powerful in western Asia, and the only obstacle to early eighteenth-dynasty Egyptian expansion there. It was made up of several vassal areas under rulers who owed obedience to the Mittanian king. This is most clearly visible in an autobiographical inscription carved on a statue found at Alalakh in which the local

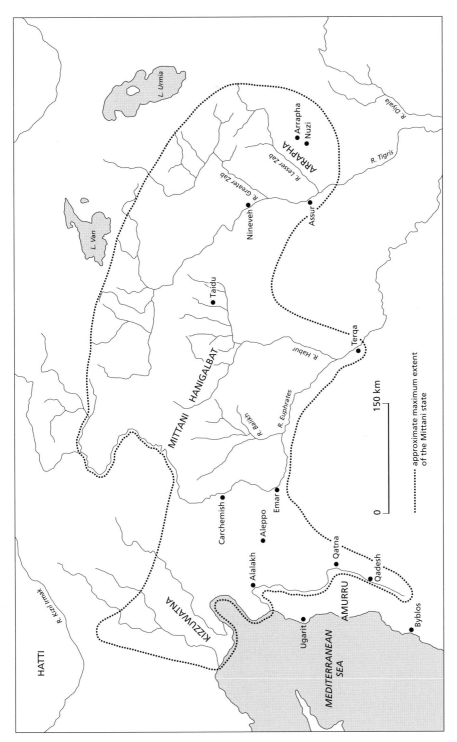

Map 8.1 The Mittani state. After Volkert Haas, ed., *Hurrier und Hurritisch* (Konstanz: Universitätverlag, 1988), p. 295.

Figure 8.1   Statue of King Idrimi. This stone statue was excavated at Alalakh in 1939 and dates to the sixteenth century. The long inscription written in faulty Babylonian cuneiform that covers most of it describes how King Idrimi came to power in that city after he left Aleppo and used *habiru* forces to seize control. British Museum, London, H. 104 cm (41 in). Credit: © The Trustees of the British Museum.

king, Idrimi, relates how he acquired power there (figure 8.1). For unspecified reasons, he and his brothers fled their hometown Aleppo for the city of Emar on the Euphrates. Unhappy at remaining an underling there, Idrimi decided to leave Emar and roam the countryside of Canaan, where he became a leader of the *habiru*, that is, social outcasts (see debate 8.1). With this power behind him he captured the city of Alalakh and its surroundings. Then he contacted the Mittanian king, Parrattarna, who endorsed Idrimi's rule and made him his vassal. The text shows the Mittani state at the height of its powers when it could determine who ruled areas far beyond its heartland. It is also clear, however, that Idrimi had taken the initiative and that the Mittani king was forced to accept him as vassal.

The dominance of Mittani in northern Syria continued until the mid-fourteenth century, and the Egyptian kings of the early eighteenth dynasty who campaigned repeatedly in the region mention the state as a significant opponent. The conflict between the two major states was not direct; both tried to make local rulers in the coastal area of Syria their vassals by threatening military action. But, after initial hostile relations Amenhotep II of Egypt (ruled 1427–1400) began to treat Mittani's King Saustatar as an ally, and soon afterwards we see how Mittani's power dissipated in a relatively short period of time. The history of this decline is complex, but in essence two branches of the royal family competed for the throne, and gave up their independence by seeking outside support for their respective claims. Tushratta, who corresponded with Egypt's King Amenhotep III (ruled 1390–1352) in the Amarna archive, had been placed on the throne by the unnamed murderer of his older brother. Initially Amenhotep had resented this state of affairs, and only after Tushratta executed his brother's assassin did he reestablish diplomatic relations and asked to marry Tushratta's daughter. But during Tushratta's reign, another brother, Artatama, established a rival kingship with initial support from the Hittites. A later Hittite treaty described the existence of two kingdoms: one of Mittani under Tushratta and one of the Hurrians under Artatama. Artatama's son, Shuttarna III, may have murdered Tushratta, and he shifted his allegiance from Hatti to the newly ascendant state of Assyria to his east. This roused the ire of the Hittite King Suppiluliuma I, who for many years had raided the land of Mittani and picked off most of its west Syrian allies. He thus took the side of a son of Tushratta, Kili-Teshub, who had sought his help. Suppiluliuma placed him on the throne of what remained of the Mittani state, and under the name of Shattiwaza made him his vassal, marrying him off to one of his daughters. The west of the state was thus under Hittite control, while in the east Assyria dominated. Egypt did not intervene in these matters at all, perhaps because it had already lost its grip over northwest Syria. From 1365 to 1335, the Mittani state went thus from a regional superpower to a divided state with both parts subservient to foreign kings.

The Hittites allowed the rump of the Mittani state to survive, and several of Shattiwaza's descendants occupied the throne. The Assyrians took advantage of a weakening of Hittite power after the death of Suppiluliuma to maintain pressure on the region. Under Adad-nirari I (ruled 1295–1264) and Shalmaneser I (ruled 1263–1234) they turned the core of the state gradually into Assyrian territory. They left a native dynasty in place, but its rulers were vassals. The remnants of the Mittani state, which the Assyrians always referred to as Hanigalbat, regularly resisted the Assyrians, seeking help from Hittites and Arameans, a new people in northern Syria who would become very important later on. They had little success, however. The Assyrians established administrative centers throughout their territory as far west as the east bank of the Euphrates River, where they faced Hittite fortresses on the west bank. They placed these centers in strategic locations to control trade and military movements. The death of the last strong Assyrian king, Tukulti-Ninurta I (ruled 1233–1197), coincided with the upheavals that shook the western Near East around 1200, and the disappearance of political centralization in the Mittani region was probably related to those events.

We have to base the study of Mittani society on documents found in cities outside the state's core, which in the fifteenth century were governed by local dynasties that were subject to the Mittani king: Alalakh in the extreme west and Nuzi in the extreme east. Idrimi's descendants made up Alalakh's royal house, while Nuzi had a "mayor" who was dependent on the king of Arrapha, himself a vassal of the Mittani ruler. Yet, Nuzi had a large central building and its texts referred to a "palace." The political structure of the Mittani state is poorly known, but the king's interference in local matters is clear from the use of the same royal seal on records from various places and from references to his legal authority in contracts. The different territories of the state shared certain common elements: agriculture depended on rainfall and village communities were strong. The courts and other urban residents relied on these villages for their support, and, as stated before, the relationship between the city and countryside was exploitative. The local palaces held censuses in order to calculate exactly how much taxation and corvée labor they could impose. In their records they divided the population into groups whose meanings are not fully clear to us, but they made a distinction between palace dependents and free villagers. Men designated with the term *mariyannu* dominated the first group. Their role initially had been in the military as charioteers, but they became involved in all aspects of life and seem to have formed a privileged urban class. In the countryside, people owed labor service to the palace as a result of its ownership of the lands they worked. Labor was in short supply and the palace and private landowners competed for access to it. At Nuzi a strange legal procedure existed that enabled well-off individuals to acquire land while keeping its original owners as farmers. In private archives from that city appears a type of contract, called "sale-adoption," in which a buyer had him- or herself "adopted" by the seller. A man named Tehip-tilla, for example, was adopted some fifty times. It seems that this fiction allowed him to use his new parents as *de facto* tenant farmers. Likewise he acquired indentured labor by paying off the debts of men who from then on had to take care of his fields and orchards. These practices were possible because of the high level of debt that the peasants carried. When they had to take out loans, interest rates were usually 50 percent and, unlike in earlier periods, the palace did not help these people out by periodically annulling outstanding debts. On the contrary, the king of Arrapha himself is known to have taken advantage of such practices to obtain access to labor and land. The peasantry was at the mercy of urban moneylenders, who could set any terms they wanted and acquired control over their resources.

The Hittites referred to the Mittani state as the "land of the Hurrians," and indeed one of the official languages of the state was Hurrian. Spoken in northern Syria and Mesopotamia for a millennium before, it never managed to become a commonly written language. Akkadian always dominated, including in the second half of the second millennium, when the administrative and legal texts from the entire Mittani state were written in the Babylonian dialect. The rarity of Hurrian texts may be due to a large extent to the fact that the Mittani capital, Washukanni,

---

Document 8.1 *Hurrian writings*

Relatively few texts that are written entirely in the Hurrian language exist, and they come mainly from the cities of Ugarit, Emar, and Hattusa. This scarcity does not give an accurate reflection of the importance of the language in the Near East of the second millennium, however. Many personal names over a wide area of Anatolia, northern Syria and Mesopotamia, and the Syro-Palestinian area, including the names of kings, were Hurrian. The common use of the language in speech is also clear from passages in Hittite texts, which regularly include Hurrian phrases or terms. This occurs often in descriptions of rituals where the cult official is quoted as speaking in Hurrian. The following passage appears in a Hittite tablet describing rituals of a priest identified as AZU:

Now the AZU-priest takes a goose with the left hand, and with the right hand he lifts the cedar wood from the incense-burner. Then he drips oil in a cup of water and performs the *katkiša* (Hurrian term) of the goddess Hepat. He puts the cedar in the cup of water, lifts the cup of water up, and pours the water towards the goddess.

He says the following in Hurrian: "*ašseš Hepat šuunip šiaai ahraai unamaa kešhepwe kelteieni ambaššini kelu.*" Then he pours water towards the one who commissioned the offering and sets the cup of water down on the table of woven reed.

Then the AZU-priest takes the cedar wood from the incense-burner and throws it in the *huprushi*-vessel (Hurrian term) on the hearth, and says in Hurrian: "*aharreš laplihhineš,* etc." And he holds the goose out to the one who commissioned the offering and puts his hand on it. The AZU-priest takes a piece out of its breast, dips it in oil from the incense-burner, throws it in the *huprushi*-vessel on the hearth, and says in Hurrian: "*anahiteneš tatuššeneš kelu.*"

Translation after Salvini & Wegner 1986: 40–2.

---

has not been identified and excavated. A long letter by Tushratta fully written in Hurrian, found at Amarna, demonstrates that the Mittani court did have a chancellery with scribes who could write the language. In content the letter parallels those written in Babylonian, so we do not know why its writer used that language and who in Egypt was able to read it. Other texts or passages in the Hurrian language appear in the archives of such cities as Ugarit, Qatna, and Hattusa, while people with Hurrian names lived all over Anatolia, Syria-Palestine, and eastern Mesopotamia (see document 8.1). This reveals how widely the language was spoken outside the Mittani state.

8.2 The Hittite New Kingdom

The central area of Anatolia in the second millennium was the core region of the kingdom of the Hittites, called Hatti in ancient sources. Its capital city, Hattusa, is our predominant source of texts, which contain much information on political history (see box 8.1). The treaties that the Hittite kings regularly concluded had introductions that outlined past relations between the two states, and these provide some of our best evidence, albeit very biased, on their political histories. Yet, the writing of Hittite history is faced with many chronological difficulties. Several of the Hittite kings bore the same names, for example, Tudhaliya or Arnuwanda,

---

Box 8.1   *Hittite historiography*

The reconstruction of Hittite history is to a great extent based on accounts the Hittites themselves wrote, covering events in a chronological sequence over several reigns or in successive years of a single reign. These are found as freestanding texts or included in edicts and international treaties. Among the first group are annals, year-by-year accounts primarily of military campaigns, which appear already in the Old Kingdom when Hattusili I left a bilingual Hittite–Akkadian account of his military accomplishments. This type of text became very widely written in Assyria after the disappearance of the Hittite state in the twelfth century. It is likely that the Hittite practice inspired the Assyrian genre, one of our main sources for the reconstruction of first-millennium history.

From the Old Kingdom on, the Hittites also summarized, mainly military, events over several reigns. The sixteenth-century edict of Telipinu, for example, recounts the campaigns of preceding kings as far back as the founder of the dynasty, Labarna (see document 6.2). Also in international affairs they kept track of former relations between Hatti and other states. Treaties customarily described the previous hostile and friendly interactions between the partners over several generations. In this sense they were not followed by the Assyrians, who both in their annalistic accounts and in their, admittedly few, treaties focused on the present.

Not only did the Hittites record annals, but they also preserved these texts in later centuries. Much of the Hittite textual record available to us comes from the last century of Hattusa's existence, the thirteenth century, and it includes newly made copies of historical documents from many centuries earlier. While we cannot always determine when they were composed, some fragmentary older manuscripts show that the Annals of Hattusili, for example, were compiled in or close to his reign.

Why the Hittites had this concern with past events in previous reigns is difficult to determine. While they saw some causal relations between the past and the present (in prayers to the gods, King Mursili II asked what deeds in the past had caused a plague), they did not seek explanations beyond the fact that it was the wish of the gods. In that sense, they shared the ideas of their contemporaries. Hittite historical records are very detailed and structured in such a way that modern historians are tempted to use them as a template for their reconstructions of Hittite political history, but they have to be treated with great caution. They often portray the idea that the present king's actions led to a good situation, while those of his predecessors caused misery. Our accounts of Hittite history are mostly based on this heavily biased evidence, as we often lack external data to verify statements. We have to remain alert then to the aims of the authors.

and while today we number them I, II, etcetera, this was not done in the native sources. Thus, often we cannot determine the ruler to which a text relates. The absolute chronology is problematic as well. The Hittites did not leave us king lists and even for the creator of the New Kingdom state, Suppiluliuma I, we have different suggestions for the length of his rule, varying from twenty-two to forty years. Not a single moment of Hittite history can be dated without synchronisms to Egypt, Assyria, or Babylonia, and the points of contact we have are few and mostly from the later part of Hittite history. While in practice we assign absolute dates to the individual rulers, these are always approximate and may need revision, especially according to changes in our understanding of Egyptian chronology.

Geographically, the Hittite state's borders shifted constantly. The capital city was in central Anatolia in the basin of the Kızıl Irmak River, and military expansion was especially directed toward the south, where in its heyday Hatti controlled western Syria. It is unclear whether its borders in the north and west extended as far as the shores of the Black and Aegean seas, which were closer to Hattusa than was Syria (see map 8.2). As the state's political structure was not one of direct territorial control but of domination over vassals, the relative dependence of regions within the Hittite sphere of influence determined the borders more than actual hegemony. Throughout the period discussed here, there was clearly a greater interest in Syria than in the peripheral areas of Anatolia, and the political center of the state lay at its northern edge.

The Hittite state existed for a comparatively short time, from about 1800 to 1200. It knew two periods of great strength, one in the seventeenth century referred to as the Old Kingdom, the other from about 1400 to 1200, the New Kingdom period (for a list of kings, see Sections 9 and 11 of the King Lists at the end of the book). Sometimes the term Middle Kingdom is used to refer to the period in between, but as Hatti was in decline, the historian's grasp of what happened then is very weak. A number of poorly documented rulers led the road to recovery. They reaffirmed Hittite dominance over central and southern Anatolia, including the area of Kizzuwatna on the southeast coast, which Mittani had ruled before. Moreover, Aleppo, the foremost city in northwestern Syria that was vital for access to regions farther south, had to shift allegiance from Mittani to Hatti. The Hittites' competitors in the region were Egypt and Mittani, two states that had fought each other before, but in the early fourteenth century they joined forces perhaps in reaction to the Hittite advances. Egypt also tried to establish good relations with Arzawa to the west of Hatti, including the proposal of a diplomatic marriage, in order to contain the emerging power. And indeed, the west and north presented great difficulties to Hatti: a vassal of the west, King Madduwatta, conquered southwest Anatolia and Cyprus in the mid-fourteenth century, and the Kaskeans, a people from the south coast of the Black Sea, attacked and perhaps even destroyed Hattusa.

Suppiluliuma I (ruled 1344–1322), one of the Hittites' ablest military leaders, reversed these setbacks, however, and he was the true founder of the Hittite New Kingdom. After solidifying his control over Anatolian regions to the south and east of the Hittite heartland, he invaded the Mittani state from the north

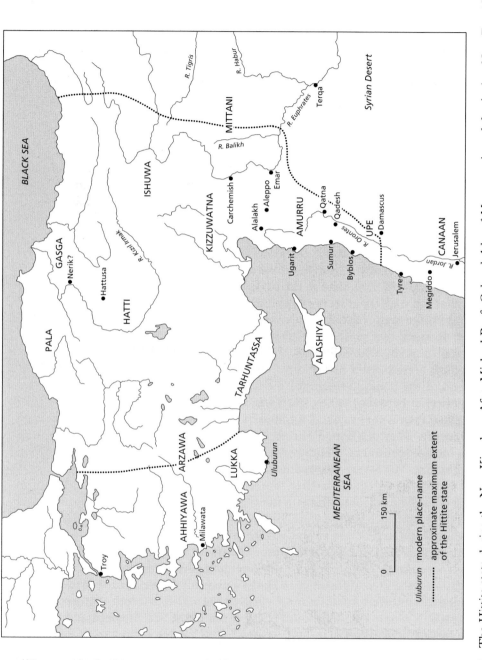

Map 8.2 The Hittite state during the New Kingdom. After Michael Roaf, *Cultural Atlas of Mesopotamia and the Ancient Near East* (Oxford: Equinox, 1990), p. 139.

and occupied its capital, Washukanni. Western Mittani became his vassal. Along the Syrian coast to the west of the Euphrates he extended Hittite control as far south as Damascus and forced the rulers of the small states there into submission. Niqmadu of Ugarit came to him in Alalakh offering to become his vassal, Aziru of Amurru switched allegiance from Egypt to him, and in Qatna Suppiluliuma placed a new king friendly to him, Idadda, on the throne. His main competitor in the region, Egypt, was at the time less attentive to its Asiatic territories, and did not counter Hittite expansion directly. The highly unusual request by the recently widowed queen of Egypt for a son of Suppiluliuma to become her husband, mentioned in the previous chapter, came at this moment. If the union had taken place it would have given Suppiluliuma influence over a gigantic area, but unknown Egyptians prevented it by assassinating Zannanza, the son he sent.

The reign ended in disaster, however. Probably Suppiluliuma himself and his first successor both died of a plague that soldiers had brought home from Syria when they retaliated for Egypt's murder of Zannanza. Another son, Mursili II (ruled 1321–1295), was young when he ascended the throne, but he was able to maintain control over Syria, where many vassals rebelled, and also devoted attention to the Anatolian areas his father had ignored. He defeated Arzawa in the west and attacked the Kaskeans in the north. The latter continued to present a threat, however, even taking the capital Hattusa in the reign of Muwatalli II (ruled 1295–1272). This suggests that Hatti left its northern flank ill-guarded because of its preoccupation with Syria. And Muwatalli was very much focused on Syria, to the extent that he moved his capital to a previously obscure city in the south of Anatolia, Tarhuntassa (exact location unknown).

Egypt's reemergence under the nineteenth dynasty and its incessant campaigning in Syria culminated in the battle of Qadesh between Ramesses II and Muwatalli in 1274 (discussed in the previous chapter). The Egyptian gave this event enormous attention in inscriptions and representations, despite the fact that he lost the battle, something he failed to acknowledge but which is evident from the subsequent expansion of Hittite control over southern Syria. The battle presents the climax of the centuries-long rivalry between Egypt and Hatti over Syria, one in which the Hittites typically had the upper hand. In order to concentrate on Syria, Muwatalli left his brother, the future King Hattusili III, in charge of the northern areas of the Hittite state. The latter liberated Hattusa as well as the cult center of Nerik, which had been lost to the Kaskeans many years before. But when Muwatalli's son, Urhi-Teshub, came to power under the throne-name Mursili III (ruled 1272–1267), Hattusili III used the north as a power base from which to undermine the young king. Although Urhi-Teshub as legitimate heir may have had the support of Egypt and Babylonia, Hattusili III managed to remove him after several years of intrigue. Hattusili remained king of Hatti for another thirty years (1267–1237), and his peace treaty with Egypt's Ramesses II was the major accomplishment of his reign. In 1259, fifteen years after the battle of Qadesh, the two kings concluded a detailed arrangement to end hostilities, establish a defensive alliance, and exchange political refugees. The threat of Assyria, now in full control over much of the Mittani area, probably inspired their alliance. Most likely, Hattusili was also concerned about rivalries inside the Hittite court and his own succession, and later events show how well founded his fears were. While the relations between the two powers may not have been as cordial as was hoped, the struggle over Syria was over.

Hatti declined rapidly, however, due to problems similar to those that had confronted Mittani a hundred and twenty years earlier. Internally, the designated heir to the throne, Tudhaliya IV (ruled 1237–1209), had to deal with a powerful claim by a son of Muwatalli, Kurunta, whom Hattusili III had made "king of Tarhuntassa." Kurunta may have temporarily deposed Tudhaliya IV in 1228–1227, when he appeared as "Great King" on sealings found at Hattusa. In any case, Tudhaliya regained the throne. External pressures were great as well. Tukulti-Ninurta I of Assyria (ruled 1233–1197) attacked the Hittite state from the east, and vassals in the west and southwest of Anatolia rebelled. Trouble in the regions adjoining the Aegean sea may have been inspired by an elusive "king of Ahhiyawa," certainly a major player in the area, but hard to pinpoint in space and time. Tudhaliya IV was able to take Milawata (classical Miletus) from them, but in the end Hatti's grasp over western Anatolia seems to have slipped.

When Suppiluliuma II came to the throne in 1207, the fall of Hatti was imminent. The causes of its collapse as a territorial state are not fully clear to us (see debate 10.1). Archaeology shows that the public buildings in the capital Hattusa were burned down, but the court had abandoned the city beforehand. Other important cities under Hittite control, such as Ugarit, Alalakh, and Emar, disappeared and Egyptian sources evoke a general devastation of the entire Anatolian and west Syrian region. But certain Hittite cities survived, most prominently Carchemish, where members of a branch of the Hittite royal family continued to refer to themselves as "Great Kings" for centuries to come. The end of Hattusa must be seen within the context of the collapse of the entire regional system around 1200, which we will discuss in a later chapter, but in contrast to other areas, no Hittite state would ever reappear in central Anatolia.

Hittite history was to a great extent determined by events in the west and north of Anatolia. It is clear that major states existed there, such as Arzawa whose king corresponded with Egypt's as an equal. The most important kingdom west of Hatti in the later part of the period was that of Ahhiyawa. The writing of its history is complicated by the question of whether or not it had anything to do with the Mycenaean Greeks, who certainly established commercial outposts on the Anatolian coast. The similarity between the names Ahhiyawa and Achaians, Homer's term for the Greeks, has suggested this equation from the first discovery of the name Ahhiyawa. A scholarly consensus is growing that such is indeed the case and that we find evidence of Mycenaean political and military interactions with the Hittites in texts from Hattusa. We can thus connect the rich archaeological culture from Mycenaean Greece to the history of the eastern Mediterranean at this time (figure 8.2). From the fifteenth century on Ahhiyawa appeared in Hittite sources, but it remained of minor importance until two centuries later. At that time, Hattusili III, attempting to restore order in western districts, wrote to Ahhiyawa's king and addressed him as brother, in order to convince him to

Figure 8.2 Lion gate at Mycenae. If indeed the Ahhiyawa of Hittite texts are the same as Homer's Achaeans, the rich archaeological remains of the Mycenaean culture on mainland Greece and the Aegean islands become an integral part of ancient Near Eastern history. Those remains attest to a rich warrior society with heavily fortified fortresses and lavish tombs. Shown here is the entrance gate to the citadel of Mycenae built with massive monoliths around 1250. The sculpture representing lions had parallels in the entrance gates found at Hattusa and other Hittite cities. Credit: akg images/Album/Prisma.

control rebels active in his territory. His successor, Tudhaliya IV, invaded the territory of Ahhiyawa and clearly regarded it as a major state. In his treaty with Shaushga-muwa of Amurru he listed those kings who he considered to be his equals: Egypt, Babylonia, and Assyria. The king of Ahhiyawa completed that list, but after writing it down the scribe erased the words. Whatever the meaning of that erasure, it is evident that the latter's status around that time had been regarded as that of a Great King. After Tudhaliya IV textual information regarding the Ahhiyawans disappears, possibly because of the disturbances in Greece at that time.

In the area north of Hattusa the Kaskean people were in control, and the Hittites always portrayed them as aggressive and wild tribesmen who raided and captured cities. One of Hattusili III's duties during his brother's reign had been to regain territory occupied by the Kaskeans. These people may have contributed to the troubles that ended Hittite history, but we are uninformed about the details. The west and north of Anatolia were thus never fully integrated into the Hittite state, although they were the targets of many military campaigns. Nevertheless, their interactions with Hatti tied them into the political system of the Near East.

The political structure of the Hittite state is often compared to that of medieval western European vassalage. The Great King of Hatti directly governed the core area, but used vassals to control most regions of Anatolia and Syria. These were locals who swore allegiance to him, but who could switch it to other powers. Although Hittite princes administered certain key places such as Carchemish and Aleppo at strategic points in northern Syria, other regions kept indigenous dynasties while under Hittite supremacy. Two such centers are well known through their own sources – Ugarit on the Syrian coast and Emar of the kingdom of Astata on the Euphrates. The Hittite overlords seemingly continued to respect local traditions and did not attempt to unify the entire region in political or cultural terms. In this sense, the organization of the Hittite state seems to parallel that of Mittani, and the people of northern Syria were thus able to maintain their own cultures and political hierarchies.

The king's supreme status was beyond doubt, however. He bore a set of titles that clearly identified him as such, including that of "Great King" and of "the Sun." He also had an old Hattic title, Labarna or Tabarna, which may refer to the name of the first ruler of the dynasty, while his wife was given the title Tawananna, probably alluding to the first queen. She had much power, which she exercised even upon her husband's death, and she engaged in diplomacy with foreign courts on her own. Hattusili III's wife Puduhepa, for example, personally corresponded with Ramesses II about his marriage to her daughter. There were repeated problems with royal succession; oftentimes the father–son sequence was not respected and a brother became king. This led to one of the best-documented struggles for kingship in Near Eastern history between the son and the brother of Muwatalli. Urhi-Teshub, the latter's son with a concubine, came to the throne under the name Mursili III, but Hattusili III, Muwatalli's brother, rebelled and overthrew his nephew after five years. The usurpation of power was a sufficient breach of the law for Hattusili to compose a long document, his *Apology*, in which he explained his actions. In it he described how he was put in charge of the northern territories while his brother had moved the capital to the southern region of Tarhuntassa, and how he successfully conquered peripheral areas for his brother. When Muwatalli's son came to the throne, Hattusili initially supported him but became increasingly frustrated with his nephew. In order to preserve his power and that of his friends, Hattusili rebelled. He deposed Urhi-Teshub and sent him into exile in an outlying part of the state – he managed to flee to Egypt later on. In order to justify this act, Hattusili made accusations that Urhi-Teshub had used magic, which shows the weakness of the legality of his claim to kingship.

The titulary and names of the rulers of Hatti demonstrate the multicultural character of the state. The title Tabarna and the royal throne names were Hattic, that is, of a group of Anatolian people who had perhaps dominated the area of Hattusa many centuries earlier. But the birth-names of the kings were of different origin: Urhi-Teshub, for example, was clearly a Hurrian name. Yet the official language of the chancellery at Hattusa was Hittite. Moreover, the archives excavated there also held texts in other Anatolian languages, such as Luwian and Palaic, while scribes who could write in the Mesopotamian languages Akkadian and Sumerian worked there as well. All of these texts were written in cuneiform. Simultaneously, an Anatolian hieroglyphic script was used on official monuments

Figure 8.3   Letter from King Tudhaliya IV of Hatti to the king of Ugarit. In this brief
message in Akkadian Tudhaliya informs Ugarit's king of his decision that no horses from
Hatti can go to Egypt and vice versa. In the center of the tablet the scribe impressed
Tudhaliya's official seal, inscribed with the two official languages of the court. On the rim the
king's name and titles are written in two lines of cuneiform, while the center provides the
information in Luwian hieroglyphs. Louvre Museum, Paris, AO20191. H. 10 cm; W. 7.8 cm
(4 × 3 in). Credit: akg images/Erich Lessing.

and personal seals and rendered the Luwian language. That script survived the
end of the Hittite state (figure 8.3).

The literature recorded at Hattusa derived from a great variety of sources.
Hurrian traditions are represented in a number of myths translated into Hittite.
Hattic elements are often found in shorter stories, while original Hittite material seems to have been rare. Certain literary texts from Babylonia were imported
wholesale, translated into Hittite, or adapted to local tastes by changing the leading deities to reflect Hittite preferences. The scribes of Hattusa copied lexical lists
from Mesopotamia, sometimes adding Hittite and Hurrian translations and information on how to pronounce the Sumerian terms. Many Anatolian myths seem
to have had a ritual function and the prescriptive rituals show a great variety of
languages, including Hattic and Hurrian. The Hittites also imported Canaanite
mythology from the Syro-Palestinian areas they had conquered.

Hatti was thus certainly one of the most important states of the Near East
in the second half of the second millennium, and a leading participant in the

international culture of the time (see figure 8.4). Its location at the edges of the Near Eastern world exposed it more to outside pressures than its colleagues and its internal political structure was relatively loose. Consequently, its collapse was sudden and almost total. Central Anatolia in the first millennium would be very different from what we observe in the New Kingdom period.

8.3 Syria-Palestine

Located in between the powerful states of Egypt, Hatti, and Mittani, the Syro-Palestinian area remained politically fragmented. It was where the great powers competed for hegemony and its inhabitants bore the brunt of the numerous military campaigns that characterize the period. The region stretched from the south of Anatolia, between the Mediterranean and the Euphrates, to southern Palestine, where it bordered the Sinai Desert. It ran along the coast in a band that became increasingly narrow the farther south one went, from some 200 kilometers (125 miles) in the north to some 70 kilometers (45 miles) in the south. The Syrian Desert and the Jordanian mountains, regions where urban settlement was impossible, set its eastern border.

We can reconstruct the history of this area not only through documents from the nearby great powers, but also from an increasing number of texts found in excavations in the region itself, as every palace employed scribes for bookkeeping and to maintain contacts with foreign leaders. The Amarna correspondence includes letters from some forty Syro-Palestinian vassals to the king of Egypt. Some cities have yielded substantial numbers of written documents, especially three in the north – Ugarit, Alalakh, and Emar – where they appeared not only in palaces and temples, but also in private residences. Smaller collections were excavated at Kummidu and Qatna. The language of most of the texts was Babylonian but local vernaculars often heavily influenced the scribes' writing. In the Amarna correspondence appear many traces of the west Semitic dialects people spoke, while at Qatna scribes inserted a large number of Hurrian expressions into their texts. Simultaneously, local languages and alphabetic scripts were in use, very poorly attested except at Ugarit, where a cuneiform alphabetic script written on clay tablets existed. Scribes in the region thus had to be able to work with multiple languages and scripts. Clearly Babylonia provided the paradigm of how to write, that is, in syllabic cuneiform on clay tablets, and while the most respected language seems to have been Babylonian, the scribes readily penned down other languages as well.

The political fragmentation of the region made it an easy target for expansion by the great powers surrounding it, and its wealth and technological expertise made it an appealing prey. Throughout the period under consideration outsiders constantly dominated almost the entire area, and their point of view dictates our reconstruction of political history. When the obscure centuries of the mid-second millennium ended, Mittani ruled northern Syria and governed the region west of the Euphrates through a system of vassals. Mittanian control extended as far south as Qadesh and as far west as Kizzuwatna in southern Anatolia. But with the rise of the eighteenth dynasty, Egypt expanded rapidly into the region. After conquering Palestine, sometimes inflicting severe destruction on cities there, Egypt picked off Mittanian vassals farther north, reaching Ugarit on the coast and Qadesh inland. The two powers fought over the states bordering on Mittani. Egypt's army raided as far as the Euphrates valley, while Mittani supported local resistance to those raids.

Egypt's control over the regions it had conquered, well documented in the Amarna letters, was more direct than that of Mittani. It set up three provinces, Amurru, Upe, and Canaan, each with an administrative center under an Egyptian official, who was responsible for collecting critical resources directly. Native dynasts continued their rule over the small states but had to provide annual tribute. The vassals wrote many letters to the king, asking for help against trouble-some neighbors, pledging obedience, promising payments, and so on. Egypt remained aloof to most local problems and focused its attention on the collection of tribute, which it could do without a substantial military presence. During this period, we find little evidence of Egyptian campaigning in Asia, probably because its grasp on the region was firm and because Egypt and Mittani had become allies rather than enemies.

The threat to this arrangement came from Hatti in the north, whose king, Suppiluliuma I, had subdued Mittani shortly after 1340, and then expanded into territory Egypt saw as its own. Ugarit, Qadesh, Amurru, as well as all northern Syrian states previously dependent on Mittani, became Hittite vassals. The Hittite king placed his sons as viceroys in the key cities of Carchemish and Aleppo, and kept the Mittanian system of vassalage elsewhere. The governmental arrangements are well documented at Ugarit on the coast and Emar on the Euphrates River, where native dynasties continued to take care of most local affairs. The viceroy at Carchemish settled conflicts between vassals, while the king of Hatti received tribute and made arrangements of political and economic importance to the entire state. The treaties between the Hittite overlord and the vassals were expressed as personal agreements between two men, and were renewed whenever a new king ascended the throne. From such information we can recover the names of the local rulers, but we know little else about their political careers.

The division of Syria-Palestine between Hatti and Egypt remained stable until the beginning of the nineteenth dynasty in Egypt, when kings Sety I and Ramesses II tried to extend their control farther north. Muwatalli of Hatti thwarted this attempt at the battle of Qadesh (1274), and fifteen years later the two states con-cluded a peace treaty, probably under the pressure of Assyrian expansion into northern Syria. Egypt lost control over southern Syria and northern Palestine and Ramesses II built a line of fortresses close to the Egyptian border, while Hittite administration over the north continued according to the earlier pattern.

Amurru, a kingdom extending from the Mediterranean coast in northern modern-day Lebanon to the plain of Homs in Syria inland, can serve as an exam-ple of how Syro-Palestinian states interacted with their powerful neighbors (for a list of kings, see Section 12 of the King Lists at the end of the book). We know its history only from texts found outside the state, in the records of Hatti, Egypt, and Ugarit. Initially Amurru belonged to the Egyptian sphere of influence, probably as a result of campaigns by Tuthmose III (ruled 1390–1352), and it figured prominently in the Amarna correspondence. The early letters from that archive reveal that a man called Abdi-Ashirta seized control over several city-states, and that he even conquered Sumur, Egypt's administrative center in the region. He wanted to gain recognition as an Egyptian vassal, but he may have been too ambitious and the Egyptians were suspicious of his motives. His death, perhaps an assassination by one of his own courtiers, put an end to his accomplishments around 1345. Several of his sons (three or four) took over the rule of Amurru and one of them especially, Aziru, fought hard to make it the dominant power in central Syria. He too captured Sumur, which caused the pharaoh to order him to come to Egypt. When he was there he was officially made Egypt's vassal and king of Amurru – Egypt probably had little choice in the matter. His visit coincided with the start of Hatti's expansion into Syria under Suppiluliuma I, however, and he returned home to face the threat on Egypt's behalf. But Aziru realized that Hatti was more powerful and concluded a treaty with Suppiluliuma. His neighbors complained loudly to the pharaoh that he threatened their independence and urged them to betray Egypt. Rib-Adda of Byblos in particular wrote numerous letters that accused Aziru of trying to overthrow him. We do not know how much truth there was in these allegations. Rib-Adda certainly used hyperbole, but when Egypt's court called Aziru to account he refused to return there. Amurru was now firmly in the Hittite camp and settled its borders with other Hittite vassals such as Ugarit by treaty.

Aziru's second successor, Tuppi-Teshub, renewed the treaty with Hatti's King Mursili II, who was especially worried about the vigorous Egyptian expansion into Syria under the early nineteenth-dynasty rulers. But the next ruler of Amurru, Benteshina, thought that he could take advantage of Egypt's military successes and forsake Hatti. After the battle of Qadesh, Muwatalli II retaliated, defeated Benteshina and deported him to Hatti, where he placed him in the care of his brother who would later rule as Hattusili III. Muwatalli put one Shapili on the throne of Amurru, who was a reliable vassal for some fifteen years. But the political changes in Hatti had repercussions in Amurru politics as well: when Hattusili III grabbed power, he reinstated Benteshina as king of Amurru. The two kings concluded a treaty and confirmed their alliance through a dual marriage: Benteshina to Hattusili's daughter and Benteshina's daughter to Hattusili's son. Benteshina remained loyal and his son Shaushga-muwa in turn concluded a treaty with Tudhaliya IV, his brother-in-law and uncle (see document 8.2). The treaty stipulated that Amurru had to follow Hatti's lead in international relations. Its attitude toward Egypt and Babylonia should depend on that of Hatti, while Shaushga-muwa had to contribute troops to Hatti in its war with Assyria. Moreover, he was barred from sending merchants to Assyria, had to arrest and extradite Assyrian merchants, and intercept traders moving between Assyria and Ahhiyawa. The last reports about Amurru derive from Ugarit and involve the divorce of its ruler Ammistamru II from Benteshina's daughter. The affair was of sufficient concern to the king of Hatti that he personally intervened.

Document 8.2   *Excerpts from the treaty between Tudhaliya IV of Hatti and Shaushga-muwa of Amurru*

Almost all the later second-millennium treaties preserved derive from Hattusa, the Hittite capital. They stipulate the interactions between the Hittite overlord and his vassals and obviously focus on obedience but also guarantee protection in return. In its competition with the other great states it was crucial for Hatti that its vassals did not pursue independent foreign policies and the treaties specify what powers were friendly and what powers were not. In this case, Hatti was on good terms with Egypt and Babylonia, but at war with Assyria. Thus the king of Amurru had to ban Assyrian merchants from his territory and gather troops in support of Tudhaliya's war against Assyria. Of special interest in this treaty is that Ahhiyawa was originally listed as equal to Hatti, but that the name was erased from the tablet.

[Thus says Tabarna, Tudhaliya], Great King, [King of] Hatti, hero, beloved of the Sun-goddess of Arinna, [son of Hattusili, Great King, King of] Hatti, hero, [grandson of] Mursili, Great [King], King of Hatti, hero, [descendant of] Tudhaliya, [Great King, King of] Hatti, hero:

I, my Sun, [have taken you] Shaushga-muwa [by the hand], and have made you my brother-in-law. And you [shall not change the words] of this treaty tablet.

. . .

When [the king] of Egypt is my Sun's [friend], he will also be your friend. [But] when he is my Sun's enemy, he shall also be [your enemy]. And the kings who are equal to me in rank are the King of Egypt, the King of Babylonia, the King of Assyria, and the King of Ahhiyawa.[1] When the King of Egypt is my Sun's friend, he shall also be your friend. But when he is my Sun's enemy, he shall also be your enemy. When the King of Babylonia is my Sun's friend, he shall also be your friend. But when he is my Sun's enemy, he shall also be your enemy. Since the King of Assyria is my Sun's enemy, he shall also be your enemy. Your merchant shall not go to Assyria, and you shall not let his merchant into your country. He shall not pass through your country. If he would enter your country, take him and send him to my Sun. This matter [is placed] under an oath for you.

Since I, my Sun, am at war with the King of Assyria, gather together an army and a chariotry unit, as my Sun has done. Just as it is for my Sun an issue of urgency and . . . , it shall be for you an issue of urgency and . . . Gather together an army and a chariotry unit. This matter is placed under an oath for you.

No ship of Ahhiyawa shall go to him (the King of Assyria).

Translation after Beckman 1999: 103–8.
[1] The words "King of Ahhiyawa" were erased from the tablet.

Amurru's history exemplifies how dependent the Syro-Palestinian states were on their powerful neighbors. They had to yield to the political and military realities of the times, and switched allegiance between Mittani, Hatti, and Egypt whenever these powers' fortunes in the region changed. The Hittite treaties show how diplomatic agreements were expressed in personal terms and had to be reaffirmed whenever one of the rulers changed. The supremacy of the great states was evident, but it is also clear that often they could only endorse situations local rulers had created.

The Syro-Palestinian region illustrates most clearly the tension that existed between the lavish lifestyle of a small elite and the impoverished situation of the mass of the population. There were fewer cities in the region than in the preceding period, but those remaining were richer than before. A city like Ugarit had several palaces, large residences, and temples. The region was famed for its crafts: Egyptian tomb paintings often show Syrian tribute bearers as carrying elaborately manufactured furniture, vessels, ornaments, and so on. Artistic production was of very high quality, as archaeological finds document: works in gold, silver, and ivory appear throughout the region. Texts record the existence of guilds of craftsmen, such as jewelers, scribes, builders, etcetera, and show a high level of labor specialization in the cities.

This system collapsed around 1200 in a process that took several years. Many cities were sacked not by the regular armies of the past but by newcomers on the scene. The dates when this happened are not easy to establish. On the basis of radiocarbon dating archaeologists claim that the Syrian harbor of Gibala was destroyed between 1192 and 1190; Ugarit's correspondence with Egypt shows that it still existed in 1191 and the city seems to have disappeared between 1190 and 1185; Emar, located inland on the Euphrates, ceased to exist in or soon after 1185. Documents show that in its last years Ugarit faced much trouble, including attacks by seaborne raiders, and invasions of the Sea People reported in Egyptian sources were certainly partly responsible for the widespread upheavals. Other cities survived, however, albeit at a much poorer level, and the entirety of Syria-Palestine fell into historical obscurity lasting several centuries.

Highly trained men were also responsible for the composition and preservation of the literature of the region. These works are the only extensive remnants of literature from the Syro-Palestinian area in ancient Near Eastern history, except for the later Hebrew Bible, and they, together with some material remains, give an insight into the religious ideologies of the time. Ugarit provides the largest selection of texts, but cities such as Emar have yielded literary material as well. At Ugarit scribes composed a set of religious texts involving the native pantheon. The storm god Ba'al, a very important deity in Syria, was the main character of a cycle of myths that describe how he defeated the forces of chaos and rose to kingship over the gods. Human actors were also important, less as great warriors than as the ancestors to living kings. Tales of the mythical kings Aqhat and Keret relate their difficulties in having children, and the gods' intervention in this matter. The texts deal not only with the creation of a dynasty, but also with the cult of ancestors, which was of great concern in ritual texts as well. The Ugaritic accounts provide the most extensive record of what is often called Canaanite culture, the literary and religious traditions of western Syria and Palestine in the second millennium. These texts were recorded in the Ugaritic language and the cuneiform alphabet of that city, one that was relatively easy to learn with its reduced set of characters (see figure 10.3). But the scribes there also knew how to write in the Akkadian, Hurrian, and Hittite languages, using the Babylonian syllabic cuneiform. They were trained to do so in the same way as the Old Babylonian students, using a series of increasingly difficult tools: sign lists and lexical texts, which sometimes have added to them Ugaritic and Hurrian translation columns. They completed their training by copying literary texts. This instruction took place in the houses of accomplished scribes, and often the work was signed, so we know the name of the writer. Whereas the literature shows strong Babylonian influences, it is clear that the Egyptian presence in the region also had its cultural effects in the visual arts. Images of local gods appear with Egyptian crowns, for example.

Relatively small hinterlands and sparse populations supported the Syro-Palestinian cities. Estimates of their numbers are difficult to make, but records from Ugarit, for example, suggest that a rural population of 20,000 to 25,000 living in some 150 villages had to provide for an urban population of 6,000 to 8,000 people. Labor was thus in short supply, and palace policies exacerbated the situation. They made a distinction between the people they employed directly, the "people of the king," and those who were theoretically independent, "the sons of Ugarit." The former included the urban elites, who received full palace support, with a mixture of payments and agricultural land, sometimes even entire villages. Although these elites held their estates originally only for as long as they provided service, some were able to pass them on to their children and run them virtually as private property. While land was perhaps sufficiently available, labor was not, and independent villagers were conscripted by making them indebted to the urban residents. They were obliged to contribute taxes and corvée labor, but because of their restricted numbers the demands were often excessive. In order to meet taxes, they had to take out loans, and contracts from the period often include the statement that they had to provide service in return. This reduced their ability to work their own fields and led to an increased dependence on urban residents. Even kings recruited labor in this way, and they did not abolish debts as had been customary in the early second millennium. Debt-slavery boomed at this time.

The only way out for the laborers was to flee the land, and this they seem to have done in great numbers. Throughout the Syro-Palestinian area there was an increased presence of men and women who had cut ties with their political and social communities and joined groups of outcasts beyond the reach of the states. They lived in inaccessible areas in the steppe and the mountains. The urban residents whose texts we read regarded them with disdain and fear, and grouped them under the derogatory term *habiru*, which translates as "bandit" or "vagabond." All states of the Near East of this period refer to them. The *habiru* were not an ethnic or tribal group but a social one, made up of people who had fled their states and communities. The states' attitude toward them was consistently hostile, and the Amarna letters, for example, depict them as a great threat to stability in the region. Although there is a degree of urban prejudice here, these descriptions were not pure rhetoric. Relations between *habiru* and the states were antagonistic and raids on villages and cities frequently occurred. On the other hand, the states had to turn to *habiru* for manpower, and they appear in records as mercenaries and laborers, now possibly being able to set their own terms. The diplomatic exchanges between states often discussed this issue: refugees had to be returned, and Hattusili III, for instance, declared that he would not accept any person from Ugarit as a *habiru* in Hatti. The discrepancy between the high demands of urban elites and the limited supply of labor was so great, however, that the resulting tensions probably caused the collapse of the palatial system that characterized the Syro-Palestinian region in the second half of the second millennium.

Debate 8.1   *Who were the* habiru?

When in the 1880s the Amarna letters first became known, scholars soon noticed the many references to a people in the Syro-Palestinian area called *habiru*. Over time the evidence on them increased sizably: the name appeared in later second millennium records from Alalakh, Nuzi, Hattusa, Ugarit, Nippur, Babylon, and Egypt. Far fewer references from earlier Babylonian periods also exist (see Bottéro 1972–5 for a complete list up to then). By far the most attestations were in Babylonian cuneiform, either written syllabically *ha-bi-ru* or with the Sumerian word-signs SA.GAZ; Ugaritic scribes wrote ʿprm in their alphabetic script, the Egyptians ʿpr.w. This evidence allows for different readings of the name: *habiru*, *hapiru*, and *ʿapiru*.

Who were the *habiru* (I use this spelling for simplicity's sake)? The name by itself almost immediately called to mind that of another people in the region, the Hebrews (ʿibri) of the Bible. Already in 1888 a scholar suggested this equation. Abraham, who is called "the Hebrew" in the Book of Genesis, could have been a *habiru* of the Amarna period, and the evidence on these people could serve as a complement to the biblical stories about the early history of Israel. For a long time, the question of whether or not *habiru* and Hebrew were the same occupied scholars of the ancient Near East and the Bible, involving philological, sociological, and historical arguments. Conferences (e.g., Bottéro 1954), doctoral dissertations (e.g., Greenberg 1955), and monographs (e.g., Loretz 1984) dealt with the question, and gradually a consensus arose that the equation was false (although some scholars continue to see a connection, e.g. Liverani 2005a: 27; Milano 2012: 275).

So what does the term mean? *Habiru* were not a clearly defined group of people. No one was born a *habiru*, but one chose to become one as the story of Idrimi shows. They came from communities all over the Syro-Palestinian region and beyond: when texts provide places of origin, they include many cities and regions (von Dassow 2008: 345) and their names show that they spoke different languages, among them Hurrian, Semitic, and even Egyptian. They were "refugees" who ended up in foreign territories (Liverani 1965). Unlike the Amorites, for example, they had no tribal structure or clearly identified leaders. They were feared and the authors of the letters about them always accused them of aggression. When they wrote out the name in Sumerograms rather than syllabically they used SA.GAZ, a word that meant "robber" in other contexts. Whenever a Syro-Palestinian vassal wanted the pharaoh to distrust a neighbor, he accused him of collaborating with the *habiru*.

At the same time, however, these same vassals had *habiru* in their service and regularly *habiru* appeared in records as palace dependents, oftentimes as soldiers. In a letter to Damascus Egypt's king asked for a detachment of them so that he could station them in Nubia (Edzard 1970: 55–6). We find thus the same contradiction as with other non-urban groups: all depictions of these people were negative, but they were also considered useful in certain ways, especially as mercenaries. But, the *habiru* were not like the Amorites, for example, because they were much more heterogeneous.

Scholarly consensus today is that the *habiru* were people, mostly from the Syro-Palestinian region, who abandoned their communities because of financial or political pressures and formed bands in areas outside state control. The region had many inaccessible zones where regular armies could not function, but which small and mobile groups could use as a base from which to prey on settled communities (e.g., Rowton 1965; Bottéro 1981). Their ferocity and lack of ties made them ideal mercenaries, and men like Abdi-Ashirta of Amurru may have exploited their discontent for his own political purposes (Liverani 2005a: 26–9). They presented a nuisance, but as in any situation with much warfare they also provided a ready source of men for hire. And from that basis, they were able to reintegrate themselves in urban societies and rise through the ranks in other areas of life.

9

Kassites, Assyrians, and Elamites

3000	2500	2000	1500	1000	500

1595	End of the Old Babylonian dynasty
ca. 1475	Kassites control Babylonia
ca. 1400	Unification of Susiana lowlands and highlands of Anshan
ca. 1350	Assyria emerges as a major state under Assur-uballit I
1305–1207	Sustained Assyrian military expansion
1225	Tukulti-Ninurta I of Assyria sacks Babylon
1155	End of the Kassite dynasty
ca. 1110	Nebuchadnezzar I of Babylon sacks Susa

The eastern part of the Near East, and especially Babylonia, had been the focus of political and cultural developments for the centuries before 1500, and provided the historian with the most detailed sources for study. The situation changed in the second half of the second millennium, when in political terms the states there became integrated in the greater Near Eastern system as equals of those in the west and when sources are abundantly available from the entire Near East. At first, Babylonia, Assyria, and Elam were perhaps less powerful than their western neighbors (Hatti, Mittani, and Egypt), but after 1400 they developed into significant territorial powers, closely interacting with one another. Babylonia was the earliest to gain the status of a great kingdom, and Assyria to its north followed

A History of the Ancient Near East ca. 3000–323 BC, Third Edition. Marc Van De Mieroop.
© 2016 John Wiley & Sons, Inc. Published 2016 by John Wiley & Sons, Inc.

Map 9.1   The Middle Assyrian, Kassite, and Middle Elamite states.

around 1350. Elam in the east became a crucial player on the international scene only after 1200, the time of the major disruptions in the west. The eastern states suffered from the collapse of the regional system, and by 1100 they became isolated and weak kingdoms.

9.1   Babylonia

A power vacuum emerged after the Hittites sacked Babylon in 1595. The ancient political structures vanished and much of the population of Babylonia no longer lived in cities. A people using the name Kassites took advantage of this situation and seized the throne of Babylon perhaps soon after its sack. The first-millennium *Babylonian King List A* places its rulers among the dynasties that governed in succession from Hammurabi's to the beginning of the Neo-Babylonian dynasty (in 626 BC), and assigns the Kassite dynasty the longest rule of all: thirty-six kings who reigned for 576 years and nine months. We can date the dynasty's end to 1155. Adding the years given by the king list to that date would place its beginning in the eighteenth century, when Samsuiluna securely held Babylon. It is thus clear that ancestors of the Kassite kings appear in the king list and the date of accession to Babylon's throne remains unknown to us. When outside forces terminated Kassite rule in 1155, a dynasty the *Babylonian King List* claims to be from Isin took control over the land (for a list of rulers, see Section 13 of the King Lists at the end of the book). Its rulers saw the country slide into a general decline that would last for more than four hundred years. The Kassites were recent immigrants in Babylonia, distinct from the older populations, and they spoke a language without a linguistic relationship to any other language we know. Until the thirteenth century, all their kings had Kassite names, and subsequently only a few took Akkadian ones. Despite the official adherence to Kassite, this language did not have much influence on Babylonian culture. No complete texts written in it have been found, and only a few words in Kassite appear in other contexts. There exist two Akkadian–Kassite vocabulary lists that indicate that the Kassite language was of interest at least to scholarly circles, but these scholars did not compose Kassite works. Similarly, the Kassites had their own pantheon, known to us primarily from people's names. Their gods did not become prominent in the cult of Babylonia, however. The only gods for whom shrines were built were the patron deities of the king, Shuqamuna and Shumaliya. They were important in coronation rites and had a chapel in the palace. But otherwise, Kassite kings honored the ancient Babylonian gods as their own (figure 9.1). As was the case with the Amorites earlier, the Kassites acquired political power but did not have a cultural impact.

They may have fundamentally affected the social structure of Babylonia, however. The Kassites were organized in family and tribal units, and they continued to refer to such units after they had taken control over cities. They identified people as belonging to the "House of so-and-so" (in Akkadian *Bit* + name of a person), named after an ancestor, who may have been a real person or a fictitious character. The men were "sons" of that ancestor. These houses incorporated several villages and areas of agricultural land and became administrative entities. After the Kassites lost political control, they stayed in Babylonia and the neighboring areas and maintained their organization in houses with ancestral Kassite names. These remained the administrative units of some areas after the disappearance of the dynasty, so the Kassite influence on Babylonian social structure was lasting.

We do not know how these units related to the royal power in the capital. Kings in other Near Eastern states referred to their Kassite colleagues as "kings of the land Karduniash," the latter being a term for Babylonia that may have been Kassite in origin. In some Assyrian sources the Babylonian ruler was called "king of the Kassites." This duality probably reflects the political reality. The Kassites held political power, but they remained sufficiently distinct from the rest of the population to be regarded as a separate group. Their lack of roots in a single city facilitated the development of an ideology that they ruled a territorial state. In

Figure 9.1   Kassite stele of the Babylonian goddess Lama. Although the Kassites had their own pantheon they continued to honor Babylonian deities of old and devoted traditional cult objects to them. The 16-line Sumerian inscription on this stele states that an official with a Kassite name set up the figure of the goddess Lama for the life of King Nazi-Maruttash and dedicated it to the goddess Inanna. A mirror image of the stele with the same inscription was excavated at Uruk. The Metropolitan Museum of Art, New York. Gift of E. S. David, 1961 (61.12). Gypsum alabaster. Dimensions: 83.82 × 30.48 × 20.32 cm (33 × 12 × 8 in). Credit: © 2014 The Metropolitan Museum of Art/Art Resource/Scala, Florence.

the Kassite period, the idea of the land of Babylon, that is Babylonia, was firmly established.

The creation of that state took place in the sixteenth and fifteenth centuries, which are extremely poorly known. Texts from Tell Muhammed on the outskirts on modern Baghdad mention the names of two early Kassite kings on tablets dated between thirty and forty-one years "after Babylon was resettled," which suggests that Kassites took control there soon after the Hittite raid of 1595. Around 1475, a Kassite named Ulamburiash became lord of the Sealand and replaced the "Sealand dynasty" that had ruled southern Babylonia perhaps since the disappearance of Babylon's control in the eighteenth century. He thus recreated the unified Babylonia of Hammurabi's days, and by the fourteenth century his successors had extended Kassite control beyond these borders. The Diyala region east of the Tigris was in their hands and a Kassite governor resided on the island of Dilmun (modern Bahrain) in the Persian Gulf. Thus Babylonia rightfully belonged to the great powers of the time, and indeed its neighbors acknowledged it as such. The Amarna correspondence of the kings of Egypt contains fourteen letters to and from Babylon. Two successive kings there were the correspondents: Kadashman-Enlil I (ruled 1374?–1360) and Burnaburiash II (ruled 1359–1333). Their letters were almost wholly concerned with diplomatic marriages and the exchange of substantial bridal gifts and dowries. Some political problems arose, however, and demonstrate the change in power relations in Mesopotamia. Assur-uballit I of Assyria had contacted Egypt, which caused Burnaburiash to claim angrily that he was a Babylonian vassal and could not act independently in such affairs (see chapter 6).

Babylon's claim to sovereignty over Assyria was certainly unrealistic by then, if it had ever existed. Assur-uballit I (ruled 1363–1328) had made Assyria so powerful that Burnaburiash took his daughter as his main wife. When the Babylonian king died, their son Kara-hardash inherited the throne, but rebels assassinated him. Assur-uballit did not appreciate his grandson's murder, and invaded Babylonia to place Kurigalzu II (ruled 1332–1308) on the throne. Assyria's importance could no longer be doubted. Babylonia did not live under Assyrian domination, however. It remained one of the great states of the time and, as such, other kings who needed to legitimate their own rule courted Babylon's king. Thus we see that Hattusili III of Hatti contacted Kadashman-Enlil II (ruled 1263–1255) when the latter ascended the throne, in order to plead for a continuation of good relations.

A very substantial administrative archive that was excavated in Nippur and is principally concentrated in the reigns of Burnaburiash II to Kashtiliashu IV (ca. 1360–1225) is our primary source on the socioeconomic history of the period. Unfortunately, of the 12,000 or so tablets found only one-eighth has been published so far. They show a highly centralized administration under a governor, who was in charge of the province of Nippur. He headed an agricultural office that collected harvests and animal products, often in huge amounts. These were redistributed to institutional dependents as rations, the quantities of which depended on the recipient's rank in the hierarchy. Recipients included administrators, cult officials, military personnel, and laborers. While the governor's position was secular, he could also hold the high priesthood of Nippur's patron, Enlil. That god's temple seems to have been one of the most important institutions in the land at the time, and control over its assets made Nippur's governor second in rank only to the king. The temple provided people with loans and advances, possibly in return for labor, which may have led to a situation of indebtedness found elsewhere in the Near East at this time. There are few texts from other parts of the Kassite state, and the study of its economy and society is difficult. While the level of urbanization in the region was lower than that in the early second millennium, there was much reconstruction of old cities. The Kassite kings patronized building activity all over Babylonia. Among these projects was the construction of a new

Figure 9.2   Remains of the ziggurat at Dur-Kurigalzu. The core of the ziggurat city of Dur-Kurigalzu, near modern-day Baghdad, is relatively well preserved because its builders laid reed matting soaked in bitumen at regular intervals to drain the rainwater. The remains are still about 57 meters (187 feet) high and after excavation the archaeologists restored the lowest levels of this temple tower. Credit: Marc Van De Mieroop.

capital city, named Dur-Kurigalzu, "fortress of King Kurigalzu," in the far north of Babylonia. It extended over some five kilometers and included a vast palace and temple, including a high tower made up of a set of mud brick platforms (figure 9.2). Such a tower is called a ziggurat in modern scholarship after the Akkadian word *ziqqurratu*. The otherwise barely known Kurigalzu I built the city in the early fourteenth century, which shows that the court at that time already had the ability to command large resources for itself.

The end of the dynasty was the result of the combined pressures of Assyria and Elam. Tukulti-Ninurta I (ruled 1233–1197), continuing a gradual expansion of Assyria that had started in the early thirteenth century, invaded Babylonia and deposed Kashtiliashu IV (ruled 1232–1225), whom he took in chains to Assur. The end of the Nippur archive at this time was probably not coincidental. After assuming kingship of Babylon for a short time, Tukulti-Ninurta appointed a series of puppet rulers, who represented Assyrian interests for a decade. Elamite pressure and a successful Babylonian rebellion returned Babylon to Kassite control, but Elam's raids eventually led to the collapse of the Kassite dynasty in 1155. In later literary texts the capture of the statue of Marduk and its exile to Susa symbolized the end of this era. The Elamites did not take control over Babylonia; that role was taken by a non-Kassite dynasty, which later king lists referred to as the second Isin dynasty. Its most forceful and famous ruler was Nebuchadnezzar I (ruled 1125–1104), who took revenge on Elam, ransacked Susa, and recovered Maduk's statue. His own success was short-lived, however, and soon after his rule Babylonia drifted into historical obscurity. The decline of the region is usually blamed on invasions by the Arameans, but it has to be considered within the larger context of the end of the general Near Eastern system at the time, which we will discuss in the next chapter.

One practice of the Kassite dynasty that was continued under the second Isin period was the king's granting of substantial areas of land to members of his family, officials, priests, and military personnel. These grants were recorded on stone stelae, decorated with symbols representing gods and inscribed with a declaration in which the king stated in detail what area was given to whom. The stones themselves were referred to by the Akkadian term *kudurru*, which also means "boundary." The reasons for such grants are rarely given, but they seem to have been rewards for special services or offered in support of a cult. The areas involved could be extensive, on average sufficient to feed two hundred people. Sometimes the labor of villagers was included in the donations, or the estates were exempt from taxes. These properties were granted in perpetuity to select members of the elites, but for special purposes only, and it seems doubtful that the stelae document the regular practices of land tenure at the time.

While the Kassite rulers were originally foreign to Babylonia and maintained their own language, at least in their names, they did not slow down the development of Babylonian culture. On the contrary, these centuries were crucial for the creation of a Babylonian literary corpus in the Akkadian language, an activity that the Kassite court patronized. Scribes and authors did not abandon Sumerian as a language of culture and the cult, and they preserved a part of the literary corpus from the Old Babylonian period in that language. They provided several of the texts with an Akkadian translation, recorded in a format where an Akkadian counterpart immediately followed each Sumerian line. Moreover, they used a quite artificial form of Sumerian to compose additional literary and religious texts and royal inscriptions, and inscribed many cylinder seals of the time with prayers in the Sumerian language. It is clear that a literate elite took the initiative to preserve Sumerian as a language of high culture.

It is in the Akkadian literary production that we see most of the creativity in this period. A literary dialect developed, which modern scholars call Standard Babylonian, and it was heavily inspired by the Akkadian of the Old Babylonian period. Standard Babylonian remained the literary dialect for the rest of Mesopotamian history, both in Babylonia and in Assyria, and while vernaculars influenced it, it preserved its distinct grammar and vocabulary. Much of the literature of this period is known only from first-millennium manuscripts or from late second-millennium manuscripts found outside Mesopotamia. It is evident, however, that they were composed in second-millennium Babylonia, and in the first millennium the importance of writers from this period was acknowledged. First-millennium Babylonian scribes were grouped into "families," whose eponymous ancestors had the names Sin-leqe-unninni, Hunzu'u, Ekur-zakir, and Ahhutu, and it was suggested that these families dated back to the Kassite period. Sin-leqe-unninni was also credited with having composed the version of the *Epic of Gilgamesh* that became the standard in the first millennium. These finds suggest the importance of Kassite-period literary production, which was also extremely varied in nature. They reflect the palace culture of the time, and several kings were praised in hymns for their military and cultic acts. During the second Isin dynasty, there is a sense that the individual is less secure than in the Old Babylonian period. Man is portrayed as victim to the whims of the gods, for example, in the *Poem of the righteous sufferer*. It is a monologue in which the speaker describes how he fell from fame and fortune to disgrace, destitution, and disease. There is no explanation for this suffering, except that the god Marduk inflicted it for unknown reasons.

Military and cultic events inspired the composition of some literary texts. In this period, the importance of the god Marduk in the cult increased over the entirety of Babylonia. During the New Year's festival, a ritual of renewal and regeneration, his statue had to be reintroduced into the city of Babylon. The absence of that statue thus had a disastrous effect on the cult, and its recovery was a significant feat. Several texts deal with this issue. In one, the so-called *Marduk prophecy*, the god narrates how he left Babylon three times in this period, to go to Hatti, Assur, and Elam. These seem to be references to the sacking of Babylon by Mursili I, Tukulti-Ninurta I, and Kutir-Nahhunte. Another literary text credited the first recovery to an otherwise unknown Kassite king, Agum, who may have lived in the sixteenth century. One of Tukulti-Ninurta's successors seems to have returned the statue voluntarily in the mid-twelfth century, and Nebuchadnezzar I recaptured the statue from Elam, a feat that was acclaimed repeatedly in literature. Nebuchadnezzar's accomplishment probably led to the composition of one of the most famous pieces of Babylonian poetry, the so-called *Creation myth*. It describes how Marduk rose to kingship among the gods after defeating the forces of chaos, personified by the sea, Tiamat. Subsequently, he organized the universe and built the city of Babylon as the earthly residence for the gods. The myth thus reflects an ideology that the city held a position of universal importance.

And indeed, Babylon's culture had an impact on the entire Near Eastern world. In all the courts of the second half of the second millennium, manuscripts of Babylonian literary and scholarly texts were kept, copied out, and imitated. Thus the palace at Hattusa, for example, owned copies of lexical texts, hymns, incantations, and medical texts, some of which were bilingual Sumerian and Akkadian. Moreover, several versions of the Gilgamesh epic were preserved: a Babylonian version and translations into Hittite and Hurrian, and there were tales about the Old Akkadian kings Sargon and Naram-Sin in Babylonian. In smaller courts the same situation existed. At Emar in Syria, the corpus of Babylonian texts included omens and incantations, lexical lists, and fragments of the Gilgamesh epic and other Sumerian and Akkadian literature. Even in Egypt, with its very distinct literary tradition, manuscripts of Babylonian literary and lexical texts were found at Amarna. These include the myths of Adapa and of Nergal and Ereshkigal, and a tale about Sargon of Akkad. They were the products of palace scribes trained to maintain the Babylonian-language correspondence between the courts. While these men may originally have come from Babylonia itself, at least in the larger courts, locals learned how to read and write Babylonian and passed their skills on to their sons. The literary remains had a utilitarian purpose in the training of scribes, but it is very possible that familiarity with them was part of the elites' way of distinguishing themselves from the general populations.

It is at this time that Assyrian literature became fully inspired by Babylonia, and from this period on there is no clear distinction between the two traditions. This influence was partly a result of the general Near Eastern admiration for Babylonian literature. But political acts sometimes speeded up the process of adoption. After Tukulti-Ninurta I sacked Babylon, for example, he took home literary and scholarly tablets as booty, and he may thus have laid the foundation of a royal library in Assyria filled with Babylonian manuscripts. These influenced local authors. Assyrian literary compositions of the time included genres unknown in Babylonia, such as the royal epic, but in style and language they conformed to the Standard Babylonian dialect. Local imitations of Babylonian texts were not always successful. For example, in Elam, cylinder seals in the Kassite style were carved with inscriptions in Sumerian or Akkadian. The carver's ignorance of those languages sometimes led to incomplete lines being written. While Babylonian influence was strong everywhere, it did not replace local cultural and literary traditions. In most places it became part of a multiplicity of cultural heritages. Thus in Ugarit, for instance, literatures in Ugaritic and in Hurrian coexisted with Babylonian. The patronage of literary culture came from the palaces. The fact that Babylonian literature was known everywhere in the region indicates the strength of the palace culture in this period. In the cultural heartland, Babylonia, this creativity was supported by a foreign dynasty, the Kassite, which may be credited with providing that region with its longest era of stability.

9.2   Assyria

The Assyrians themselves presented their history as a long succession of kings – from a distant pre-sedentary past to the late seventh century – who ruled the city of Assur. Royal power passed from one family to another many times, but we are unable to subdivide the history on that basis as a sequence of dynasties as we do for other kingdoms in the Near East. Instead, modern historians use a vaguely defined tripartite division of Old, Middle, and Neo-Assyrian periods, which correspond to periods with relative textual riches, each reflecting a stage of the Assyrian language. The middle to late second millennium is often called the Middle Assyrian period.

The history of these centuries is usually written with a particular focus on individual kings who were militarily very active and successful. From the fourteenth to eleventh centuries Assyria was able to turn itself from a small state around the city Assur to a sizeable territorial state and leading player in regional affairs. Our sources, mostly royal annals (see box 9.1), present this feat as the result of incessant campaigning. This bias is reflected in our modern histories, but we should not ignore the diplomatic means by which Assyria gained its status on the international scene, surely backed by military might.

The first ruler of importance in this period was Assur-uballit I (1353–1318). He was able to establish firm control over the heartland of Assyria, that is, the Tigris valley and plains to the east, from the city of Assur to the Taurus Mountains in

Box 9.1 *Assyrian royal annals*

In the late Middle Assyrian period, in the reign of Tiglath-pileser I (1114–1076), there appeared a new genre of royal inscription that provides the most detailed chronologically organized account of military events: the royal annals. Accounts of this type became increasingly numerous and elaborate, and by the late Assyrian period the corpus each individual ruler left is vast. Annals describe year by year where the king campaigned, what places he conquered, and what booty he brought back with him. While there are some annalistic texts that describe one year only, the majority involves several years up to the moment the text was composed. Each year became identified with a campaign. Versions of the same campaign written at different times often provide various accounts of events. This could be an abbreviation of the original report, as more emphasis and detail were given to what happened immediately before the composition. But there could also be a rewriting of episodes to reflect changes in the political situation. For example, King Sennacherib (ruled 704–681) had great difficulties with Babylonia and campaigned there repeatedly in order to establish a government loyal to him. One solution he tried out was to place a local man, Bel-ibni, on the throne, and in the earliest annalistic accounts he stated so. But this solution did not work out, and after three years Bel-ibni had to be replaced by an Assyrian prince. Annals written after that date did not mention Bel-ibni, even when talking about rule in Babylon, as that man no longer had any relevance. While annals may seem to us to be factual, albeit heavily biased, they have to be used critically as historical sources.

Many of the annalistic texts were part of building inscriptions and were structured in three main sections: the titles and genealogy of the king, a year-by-year narrative of his military actions up to the moment of composition, and a description of the building project undertaken at that time. As a result, they provide a chronological framework for building activity. They were written on clay tablets, barrels, and cylinders, often buried in foundation deposits, or carved on stone reliefs and stelae. The objects were often carefully fashioned (figure 9.3). The annals' focus on warfare and the abundance of details about campaigns have led to the situation that modern reconstructions of Assyrian history are primarily military. We should not conclude from them that the Assyrians were more militaristic in their behavior than were their neighbors, whose inscriptions do not have this emphasis.

the north. Previously, Assyria had never been more than a city-state, the city of Assur and its hinterland, and in the fifteenth century the Mittani of northern Syria probably dominated it. Nuzi, to the east of Assur, was certainly under Mittani rule, and likely the king of Assur was a vassal as well. When the Hittites attacked the Mittani kingdom from the west, Assur-uballit was able to annex its eastern territories. He established himself as a figure of international importance. Two letters he wrote to the king of Egypt were found at Amarna, in which he tried to claim a status at least equal to that of the king of Mittani. The diplomatic opening to Egypt prompted an angry reaction by Burnaburiash II, who urged his Egyptian

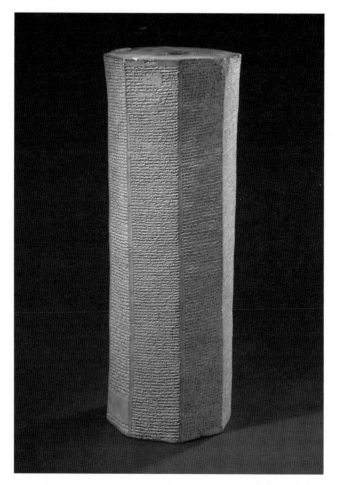

Figure 9.3   Octagonal prism with dedicatory inscription of Tiglath-pileser I, from Assur. This eight-sided prism is an excellent example of how elaborate the building inscriptions of Assyria could become, and how carefully fashioned the objects could be. It is the first-preserved example of annals that provide a year-by-year account of the military campaigns in a king's reign up to the date of the text, that is, the fifth year of Tiglath-pileser. The text is known from numerous octagonal prisms and fragments, which were placed in the foundations of the Anu-Adad temple at Assur. Vorderasiatisches Museum, Staatliche Museen, Berlin (Inv. VA 8255), 1109 BCE. Terracotta, H. 56 cm, Diam. 17.5 cm. (22 × 6.9 in). Credit: © Photo Scala, Florence/BPK, Bildagentur für Kunst, Kultur und Geschichte, Berlin.

counterpart to regard Assyria as Babylon's vassal. Yet, Assyria's importance could not be denied, and the Babylonian king himself married an Assyrian princess, Muballitat-sherua. When their son, Kara-hardash, was murdered in an uprising, Assur-uballit intervened, deposed the Kassite claimant to the throne, and replaced him with Kurigalzu II.

Assur-uballit's death caused a temporary setback in Assyria's international stature, but soon afterwards three long-lived kings, whose rule spanned almost an entire century, turned the country into a major force: Adad-nirari I (1295–1264), Shalmaneser I (1263–1234), and Tukulti-Ninurta I (1233–1197). The primary focus of their military activity was the west, where they gradually turned the area of the former Mittani state east of the Euphrates into directly controlled Assyrian territory. At first the king of what the Assyrians called Hanigalbat became a vassal. But when he rebelled, Shalmaneser I occupied the southern and eastern parts of his state and established fortresses and administrative centers. A later rebellion by northern and western areas led Tukulti-Ninurta I to annex the entirety of northern Syria east of the Euphrates, where he faced the Hittites, who remained in control of western Syria. The two states had a contentious relationship. At first Tukulti-Ninurta offered peace to his colleague Tudhaliya IV, but simultaneously he prepared to invade eastern Anatolia and defeated a Hittite army that came to confront him. He also started diplomatic overtures to some Hittite vassals in western Syria and crossed the Euphrates at least once. He claimed to have "uprooted 28,800 Hittite people," but annexed no territory.

The diplomatic acceptance of Assyria into the league of great states was slow. After Adad-nirari had established *de facto* control over the Mittani area, he wrote to the king of Hatti and called him brother. The Hittite ruler replied rudely: "On what account should I write to you about brotherhood? Were you and I born from one mother?"[1] Soon afterwards the reality that the Assyrian kings were among the great rulers could no longer be denied. Successive Hittite kings engaged in diplomatic exchanges with Adad-nirari I and Shalmaneser I. They used both friendly approaches and threats, but probably wanted to avoid direct conflict. At times the two countries were officially at war. When Tudhaliya IV in the late thirteenth century concluded a treaty with Shaushga-muwa of Amurru, he demanded support troops from his vassal against Assyria. As we saw, that treaty also sought to restrict Assyria's commercial access to the Mediterranean, prohibiting Amurru to deal with Assyrian merchants (see document 8.2).

Assyria's administration of western territories was centered round settlements placed in strategic locations and connected by canals and roads. The latter sometimes ran through the steppe and were provided with wells at regular intervals. The Assyrian centers were probably situated in places where they protected trade routes and controlled the districts surrounding them. The records found in them document that the Assyrian officials stationed there ran affairs without much input from the local populations. There was no attempt to turn the Syrian people into Assyrians, or any adaptation of local practices. The main concern of the records was agricultural production. Groups of laborers cultivated fields and were directly dependent on the Assyrian administration, which supported them with rations. Shalmaneser I introduced a new method of control of the local populations: he displaced entire groups within Hanigalbat itself, with their families and properties. Tukulti-Ninurta I expanded this practice by deporting north Syrian people to Assyria, where they were set to work on public projects and in agriculture. Northern Syria thus became an important source of agricultural produce and laborers for Assyria.

Assyrian expansion in the thirteenth century was not limited to the west. The campaigns extended into territories to the north of Syria, in eastern Anatolia, and Assyrian pressure may have pushed the local people there into forming states or federations. The accounts start referring to regions such as Nairi and Uruatri, where in the early first millennium the important state of Urartu developed. Mountain tribes to the east, which the Assyrians referred to with antiquated names, such as Gutians and Subarians, were also the targets of campaigns. Babylonia once more came under Assyrian control when Tukulti-Ninurta I defeated Kashtiliashu IV, an event described in a long epic poem. He took the titles "King of Assyria and king of Karduniash, king of Sumer and Akkad, king of Sippar and Babylon, king of Dilmun and Meluhha, king of the Upper and Lower Seas, king of the extensive mountains and plains, king of the lands of the Subarians (and) Gutians, and king of all the lands of Nairi,"[2] thereby claiming control over a wide expanse. But this period of strength was abruptly terminated by his assassination and the subsequent confusion in Assyria, which gave non-sedentary people the opening to gain political influence in eastern Anatolia and northern Syria. In Syria, Arameans took control over many cities. Two kings temporarily halted Assyria's decline: Assur-resha-ishi I (ruled 1132–1115) stabilized the region internally, and Tiglath-pileser I (ruled 1114–1076) campaigned aggressively in all directions. In the west, he fought against Arameans and Mushku and reached the Mediterranean Sea. In the south, he raided Babylonia, which was, however, also able to retaliate and capture Ekallatum, near Assur. In the north, Tiglath-pileser reached the shores of Lake Van. His successes were ephemeral, however, and by 1050 Assyria was reduced to its heartland, with Arameans in control of most of northern Syria and large parts of Mesopotamia. A one hundred year period of total obscurity followed.

The military successes provided the economic resources for building activity in Assyria itself. The greatest project was Tukulti-Ninurta's construction of a new capital city, named Kar-Tukulti-Ninurta, opposite Assur on the Tigris River. He built it after he had defeated Babylon, and used the spoils of that campaign to do so. The city was founded on virgin soil and covered an enormous area, some 240 hectares (593 acres), if not more. Its center contained a massive walled inner city, with a temple to the god Assur and two large palaces. Documents reveal that Syrian deportees provided the labor. The city's life as a capital was short, however. After Tukulti-Ninurta's assassination it became a place of secondary status.

Middle Assyrian society very much reflected the state's militarism. In the heartland of Assyria, the crown held much of the agricultural land and awarded it as concessions to men and their families in return for their labor. When someone was called up for service, he was said to join the "army," although not all duties were purely military. For instance, participation in building projects was also required. In return, the state gave fields that could be treated almost like private property: the lots were passed on from father to son, and could be sold to someone else without palace interference. But when the holder defaulted on his duties or had no heirs, the land reverted to the palace, even if it had been sold. To fulfill the service requirements people could substitute another person, who was usually indebted to them. As in other Near Eastern societies of the period, in Assyria the level of indebtedness was high and many of the contracts preserved are loans backed up by the debtor's labor.

Among the official records of the period are a set of tablets we call the *Middle Assyrian Laws* and the *Palace Decrees* (see document 9.1). These indicate that social rules were very strictly regulated and austere, especially for women, who were wholly dependent on their husbands and fathers for support and were severely punished for any transgression. A wife whose husband had been captured by an enemy had to wait two years before she could remarry. In the meantime her father or sons supported her or, if they were not present, the community did. If her first husband returned after more than two years, he had to take her back, although her children by the second husband would remain with the latter. Punishment for crimes was often bodily mutilation. A woman who was caught stealing would have her ears cut off by her husband, or her nose by the victim. Public behavior was rigidly controlled. Although married women were allowed to go outside the house on their own, they had to cover their heads, but unmarried women, slaves, and prostitutes were forbidden to do so. A prostitute who covered herself received fifty lashes and had her clothes taken away and hot pitch poured over her head. Anyone who did not report such a transgression would be penalized equally severely. The *Middle Assyrian Palace Decrees* regulated behavior within the court, and also dealt primarily with women. Access to women was monitored and outsiders were checked, possibly to see whether they were castrated. If a palace woman met with a man without an attendant, both would be killed. If a servant spoke to a palace woman with bare shoulders, he would be given one hundred lashes. The *Laws* and *Palace Decrees* portray a society with very strict and harsh court-imposed rules of conduct.

9.3 The Middle Elamite Kingdom

On the eastern border of the Near Eastern world of the late second millennium, the state of Elam developed along the lines of its great neighbors, although its role in the international system remained of secondary importance (for a list of kings, see Section 14 of the King Lists at the end of the book). After Hammurabi of Babylon had defeated Elam in the eighteenth century, its earlier political unity probably shattered. This situation was reversed only around 1400, but already from 1500 on rulers in Susa referred to themselves as "Kings of Susa and Anshan" in Akkadian, or as "Kings of Anshan and Susa" in Elamite. After 1400 the lowlands of Susiana in the west were unified with the highlands of Anshan, some 500 kilometers (310 miles) to the southeast, and the shore of the Persian Gulf, some 400 kilometers (250 miles) to the south. The Elamite state was thus a large geographical entity, uniting people from various cultural backgrounds. Mesopotamia had much influence over the western lowlands, while the highlands preserved local traditions. This distinction is clear in the usage of languages and in religious practices. The Akkadian of Babylonia had been used in earlier periods of Elamite history, and in this era it was at first the official language. After 1400, the Elamite language took over that role. Likewise, in the early part of the period, Mesopotamian deities were popular in Susa, even though Elamite gods were worshipped there as well. After 1400, Elamite gods came to dominate the official cult.

Document 9.1   *Excerpts from the Middle Assyrian Laws*

In contrast to the unified corpus of laws in the Code of Hammurabi, the so-called Middle Assyrian Laws are a series of cuneiform tablets (labeled A through O in modern scholarship), each with a collection of clauses. Only tablet A is well preserved, the others are mostly fragmentary. Middle Assyrian Laws A concentrates on issues with women as victims and principal actors in different contexts: inheritance, sexual assault, debt, etcetera. The clauses use the same format as Hammurabi's Laws, "If ... then," but tend to be much longer than in earlier codes. Although the collections date to the fourteenth century, we only know them from eleventh-century copies.

Tablet A, Paragraph 45

If a woman is married and the enemy seizes her husband, and she has no father-in-law or son, she shall wait for two years for her husband. If she has nothing to eat during these two years, she shall come forward and say so. If she belongs to a community dependent on the palace, her [father?] shall feed her, and she shall work for him. If she is the wife of a low-ranking soldier, [ ] shall feed her, [and she shall work for him]. [If she is the wife of a man whose] field and [house cannot support her?], she shall come forward and say to the judges, "I have [nothing to] eat." The judges shall question the mayor and city-leaders, and according to the going rate of fields there, they shall assign a field and house to her for her support for two years and give it. She shall live there and they shall write a tablet to that account. She shall let two years pass, and then she can go and live with the husband of her choice. They shall write a tablet for her as if she is a widow. If later on her missing husband returns to the country, he shall take back his wife who had married outside the family. He will have no claim over the sons she had with her new husband. Her new husband shall take them. As for the field and house that she had sold at full price outside the family to support herself, if it has not become a royal holding, he shall pay as much as was given and take it back. If he does not return and dies abroad, the king shall give his field and house wherever he wants.

Tablet A, Paragraph 47

If either a man or a woman should be caught practicing sorcery, and should they establish and prove the charges, they shall kill the one who had practiced sorcery. A man who heard from the mouth of someone who observed sorcery: "I saw it myself," shall go and tell it to the king. Should the eyewitness deny what was told the king, the hearsay-witness shall say in front of the divine Ox, son of the sun god: "He did indeed tell me," and he shall be clear. As for the eyewitness, who (first) spoke but then denied, the king shall question him as he likes and investigate him. An exorcist shall make the man speak when they purify and he himself shall say: "No one shall release you from the oath that you swore to the king and his son. According to the tablet you swore to the king and his son."

Translation after Roth 1997: 170–3.

To write the history of this period, we must rely primarily on building inscriptions, as only the attestation of a king's name in several places allows us to determine the extent of his state. Moreover, the inscriptions often provide genealogical information, so we can reconstruct the sequence of kings with some certainty, although scholars still disagree. In order to date any of these rulers, we have to rely on synchronisms with Mesopotamia. Babylonian sources sometimes relate military clashes with Elam, and there are some letters that deal with dynastic marriages. In general, however, our knowledge of events is vague.

Three dynasties in succession ruled Elam in the centuries between 1500 and 1100. We are the least informed about the first, which governed until around 1400. All we have is a list of the names of five rulers, without their affiliation, so we are not even certain that they formed a dynasty. Almost all of them held the title "King of Susa and Anshan." This may have been a fiction, however, as we have no evidence of control outside the Susiana plain. It is even possible that the ruler's power was also limited there. The best-attested act of one of them, Tepti-ahar, was the building of a new settlement, Kabnak (modern Haft Tepe), some 20 kilometers (12 miles) from Susa. It has been suggested that loss of control over Susa forced the move, but there is no clear evidence for this. In any case, if the early Middle Elamite rulers had a wide geographical reach, they did not have the ability to leave a mark on more than the western lowlands.

The formation of the Middle Elamite state was the work of the second dynasty of the period, whose founder was Igi-halki. It held sway for some two centuries. The succession of kings was unusual for the period in that the throne moved back and forth between the descendants of two sons of Igi-halki. The first successor, Pahir-ishshan, was followed by his brother Attar-kittah, whose son and grandson succeeded him. Then the throne reverted to two sons of Pahir-ishshan in succession, and descendants of Attar-kittah followed them. There may have been friction between the two branches of the family, as we saw in other states of the time, but the situation is unclear. The dynasty's control over the lowlands is well documented by its building inscriptions, however, and included work in Liyan, a harbor on the Persian Gulf. The largest project by far was the construction in the late fourteenth century of a new city 40 kilometers (25 miles) from Susa, Al-Untash-Napirisha, named after its founder, Untash-Napirisha. Its center was a massive ziggurat surrounded by an inner enclosure with numerous temples. Inside a second enclosure, more secular buildings were located. The ziggurat was devoted to Napirisha, the great god of Elam, and Inshushinak, the patron deity of Susa. The construction was truly monumental: it contained millions of bricks, a substantial part of which was baked at great expense of fuel. A 2 meter thick layer of baked bricks encased the inner core of sun-dried brick. Every tenth layer of the outer casing had a row of bricks inscribed with a dedication from Untash-Napirisha to Inshushinak. Because of the solidity of its construction, this is the best-preserved ziggurat in the Near East. Many of the temples in the inner enclosure were devoted to purely Elamite deities, while some of the others honored Mesopotamian gods popular in Susa. There was thus an increased attention to Elamite traditions. Another move away from

Mesopotamian influences was the shift to the Elamite language in the official records of the state. With few exceptions, building inscriptions were no longer written in Akkadian. Al-Untash-Napirisha, like many other new foundations of the time, did not survive its creator as a capital. While not abandoned, it had secondary status to Susa soon after the death of Untash-Napirisha.

The last rulers of this dynasty became militarily involved in Babylonia. When that state was under the control of Tukulti-Ninurta I of Assyria, who appointed a string of puppet rulers, Kidin-Hutran III attacked the eastern Tigris region. Twice he entered Babylonia, the first time taking Nippur, the second attacking Isin. Soon after the Kassites regained control over Babylonia on Tukulti-Ninurta's death in 1197, Kidin-Hutran also died and a change of dynasty took place in Elam.

The details of this change are unknown to us. The building inscriptions at Susa of the early twelfth century report the activities of a Shutruk-Nahhunte, son of Hallutush-Inshushinak, and we can document that his descendants ruled Elam for the rest of the century. Shutruk-Nahhunte was married to the eldest daughter of the Kassite Meli-Shipak (ruled 1186–1172), but relations with Babylonia became extremely strained. In 1158, Shutruk-Nahhunte invaded Babylonia, ransacked its cities – 700 according to an Elamite inscription – and removed the Kassite king from the throne. He brought back an enormous quantity of spoils from all the important cities there, including some of the most famous early Babylonian monuments, such as the stele of Naram-Sin and the law code of Hammurabi. On several of these monuments Shutruk-Nahhunte inscribed an Elamite text, in which he commemorated their capture, identified where he took them, and stated that he presented them to the god Inshushinak (document 9.2). This explains why so many Babylonian monuments were excavated in Susa. The king also collected objects from Elamite cities, including Al-Untash-Napirisha, and rededicated them in Susa.

Shutruk-Nahhunte may have been assassinated by his own son, Kutir-Nahhunte. The new ruler was the main character in a set of Babylonian literary texts, all preserved in later manuscripts that mostly date to the Persian era. As son of a Babylonian princess, he felt that he should have become king of Babylon. In a perhaps fictional letter he complained: "Why have I, who am a king, son of a king, descendant of a king, who am king in the lands of Babylonia and of Elam, of the lineage of the eldest daughter of the mighty king Kurigalzu, not taken my rightful place on the throne of the land of Babylonia?"[3] After the Babylonians rejected his claim he invaded the country in 1155, ransacked more cities, and took Marduk's statue to Susa. He put an end to the Kassite dynasty, but did not ascend the throne of Babylon – the second Isin dynasty took over there. His brother and successor, Shilhak-Inshushinak, claimed to have raided Babylonia and Assyria repeatedly and to have established control over the area east of the Tigris as far north as Nuzi. The collapse of Kassite authority and the weakening of Assyria must have made that region an easy target, and Elam became the strongest power in the region. The kingdom also flourished economically at this time and developed its eastern areas. Babylonian resurgence under Nebuchadnezzar I of the second Isin

---

Document 9.2   *Middle Elamite inscriptions*

When Shutruk-Nahhunte took a large number of monuments from Babylonian cities as loot back home to Susa, he inscribed several of them with a text in the Elamite language, identifying the original patron of the monument and where he captured it. Those inscriptions were carved in prominent locations on the monuments and showed clearly that they belonged to the Elamite king. Three of them are translated here.

1. On the stele of Naram-Sin, captured in Sippar (see figure 4.1)
I am Shutruk-Nahhunte, son of Hallutush-Inshushinak, the beloved servant of the god Inshushinak, king of Anshan and Susa, who has enlarged the kingdom, who takes care of the land of Elam, the lord of the land of Elam. When the god Inshushinak gave me the order, I defeated Sippar. I took the stele of Naram-Sin and carried it off, bringing it to the land of Elam. For Inshushinak, my god, I set it up as an offering.

2. On a statue of Manishtushu, captured in Akkad
I am Shutruk-Nahhunte, son of Hallutush-Inshushinak, the beloved servant of the god Inshushinak, king of Anshan and Susa, who has enlarged the kingdom, who takes care of the land of Elam, the lord of the land of Elam. When the god Inshushinak gave me the order, I defeated Akkad. I took the statue of Manishtushu and carried it off to the land of Elam.

3. On a statue of Manishtushu, captured in Eshnunna
I am Shutruk-Nahhunte, son of Hallutush-Inshushinak, king of Anshan and Susa. When the god Inshushinak gave me the order, I defeated Eshnunna. I took the statue of Manishtushu and carried it off to the land of Elam.

Translation after König 1965: 76–7.

---

dynasty put an end to this prosperity, however. The Babylonian king recovered Marduk's statue from Susa and the Elamite state disappeared from our records for three centuries.

Despite the fact that this period is the best documented for the entire history of Elam, our grasp on it remains limited. Although the state was a late arrival on the scene whose international influence was restricted to Babylonia and Assyria, it cannot be ignored as a significant force. The fact that Elam does not figure in international correspondence probably results from its rise after the Amarna archive and its distance from Syria. Contacts with the Kassites in Babylonia were close, but we lack the Babylonian royal archives from this period, so we have no letters from Elam, except in late copies, which may be fictional. Elam shows strong Babylonian cultural influence, but also resistance against it. At first scribes used Akkadian, but after 1400 that language played only a minor role when compared to Elamite. On the other hand, the visual arts of the period imitated Babylonian practices and styles (see figure 9.4). This mixed behavior may be a result of the heterogeneity of cultural traditions in Elam itself, with neither the Mesopotamian-influenced lowlands nor the Elamite highlands fully dominant.

Debate 9.1   *Why did Shutruk-Nahhunte carry Babylonian monuments off to Susa?*

One of the great surprises of the French excavations at Susa in western Iran around 1900 was that they brought to light a large group of monuments that were clearly made in Babylonia. They included very famous works we have mentioned before, such as the stele of Naram-Sin and the code of Hammurabi, but the group was much larger (see Potts 1999: 235 for a list). It included monuments that were more than a thousand years old, but also a number of recent *kudurru* boundary stones. These were all heavy stone objects and not easy to transport. Some of them were especially massive, such as the 225 cm (7.2 ft) high stele of Hammurabi, the life-sized statue of Manishtushu, and a seated statue, dimensions 89 by 52 cm (35 × 20.2 in), all in solid stone (see figure 6.2 and Harper 1992: 165 and 173 for images). Not all of them were inscribed, but those that were indicate that Shutruk-Nahhunte took them from various cities in Babylonia (e.g., Sippar, Akkad) and areas to its east (e.g., Eshnunna). Although he may not have taken all the Babylonian objects found at Susa, he certainly carried off a large number of them during his campaign of 1158.

Why did he bother to do this – the transport must not have been easy – and what happened to the monuments afterwards? One can look at it as simply a "trophy collection" (Carter & Stolper 1984: 40), akin to the German looting of European art collections in World War II. The theft and display of Babylonian monuments could have been an attempt to announce that Susa had become a major city and that its rulers were legitimate heirs to the Kassites (Carter 1992: 122). It has also been suggested that Shutruk-Nahhunte wanted to protect the monuments from further damage and that he inadvertently exposed them to later violence when the Assyrian King Assurbanipal sacked Susa in 646 (Harper 1992: 161–62).

These explanations do not take into account the power of such images, however. Texts and visual representations show that the abduction of royal monuments was a common act of war in the ancient Near East. When Shutruk-Nahhunte seized these objects they were not just memorials of the past, but they continued to be manifestations of the rulers they represented. Naram-Sin was present in his stele and still exercised his military prowess in it. Hammurabi was still a great king of justice through his law code. By taking control over these monuments and inscribing his own name on them, Shutruk-Nahhunte usurped the powers of these past rulers (Bahrani 1995). He did not shy away from acknowledging who had set them up, although he may have erased the original inscriptions partly, but he asserted that he was now in control of them. He set them up for public display to show this, and some of them may have stood so for many centuries afterwards. A Persian-era tablet found at Sippar claims that its scribe copied the text straight from Hammurabi's stele as it stood in Susa (document 15.2).

NOTES

1   Beckman 1999: 147. The name of the Hittite king is lost. Scholars have suggested Muwatalli II, Mursili III, and Hattusili III.
2   Grayson 1987: 275.
3   Foster 2007: 21.

10

The Collapse of the Regional System and Its Aftermath

3000	2500	2000	1500	1000	500

1209	Merneptah of Egypt fights "Sea People"
ca. 1200	End of Mycenaean culture
ca. 1190	Sack of Ugarit
ca. 1185	Fall of Hatti
ca. 1185	Sack of Emar
1177	Ramesses III of Egypt fights "Sea People"
1155	End of Kassite dynasty
ca. 1120	End of the Middle Elamite period
ca. 935	Reemergence of the textual record in Assyria

The twelfth century was extremely eventful in the Near East and the surrounding areas, and introduced radical changes in many aspects of people's lives. There was much destruction of long-existing cultural practices. Yet, elements of continuity are also visible and certain regions were less affected by the events than others. Because of the disruption of standard bureaucratic and other recording practices, it is difficult to ascertain what exactly happened in various places, and in addition the chronology of the incidents we observe is often doubtful. Even more difficult is their interpretation: no single cause can explain what went on in all regions and states. Local circumstances modified the impact of wide

A History of the Ancient Near East ca. 3000–323 BC, Third Edition. Marc Van De Mieroop.
© 2016 John Wiley & Sons, Inc. Published 2016 by John Wiley & Sons, Inc.

regional changes. The end result was the total disappearance of the system that had characterized the Near East in the preceding centuries. The unraveling of that system certainly exacerbated the various difficulties that individual localities experienced and ultimately becomes the framework in which this period has to be explained.

10.1   The Events

The available documentation focuses most on disruptions and disturbances. Archaeologically, the burning down of a city is more visible than its survival, and royal inscriptions, with their attention to warfare, highlight battles rather than peaceful conditions. The story of the twelfth century is therefore primarily one of upheaval, but there were also strong elements of continuity and of gradual change. The latter are harder to examine, but should not be forgotten. There is much scholarly debate about the relative importance of the forces of continuity and change. All scholars agree, however, that the Near Eastern world in 1050 was very different from what it had been in 1250. What happened, why, and exactly when, is more controversial.

We observe that the forces of disruption were strongest in the area of the eastern Mediterranean, that is, the Aegean and Anatolia, and extended eastward with less force. Coastal Syria and the Levant were more fundamentally affected than the inland areas. The great states of Mesopotamia and Egypt were able to hold out against the major destructive forces, but did suffer from the repercussions of what happened outside their borders and finally went into decline. The following description will thus move from west to east (see map 10.1).

The Aegean world of the Mycenaeans was on the fringes of the Near Eastern system that characterized the fifteenth through thirteenth centuries. The precise nature of Mycenaean social and political organization is still unclear, but the massive fortresses built as residences for wealthy elites in places such as Mycenae and Tiryns suggest the existence of strong central powers in various regions. Mycenaean influence had extended over a large part of the Greek mainland, the Aegean islands, including Crete, and the Anatolian coast, and there had been much trade with Cyprus and the Levant. That world disappeared in the early twelfth century: overseas trade ceased, people were no longer buried with lavish grave-goods, and several of the fortresses were destroyed or substantially reduced in size. The Bronze Age palace culture vanished. The destruction did not happen all at once, but was spread over several decades. Although the subsequent archaeological culture can still be described as Mycenaean in character, it was impoverished and had lost its wide geographical extent. While decline and disruption are visible in most of the Aegean world, the island of Cyprus seems to have developed in the opposite direction: around 1200, there was increased urban expansion and metal production, as well as international contacts with Egypt, the Levant, and the central Mediterranean. The disappearance of Mycenaean power may thus have enabled the Cypriots to fill a void.

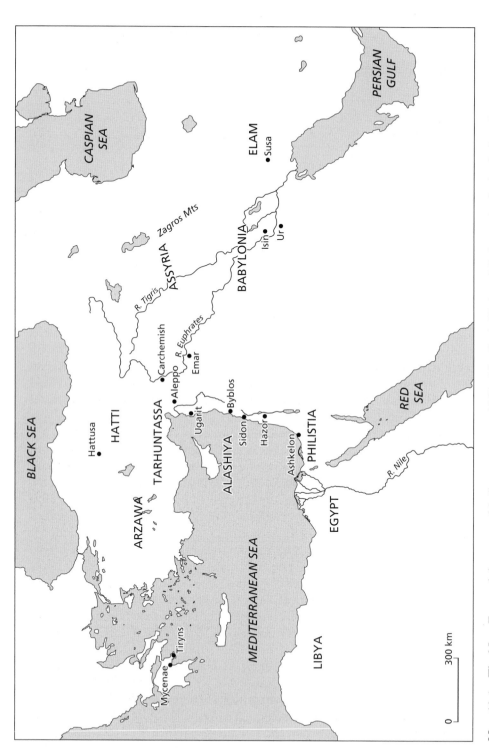

Map 10.1 The Near East and the eastern Mediterranean, ca. 1200. After L. de Blois and R. J. van der Spek, *An Introduction to the Ancient World* (London and New York: Routledge, 1997), p. 21.

Anatolia underwent fundamental political changes around 1200: the state of Hatti that had dominated the region for centuries disintegrated, but again the circumstances are mysterious (see debate 10.1). Several elements played a role. Already in the late thirteenth century the king in Hattusa had to deal with a competing royal house in the south of Anatolia, in the region of Tarhuntassa. The kings there also claimed descent from the earlier great rulers of Hatti, and carved out an almost independent state of their own. Simultaneously, western Anatolia needed to be brought under military control, and Hatti's last king, Suppiluliuma II, engaged in sea battles over the kingdom of Alashiya on Cyprus. Based on references to grain deliveries in Egyptian and Ugaritic texts, some scholars have suggested that a famine struck the region; the unstable agricultural base of Anatolia with its many poor harvests may explain these isolated references better than a sustained famine, however. The end of Hatti was due to violence, but the destruction was far from uniform over the region. In the capital city Hattusa, the royal fortress was burned down along with some individual public buildings in the lower town, though private residences were untouched. It seems that the court had abandoned the city long beforehand, as if it had warning of what was about to happen. Throughout Anatolia a similar pattern is visible: on those sites where destruction took place, it was not complete. Many settlements were left unscathed, but were nevertheless abandoned. As a result, Hatti disappeared as a political power. In the south, the previously dependent Hittite viceroy of Carchemish survived, however, and claimed to be the descendant of earlier Great Kings, prolonging the history of the Hittite royal house. The succession of rulers there could not keep the region unified, and an increasing number of small states developed by 1100.

With the end of Hittite dominance the Syrian cities became independent, but several were destroyed, especially those in the coastal area. The events are best documented at Ugarit. Its last king, Ammurapi, was a faithful vassal to the king of Hatti and maintained direct contact with the Hittite viceroy at Carchemish. As such, he supported Hatti with grain deliveries and troops. He also corresponded with several rulers of the region, who warned him about the imminent danger of raiders on the sea. The Hittite king identified one of the groups involved as "Shikalayu, who live on ships,"[1] and he instructed Ugarit to send him a man they had captured so that he could be interrogated. The king of Alashiya advised Ammurapi to fortify his towns and gather his warriors and chariots. But the reply presented a distressing picture: several villages had already been sacked, and most of Ugarit's troops were in Hatti, while its ships were on the south coast of Anatolia (see document 10.1). The excavator of Ugarit, Claude Schaeffer, claimed that these letters were found in an oven, where they would have been baked before their dispatch, and that the city had been sacked before they were ready. This gave a dramatic context to these texts, as if they were written while enemy troops were advancing and were never sent because Ugarit was sacked first. Now, it seems that this was an archaeological phantom. The enemy was not at the gate when the letters were written, and we have here an accidental grouping of texts written on different dates. In any case, we know what happened. Ugarit was destroyed

Document 10.1   *Letters from Ugarit*

The rich city of Ugarit on the Mediterranean coast of northern Syria was the target of hostile forces coming from the sea around 1200. It is clear that its inhabitants were forewarned as correspondence with Cyprus found in its ruins shows. Small numbers of enemy ships were involved, but Ugarit's army seems to have been requisitioned to defend Hatti. The outcome is clear: Ugarit was destroyed never to reemerge.

Letter from the king (of Alashiya) to Ammurapi of Ugarit

Thus says the king, tell Ammurapi, king of Ugarit: May you be well and may the gods guard your well-being.

Regarding what you wrote me before: "Enemy ships were observed at sea!" If it is true that ships were observed, reinforce yourself. Where are your troops and chariots? Are they not with you? If not, who will deliver you from the enemy? Surround your cities with walls and bring your troops and chariots into them. Watch out for the enemy and reinforce yourself well!

Letter from the king of Ugarit to the king of Alashiya

Tell the king of Alashiya, my father; the king of Ugarit your son says: I fall at the feet of my father. May my father be well. May your houses, your wives, your troops, and everything that belongs to the king of Alashiya, my father, be very, very well.

Father, the ships of the enemy have been coming. They have been burning down my villages and have done evil things to the country. Does my father not know that all my troops [and chariots] are in Hatti and that all my ships are in Lukka? They have not yet reached me, so the country is undefended. May my father be informed of this. Now the seven ships of the enemy that came have done evil things. If other enemy ships appear, send me a message so that I know.

Letter from the senior governor of Alashiya to the king of Ugarit

Thus says Eshuwara, senior governor of Alashiya. Tell the king of Ugarit: May you and your land be well.

Regarding the things that the enemies have done to the people of your country and your ships, they have done these transgressions against the people of the country. Thus, do not be angry with me.

Now, the twenty ships that the enemies earlier left in the mountainous areas, have not stayed behind. They left suddenly and we do not know where they are. I write to you to inform you so that you can guard yourself. Be informed!

Translations after Knapp 1996: 27.

and was not to be resettled for a thousand years. Its harbor, Ras Ibn Hani, was also sacked but was soon restored, perhaps by the people who had attacked it. Ugarit's destruction happened around 1190 or soon thereafter: in its ruins was found a letter from the Egyptian chancellor Bay, whom we know was executed in that year after a brief stint governing the country. He must have been alive and in charge during Ugarit's last days.

Farther south in the Syro-Palestinian area, the pattern of selective destruction continued. Prominent harbors like Byblos and Sidon survived unscathed, but cities like Ashkelon and Hazor were destroyed. The devastation was not simultaneous and a time span of several decades was involved. In Palestine, village life gradually replaced the urban culture that had characterized the region. New people gained prominence in the region, such as the Philistines, who took over control of the southern coastal area up to the Egyptian border.

Reports from Egypt are the most detailed available, but their point of view was self-centered and biased. Two Egyptian kings described in narrative and pictorial accounts what happened in the eastern Mediterranean. They set the events in the context of a war with outside invaders who always included Libyans, coming from the west. Although the accounts are separated by twenty-five years, they narrate very similar things. King Merneptah (ruled 1213–1203) claimed that in 1209 he successfully repelled an attack by Libyans and assorted people from the north, whom he called "of the countries of the sea." Although they tried to enter Egypt using military force, they brought their families and cattle, which indicated their intention to settle there. Ramesses III (ruled 1184–1153) provided more detail. After mentioning attacks from the north in his fifth year (1180), his account of the eighth year (1177) purports to provide an overview of what happened throughout the eastern Mediterranean:

> The foreign countries made a conspiracy in their islands. All at once the lands were removed and scattered in the fray. No land could stand before their arms, from Hatti, Kode (=Tarhuntassa), Carchemish, Arzawa, and Alashiya on, being cut off at [one time]. A camp [was set up] in one place in Amurru. They desolated its people, and its land was like that which had never come into being. They were coming forward toward Egypt, while the flame was prepared for them. Their confederation was the Peleset, Tjeker, Shekelesh, Denyen, and Weshesh, lands united.[2]

This account presents a clear image of an invasion by island people into the states of Hatti, Tarhuntassa, and others, and these states supposedly collapsed at once. The invaders gathered forces in northern Syria and marched on toward Egypt, where Ramesses III defeated them both on land and at sea (see figure 10.1). He identified certain groups explicitly, including Shekelesh, who must be the same as the Shikalayu mentioned before in the letter found at Ugarit. Upon closer examination, Ramesses' detailed reconstruction becomes suspect, however. Carchemish, for example, was not destroyed. More importantly, the names of the "Sea People" whom he portrayed as swooping down the Syrian coast from distant islands were already attested several decades earlier as present in the region,

Figure 10.1   Ramesses III's battle against Sea People, detail of relief from Medinet Habu. The Egyptians described their battles against the so-called Sea People in inscriptions of pharaohs Merneptah and Ramesses III and also depicted them in various gigantic wall reliefs. They portray the attacks as involving large armies that approached Egypt both overland and by sea and made a point of representing individual characteristics in the weaponry and dress of the enemies. Scholars have tried to correlate the images with the names of the Sea People in the texts, and these two warriors are often considered to be Sherden. Although Ramesses III states that they attacked Egypt as a group in his reign, we know that they had served as mercenaries in the Egyptian army since Ramesses II's battle at Qadesh. Credit: akg images/Erich Lessing.

including as mercenaries in the Egyptian and Hittite armies. In other words, Ramesses III turned what may have been chronic clashes with groups in Syria into a major battle between Egypt and an invading foreign army that had destroyed everything in its path. The interpretation of this data is very complicated. Some scholars have even suggested that Ramesses III merely repeated battle accounts by his predecessor Merneptah and claimed earlier victories for himself, something not unprecedented in Egypt. We have no way to confirm or deny this idea. Whatever the details of events, it is clear that Egypt lost most of its direct control over territories in Asia, although it still had access to mines in the Sinai. It survived as a territorial state, but the century after Ramesses III shows internal disorder and social upheaval, a reduction of contacts with regions beyond its borders, and ultimately, around 1100, a political fragmentation of the country.

Similar processes were visible in the eastern states of the region, which became cut off from western Syria and the Mediterranean. Assyria, Babylonia, and Elam continued to interact with one another, often through military clashes. Each remained a territorial state, but had internal problems and little permanent influence beyond its borders. After the militarily successful thirteenth century, Assyria abandoned its policy of constant campaigning for some ninety years. Internal problems after the assassination of Tukulti-Ninurta I in 1197 may have been responsible, and the troubles in western Syria were probably also a factor in this change of policy. These disturbances did not spill over into the region east of the Euphrates, however. The easternmost city destroyed was Emar, a Hittite dependency, where two texts mention "the year that the hordes(?) afflicted the city," and the latest dated text is from 1185. East of Emar, Assyrian outposts in Syria did not disappear, but they shrank in size and scribal activity stopped. Semi-nomadic Arameans controlled the countryside and became prominent in political life. The level of urbanization in the region declined. For three centuries Assyria was reduced to its heartland, perhaps with some outposts in the region to its west.

Scholars often regard the change of dynasty from the Kassites to the so-called second dynasty of Isin in twelfth-century Babylonia as a relatively unimportant shift in power from one royal house to another. But it demonstrates how in political terms the centralized power the Kassites had held for four hundred years disintegrated. The existence of a competing dynasty in central Babylonia, which captured Babylon's throne by 1150, shows that the strength of the state had dissipated. Moreover, the archaeological record indicates that urbanism was in sharp decline: the number of true urban centers became very small, perhaps only Babylon, Isin, and Ur, and the large majority of the settled people lived in villages. Nippur, for example, had lost its urban characteristics by 1200 and by 1000 it housed perhaps nothing more than a small population living near its ancient ziggurat. The size of the sedentary population had dwindled to 25 percent of the level of the late third millennium. There were regional variations with, for instance, a much steeper decline in the Diyala valley than in the region of Ur. But there is no doubt that the urban organization and its infrastructure of irrigation canals had collapsed by the end of the second millennium. Many of the occupants of the region reverted to a semi-nomadic lifestyle. The primary causes for this development may have been non-political. The bulk of the Euphrates water flow seems to have shifted toward western branches of the river, which deprived some major urban centers of earlier days of sufficient irrigation to support a large population. Moreover, overuse of the soil leading to salinization probably reduced yields. Certainly, a complex interaction between political and ecological factors was at work. The weakening of central power made the organization of large irrigation projects to counter these natural changes impossible. Outside military interference from Elam and Assyria may have precipitated the process of decline, and the Babylonian state lost control over its countryside.

Since we do not know the organization of the state of Elam in the preceding era well, it is impossible to determine how much it changed in the twelfth century. Earlier internal decline may have facilitated the military raid by Nebuchadnezzar I (ruled 1125–1104) that triggered the end of the Middle Elamite period. In any event, the result was similar to what happened throughout the Near East: a centralized state ended and new population groups infiltrated the region, in this case seemingly coming from the east.

10.2   Interpretation

Numerous explanations of these events have been proposed in scholarship, mostly focused on one state or on the eastern Mediterranean by itself. Invasions and migrations, social revolutions, and ecological disasters have all been suggested as the main causes for the collapse of the states. Other scholars, however, have stressed the visible continuities and have disputed the idea that the twelfth century was one of radical change. If they are correct, we need to search for an explanation to account for the differences between the late second millennium and the early first in subsequent centuries, where our data are almost completely lacking. Yet, it seems clear that changes that started around 1200 precipitated the end of the Near Eastern world of the fifteenth to thirteenth centuries, and that the causes for this end have to be sought in the twelfth century. Moreover, it cannot have been accidental that all societies experienced drastic change at this time. Since they had been tied together in a common system for centuries, the end of that system must have had wide-ranging repercussions. But, no single cause can explain this comprehensive change.

When referring to the Aegean, Anatolia, and Syria-Palestine, the ancient sources stress invasions by outsiders as a significant cause of disruption. Most prominent are the contemporary Egyptian sources. But later Greek accounts of the rise of the classical world and the biblical depiction of the creation of the ancient state of Israel also describe invasions in this period, whereas Babylonian sources portray a period of great upheaval (see document 10.2). This general image has inspired scholars to interpret other data in that light. They interpret the appearance of a new type of pottery in the Zagros Mountains, for example, as the consequence of people from the east invading the region, or they consider that references to Arameans in Assyrian texts demonstrate that these people attempted to infiltrate the state. An analysis of the textual records of invasion shows that they draw too simplistic a picture, however. They contain internal contradictions and other references provide a different image. For example, Ramesses III's statement that the Sea People came down from their islands and destroyed the states of Anatolia and Syria-Palestine in one fell swoop, only to be stopped by him at the Egyptian border, is contradicted by the fact that people with their names appeared decades earlier in the region. The archaeological record does not show a series of devastating events in a short period of time but a prolonged period in which individual sites were destroyed, while others survived yet declined in size. Military confrontations with unconventional troops, including people who originated outside the Near East, most probably took place, but they were not the result of a widespread invasion. In the eastern part of the Near East, interstate warfare is often seen as a major cause of disruption and decline. But this was not a novelty of the twelfth century. Throughout the second half of the second millennium states

---

Document 10.2   *Later reflections on the Dark Age*

During the centuries after the disturbances that engulfed the Near East in the twelfth century virtually no texts were written, or at least extremely few are preserved today. Several people from the first millennium reflected back on this period, however, and described conditions of great disorder. The classical Greeks depicted the period after the Mycenaean civilization disappeared as one of invasions of people such as the Dorians. The Bible placed the Israelite conquest of Canaan in this period as well. In Babylonia, a possible literary reflection on this period was a long poem probably written in the seventh century. Scholars often refer to it as the Erra Epic. The author identified himself at the end of the text as Kabti-ilani-Marduk of the Dabibi-family, and he claimed that the work was revealed to him in a dream. The epic relates how Erra, the god of plagues, became enraged because he felt snubbed by the other gods, and rampaged throughout Babylonia, leaving death and destruction in his wake. In Babylon the citizens rallied around him and burned down temples, until royal troops massacred them. Nomads, identified with an anachronistic tribal designation as Sutians, overran Uruk and molested Ishtar's cult personnel. Sippar's wall was torn down and Der was destroyed. The gods of those cities were horrified, and only then did Erra calm down and give Babylon his blessing to rule the whole land. The text was considered to have apotropaic values and parts of it were copied out on amulets that protected houses. The following excerpt is just a short part of a long litany of chaos and violence.

> He who did not die in battle, will die in the epidemic;
> He who did not die in the epidemic, the enemy will rob him;
> He whom the enemy has not robbed, the thief will thrash him;
> He whom the thief did not thrash, the king's weapon will overcome him;
> He whom the king's weapon did not overcome, the prince will kill him;
> He whom the prince did not kill, the storm god will wash him away;
> He whom the storm god did not wash away, the sun god will carry him away;
> He who has left for the countryside, the wind will sweep him away;
> He who has entered his own house, a demon will strike him;
> He who climbed up a high place, will die of thirst;
> He who went down to a low place, will die in the waters;
> You have destroyed high and low place alike!

Translation after Foster 2005: 905.

---

had clashed. So the effects of these wars by themselves do not provide sufficient explanation for the widespread collapse.

Other scholars have focused more on internal developments to explain change. An important characteristic of the system of great states was the existence of a palace elite that exploited the agricultural communities under its control. There was a huge discrepancy in wealth and lifestyle between the two groups. The rich grave-goods and architectural remains we admire were produced from the income of impoverished farmers and herdsmen. Rural indebtedness led to many seeking refuge outside the structures of the state and becoming *habiru* (see debate 8.1). The problem of palace dependents leaving the countryside was considered a serious threat to the palace system: labor was scarce and when more people fled palace control it was even harder to find workers. This explains the frequent references in treaties to the extradition of refugees. A shortage of laborers reduced the agricultural productivity of the states and threatened revenue. To compensate for the loss of labor, palaces may have increased demands on the remaining dependents, consequently exacerbating the problem. The laborers may have turned against their masters and joined hostile forces that challenged them, including such groups as the Sea People. The selective destruction we observe is in that case no surprise. Not all cities were sacked, but the rural infrastructure of most disappeared, which led to their reduction in size or total abandonment.

Some scholars have looked at natural causes for the collapse observed. Certain archaeological sites show evidence of earthquakes, but this could not account for the regional disintegration. Lack of food is attested in some textual sources, and scholars have used this to suggest that famines were a great problem. Both a general desiccation of the climate in the north and a shift of river courses in southern Mesopotamia have been proposed as an explanation for agricultural decline. The evidence remains ambiguous, however. Throughout the Near East the agricultural base was always unstable, and the textual references to difficulties with food supplies may simply refer to isolated instances rather than a long-lasting famine. If a drying of the climate had indeed taken place, it would certainly have exacerbated the already severe problems of insufficient support for the lavish lifestyles of the elites. Nevertheless, environmental stress by itself does not seem adequate to explain all the changes that we see in the Near East.

Since all these explanations have some foundation in the historical record, we may conclude that a variety of causes were probably at the root of the changes we observe, but in each case local circumstances played an important role. What happened in Hattusa, for example, was not necessarily repeated elsewhere. Military clashes and social rebellions may have been the main reason for the destruction of individual sites. What made each separate cause more important was that it contributed to the unraveling of an entire system that had characterized the region and had provided its stability from 1500 to 1200. The states had not existed in isolation, but had been closely tied to one another. The contacts between them had been vital for maintaining their internal organizations. The disruption of those contacts had a fundamental impact on all of them. When the Hittite state disappeared and Syria-Palestine was in turmoil, Egypt was cut off from Asia. It had no other equals with whom to interact, as Babylonia and Assyria were out of reach. Trade and diplomatic exchange ceased, leaving Egypt blind to events in the north. The country had substantial resources of its own, so it could survive, but the international system that had supported its palace elites was gone. Similarly, the eastern states of Assyria, Babylonia, and Elam were reduced to a small international system with only the three of them as participants. The Mediterranean Sea and Egypt were no longer accessible, and trade routes were cut. The loss of the wide geographical infrastructure led to the disintegration of these eastern states, which allowed new people, especially the Arameans, to control areas in between them and further isolate them from one another. No one power filled the vacuum created by the decline of these states, enabling new groups and lower social strata to acquire control. When we talk about collapse of the states, we should not imagine that everyone suffered. There was a rearrangement of power, and large parts of the populations of the Near Eastern states may have benefited from the newfound freedom.

10.3   The Aftermath

As can be expected, the crisis of the palace system led to a sharp reduction in the number of sources available to the historian. Bureaucracies ceased to function and building activity was minimal. Textual and archaeological data are lacking, and the history of the Near East entered another "Dark Age." The length of this period varied from region to region. The first to come out of it was Assyria, but even there textual records were extremely rare from around 1050 to 935. Afterwards its expansionist policy drew many surrounding regions into its orbit and its increasingly detailed records document some of the circumstances there. Often the use of writing in these areas was limited until much later, however. Even in Babylonia, the region with the oldest and strongest literary tradition, we have to wait until the mid-eighth century to see a level of scribal activity beyond the isolated document.

Very little is known about the centuries from 1100 to 900. We can determine, however, that in that time important technological and social changes occurred, largely due to the disappearance of earlier structures. Social and economic life reformed itself to adapt to the new circumstances. The Late Bronze Age palaces had supported certain technological and economic practices, and when they ceased to exist, infrastructure collapsed and there was a need for change. We can see that the regions where the palaces remained stronger in this period – Assyria, Babylonia, and Egypt – became technologically backward as they carried on older methods. Developments in writing practices well demonstrate this situation. Throughout the Near East, the palaces of the second millennium had supported chancelleries where scribes read and wrote Akkadian. This was a foreign language for most of them, and it was recorded in a script, cuneiform, that was relatively difficult to master. Training and support of these skilled people was possible only in an institution that had sufficient wealth. With the end of the palaces, the support for these specialists disappeared, as did the rationale for their existence. No longer were letters written to other courts that required knowledge of the diplomatic language. Moreover, the disruption of economic routines led to a reduced need for bureaucracies. Trade was interrupted, fields and labor were no longer centrally administered, and private economic activity declined. In the states where the palaces retained some prominence, bureaucracies were preserved to some extent. This explains the continuation of cuneiform writing in Assyria and Babylonia. But in other regions, that particular recording system was no longer in use and people reverted to local practices. Egypt, with its still relatively strong palace, used only its own hieroglyphic script and its derivatives to write the Egyptian language.

Figure 10.2   Anatolian hieroglyphic inscription from the early first millennium. After the collapse of the Hittite Empire its so-called hieroglyphic writing system survived and small rulers of southern Anatolia and northern Syria continued to use it for several more centuries. This stele, probably from Maras in Turkey, is a typical example of the use of writing on their monuments. It is too fragmentary for its contents to be clear. Late ninth century (MMA X.196 H. 10¾ in × W. 12 in × D. 9 in). Credit: © 2014 The Metropolitan Museum of Art/Art Resource/Scala, Florence.

Elsewhere very few texts were written. In southern Anatolia and northern Syria, the successors of the Hittites expanded the use of what we call Anatolian hieroglyphs, with which they rendered the Luwian language. Previously, during the Hittite New Kingdom, that script had been reserved for short royal inscriptions and marks of ownership, but it was a more indigenous and perhaps more popular writing system than cuneiform. Hieroglyphic writing survived the collapse of the elite culture and became the official script of the so-called Neo-Hittite states. In the twelfth to eighth centuries courts of southern Anatolia and northern Syria carved monumental royal inscriptions in it (figure 10.2). Some administrative records on strips of lead show that the use of hieroglyphs extended into everyday life as well, and most likely letters and contracts were written with them on writing boards and parchment, which have perished. In the Syro-Palestinian area the script of choice was the linear alphabet. Developed many centuries before, it had only a limited use among a variety of scripts and languages (see box 10.1). In the eleventh and tenth centuries, it became the sole system of writing in the region. Most inscriptions known to us were from the Phoenician harbor cities that had not been destroyed during the disturbances around 1200. The alphabet used only twenty-two letters, and the direction of the script was fixed from right to left. In the ninth century, Hebrew and Aramaic were also recorded in it, and an increasing number of mostly short inscriptions were written. With the spread of Aramaic as a spoken language throughout the Near East, the script spread as well. As a simpler

Box 10.1   *Alphabetic scripts*

In the Syro-Palestinian area of the second millennium, the first evidence of what can be called alphabetic scripts appeared. Instead of indicating word signs and syllables with one, two, or three consonants, these scripts used one sign for each consonant of the language, and this required fewer than thirty characters. The Egyptian writing system may have inspired the idea, as it includes a set of hieroglyphs for single consonants only, which can be combined with any vowel. The earliest evidence of alphabetic writing derives from Serabit el-Khadim, a site in the Sinai with strong Egyptian influence in the early second millennium. In the second half of the second millennium, various alphabetic scripts coexisted. The system that survived into later periods had a set of characters whose reading was based on the acrophonic principle: for example, the drawing of a house represented the sound /b/, the first in the Semitic word for house, *baytu*. A handful of such alphabetic inscriptions of the second millennium are known, most of them with a few characters only. The forms of the letters show much variation, but a common basic system can be recognized. These texts were mainly carved on stone or metal or drawn with ink on pottery shards.

In the thirteenth century, scribes in the Syrian city of Ugarit and its territory used a much better-attested cuneiform alphabet, with twenty-seven letters, alongside the syllabic cuneiform system from Babylonia. Written on clay tablets, the Ugaritic alphabetic signs look like the syllabic cuneiform ones, but there is no obvious formal connection between the two. A large variety of texts was written in the alphabetic script, including letters, contracts, and literature. Very few texts do not record the local Semitic language, however. It seems that local affairs were recorded in Ugaritic alphabetic writing, while Babylonian was preferred for international affairs. In total, some 1,400 tablets with the Ugaritic script are preserved. Interestingly, both for the cuneiform and the other alphabetic systems, abecedaries of this period were found, which show that the sequence of letters was well established (figure 10.3).

Ugarit did not survive after 1200 BC, nor did its script. The Phoenicians adopted the linear alphabet and developed it further during the first millennium to write the Semitic languages of Syria-Palestine. With the spread of the Aramaic language in the Assyrian empire in the first millennium, and its adoption as an official language in the Persian empire in the fifth century, the alphabet became the dominant script of the Near East and far beyond. The date of transmission to Greece is controversial. Most scholars believe this took place from the Phoenician or Syrian area in the ninth or eighth centuries, but some suggest a date before 1200. The Greeks reserved a number of the signs to indicate vowels, thereby enabling the use of the alphabetic script for non-Semitic languages.

system that rendered the language locally spoken, it was much easier to learn and the scribes did not have to be as extensively trained as those who wrote cuneiform. Thus there was no need for a palace organization to support them.

A fundamental technological change also took place in metallurgy. The most commonly used metal up to 1200 had been bronze, an alloy of copper and tin. In most countries of the Near East, both metals had to be imported from different

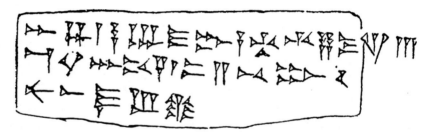

Figure 10.3 Tablet with an abecedary of the Ugaritic script. This small tablet lists the thirty letters of the Ugaritic cuneiform alphabet in sequence and was probably intended for schooling. The three last letters were not necessary to write the Semitic language, Ugaritic, but for Hurrian, either as individual words in Ugaritic texts or for texts written entirely in Hurrian. This alphabet disappeared when Ugarit was sacked around 1200. Fourteenth century. 1.3 × 5.1 cm (0.5 × 2 in). Credit: Virolleaud, 1957. Reproduced with permission from Klincksieck, Paris.

sources, and no one had access to both locally. The international trade system of the second half of the second millennium had greatly facilitated the acquisition of these metals. This is well illustrated by one of the shipwrecks of the period (Uluburun), which contained ingots of copper and tin in the correct ratio of ten to one (see figure 7.1). The palace workshops housed and supported the craftsmen needed for bronze production. After 1200, iron replaced bronze as the chief metal and had several advantages over it. It was not an alloy of two ores found in distinct locations, but derived from one ore that was available almost everywhere and did not need to be imported. Moreover, in the twelfth and eleventh centuries the technology was discovered to alloy iron with charcoal from the furnace during the smelting process, and so steel was produced, which was much harder than bronze. Iron had been in use since the third millennium, but only as a byproduct of bronze manufacture and it was reserved for special objects. After 1200, it became widely used. Scholars have explained its success in two entirely opposite ways. To some, it was the result of the scarcity of copper and tin. Because of the collapse of the Late Bronze Age system several cities, especially in the eastern Mediterranean, were cut off from new metal supplies and their bronze workshops could no longer function. People turned to iron as a substitute that suited the new social conditions perfectly. A cheap metal, superior in strength to bronze, it could be produced without the need for an elaborate trade network. As in the case of writing, the regions where the palaces remained strong, Mesopotamia and Egypt, lagged behind. Iron became common there only in the ninth century, and even then was mostly reserved for the palaces. To other scholars, the success of iron was the result of increased supplies of copper and tin in the last century of the Late Bronze Age. The value of bronze diminished, but iron did not lose its special status. On the contrary its appeal rose, and gradually it took over the role of bronze.

There was indeed a shift in the conduct of trade that may have started before 1200, but certainly became obvious after the end of the Late Bronze Age system. Private actors, who did not rely on great states for their support but were based in mercantile cities, became the leading traders. At first they originated from Cyprus and the Philistine coastal cities, then later in the early first millennium from Phoenician harbors, as we will see. They explored the entire Mediterranean and brought distant goods into the Near East without palace involvement. The disappearance of the heavy-handed palace system provided an opening for their activities to flourish.

During the Dark Age an almost complete restructuring of society took place over most of the Near East. The crisis of the states enabled foreign peoples to migrate into the region and internal population movements were numerous. There was a flux between semi-nomadic and settled people. Many urban residents turned to a pastoralist lifestyle, while some previously semi-nomadic people gained political power in cities. The situation was very confused and the movements cannot be traced accurately. We see, however, that when first-millennium records provide information on the identity of peoples, the makeup of the population in the Near East was very different from before.

Some new peoples came from outside the Near East. In central Anatolia, for example, Phrygians seem to have arrived from the Balkans in the twelfth century, and by the eighth they had formed a unified state. Some of the Sea People identified by the Egyptians settled down in the region of Syria-Palestine. There is much scholarly speculation about the destination of these groups, all based on a comparison of the names listed by the Egyptians with toponyms and the names of peoples in later texts. It is very often stated that the Peleset of the Sea People became the Philistines, who inhabited the coastal area just north of Egypt in the early first millennium. But, besides the resemblance in names, there is nothing to confirm this hypothesis. Other identifications are even less clear: the Sea People called Denyen, for example, have been associated with the Israelite tribe of Dan and with the north Syrian region Danuna around modern Adana. The evidence, purely based on name similarity, is tenuous. Whatever the origin of the Sea People and their final destinations, they did participate in the general movement of populations and the restructuring of societies. Even if the Peleset were not the Philistines, we can say on the basis of archaeological evidence that a new material culture appeared in southern Palestine, a region later called Philistia.

The most prominent among the groups who gained in importance were the Arameans. Most probably pastoralists in northern Syria for a long time before 1200, they took advantage of the weakening of the states to spread out over large parts of the Near East and to acquire political power, including in cities. They kept their tribal organization and were subdivided into groups identified as belonging to the "house of so-and-so," in Akkadian *Bit* and the name of a person, who was considered to be the tribal ancestor. Many of the states they founded appear in the first millennium with this designation, for instance Bit-Adini. In northern Syria, Arameans took control of most cities, including some that were inhabited by people who maintained Hittite cultural and political traditions. In such places certain kings had Luwian names, others Aramaic. Other cities were completely Aramean and became the core of states, such as Aram-Damascus. By the ninth century these people politically dominated the whole of Syria.

In the first millennium, Arameans also appeared in Assyria and Babylonia. In many respects the processes involved were the same as we observed before with other pastoralists, such as the Amorites, and their presence had similar results. Mesopotamian traditions continued to dominate in the court-patronized culture. Akkadian remained the official language, found in royal inscriptions, letters, administrative texts, and so on. But a large part of the population spoke Aramaic, and traces of its influence in the grammar and lexicon of Akkadian are clear. Unlike the Amorites and Kassites previously, however, Aramaic speakers introduced a parallel written tradition. First-millennium Assyrian reliefs represent two types of scribes: those writing on clay tablets and those writing on a leather scroll. The profession of a "scribe on leather" is also attested in the texts. These scribes would have written Aramaic in alphabetic script on parchment, but this material has not survived in the archaeological record, so we have no evidence of their work. The names of people remained predominantly Akkadian, yet it is clear that Aramaic speakers did take on Akkadian names, or even had distinct names in both languages. A later literary tale in Aramaic regarding a man called Ahiqar reveals this practice. The oldest preserved manuscript is from late fifth-century BC Elephantine in southern Egypt, but references to Ahiqar appear in earlier texts. In the tale he was adviser to the seventh-century Assyrian kings Sennacherib and Esarhaddon, and he helped his masters acquire a fabulous amount of gold in a competition with the king of Egypt. According to this story, the Aramean Ahiqar was a highly placed member of the Assyrian court. We would not have recognized him in the contemporary record as an Aramean, however, since he also had an Akkadian name. This is revealed by a cuneiform text from second-century Babylonia, which lists as adviser to King Esarhaddon "Aba-Enlil-dari, whom the Arameans call Ahiqar." Many of the high court officials with Akkadian names recorded in the Assyrian documentation could thus have been Arameans.

The Arameans started to raid Babylonia in the eleventh century, but occupied territories along the Tigris River only in the ninth century. At the same time a people called Chaldeans, also with a tribal organization but of a different kind, settled primarily along the Euphrates and in the south. Both groups remained distinct and used separate tribal designations, but together they controlled most of the Babylonian countryside. Also in the first millennium, Arabs from the peninsula entered central Babylonia, while until the mid-ninth century remnants of the Kassites remained in the area, especially in the Diyala valley, and they kept their own tribal organization. Often opposed to these groups were the inhabitants of the remnants of the great cities of the past, such as Babylon, Nippur, and Ur, who held on to ancient Babylonian traditions. For almost five centuries, the political situation in the region was extremely volatile, and rarely did a succession of men from the same family hold royal power. Chaldeans, Babylonians, Kassites, Elamites, and Assyrians fought incessantly over the throne, until the Neo-Babylonian dynasty was established in 626. There thus existed a stark opposition between cities and the countryside, with the former having little influence outside their walls. Often urban residents sought military support from the kings of Assyria, who had great difficulty in the eighth and seventh centuries in controlling Babylonia. But at other times the cities opposed Assyria, which sometimes violently crushed the rebellions.

During the Dark Age there also occurred a technological change that brought new populations into contact with Near Eastern states: the domestication of the camel. This happened in the Arabian Peninsula in the later second millennium and has to be related to the beginning of the overland incense trade to Mesopotamia and the Levant. Consequently, Arabs became part of the documented Near Eastern world. On the fringes of the settled societies, they were mostly seen as enemies. Anti-Assyrian coalitions in Syria often included Arab warriors and their camels. Only during the late Assyrian empire, when it experienced its greatest expansion, did kings attempt to subdue them in their own territories, but Assyrian military techniques were not suitable for a desert environment (figure 10.4). Camels enabled a new type of nomadism. Instead of sheep and goat pastoralism that utilized areas in between permanent settlements, camel nomads could traverse long stretches of the desert using oases as resting places. The latter thus became connected to the better-known Near Eastern lands, and much later the sixth-century Babylonian King Nabonidus temporarily moved his capital to one of them.

The Dark Age was, therefore, of fundamental importance in Near Eastern history, connecting two very different worlds. The radical changes that took place during this period will always remain difficult to study, since there was so much upheaval and consequently a lack of records. When the historian next becomes able to comprehend the situation, the Near East can be said to develop into an age of empires.

Debate 10.1   *What happened to the Hittite state around 1200?*

The Hittite kingdom was one of the greatest powers of the ancient Near East but it vanished around 1200 when the Late Bronze Age system collapsed. In the first millennium Central Anatolia, where its heartland had been, looked very different from before. Major Hittite cities, including the capital Hattusa, were barely inhabited, the Hittite language written in cuneiform had entirely disappeared, and the people living in the region had different political organizations and cultural practices. How could such a major power have dissolved so suddenly?

Until recently the answer was considered to be simple. Archaeologically identified destruction layers in cities like Hattusa confirmed what Ramesses III said in his inscriptions: the Sea People had wiped Hatti off the map. Perhaps old enemies of the Hittites had contributed to the end of the empire, but mass population movements triggered by the Sea People were at fault. Hittite culture disappeared in the heartland, but some aspects of it surprisingly survived in northern Syria, among the so-called Neo-Hittites (e.g., Gurney 1990: 38–40).

Closer archaeological study of Hattusa and other Hittite centers casts doubt on this picture. While there was indeed sudden destruction after a period that saw no decline in building activity, it was limited to official buildings, that is, palaces and temples. There was no evidence of a violent struggle – no dead bodies or weapons had been found in the ruins – nor did archaeological remains suggest that foreigners had taken over. Hittite culture disappeared and the early first-millennium use of imperial titles was based on reminiscences of the greatness of the region in the second millennium (Bittel 1976).

New text finds and a better understanding of Anatolian hieroglyphic inscriptions forced different interpretations. It became clear that in the last decades of Hittite history Hattusa was not the sole and undisputed center of Hittite political power. Tarhuntassa, a still-unidentified city in southern Anatolia, was home to another branch of the royal family that acted independently from and even hostile to the Great King in Hattusa. Hattusili III and Tudhaliya IV had to conclude treaties with one or more rulers of Tarhuntassa (Beckman 1999: 107–23). But in Tudhaliya's reign Kurunta of Tarhuntassa briefly assumed kingship in Hattusa and in a hieroglyphic inscription Suppiluliuma II described military action against Tarhuntassa. Internal conflict was thus at the basis of the collapse of the Hittite state (Hoffner 1992). Still scholars mostly believed that a massive conflagration put an end to Hattusa (e.g., Kuhrt 1995: 265; Klengel 1999: 312–13).

That idea too needed revision. More detailed archaeological research in the official buildings of Hattusa showed that hostile forces – be they Sea People, Kaskeans, or local rebels – did not suddenly sack them while still in use, but that the court had abandoned them beforehand and had cleaned them out of all but things too heavy or of no interest. Only years later they were burned down, perhaps by Kaskeans (Seeher 2001). This happened around 1185 (Bryce 2012: 53) or slightly later (http://www.hattuscha.de/English/cityhistory2.htm).

The commonly accepted scenario today is thus as follows: in the late thirteenth century internal divisions, rebellions by subject regions, foreign threats including from the Sea People, and food shortages made the continuation of normal imperial life at Hattusa impossible. The court abandoned the city, which fell prey to the Kaskeans, but the latter found little left to loot. We do not know where Suppiluliuma II ended up, but Hittite elites in northern Syria, at first especially at Carchemish where viceroys had been stationed for centuries, considered themselves heirs to the empire. They continued some practices, such as the choice of royal names, but also made changes: Anatolian hieroglyphs became the official writing system recording the Luwian language and Hittite cuneiform ceased to exist, and there were changes in what deities were considered to be prominent. There was no unified state any longer and parallel Neo-Hittite dynasties coexisted in southern Anatolia and northern Syria. When the Assyrians spoke of the "Land of Hatti" in the first millennium, they were not mistaken, although they no longer knew of the empire of former times (Collins 2007: 72–90, Bryce 2012: 9–31, and Genz 2013 for slightly different accounts).

NOTES

1   Gregory Mobley in Coogan 2001: 118–19.
2   John Wilson in Pritchard 1969: 262.

Part III
Empires

11

The Near East at the Start of the First Millennium

3000	2500	2000	1500	1000	500

853	Battle of Qarqar between Assyrian King Shalmaneser III and western coalition
ca. 850	Sarduri I unifies Urartian state
ca. 740	Elamite resurgence
691	Battle of Halule between Sennacherib of Assyria and Humban-nimena of Elam
646	Assurbanipal of Assyria sacks Susa
626	Nabopolassar founds Neo-Babylonian dynasty

With the start of the first millennium the political situation in the various parts of the Near East had settled and an entirely new network of states had arisen. Consequently, scribes again wrote records and kings and others once more commissioned buildings and monuments, and the historian's grasp on what happened improves drastically. The process took time, however, and it is only in the ninth century that sources start to shed light on a wide geographical region. At this time one power began to dominate, Assyria, though we have to wait until the seventh century before it became so encompassing that the entire Near East can be studied through its sources. Despite Assyria's preeminence in historical reconstructions, we have to keep in mind that other states coexisted with it. The historical evidence on them is often sparse, and to study them we must take into account somewhat

A History of the Ancient Near East ca. 3000–323 BC, Third Edition. Marc Van De Mieroop.
© 2016 John Wiley & Sons, Inc. Published 2016 by John Wiley & Sons, Inc.

earlier and later evidence as well. These states included Babylonia in southern Mesopotamia, and Urartu which developed in eastern Anatolia in the early first millennium. Elam in western Iran became a crucial actor in the eighth century only. Outside the Near East as defined in this book, Egypt remained important. In the Syro-Palestinian region and western Anatolia, a large number of smaller states existed. Some were a continuation of those of the second millennium – the Phoenician harbor cities and the Neo-Hittite states – while others were new – the Aramean states in Syria, and those of Israel, Judah, and their eastern neighbors. In Anatolia, Phrygians and Lydians created new political entities, while in the Zagros Mountains various peoples formed small states. I will discuss these states in this chapter, while the rise of the Assyrian empire within this setting will be the subject of the next.

11.1   The Eastern States

In the east of the Near East, the three states that dominated in the Late Bronze Age, Assyria, Babylonia, and Elam, continued to be important in the early first millennium, while a newcomer, Urartu, developed as an international force in the early first millennium. Our ability to reconstruct their respective histories is uneven and very much biased toward an Assyrian point of view. Still, a study of the development of the Assyrian empire has to take these neighbors into account, and a survey of their histories is provided here first.

The entire period from 1000 to 626 was a very difficult one for Babylonia. Politically, the region was in disarray with various groups vying for power, and economically it was weak because of a collapse of the agricultural infrastructure and a loss of access to trade routes. In political terms, power passed from the Kassites to the Chaldeans over a long period of instability, made especially complicated because many people, from both inside and outside Babylonia, were determined to take control. The *Babylonian King List A* lists numerous royal names between the end of the Kassite dynasty in 1155 and the pacification of Babylonia under the Chaldeans in 626. Although it groups them into a number of dynasties (second Isin dynasty, second Sealand dynasty, etc.), the kings' names reveal that they had diverse backgrounds, and rarely did two men from the same family succeed each other. They included Kassites, Elamites, Babylonians, and Chaldeans, and after 728, the Assyrians became directly involved. Their attempts to rule Babylon will be described in the next chapter. Most of these men accomplished little, and a political history of this period can easily read like a mere succession of names (for a list of rulers, see Section 15 of the King Lists at the end of the book).

The main challenge to the kings of Babylon was to control their territory. The newly arrived Arameans and Chaldeans dominated the countryside and certain regions were *de facto* independent. The Aramean tribes were most prominent along the Tigris River and seem to have settled primarily in small village communities on the fringes of the agricultural zone. Assyrian military accounts list many tribal names, most important among them being the Gambulians and the

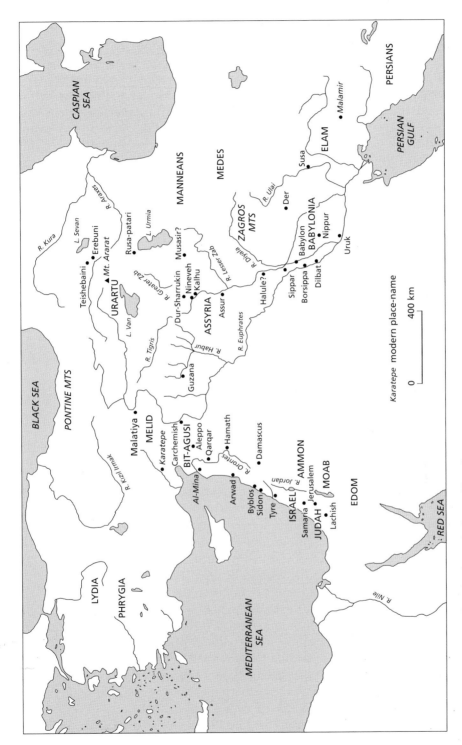

Map 11.1 The Near East in the early first millennium.

Puqudians. The Arameans did not seek integration in Babylonian society, and mostly did not have ambitions to political power beyond their own communities. By 850, the Chaldeans were firmly established along the Euphrates and in the south of Babylonia, including in fortified cities, but we do not know where they came from. Some scholars state that they were very closely related to the Arameans, but the ancient sources always keep them distinct, so this is not certain. The Chaldeans were organized in three leading tribes, Bit-Amukani, Bit-Dakkuri, and Bit-Jakin, and these affiliations remained important throughout their history. They did try to gain political authority in Babylon and were often successful in capturing its throne. Consequently, they regularly led the opposition to Assyrian expansion in Babylonia. Their greater integration into Babylonian society is visible in the fact that they frequently adopted Babylonian names.

The few texts we have from this period mention violence and warfare, not only between cities and tribal groups, but also between different cities. For instance, Nabu-shuma-imbi, governor of Borsippa in northern Babylonia in the early eighth century, wrote:

> Disorders, disturbances, revolt, and turmoil occurred in Borsippa, the city of truth and justice. During the reign of king Nabu-shuma-ishkun, the Dakkurian, the Babylonians, the Borsippians, (the people of) the town Duteti (which is on) the banks of the Euphrates, all the Chaldeans, Arameans, (and) the people of Dilbat *sharpened*(?) their weapons for many days (to fight) with one another (and) slew one another. Moreover, they fought with the Borsippians over their fields.[1]

References to warfare against tribal groups are plentiful in other texts. Part of the anti-tribal rhetoric, accusing them of hostile and destructive behavior, probably resulted from the standard negative attitude toward newcomers of the residents of ancient cities. But the highly unstable nature of the period and its warlike character cannot be denied.

The Assyrians often aggravated this volatile situation with their military actions. Already in the second half of the ninth century they were campaigning in the region, sometimes against tribes in support of cities, sometimes against Babylon's ruler. Babylon was not always the weaker party. In the mid-ninth century, its King Marduk-zakir-shumi I (ruled 854–819) asked Shalmaneser III (ruled 858–824) for help to quell a rebellion by his younger brother. That Shalmaneser III regarded him as an equal is clear from a representation on the base of his throne at Kalhu in which he is shown grasping the Babylonian king's hand. Conversely, the latter supported Shamshi-Adad V's claim to the throne of Assyria when Shalmaneser III died, and forced an unfavorable treaty on him. But Babylonian power was too ephemeral to maintain this attitude for long, and by 813 Shamshi-Adad V had captured and deported two Babylonian kings in succession. This seems to have left the country in total disarray, and perhaps there were no kings at all in Babylon for a while. Only when, in 728, Assyria tried to govern Babylonia directly did the chaos subside somewhat and even then instability persisted for another century, as we will discuss in the next chapter.

Within this confusion, cities stood out as isolated centers that preserved traditional political and cultural life. In political terms, they seem to have been important as a support for royal power, which retained its urban character of the past. The ancient cities of Babylonia were greatly reduced in size and economically weak. They did, however, provide the king with points of control in an unruly countryside. In return, the citizens could demand special privileges which, while their precise characteristics are unclear, seem to have been very encompassing. Kings were not allowed to tax or demand corvée labor and military service; they could not arrest someone or seize property. These privileges seem to have been renewed after the accession of each new king as a personal agreement, and they survived into the period of Assyrian domination. The list of cities awarded them included Babylon, Borsippa, Nippur, Sippar, and Uruk, all of them important religious centers. The gods were considered to be the guardians of the agreement, and a literary text we call *The Advice to a Prince* (the date of its composition is unknown) clearly sets out that the king would be severely punished were he to break it. Although royal governors in the cities owed allegiance to the king in Babylon, they must have had substantial autonomy at many times during the period.

These cities continued the cultural and religious traditions of Babylonia, although not much wealth could be devoted to such activity. Until Assyria's conquest of the region, little building work was undertaken and it was mostly restricted to the restoration of older structures and city-walls. In religious practices, the role of the god Marduk had substantially increased in the late second millennium, especially under King Nebuchadnezzar I, who brought back his statue from Elam. In the early first millennium Marduk's son, Nabu, the scribe of the gods, rose in prominence, as did his cult-city, Borsippa. His statue had to visit Babylon during the New Year's festival, which had become the most important royal ritual, and records kept track of when Nabu's statue failed to participate in the festival. Scribal activity was also limited because of the lack of economic and building activity. The number of legal and administrative records is paltry, and official inscriptions are rare and mostly very short. Yet, earlier literary and scholarly texts continued to be copied out. When in the seventh century King Assurbanipal of Assyria compiled his library at Nineveh, he ordered his officials to go into the Babylonian temples and private houses of priests and scholars to collect tablets that were rare and unavailable in Assyria. This suggests that the temples had become the patrons of scribal activity.

From the late eighth century on, the state of Elam in the east regularly supported Babylonian and Chaldean opposition to Assyria. The marshes of the south enabled rebels simply to flee from Babylonia to Elam to escape Assyria's army. Moreover, the Babylonians easily persuaded Elamite armies to do battle with Assyria, and often paid for these services. We know the history of Elam in the first millennium almost exclusively through Assyrian and Babylonian sources. Although some Elamite kings left inscriptions, these are few in number and contain little information. For the period of Elamite resurgence on the international scene from about 740 to 647, we know of only five kings from native sources, while Mesopotamian sources record fifteen men who claimed the throne. Despite Elam's political instability – fifteen kings in one hundred years – the state was able to cause trouble for Assyria and to acquire wealth that made it the envy of its neighbors.

After the sack of Susa by Nebuchadnezzar I around 1100 we hear almost nothing about Elam until it joined Babylonia in its struggles against Assyria. The first attested ruler was Humban-nikash, who helped in the fight against Sargon II (ruled 721–705). His successor Shutruk-Nahhunte II, in his own name and with the title "King of Anshan and Susa," referred back to the glorious past of the Middle Elamite kingdom and left inscriptions at Susa and at Malamir, a site on the way to Anshan. It is unclear whether he controlled the latter area as well, despite his official claim to it. The prolonged war with Assyria led to victories and defeats on both sides, and often had an indeterminate outcome. The various witnesses regularly differ on who won individual battles. For example, after the battle at Der in 720 between Assyria and a coalition of Babylonians and Elamites, the Assyrian Sargon II and the Chaldean Marduk-apla-iddina both claimed victory in their own inscriptions, while the *Babylonian Chronicle* credited it to the Elamite king and reported that the Chaldean did not even arrive on time. In 691, Sennacherib of Assyria confronted a coalition of Iranian states led by Humban-nimena of Elam at Halule on the Tigris. Again the Assyrian claimed victory, while the *Babylonian Chronicle* gave it to the Elamite. The battle was not decisive, and it did not prevent Sennacherib from devastating Babylon, though it did stop him from invading Elam. Afterwards there was a period of relative peace, which only ended in 664 when Elam attacked Babylonia. Ten years later the Assyrian Assurbanipal invaded Elam and fought a battle at the river Ulai, which runs near Susa. The king of Elam, Te'umman, was killed and decapitated (figure 11.1), and his head was transported to Nineveh for display in the royal garden. When Assurbanipal and his brother became engaged in a civil war in Babylonia from 652 to 648, Elam supported Babylonia. Assurbanipal defeated his brother and turned against Elam, ransacking the countryside. In 646 he devastated Susa and all other remaining Elamite centers. The destruction of the capital was as thorough as possible: the Assyrians salted the fields to make them useless and deported the population wholesale to Samaria in the west of the empire. They even emptied the royal tombs of their bones and crushed them. Yet, a small and weak state remained in existence, and Elam survived longer than Assyria, until the Persians integrated it into their empire in the sixth century.

Great instability characterized Elamite internal political life. Various families contended for the throne and those who failed often sought support in Assyria for their claims. The power of the local lords seems to have been great, and they acquired wealth that seemed fabulous in the eyes of the Assyrians. Such wealth must have partly derived from the control of trade routes, but we have no documents to study this in detail.

Elam probably controlled only the plain of Khuzestan on the western flank of the Zagros Mountains. The highlands of Anshan were home to the Persians, and other groups that had only recently entered the area inhabited the Zagros Mountains farther north. They formed various states that were at first loose

Figure 11.1 Assurbanipal's depiction of the death of King Te'umman. On an intricate wall relief in his palace at Nineveh, King Assurbanipal depicted the battle of Til-tuba in which he killed the king of Elam. The scene here shows the beheading of the Elamite king and his son. The six-line text above it states how Te'umman was wounded in battle and tried to flee into the woods with his son Tammaritu. Assurbanipal killed and decapitated them. Other parts of the relief show how Te'umman's head was taken to Nineveh and ended up hanging off a tree in the palace garden where Assurbanipal and his wife had a garden party. British Museum, London. Credit: Werner Forman Archive.

coalitions of peoples, with names only known to us from Assyrian sources. These mention Medes, Manneans, Persians, and others, originally with large numbers of kings, but later as consolidated states. It is out of this complex political situation that the principal opponents to Assyria would later develop.

To the north of Assyria in eastern Anatolia there existed one of the most enigmatic important states of the ancient Near East: we call it Urartu following Assyrian practice, but the indigenous term was Biainili, that is, "those of the land of Bia." That last term has survived today in the name of Lake Van. While it is clear that Urartu played a crucial role in the first half of the first millennium, and at one point was the most powerful state in the region, the reconstruction of its history is extremely difficult. Most information needs to be culled from Assyrian accounts, which also provide the only chronological framework we have. They bring up Urartian rulers solely in conflict situations. The Urartians themselves left inscriptions, at first in the Assyrian language, script, and formulary, and from the late ninth century on also in the Urartian language. There are quite a few Assyrian–Urartian bilingual texts. These are primarily building inscriptions that mention military campaigns and tend to be repetitious; they provide little insight into the history of the state. The textual information is thus biased toward an Assyrian view. Archaeological exploration in Urartu has focused on the mountain fortresses, and so, again, stresses military aspects of the state.

High mountains and narrow valleys, with rivers that do not form a sequential system, dominated Urartu's territory (document 11.1). The headwaters of many rivers originated there, but they flowed in all directions, and only the Euphrates was navigable. The original center of the state was Lake Van, whose waters were too saline for drinking and agriculture. The people lived in villages in the valleys, which they often could not leave during the winter because of snow. Traffic through the region was difficult, and this fact protected it from the advances of the Assyrian army, among others. The state extended in all directions and clashed with Assyria in southern Anatolia and northwest Iran, where it came close to the Assyrian heartland. Its northern and eastern borders are not clear to us, but in its heyday Urartu incorporated the region of the modern state of Armenia. Modern Yerevan is located where ancient Urartian Erebuni used to be. The name of the city is still the same after more than 2,000 years.

The first references to a political organization in this region come from the thirteenth century, when Assyrian kings campaigned to the north of Syria and encountered what they called Nairi and Uruatri, a variant of the later name Urartu. The separate political entities joined forces most likely in reaction to Assyrian aggression. From the ninth century on, Assyrian kings mention fewer, yet more formidable, opponents in the region of eastern Anatolia. The ruler who unified the state of Urartu and initiated its royal dynasty was Sarduri I, attested in the accounts of Shalmaneser III (ruled 858–824). His immediate successors turned the state into an important power. They campaigned incessantly in all directions from the heartland at Lake Van, and annexed territories as far north as Erebuni. In the west they reached northern Syria, and in the southeast they occupied the Zagros Mountains east of Assyria. They kept a number of buffer states there, however, and agreements between Assyria and Urartu existed about access to these. Urartu's expansionist policy was made easier by the internal weakness of Assyria in the late ninth to early eighth centuries. The situation was so bad that an Assyrian official in northern Syria, Shamshi-ilu, personally led the defense against Urartu's attacks rather than wait for the king. The Urartians solidified their territorial gains by building a system of mountain fortresses, such as Rusa-patari, "Small city of King Rusa," or Teishebaini, "City of the god Teisheba." Perched on top of natural heights, these controlled the agricultural plains and the trade routes that ran through them. They were administrative centers and contained huge storage areas for grain and wine. The region must have had extensive vineyards, as the amounts of wine consumed were vast. The state supported agricultural development through the construction of hydraulic works, including aqueducts that seem to have inspired Assyrian projects. The work required a large labor

> **Document 11.1**   *An Assyrian description of the Zagros Mountains*
>
> *To the Assyrians who lived in the lowlands, the Zagros and Taurus Mountains to the east and north presented formidable barriers and an unfamiliar natural environment. Military campaigns with regular armies were difficult there, and Assyrian expansion was constrained. In this region they faced the Urartian state, however, and when Sargon II decided to attack it in 714, he needed to enter the inhospitable mountains. In his report on the campaign, a letter to the god Assur written in high literary language using many metaphors from the animal world, he describes the challenges he faced in these words:*
>
> Mount Simirria, a great mountain peak that points upwards like the blade of a lance, and raises its head over the mountain where the goddess Belet-ili lives, whose two peaks lean against heaven on high, whose foundations reach into the midst of the netherworld below, which, like the back of a fish, has no road from one side to the other and whose ascent is difficult from front or back, ravines and chasms are deeply cut in its side, and seen from afar, it is shrouded in fear, it is not good to climb in a chariot or with galloping horses, and it is very hard to make infantry progress in it; yet, with the intelligence and wisdom that the gods Ea and Belet-ili destined for me and who broadened my stride to level the enemy land, I made my engineers carry heavy bronze axes, and they smashed the peaks of the high mountain as if it were limestone and made the road smooth. I took the head of my army and made the chariots, cavalry and battle troops that accompany me fly over it like eagles. I made the support troops and foot soldiers follow them, and the camels and pack mules jumped over the peaks like goats raised in the mountains. I made the surging flood of Assyrians easily cross over its difficult height and on top of that mountain I set up camp.
>
> Translation after Thureau-Dangin 1912: pls. I–II.

force and it is likely that many of the military expeditions were intended to gather people for these tasks.

In the mid-eighth century, under King Sarduri II, Urartu was at the height of its power. It controlled the trade routes from northern Mesopotamia and Iran to the Mediterranean Sea and to metal sources in Anatolia. Northern Syria itself was within its reach. The reorganization of Assyria and its subsequent expansion led thus to immediate confrontations with Urartu. These are detailed in Assyrian accounts, naturally with a strong pro-Assyrian bias. Tiglath-pileser III (ruled 744–727) fought the Urartians in the west, where they had made alliances with Syrian states such as Bit-Agusi near Aleppo. Sargon II attacked the buffer state between Assyria and Urartu by moving his troops through the Zagros Mountains east of Assyria. He plundered the city of Musasir, an important religious center of Urartu's main god Haldi, with the intent of disrupting that state's official cult. In the seventh century, Urartu was no longer a target of Assyrian campaigning but was closely watched by its spies, who sent reports to Nineveh. Diplomacy replaced warfare and Assyria contained Urartu's threat, but did not intend, or was unable, to strike the final blow.

Urartu's ultimate fate may have been determined more by people from the north whose identity is unclear. Scholars have suggested various groups as being responsible for its demise. Among them are the Cimmerians from northern Anatolia, who in the early to mid-seventh century seem to have controlled the central Zagros and may have annihilated Urartu on the way. The Medes and Scythians have also been blamed, but there is no solid evidence for this. The end of Urartu was violent, however, and archaeology shows that many of its fortresses were burned down. Certainly, by the late sixth century, Armenia had replaced Urartu when the region became incorporated into the Persian empire.

Urartian culture and religion remain poorly known. The language has no cognates except for the Hurrian of the second millennium, but it is not a later form of Hurrian. The two languages had a common ancestor; while we only have evidence for Hurrian in the second millennium, Urartian must also have been spoken at that time. The textual record from Urartu consists mostly of royal inscriptions, some of which are also preserved in an Assyrian version. A small number of economic documents and hundreds of royal sealings have been found, indicating that the state had a central administration. Many names of gods are attested in the inscriptions, but few are otherwise known. Three deities headed the pantheon, two of whom were known to the Hurrians as well: Teisheba, who was the Hurrian storm god Teshub, and Shiwini, the Hurrian sun god Shimiki. The most important god in battle accounts was Haldi, probably a god of war and not known elsewhere in the Near East. His main cult center was Musasir, which Sargon II sacked in 714.

Urartu's most impressive material remains are its metalwork, especially bronze, which was cast as vessels, furniture attachments, armor, statuettes, and so on (figure 11.2). The location of the state gave it direct access to mines, and it controlled trade routes from central Anatolia and Iran where other mineral resources were found. The focus on metalwork is therefore not surprising. Unfortunately, many of the remains were illicitly excavated and we do not know their archaeological context. Although our understanding of Urartu remains weak, it is undeniable that it was one of the most powerful states of the Near East in the first three centuries of the first millennium, and that its existence had important effects on the development of the Assyrian empire. It is a typical illustration of one of the main challenges that confronts the historian of the ancient Near East. We are aware that it was a major player on the international scene but because its indigenous sources are few and lack detail we are forced to study Urartu through the eyes of the Assyrians – consequently we tend to see the state as more marginal and less accomplished than it really was.

11.2   The West

Whereas large territorial states dominated the eastern part of the Near East (Assyria, Babylonia, Elam, Urartu), in the west political fragmentation remained

Figure 11.2 Urartian bronze plaque. The piece was originally attached to a larger object and depicts the same scene twice: two men carrying bundles of sticks followed by a chariot with a driver and probably a prominent passenger. The inscription in Urartian reads: "(King) Argishti's property." Large numbers of Urartian metalwork like this were looted from sites in modern Turkey, Iran, and Armenia, and the absence of a context makes it hard to say much about their function and use. They include modern forgeries as well. The Metropolitan Museum of Art, New York. Bronze, 6.91 × 15.24 cm (2.72 × 6 in). Credit: © 2014 The Metropolitan Museum of Art/Art Resource/Scala, Florence.

the norm. Inhabited and governed by groups who spoke different languages and had varied traditions and ancestries, the states there were still mostly centered round one city that acted as the political capital. We can distinguish between those that continued the political and cultural traditions of the late second millennium, primarily the Neo-Hittite and Phoenician states, and those that were newcomers, principally the Aramean states. It is, however, clear that political power increasingly shifted toward the Arameans, until the Assyrians conquered the region in the late eighth century.

The so-called Neo-Hittite states were located in southern Anatolia and northwestern Syria, from the Upper Euphrates valley to the Mediterranean coast. Assyrian accounts call the region Hatti, acknowledging thus a connection with the second-millennium Hittite state. And indeed there was continuity in the script and language people there used and in the political ideology. As mentioned before the Neo-Hittite states used the so-called Anatolian hieroglyphs to write the Luwian language, which had been one of the official means of expression in the Hittite kingdom. Politically, the rulers of some of the states presented themselves as descendants of the Hittite kings. Crucial in this transmission was the city Carchemish, where a viceroy of the king of Hattusa, often a prince, had resided in the second millennium. When the Hittite state collapsed, Kuzi-Teshub, the son of the last attested viceroy, declared himself "Great King of Hatti," and filled the power vacuum in northern Syria. His state was soon fragmented, however, and a set of successor kingdoms developed along the Euphrates and to its west. Most prominent was Melid around the city Malatiya on the Upper Euphrates, where rulers claimed descent from Kuzi-Teshub. Farther west there were a number of states where kings bore names such as Muwatalli and Suppiluliuma in second-millennium tradition.

We know little about the internal political organization of these states. The cities had citadels with palaces and temples surrounded by massive walls, and in that sense they continued second-millennium practices. Although there are no written records to demonstrate how the elites ruled, there are indications that they lived in a luxury that was the envy of others. The Assyrians so much admired north Syrian palaces that they imitated elements in their own royal architecture. They referred to a portico with columns as "in the style from Hatti" and their palace reliefs may have been inspired by the orthostats of the royal citadels of northern Syria. Those were set up on gates and walls, carved with scenes in a style that is typically Neo-Hittite (figure 11.3), and they often contained hieroglyphic inscriptions celebrating the king's acts. The social rebellions that contributed to the collapse of the second-millennium system seem thus to have bypassed the Neo-Hittite states.

The wealth of the Neo-Hittite region probably derived from its control over trade routes and mining areas. Several of the prominent cities, such as Carchemish and Malatiya, commanded passages over the Euphrates, and all traffic from Anatolia to Syria also had to go through the region. The strategic location and the wealth of these states made them appealing targets for their powerful neighbors. When the Assyrians expanded westward, they encountered them as soon as they crossed the Euphrates River. Neo-Hittite states were thus forced in the ninth century to pay tribute to Shalmaneser III, and in the mid-eighth century Tiglath-pileser III gradually incorporated them into his empire. In the period in between when Assyria was weak, Urartu extended its influence over these states. Moreover, Arameans were able to seize political power in some of the Neo-Hittite states. For example, by the eighth century they ruled Hamath, the southernmost Neo-Hittite kingdom in central Syria.

Another region where late second-millennium political entities survived was the Levantine coast. The Phoenician harbors of Tyre, Sidon, Byblos, and Arwad were not destroyed around 1200 and continued to function as before, even though their wealthy customers had disappeared. The change in the status of the latter is vividly portrayed in the Egyptian *Tale of Wen-Amun*. It relates how a priest of the

Figure 1.1 Göbekli Tepe view. The remains at Göbekli Tepe in southeast Anatolia show how pre-agricultural people constructed a circular ceremonial center within an artificial mound of stone debris. Stone monoliths line the circumference and the upright stones in the middle, decorated with carved reliefs of animals, stand 5 meters tall. Credit: Deutches Archäologisches Institut.

Figure 3.3 Ram in the thicket from the Royal Cemetery at Ur. This decorative object is one of an identical pair found in the Royal Cemetery. It represents a goat standing on its hind legs to reach the upper leaves of a bush. Sculpted in wood (now decayed) most of the figure was covered with gold leaf, while the goat's fleece and ears are of lapis lazuli. British Museum, London, ME 122200. H. 45.7 cm; W. 30.48 cm (18 × 12 in). Credit: © The Trustees of the British Museum.

Figure 5.3 Fresco fragment from the Mari palace. The Mari palace was renowned throughout Syria for its grandeur and opulence. It walls were decorated with frescoes traces of which archaeologists were able to recover in five rooms. This fragment shows a bearded man leading a bull by a rope fastened on a nose ring. The tips of the bull's horns are covered with metal and a crescent decorates its forehead. National Museum Aleppo, Syria M10119. H. 52 cm; W. 47 cm. (20.4 × 18.5 in). Credit: akg images/Erich Lessing.

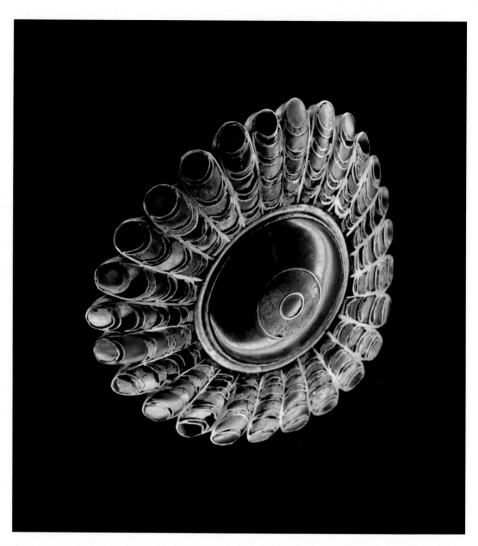

Figure 7.3 Object from the royal tombs at Qatna. The finds in the tombs beneath the palace at Qatna are typical of the wealth urban elites of the second half of the second millennium accumulated. The object here is made of gold, lapis lazuli, and carnelian and has a diameter of 6.9 cm (2.7 in) and shows a remarkable degree of craftsmanship, each of the twenty-six petals carefully made with nine gold compartments inlaid with stone. Credit: Marc Steinmetz/VISUM Foto.

Figure 8.4 Hittite vessel in the form of a stag. This silver vessel with gold inlay in the form of a stag is a typical product of Hittite metalwork. There is a hole in the stag's chest from which liquids could be poured and the frieze on the vessel's rim probably depicts the religious festival in which it was used. The Metropolitan Museum of Art, New York, Gift of Norbert Schimmel Trust, 1989 (1989.281.10), H. 18 cm (7 in). Credit: © 2014 The Metropolitan Museum of Art/Art Resource/Scala, Florence.

Figure 9.4 Statue of Queen Napir-asu, wife of Untash-Napirisha. This statue shows the great skills of Elamite metalworkers of the later second millennium. They used some 1,750 kg (3,760 pounds) of metal to make it and cast the object in two parts: the outer shell was first made with the lost-wax method from copper and tin, and then the interior was filled with a bronze and tin alloy. The two parts are held together with pins. The decoration on the outside was mostly cast but the inscription and additional details were carved, and gold and silver decoration was probably attached. The text in Elamite states that it is the statue of Napir-asu and curses whoever would damage it. Louvre Museum, Paris. Copper and bronze, H. 129 cm (4.2 feet), excavated in Susa. Credit: akg images/Erich Lessing.

Figure 10.4 Assyrian relief with domesticated camels. When the camel became domesticated around the tenth century the desert became more integrated into the Near Eastern world as people could travel through it and use oases as places of residence. Arabs appear in Mesopotamian texts from that moment on, albeit still as remote people. When Assyrian expansion was at its height its rulers wanted to gain control over the desert populations as well and we see them appear in representations of war. Palace of Assurbanipal, Nineveh. Seventh century. British Museum, London. Credit: Werner Forman Archive.

Figure 12.2 Reconstruction of palace at Kalhu. The nature of Mesopotamian ruins is such that it can be hard to image what the buildings looked like when in use. Early explorers were perhaps more daring in their reconstructions than today's archaeologists are. This engraving was made in 1853 on the basis of information Sir Austen Henry Layard provided after his excavations at Nimrud (ancient Kalhu). It shows the royal throne room lined with colorfully painted reliefs depicting scenes of war, hunts, and cultic actions. Although one can question its accuracy, the scene does give a sense of past reality. Credit: The Art Archive/Gianni Dagli Orti.

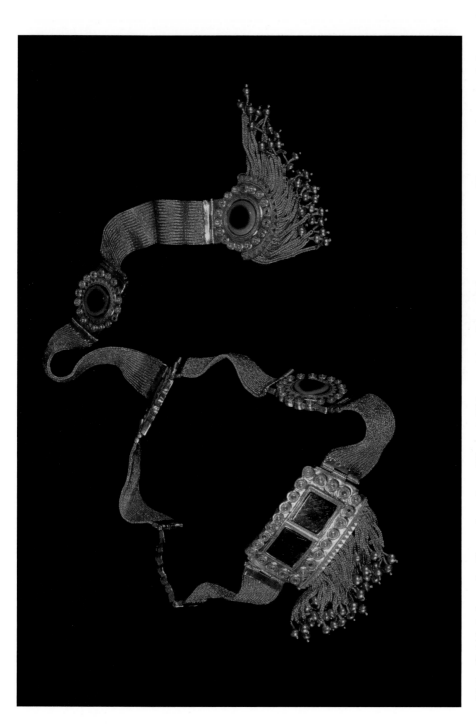

Figure 12.3 Gold belt from the Queens' tombs at Nimrud. This exquisite piece weighs more than one kilogram and was made by weaving fine gold wires in a broad band to enclose several ornaments of semi-stone; round pieces of banded agate and rectangular pieces of black agate. This is just one of the numerous works of jewelry found in these tombs, and a vivid illustration of the wealth of Assyria's court. Iraq Museum 105696. Weight: 1.1027 kg. Credit: Barry Iverson/Alamy.

Figure 13.4 *Death of Sardanapallos*, by Eugène Delacroix. When Delacroix made this painting in 1827 knowledge about Assyria was restricted to information from the Hebrew Bible and ancient Greek authors, such as Ktesias, who portrayed the Orient as the antithesis of Greek vitality and as decadent. Sardanapallos lies back in apathy while his harem women are being slaughtered and his treasures looted. The painting serves as a perfect example of how the ancient Near East was perceived before archaeological and textual discoveries revealed the details of its history. Louvre, Paris. 392 × 496 cm (145 × 195 in). Credit: akg images/Erich Lessing.

Figure 14.3   The Ishtar gate as exhibited in Berlin. German archaeologists took the best-preserved gate of Babylon in its entirety to Berlin. Its surface is made up of colored glazed baked bricks that represent the dragon of the god Marduk and the bull of the god Adad as protectors of the city. The yellow-colored animals were molded in relief on the dark blue background presented an awesome view to anyone approaching the gate. Baked brick, 14 meters high and 30 meters wide (47 by 100 feet). Credit: © Photo Scala, Florence/BPK, Bildagentur für Kunst, Kultur und Geschichte, Berlin. Staatliche Museen zu Berlin.

Figure 15.1 Representation of the Persian archers from Susa. The walls of the palace of Darius at Susa were decorated with panels of glazed baked brick, many of them representing elite soldiers of the Persian army. The men are shown in full military outfit holding a spear, armed with a bow and arrows, and dressed in a long robe. They are life-sized and probably were intended to provide constant protection to the king. Polychrome glazed siliceous brick, H. 4.75 m; W. 3.75 m. Louvre Museum, Paris. Credit: akg images/Erich Lessing.

Figure 11.3 Neo-Hittite orthostat from Guzana. The scene depicts two bull-men holding up a winged sun disk in front of a seated man, probably the king. Sculpted slabs of stone like this one decorated the palaces of Neo-Hittite rulers in southern Anatolia and northern Syria and may have inspired the Assyrian concept of palace reliefs of the later first millennium. The Metropolitan Museum of Art, Rogers Fund (1943.135.1). ca. 9th century BC. Limestone, 68 × 107 × 51 cm (26³/₄ × 42¹/₈ × 20¹/₁₆ in). Credit: © 2014 The Metropolitan Museum of Art/Art Resource/Scala, Florence.

god Amun of Thebes in Egypt around 1100 traveled to Byblos to obtain cedar wood. Robbed on the way, he was unable to pay for the wood, and when he appealed to the customs of gift exchange that had regulated trade in luxury items in the second millennium, the ruler of Byblos told him he was no servant of Egypt and demanded payment. Only after Wen-Amun procured funds did he receive the wood. The Phoenicians were famous for their control of luxury goods, such as hardwoods, metals, and craft products, and their highly skilled craftsmen. Thus, when the biblical authors wanted to portray Solomon as a rich and powerful king, they imagined him as receiving wood and specialist builders from Hiram, king of Tyre.

The greatest distinction of the Phoenicians, however, was their ability as seafaring merchants. With technically improved ships that had a large loading capacity, they sailed as far west as Morocco and Spain, where they established colonies from the tenth century on. These were true trading ports, where merchants collected resources from the interior and shipped them home (see box 11.1). Likewise, in the Near East itself groups of Phoenicians resided in other cities and states in order to conduct business. Unlike the records of early second-millennium Assyrian merchants in Anatolia, those of the Phoenicians are no longer extant, as they were written on perishable parchment and papyrus. At first the Neo-Hittite and Aramean states provided lucrative markets, as their elites desired luxury goods; later on the Assyrian empire continued the demand. When the Assyrians came to control Syria in the eighth century, they exacted large amounts of tribute but

Box 11.1   *The Phoenicians in the western Mediterranean*

The small city-states on today's Lebanese and Syrian coasts – Tyre, Sidon, Byblos, and Arwad – had an astounding reach beyond the Near East. As mercantile centers they established colonies throughout the western Mediterranean and even beyond the Strait of Gibraltar in southern Spain and Morocco. All the colonies were on the coast, strategically located to acquire natural resources, especially metal ore. The Phoenician objectives are perhaps the clearest on the Atlantic side of southern Spain. According to Greek and Roman authors, merchants from Tyre set up a colony there around 1100 (a date that is probably too early) and archaeology confirms their presence at the latest from the eighth century onward. They founded the settlement of Cadiz on what was then a set of islands in the bay at the mouth of the Guadalete River. This location gave it access to immensely rich silver and gold mines in inland Spain, whose revenue was transported to the coast and Cadiz. The largest deposits were at Rio Tinto, near modern Seville, an area that was mined until 1887 AD. The remains of ore refining from the first millennium BC are spread out over an area of a mile by a third of a mile and suggest that some six million tons of silver were mined then. Local people did all the work, probably under Phoenician supervision, and the refined silver was shipped from Cadiz mostly to the Near East. The merchants had little cultural interaction with local populations, it seems. Cadiz itself had a small and compact community with three temples devoted to the Phoenician gods Astarte, Ba'al-Hammon, and Melqart, and archaeology all over the western Mediterranean shows that local influence on the Phoenicians was limited and vice versa. Only on Malta, a halfway point on the long haul from the Levant to the western colonies, did the cultures mix. The Phoenicians brought thus traditions from the Near East into the western Mediterranean world, although their impact became more tangible only after Carthage in North Africa took a leading role. Their colonies show how already at this early date commercial interests inspired long-distance exploration. The idea that Phoenician sailors reached Latin America was popular in the eighteenth and nineteenth centuries AD and in the twentieth century some very prominent scholars argued that an authentic Phoenician inscription had been excavated in Brazil. That turned out to be a forgery, however, and no positive evidence of Phoenicians in the Americas exists.

left the Phoenician cities independent. This arrangement provided them with access to the foreign goods they wanted without having to manage a trade infrastructure in distant lands. The Phoenician colonization of North Africa became more intense with the establishment of Carthage on the Tunisian coast in the early eighth century. The increased Phoenician focus on the west caused intense competition there, at first with Greeks who founded colonies along the northern Mediterranean, and centuries later with emergent Rome, which sacked Carthage in the mid-second century BC.

Despite the fame of Phoenician artists and craftsmen in antiquity, relatively few examples of their work are preserved. This is partly due to the fact that the cities have been continually occupied to this day and are very difficult to explore

Figure 11.4 Syrian ivory in the Phoenician style. This piece of ivory carving shows a frontal nude goddess who holds a lotus flower and two lions in her hands. The representation contains many Egyptian elements of decoration, but was probably carved in Phoenicia as it combines Syrian iconographic elements with Egyptian ones. It was excavated in the Assyrian capital city Kalhu, where it was one of the many high-quality pieces of Syrian craftsmanship imported. The piece was used as a face piece for a horse. The Metropolitan Museum of Art, Rogers Fund, 1961 (61.197.5). ca. 9th–8th century BC. Ivory, 16.21 × 6.6 cm (6.38 × 2.6 in). Excavated in Nimrud (ancient Kalhu). Credit: © 2014 The Metropolitan Museum of Art/Art Resource/Scala, Florence.

archaeologically. Only portable items are known from outside Phoenicia, and it is not always certain whether they were Phoenician imports or local imitations. The art is best known from carved ivories, where Egyptian motifs were often employed (figure 11.4). They demonstrate a very high level of craftsmanship, which we imagine was visible in the other works as well. Phoenician textiles were extremely prized – the Greek name Phoenicia was also used to indicate the purple color used in cloth-dyeing – but no examples have survived. In addition, the written remains of these people are scarce, though they were of seminal importance for the development of writing throughout the ancient world. Since Phoenicians used the linear alphabet on papyrus and parchment, all records of daily transactions have disintegrated over time, and only a few monumental inscriptions carved in stone are known. Classical sources make reference to Phoenician histories, but the Greek and Roman accounts seem extremely garbled. The longest Phoenician inscription was found in the southern Anatolian site of Karatepe and has a Luwian translation written in Anatolian hieroglyphs. It is an account by Azatiwata, a servant of the king of Danuna, who commemorated the building of a city, named Azatiwataya after him. It dates to the late eighth or early seventh centuries, and we can therefore be certain that the Phoenician language and alphabet had expanded into the rest of Syria and southern Anatolia by then.

The role of the Phoenicians in the spread of the alphabet is their most renowned cultural accomplishment. Having preserved the use of the script in the Dark Age after 1200, the Phoenicians inspired all the alphabetic writing systems of their neighbors. In the Near East, the Hebrew and Aramaic scripts derived from the Phoenician. Of major importance to Europe was the adoption of the Phoenician alphabet by the Greeks, either directly from Phoenicians or through intermediaries in Syria or Anatolia. Classical sources were clear about this debt: the Greeks called their letters Phoenician. The date of the borrowing is controversial, however, and scholarly arguments are based almost solely on the forms of individual letters, which were notoriously diverse. The first Greek inscriptions can be dated to the first half of the eighth century, but considering the scarcity of earlier inscriptions in the Near East, it would hardly be surprising if older Greek ones have not yet been found. So some scholars have suggested a date of transmission of the alphabet to the Greeks as early as the thirteenth century, which seems unlikely.

The Phoenician city-states were thus very important for the preservation of second-millennium traditions into the first millennium, and were perhaps the least affected by the events of 1200. Other states inland may also have adhered to Canaanite traditions. In Israel and Judah the language, Hebrew, was similar to what was spoken in the region in the second millennium. Gods, myths, and cultic practices attested in the Ugaritic texts, for example, found their way into the biblical account, most likely because in certain localities they survived into the first millennium. The two kingdoms of Israel and Judah had separate, yet closely related, histories. These are almost always reconstructed on the basis of the Hebrew Bible, a very difficult source for the historian to use (see debate 11.1). It was written from a Judean point of view, and used religion as its primary point of reference to represent people's actions. In post-exilic times, that is, after the fifth century BC, the religious ideology of the area of Judah was a monotheistic devotion to Yahweh, the god of the temple in Jerusalem. At that time all earlier history was judged by how people related to him, but it is clear that prior to the exile other gods were tolerated as well. Archaeology has revealed, for example, the existence of the cult to Yahweh's wife Asherah both in Israel and in Judah. The biblical text suggests that the two states were quite different. Israel's rulers were in much closer contact with their neighbors than were those of Judah, and they were more open to Canaanite traditions and cults like those of Ba'al and El. It is thus possible that Israel was a survivor of a second-millennium state, while the archaeological record of Judah reveals greater changes at the beginning of the first millennium. That state was probably made up of new populations that had settled in the region and introduced new social and cultural practices.

The biblical text and the intensive archaeological research in the territories of ancient Israel and Judah may suggest that these states were unusual for their time. That was not the case, however. Like all their neighbors, Israel and Judah were small kingdoms centered on their capital cities. According to the biblical account, which cannot be checked fully from independent sources, Israel had nineteen rulers in the two centuries preceding the Assyrian conquest in 722. The kings were members of various families, who often relied on outside support for their claims to the throne. The kingdom was most powerful in the first half of the ninth century. Omri (ruled ca. 885–874), the creator of a new dynasty, founded a capital city at Samaria and strengthened Israel's ties with the Phoenician city of Tyre. The Assyrians referred to Israel as "the house of Omri" even after his dynasty had ended. Omri's son and successor, Ahab (ruled ca. 874–853), contributed 2,000 chariots and 10,000 troops to the coalition that fought Shalmaneser III at Qarqar in 853, the second largest contingent. Twelve years later a man called Jehu (ruled ca. 841–814) put a violent end to Omri's dynasty and massacred the entire family. Later on in his reign he was represented on the Black Obelisk of Shalmaneser III as submitting to that king, the only representation of an Israelite ruler in existence today.

Rule in the kingdom of Judah was more stable and a dynasty, called the "House of David" in an Aramaic inscription of the late ninth century, seems to have stayed in power from the state's creation, probably in the ninth century, to its annexation by the Babylonians in 587. The only exception was a seven year period (ca. 841–835) when Athaliah, the daughter of Omri and wife of the deceased Judean king, ruled on her own. The Bible lists nineteen kings for the 350 year period of Judah's existence, who all used Jerusalem as their capital. Judah was smaller and weaker than Israel and in the late ninth century the history of both states became dominated by the kingdom of Damascus, a situation that lasted until Assyria invaded the west in the mid-eighth century. The subsequent history of Israel and Judah was determined by the Mesopotamian empires and will be discussed in later chapters.

It was the Arameans who formed the most important new population group that held political power in the west. During the Dark Age they seized control over states throughout Syria and expanded their political influence, at the expense of the Neo-Hittites and others, up until the eighth century. Their states were often referred to as the "House of" an ancestor, and the inhabitants were identified as his sons, acknowledging a tribal background. Some of these ancestors are attested as historical figures. For example, Gusu, the ancestor of Bit-Agusi, was the opponent of the Assyrian Assurnasirpal II around the year 870. But the control over urban centers led to different designations of the states at the same time. When the Bit-Agusi turned Arpad, some 30 kilometers (20 miles) north of Aleppo, into a major city, their kingdom was also called Arpad. Another designation of certain Aramean states, especially in the Bible, included the term Aram, usually coupled with the name of a region or a city, for example Aram-Damascus. When that state became the strongest opponent of Assyria in the area, it was sometimes just given the name Aram, including in the texts of its Aramean neighbors. The multitude of designations shows that the ideological basis of these states was varied. They could be regarded as belonging to a tribe (Bit-X), as territories around a city (e.g., Arpad), or as governed by a particular people (Aram-X).

Despite the variety in designations of the states, the idea that a king, with the support of the local god, held supreme power in them was preeminent. When Assyria expanded into the west, the local rulers at first remained in office, but as Assyrian vassals. This led to a dual status: to the people of their state they were kings, to the Assyrian overlords they were officials. This duality is expressed in the statue of Hadad-yith'i, ruler of Guzana in northern Syria, probably in the mid-ninth century. On it was carved a bilingual inscription in Aramaic and Akkadian. The first calls him "king of Guzana," the second "governor" (see document 11.2; figure 11.5).

The political histories of these states are usually reconstructed on the basis of testimonies from outsiders, especially the Hebrew Bible and Assyrian military accounts, because local inscriptions are limited in number. All sources attest to a great deal of internecine warfare. While the states would unite against the common enemy of Assyria, they turned against each other when there was no outside threat. It seems likely that smaller states formed coalitions to protect themselves within these conflicts, and that in general larger polities developed over time. Power seems to have shifted from the Neo-Hittites to Arameans in northern Syria, and in the south Damascus became dominant.

To the south of Syria new states, with closely related histories, arose under people with non-Aramean backgrounds. In Israel, Judah, Ammon, Moab, and Edom people spoke Canaanite languages instead of Aramaic. On the southern Mediterranean shore, Philistines controlled five city-states that regulated access to Egypt and were at the end of overland trade routes from the Arabian Desert. Arabs from the peninsula, who were camel nomads, were in close contact with the Syro-Palestinian region and provided luxury goods such as incense from Yemen.

The history of the entire west was determined by its relationship to Assyria, which from the ninth century on campaigned there with great regularity, a process we will study in the next chapter. The numerous states would ally themselves to meet the threat, although some would seek support in Assyria to remain independent of their neighbors. Yet, the alliances could be massive. When Shalmaneser III crossed the Euphrates in 853 and engaged in a major battle at Qarqar, by his own account he was confronted with:

> 1,200 chariots, 1,200 cavalry, and 20,000 troops of Hadad-ezer of Damascus; 700 chariots, 700 cavalry, and 10,000 troops of Irhuleni, the Hamathite; 2,000 chariots and 10,000 troops of Ahab, the Israelite; 500 troops of Byblos; 1,000 troops of Egypt; 10 chariots and 10,000 troops of the land of Irqanatu; 200 troops of Matinu-ba'al of the city of Arwad; 200 troops of the land of Usanatu; 30 chariots and [ ],000 troops of Adon-ba'al of the land of Shiannu; 10,000 camels of Gindibu' of Arabia; [ ] hundred troops of Ba'asa of Bit-Ruhubi, the Ammonite.[2]

While this coalition most likely succeeded in holding Assyria back, it did not last long and local competition soon resurfaced.

Document 11.2   *The Akkadian–Aramaic bilingual inscription of Hadad-yith'i*

In 1979 a farmer in northern Syria found the life-size statue of a standing man, on which was carved a bilingual Akkadian–Aramaic inscription. It identified the man depicted as Hadad-yith'i, ruler of Guzana, and on the basis of the style of representation and the character of the language used most scholars believe that the statue dates to the third quarter of the ninth century. The inscription is the oldest preserved long Aramaic text and the only known extensive Akkadian–Aramaic bilingual. The text has two separately composed parts. The first (I) was originally written in Akkadian and the Aramaic version is a literal translation. The second part (II) was written for this statue specifically and the Akkadian and Aramaic versions are more divergent. The basis of the translation here is the Akkadian version.

(I) To Adad, the canal inspector of heaven and earth, who causes it to rain abundance, who gives well-watered pastures to the people of all cities, and who provides portions of food offerings to the gods, his brothers, inspector of the rivers who makes the whole world flourish, the merciful god to whom it is sweet to pray, he who resides in the city Guzana.

Hadad-yith'i, the governor [Aramaic version "king"] of the land Guzana, the son of Sassu-nuri, also governor [Aramaic version "king"] of the land Guzana, has dedicated and given (this statue) to the great lord, his lord, for his good health and long days, for making his years numerous, for the well-being of his house, his descendants and his people, to remove his body's illnesses, and that my prayers will be heard and that my words will be favorably received.

May whoever finds it in disrepair in the future, renew it and put my name on it. Whoever removes my name and puts his own on it, may Adad, the hero, be his judge.

(II) Statue of Hadad-yith'i, the governor [Aramaic version "king"] of Guzana, Sikani, and Zarani. For the continuation of his throne and the lengthening of his reign, so that his words will be agreeable to gods and men, he has made this statue better than before. In front of Adad who resides in the city Sikani, lord of the Habur River, he has erected his statue.

Whoever removes my name from the objects in the temple of Adad, my lord, may my lord Adad not accept his food and drink offerings, may my lady Shala not accept his food and drink offerings. May he sow but not reap. May he sow a thousand (measures), but reap only one. May one hundred ewes not satisfy one spring lamb; may one hundred cows not satisfy one calf, may one hundred women not satisfy one child, may one hundred bakers not fill up one oven! May the gleaners glean from rubbish pits! May illness, plague and insomnia not disappear from his land!

Translation after Greenfield & Shaffer 1983.

The entire west from southern Anatolia to the Egyptian border has to be seen as a multicultural zone where people with many different backgrounds interacted closely, mixing languages, traditions, and devotion to various gods. Some maintained second-millennium traditions – the kings of Hamath had Hurrian names

Figure 11.5   Statue of Hadad-yith'i. The statue is made from a type of basalt that is common in the region of northeast Syria where it was found. It is almost intact but for damage to the nose. It shows the full figure of a standing man, clasping his hands together, probably in veneration to the god Adad who is invoked in the inscription. The Akkadian text on the front of the skirt is carved in vertical columns which was a very archaic practice at the time. The Aramaic on the back is written in horizontal lines. National Museum, Damascus, Syria. Basalt; total height 2 m (6 ft 6 in); figure's height 1.65 m (5 ft 5 in). Credit: akg images/Erich Lessing.

until 800 – but there was no resentment of, or resistance to, new ones. A king could write inscriptions in Luwian and Phoenician at the same time. Artistic styles mixed various influences without difficulty. People seem to have maintained an international spirit and were outward-looking. They welcomed merchants from abroad. In coastal towns, such as Al-Mina at the mouth of the Orontes River, the Greeks were allowed to set up trading settlements. East Arabian traders entered Philistine cities. People of the Near East also sought goods in distant places, traveling there themselves, with the Phoenicians playing a leading role in this activity.

It is thus no surprise that the cultural contacts between the Near East and the emerging Greek world were close. The transmission of the alphabet has been mentioned before. But many works of art, especially metalwork and ivories, also entered Greece from the Near East and influenced local production to such an extent that Greek art of the seventh century is called "Orientalizing." Other, less tangible, influences on Greek culture are clear, yet it is often difficult to demonstrate that they were directly borrowed, and, if so, when. Greek material may also have contained survivals from the second millennium, when the Aegean was integrated in the regional system of the Near East. The elements where Near Eastern influence on Greek culture has been suggested include loan words, literary motifs, ideals of kingship, diplomacy, astronomy, divination, cultic procedures, mathematics, measures and weights, economic practices such as interest, and so on. The enthusiasm of scholars for finding connections depends largely on whether they see Greece as the beginning of western civilization or as located in a cultural evolution that dates much further back in time. It is usually difficult, if not impossible, to prove that Greeks were aware of a specific Near Eastern practice and consciously copied it. For example, Hesiod's *Theogony*, written around the year 700, has close parallels with second-millennium Hittite mythology. Did Hesiod personally know those texts, which would then have been preserved in Anatolia into the first millennium, or was he influenced by traditions that at some earlier moment in time had inspired Hittite tradition as well? The influence of the Near East on early first-millennium Greece has certainly been underrated in classical scholarship, but it is also easy to go too far in the other direction and find a Near Eastern background too readily. Be that as it may, the Syrian cultures of the early first millennium were not provincial or self-centered. The region flourished in many respects, economically and culturally. A new urban culture had arisen, and there was great artistic activity. Babylonia was no longer seen as the source of all civilized life, and people developed local traditions and cultural tastes. The western Near East was so successful that it presented an inviting target for the emergent Assyria.

Debate 11.1 *On writing the ancient history of Israel*

There is no doubt that the most influential text produced in ancient Near Eastern history is the Hebrew Bible (or the Old Testament in Christian tradition), a complex blend of prose narratives, poetry, laws, genealogical tables, and other kinds of writing, oftentimes of high literary value. It includes an account of world history from the moment of creation, but soon focuses on the affairs of one people only, the people of Israel. It is that story that is of most interest to the historian of the ancient Near East. In much-simplified terms we can say that it chronicles in succession the nomadic existence in the days of the Patriarchs, the conquest of Canaan after the exodus from Egypt, the United Monarchy, the division into the two states of Israel and Judah, both of which succumbed to Mesopotamian empires, the exile, and a return under the Persian empire. Although dates are not provided we could place these events between 2000 and 400 BC. But the Bible is much more than an ancient narrative of a people's history. It is one of the seminal religious texts in the world today and has been so for some 2,000 years. And it has immense ideological value beyond the religious sphere as one of the pillars of western civilization. It is a text that is constantly interpreted within ever-changing contexts.

How are historians to use the text? How much of its content is reliable for the study of the people of Israel and of those who surrounded them – Canaanites, Egyptians, Assyrians, Babylonians, Persians, and others? There is enormous disagreement on this question. A recent sober assessment states:

> No one familiar with the literature can doubt that there is currently a problem of method in the academic study of the history of ancient Israel. The depth of the problem, which some would even label a crisis, may be gauged by the fact that in some circles the level of debate has descended to that of name calling rather than to a dispassionate evaluation of the evidence and rational debate about its implications. (Williamson 2007: xiii)

In essence, the question is the same as that regarding later traditions about the dynasty of Akkad (see debate 4.1). There are maximalists who, in an extreme form, accept everything in the biblical text unless it can be proved wrong and minimalists who, in an extreme form, consider the whole Bible narrative a Persian-era or Hellenistic fiction without historical value. Many intermediate stances exist. Because the stakes are high – they involve a wide range of religious sentiments and attitudes toward the political situation in the modern Middle East – the debate can become nasty. One gets a good sense of this by looking at three recently published volumes based on conferences held between 2003 and 2005 (Liverani 2005b; Williamson 2007; and Grabbe 2011). There is no need to go into detail, but one accusation that is commonly made against members of the opposing party is that they are not historians and do not know what history is (e.g., Dever in Liverani 2005b against minimalists, whom he calls nihilists, and Whitelam and Grabbe in Williamson 2007 against maximalists).

Criticism of the biblical narrative is nothing new and started in the eighteenth century AD when the identification and analysis of sources that inspired the texts we read from ancient cultures became standard. But up to the 1970s acceptance of the Bible's basic outline of history was usual, even if the existence of various and sometimes contradictory sources was clear. Extra-biblical sources from archaeology and other ancient Near Eastern cultures were mainly used to clarify the biblical text. In the USA the so-called Albright school led in this approach and produced a series of very influential and popular histories of Israel and Judah, combining biblical data with extensive extra-biblical material (e.g., Bright 1959, 1972, 1981, 2000). But since then increasing numbers of scholars have begun to reject the historical truth of the Patriarchal narratives and, somewhat later, of the United Monarchy under kings David and Solomon, for which no explicit extra-biblical confirmation exist. Some remarkable facts make research more difficult. Unlike most of their neighbors the kings of Israel and Judah did not leave behind royal inscriptions or none are preserved. It is possible that later on there was a purposeful erasure of the memory of kingship (Garbini 1988: 17–18). Some inscriptions mentioning biblical figures, such as Baruch the scribe of the prophet Jeremiah, have been suspected as forgeries and caused heated arguments (cf. Grabbe in Williamson 2007: 62–4). Even when biblical kings appear in records from other states – Moab, Aram, Assyria, Babylonia, etcetera – the information there can be so dissimilar from what we find in the Bible that complicated explanations are needed to make the sources agree. For example, Sennacherib's account of his campaign in Judah and the biblical stories of his attack are so unlike that many scholars used to suggest that they speak of different events. In their opinion the Assyrian would have invaded the region twice – successfully the first time as he reports in his annals, and with disastrous consequences the second time as recounted in the Bible but ignored in his own records (e.g., Grayson 1991a: 109–11). There are strong arguments against this idea, however (Cogan and Tadmor 1988: 246–51). The areas of ancient Israel and Judah are possibly the most extensively excavated in the world and archaeological data can verify some biblical elements. But oftentimes archaeologists interpret their finds in a biblical light, which leads to circular reasoning, of course.

It is impossible for any historian of the ancient Near East to ignore the biblical narrative – the text is too powerful in cultural consciousness. It is an important source, and unique, as it presents reactions to the great empires of Assyria, Babylonia, and Persia, even if they were redacted or even composed much later. It contains a memory of these dominant empires from the point of view of the victims. The text also inspires us to study how people from the ancient Near East created narratives about their past and we can wonder why they did so in the ways known to us (Liverani 2005b). It is a very meaningful text, but also a most challenging historical source.

NOTES

1 Frame 1995: 124.
2 K. Lawson Younger, Jr. in Hallo 1997–2002, volume 2: 263–4.

12

The Rise of Assyria

3000	2500	2000	1500	1000	500

ca. 880–830	Sustained Assyrian military expansion
ca. 878	Assurnasirpal II chooses Kalhu as his new capital
827–823	Rebellions in Assyria's heartland
823–745	Period of Assyrian decline
717	Sargon II founds new capital at Dur-Sharrukin
704	Sennacherib moves Assyrian capital to Nineveh

One power dominated the Near East's history in the first millennium until the late seventh century: Assyria. Through its military might, this state expanded its control over a vast area from western Iran to the Mediterranean and from Anatolia to Egypt, and it dictated all aspects of political and economic life. A series of able military rulers who led the army on campaigns almost every year created this empire, but progress was neither smooth nor linear. We can distinguish two phases of expansion in the history of what scholars call the Neo-Assyrian empire: a first in the ninth century, which essentially restored Assyria's reach to that of the late second millennium, and a second, longer lasting, phase that started in the mid-eighth century and turned it into the foremost power of the Near East. While there are many similarities in Assyria's actions in these two periods, only the second phase displays a conscious and systematic approach toward the formation of a unified empire. This chapter will highlight some of the patterns of behavior that

A History of the Ancient Near East ca. 3000–323 BC, Third Edition. Marc Van De Mieroop.
© 2016 John Wiley & Sons, Inc. Published 2016 by John Wiley & Sons, Inc.

characterized the entire period, and focus on the first phase of Assyrian expansion. The next will discuss the empire at its height.

12.1   Patterns of Assyrian Imperialism

Assyria was a militaristic society. The army provided its basic structure and hierarchy. All men could be called up for military service and all state offices were designated as military ones, even if they had non-military duties. The king was at the top of this structure and his primary role was to conduct war for the benefit of the god Assur and the state. Thus there existed an ideology that the king in person should lead his army into battle: in theory, he headed every campaign and every year of his reign was identified with a campaign. While it is clear that military activity was constant, the idea that year after year a major campaign took place under the leadership of the king was a fiction. That he was actively involved is clear, however: King Sargon II died on the battlefield and his body could not be recovered for proper burial, an event that traumatized his son, who saw it as a punishment of the gods. Beneath the king was a large, pyramid-shaped hierarchy of officers, who between them took care of all state functions. Those with the highest ranks were also governors of provinces in the interior of Assyria. For example, the commander-in-chief was governor of the strategic province that stretched over northern Syria from Harran to the Upper Euphrates valley. Originally these men were members of prominent Assyrian families, but in the mid-eighth century the king replaced them with eunuchs, who could not have sons, in order to avoid them creating their own dynasties.

Campaigns were at first only fought during the summer, in the period after the harvest when agricultural tasks were limited and men were available, and when mountain passes were open and rivers could be easily crossed. In the late phase, a newly formed standing army could fight at any time. The number of soldiers is sometimes estimated at several hundreds of thousands as accounts of deaths among opponents can add up to more than 100,000. This figure seems unreasonably high, however. At the battle of Qarqar in 853, Assyria's opponents fielded some 50,000 men, so the Assyrian army was probably similar in size. In any case, the number of men required for military service surpassed the resources of Assyria's heartland, and conquered people had to be integrated into the army. Texts from the armory at Kalhu indicate, for instance, that soon after the conquest of Samaria in Israel, chariot teams from there were incorporated into the Assyrian army. Since Assyria had no navy, it engaged Phoenician ships and sailors for battles in the Mediterranean and in at least one attempt to subdue Chaldean rebels in the marshes near the Persian Gulf. Deportees from conquered regions were also regularly used particularly in mobile forces that could be moved around the empire at short notice. So the army contained a diverse group of men speaking different languages and with multiple places of origin.

Despite its prominence in Assyrian society, we know remarkably little about the organization and infrastructure of the army. It is not clear how exactly troops were levied and organized. At first governors were responsible for recruitment, but with the reorganization of the state in the eighth century it was directly in the hands of the central government. Soldiers were grouped into units of fifty men each. We have no information on how these units were integrated into larger ones to make up the entire army, however. The provisioning of the men with uniforms and weaponry must have been a major enterprise requiring the labor of substantial numbers of craftsmen. The cities in the heartland had large armories where troops and horses were trained and equipment was stored. A few records give us some insight into the quantities of barley needed to feed the troops and their animals. In the time of Sargon II, those stationed in the eastern city of Kar-Assur required daily 70,500 liters of barley for rations and 57,800 liters for fodder, a monthly outlay of 3,849,000 liters. And that was only for one segment of the army. Royal granaries provided most of the barley, but about a fifth was the responsibility of government officials.

Notwithstanding the royal rhetoric, the army rarely moved out in full force or engaged in large battles in the open field. Its tactic was often one of terrorizing the opponent into submission. Massive forces approached enemy territory and, if its people did not surrender immediately, they attacked cities and villages that presented easy targets. When conquered, the inhabitants were severely punished to set an example. They were tortured, raped, beheaded, and flayed, and their corpses, heads, or skins were publicly displayed (figure 12.1). Houses were razed, fields covered with salt, and orchards cut down. If this did not convince the capital city to give in, the Assyrians laid siege to it. Emissaries addressed the population directly and urged it to capitulate against the ruler's wish. As sieges were expensive, they were carried out selectively. The Assyrian king, never willing to admit failure in the official record, stated that he locked up the enemy like a bird in a cage. The royal accounts describe complete destruction after a tenacious city had been conquered, but probably used a great deal of hyperbole. The psychological edge of Assyria's behavior was important. This has been called "calculated frightfulness," the idea being that the results of defeat would be so calamitous that it was better to yield immediately.

As a direct result of their campaigns, the Assyrians acquired huge quantities of resources from all over the Near East. The royal inscriptions were eloquent about the spoils they took from the treasuries, palaces, and temples of conquered cities. The influx of precious goods, metals, artifacts, weaponry, and so on was enormous, as many of Assyria's victims had been extremely wealthy. In addition, cattle, sheep and goats, horses, and camels were part of the booty. Accounts sometimes boast that the result was a glut that made exclusive items available to commoners. After the submission of a foreign state, the Assyrians set a level of tribute, to be paid annually, which often included specialties of the region. For example, the Phoenicians had to provide purple cloth and cedar logs, the Zagros people horses. The amounts were not set out in the few Assyrian treaties we have, so we do not know their size. But the burden must have been a heavy one, as tributary states often rebelled despite Assyria's clear military superiority. Massive resources flowed into the heartland.

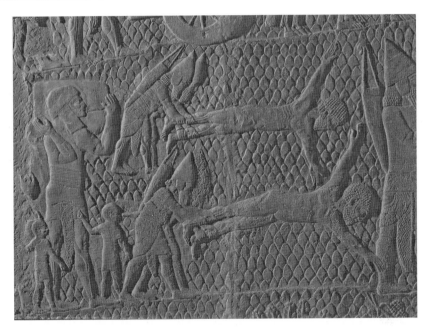

Figure 12.1 Siege of Lachish. The representations of warfare in the Assyrian palaces often included scenes of violence against those who dared to resist. Shown here is a detail of the portrayal of the siege of Lachish, which took up a full room in Sennacherib's palace at Nineveh. It shows two fates Assyrian enemies faced: the men of Lachish were deported with their wives, children, and some of their belongings, while, more gruesomely, the local officials who organized the resistance were flayed alive. British Museum, London. Gypsum, H. 256.54 cm; W. 101.6 cm (101 × 40 in). Credit: © The Trustees of the British Museum.

The same was true for manpower. Assyria had a desperate need for laborers to work in agriculture and on the great building projects it undertook, to replace Assyrians who were enlisted in the army. It also required inhabitants for the massive cities kings founded in its heartland. Throughout ancient Near Eastern history victorious armies had deported populations, but the Assyrians of the first millennium greatly expanded this practice, especially after the mid-eighth century. Again, the royal inscriptions are explicit about the numbers moved. It has been estimated that 4.5 million people were deported in the three centuries of the Assyrian empire.[1] Entire communities of men, women, and children were forcibly moved from one corner of the empire to another. Different levels of deportation existed. At first only specialist craftspeople were selected, in order to assist in building projects. But if a region remained defiant, the majority of the population could be moved. This practice had several strategic benefits for Assyria. It reduced opposition in peripheral territories as rebellious populations were resettled in foreign environments where they needed imperial protection against local hostility. Moreover, they would not run away, as they were unfamiliar with the country. The threat of deportation could be used when the army was approaching an area in order to encourage immediate submission.

The territories of deported people were selectively resettled with other groups when they were crucial for trade or the production of materials and goods. When there was no clear benefit, they were left with only a minimum of people. For example, the northern parts of the ancient state of Israel were almost completely deserted after the Assyrian conquest. A side-effect of the deportations was a mixture of populations throughout the Near East, including the spread of the Arameans and their language and alphabetic script. If the estimates of the numbers of people involved are correct, deportations caused great demographic changes. Those subjected to it were forced to walk the entire distance from their homeland to their destination, some in chains, others barefoot. Part of the population from Samaria in Israel, for example, ended up in the Zagros Mountains, some 1,200 kilometers (750 miles) away. The logistics of supervising and feeding large numbers of people during voyages of several months must have required an enormous organization. The Assyrians wanted them to arrive safely at their destination, so they took care of them. Some letters indicate that governors of the territories on the road had to supply food and protection, and they report that some deportees became ill. But, although there are some administrative lists of deportees, this massive enterprise remains poorly documented.

The Assyrian heartland was the main beneficiary of the immense resources of labor and goods acquired. There was a direct correlation between successful campaigns and major building projects. Victorious warriors were also great builders, and undertook the largest projects after they returned with their immense spoils. The construction projects of this period included several new large cities. Assur, the traditional capital, was too small for the enormous state apparatus and soon after Assyria initiated its first phase of expansion the capital was moved. The builder, Assurnasirpal II (ruled 883–859), chose the site of a Middle Assyrian city, Kalhu, but completely rebuilt it, a task that took some fifteen years. He laid out a city-wall 8 kilometers (5 miles) long and enclosing an area of 360 hectares (890 acres), and on top of the large citadel in the southwest corner constructed his palace, several temples, and a ziggurat. The palace was over 200 meters long and at least 120 meters wide, built around a vast courtyard. Not only was its architecture monumental, but the staterooms were also decorated with stone wall reliefs depicting battles, royal hunts, and cult scenes (figure 12.2). Huge human-headed bulls in stone guarded the entrances. A text commemorates the inauguration of the palace with a ten-day banquet which 69,574 people attended:

> When I consecrated the palace of Kalhu, 47,074 men and women, who were invited from every part of my land, 5,000 dignitaries and envoys of the people of the lands Suhu, Hindanu, Patinu, Hatti, Tyre, Sidon, Gurgumu, Malidu, Hubushku, Gilzanu, Kummu, and Musasiru, 16,000 people from Kalhu, and 1,500 palace officials, all of them – altogether 69,574 (including) those summoned from all the lands and the people of Kalhu – for ten days I gave them food, I gave them drink, I had them bathed, I had them anointed. (Thus) I did honor to them and send them back to their lands in peace and joy.[2]

Later kings constructed additional palaces and Assurnasirpal's immediate successor, Shalmaneser III, built a large arsenal in the southeast corner of the city. Kalhu remained Assyria's capital for one hundred and fifty years, when Sargon II (ruled 721–705) decided to build an entirely new one on virgin soil, and called it Dur-Sharrukin, "Fortress of Sargon" (document 12.1). This again was an

---

Document 12.1 *King Sargon and Dur-Sharrukin*

The chief building project Sargon II undertook was the construction of a massive new capital, called Dur-Sharrukin, "fortress of Sargon." He celebrated its foundation in inscriptions that highlight his personal involvement: he developed the idea, laid out the plans, and oversaw the construction. That he was heavily immersed in the project is clear from his official letters, preserved in the cities of Nineveh and Nimrud. A total of 113 letters can be associated with the building of Dur-Sharrukin, a tenth of all preserved letters from his reign. They involve twenty-six provincial governors and show how resources from the entire empire were used. Six letters seem to have been written by the king himself, demanding materials and labor; three of them are translated here. The project put so much pressure on the region's resources that some officials complained. The last letter translated here is from a high court official, who protested that so much straw in the territory he administered was requisitioned for the building of the city – probably to mix with clay for brick-making – that no fodder for pack animals remained.

1 *Royal letter found in Nineveh*
   The king's word to the governor (of Kalhu): 700 bales of straw and 700 bundles of reed, each bundle more than a donkey can carry, must arrive in Dur-Sharrukin by the first of the month Kislev. Should one day pass by, you will die.

Translation after Parpola 1987: no. 26.

2 *Royal letters found in Kalhu*

   a) The 1100 limestones that Bel-lishir-talaktu is loading, let them be brought to me in Dur-Sharrukin quickly! [ ]. (Addressed to the) second vizier.
   b) 700 limestones that Bel-lishir-talaktu is loading, quickly bring them to me in Dur-Sharrukin! (Addressed to the) eunuchs.

Translation after Parker 1961: 37 (ND 2606) and 41 (ND 2651).

3 *An official complaint found in Nineveh*
   To the king my Lord: your servant Gabbu-ana-Assur. The entire straw supplies of my country are consumed by Dur-Sharrukin. Now my cavalry officers are running after me because there is no straw for the pack animals. Now, what does the king command?

Translation after Lanfranchi & Parpola 1990: no. 119.

immense city, with a wall of some 7 kilometers (4.3 miles) enclosing 300 hectares (740 acres), and contained two citadels with monumental buildings decorated with reliefs and bull statues. The city was abandoned upon Sargon II's death and his successor, Sennacherib (ruled 704–681), entirely refurbished the old city of Nineveh as his capital. He extended it to 750 hectares (1850 acres) enclosed by a 12 kilometer (7.45 miles) wall, and developed two citadels with public buildings, again all decorated. These massive cities were clear markers of Assyria's wealth. Although we cannot estimate their populations with any degree of certainty, it is likely that they greatly surpassed what the surroundings could support and had to be fed and maintained using the resources of the whole empire. They were also much too large to be populated only by inhabitants from the region, so people were imported from all over to live there and to serve the state bureaucracy.

Simultaneously, public buildings in other cities of the heartland were restored and expanded, and provincial centers in the territory near Assyria, such as Dur-Katlimmu, were completely redesigned. Moreover, when the Assyrians conquered Aramean cities in western Syria, for example, they turned them into Assyrian cities. In 856 they changed the name of Til-Barsip in the land of Bit-Adini on the Euphrates to Kar-Shalmaneser ("Shalmaneser's harbor") after its conqueror Shalmaneser III, probably expanded the city in size, and provided it with Assyrian public buildings and residences. The state thus displayed its power by constructing highly visible symbols of its presence.

The building activity required manpower and resources that only the empire could provide. The cities and palaces were certainly lavishly decorated and became the depositories of precious goods from all over the Near East. The archaeological record is much less complete for movable items – rugs, carpets, jewelry, and so on – but there are some indications of the wealth that was displayed in the Assyrian court. Ivory attachments to furniture, carved in the various styles of the western part of the empire, were found in great abundance at Kalhu (see figure 11.4). Most spectacular has been the recent find in the same city of four vaulted tombs from the ninth and eighth centuries constructed beneath the palace floor in baked bricks; two of them were undisturbed and contained the original grave goods. Inscriptions indicate that the people buried included four queens: Mullissu-mukannishat-Ninua, wife of Assurnasirpal II; Yaba, wife of Tiglath-pileser III; Banitu, wife of Shalmaneser V; and Atalia, wife of Sargon II. Their bodies were covered with an abundance of gold jewelry, some 35 kilograms in total, which displays the great skills of the craftsmen who made the items and gives some idea of the treasure that was available to the royal family (figure 12.3). If we remember that most of the luxury items were lost over time, we can only vaguely imagine how spectacular the wealth displayed in the palaces must have been.

Prosperity trickled down to the elite members of Assyrian society, a group whose size we cannot ascertain. The almost exclusive focus of archaeological research on monumental architecture has led to a paucity of detail concerning private citizens, even those from the upper classes. A few houses have been excavated, but there is scant information about their material contents. Textual information from contracts and deeds shows that the high officials of the state had considerable assets in silver and landed property. Unfortunately, the extent of an entire holding cannot be reconstructed. Some men are known to have lent large amounts of silver, perhaps more than 500 kilograms (1,100 pounds) at one time. The king also gave them landed estates for their services, which they could expand through acquisition of more land, but the sizes of these estates are also a matter of pure guesswork. The donations included entire villages, houses, fields, orchards, and the populations to work them, and were often located in different regions, so they did not form one large, coherent domain. The kings regularly granted tax exemption to the owners of these estates, which certainly increased their disposable wealth. There is little doubt, then, that the upper echelons of Assyrian society benefited from the empire.

Large parts of the population were not in that situation, however. Assyria always remained an agricultural society, and the majority of its people lived on the land they worked. Again, we are not directly informed about conditions here and scholars disagree on the status of the lower classes. The Assyrian policy of developing the countryside by establishing villages and settling deportees there must have led to a substantial number of people being directly dependent on the state. Along with them free peasants seem also to have existed, but the degree of their autonomy is often thought to have been so limited as to make them no different from state dependents. Since entire villages could be sold, their residents probably had little freedom.

A group of seventh-century texts, often called census lists, although their purpose is enigmatic, gives detailed inventories of rural families, seemingly all part of the properties of wealthy men. For example:

> Idranu, farmer; his brother; one son; three women, twenty hectares (fifty acres) of arable land; one house; one threshing floor; one garden. Total, in the town of Badani, near Harran.[3]

The families recorded were small, with one wife and, on average, fewer than two children accounted for; some scholars have suggested that the landowners enforced the breakup of families to make them more controllable. In the service of the estate owners, these common people worked small plots of land, tended vines and vegetable gardens, and had a few oxen, sheep, and goats. The census lists probably reflect the circumstances of most of Assyria's population. The social structure of the state had great inequalities, with a small and extremely wealthy upper class and numerous families living at subsistence level.

12.2   The Historical Record

Since there is a direct correlation in Mesopotamian history between the strength of the state and the size of the documentary record it produced, it is no surprise that the sources for the Assyrian empire are plentiful. They derive almost exclusively from the palace and focus principally on the activities of the king, especially as a warrior and a builder. Military actions also figure prominently in the pictorial record carved on reliefs that were displayed in the palaces (see box 12.1), so we have much factual data in that aspect of history. This tends to underrate the Assyrians' other endeavors and leads to a primarily military history of the period.

The royal annals, year-by-year accounts of military campaigns, provide the most detailed record (see box 9.1). For each year they present a sequence of opponents the king defeated, sometimes merely listing their names, sometimes describing the Assyrian actions in great detail. The yearly campaign was such a fundamental concept in the Neo-Assyrian period that it came to structure the chronology of a king's reign. In his annals a king did not state "in my fifth year,"

Box 12.1 *Assyrian relief sculpture*

One of the consequences of the enormous building activities of Neo-Assyrian kings is the existence of an especially articulate kind of record available to the historian: the pictorial relief. All palaces at Kalhu, Dur-Sharrukin, and Nineveh had elaborate wall reliefs that represented some of the military campaigns its builders undertook. Often, short inscriptions identify the persons and cities represented, so that we know what events are depicted and have a record parallel to that from the annalistic accounts.

While Assyrian relief sculpture dates back to the second millennium, it is with Assurnasirpal II that the decoration of the palaces we have excavated becomes more expansive. Carved limestone slabs some 2 meters high lined the walls of public spaces. In antiquity the reliefs were painted, but only traces of this have survived. Sennacherib's palace at Nineveh has the most extensive record available to us. In it were represented such military campaigns as the siege of Lachish in Judah and attacks on the marshes in southern Babylonia. Why he selected these campaigns for display is not clear, as they were not the most important military actions in his reign. While some of the images depicting the siege of Lachish, for example, can be confirmed through archaeological information from that site, we cannot see the reliefs as intended to present an accurate historical record. Just like the annals and other royal inscriptions they provide a complex message that seeks to show the ruler in control of the entire world. The historian thus has to interpret these scenes with analytical techniques similar to those applied to the textual accounts.

Besides war scenes, the reliefs also contain representations of cultic acts and of the king as hunter. The decorative layout of the palace rooms was carefully planned to portray the king as the one who guarantees order in the universe: he defeats the forces of chaos – enemies and wild animals – and he maintains proper relations with the gods. Moreover, the reliefs had the function of protecting the palace rooms. Integrated within them were massive bull sculptures that were invoked to ward off evil. In order to understand the individual scenes, we have to study them within their architectural context and in relation to the other scenes that surround them.

for example, but "in my fifth campaign." Simultaneously, the ancient Assyrian custom of naming each year after an eponymous official was continued and lists of these names were drawn up, some of them with an indication of where the army campaigned that year (document 12.2). We have a full sequence of eponyms for the years 910 to 649, and there is a chronological anchor in the statement that "in the year of Bursagale from Guzana, there was an uprising in the inner city, and in the month Simanu there was an eclipse of the sun."[4] That eclipse can be dated to June 15, 763 BC, and we have thus a firm absolute chronology for the entire period.

Assyria's state bureaucracy was vast, and naturally it produced numerous records. Some of the imperial archives, albeit surprisingly few, were excavated in the cities of Assur, Kalhu, and Nineveh. The more than three thousand letters officials throughout the empire wrote to the kings provide a rich source of information. They discuss mostly administrative and military matters. It is certain that in addition to clay tablets inscribed with cuneiform, the Assyrians also wrote on papyri and parchments in alphabetic script. These have not survived in the archaeological record owing to the Near Eastern climate, and we are thus denied access to what may have been a substantial part of the bureaucratic apparatus. Moreover, the nature of our record is almost totally palatial, as archaeologists have concentrated on the spectacular architectural works of the kings. In the capital cities Kalhu, Dur-Sharrukin, and Nineveh only the citadels have been explored, while the immense lower towns have been left untouched. There is thus virtually no knowledge about people outside the palace sector. Even though the palace was certainly dominant, our documentation's exclusive focus on it is undoubtedly misleading.

12.3   Ninth-Century Expansion

The troubles of the twelfth through tenth centuries had forced Assyria to surrender control over the northeast Syrian area that it had colonized in the Middle Assyrian period. The administrative centers they had established then did not disappear, however, and local rulers who showed some affiliation with Assyria remained in power. How dependent they were on the heartland is a point of debate, and many scholars argue that Assyria had lost all influence. The Arameans certainly dominated the countryside, however, and gained power in various cities as well. The records suggest that into the ninth century, permanent settlement in northeast Syria was limited. When Assyrian armies campaigned there they encountered virtually no villages, so tribal groups must have been the primary inhabitants of the region. But all through the Dark Age kings of Assyria maintained control over the state's heartland, that is, the plains to the east of the Tigris from Assur northward somewhat beyond Nineveh, a region the size of Wales in the United Kingdom today. In the last third of the tenth century the Assyrians initiated a policy of regular military campaigns to turn around the situation. Their primary target was the area to the west, which they considered to have been taken from Assyria by the Arameans. In essence, their aim was to restore the state to

Document 12.2   *Excerpt from the Eponym Chronicle*

Ten manuscripts found in various sites in Assyria contain lists of years identified by the eponym, with a summary note about what happened then, most often the destination of a major military campaign. Such lists provide us with an accurate way to date a long stretch of Neo-Assyrian history, and give us an idea of the military exploits that were considered most important. In the translation here the years BC *are added.*

719	[In the year of]	Sargon, king [of Assyria]	[ent]ered
718	[In the year of]	Zer-ibni, governor of Ra[sappa]	[to Ta]bal
717	[In the year of]	Tab-shar-Assur, chamberlain	[Dur-Sharru]kin was founded
716	[In the year of]	Tab-sil-Eshara, governor of the citadel	[to] Mannea
715	[In the year of]	Taklal-ana-beli, governor of Nasibina	[ ] governors appointed
714	[In the year of]	Ishtar-duri, governor of Arrapha	[to Ur]artu, Musasir, Haldia
713	[In the year of]	Assur-bani, governor of Kalhu	[the] nobles in Ellipi, he entered the new house, to Musasir
712	[In the year of]	Sharru-emuranni, governor of Zamua	in the land
711	[In the year of]	Ninurta-alik-pani, governor of Si'mme	[to] Marqasa
710	[In the year of]	Shamash-belu-usur, governor of Arzuhina	to Bit-zeri the king stayed at Kish
709	[In the year of]	Mannu-ki-Assur-le'i, governor of Tille	Sargon took the hands of Bel
708	In the year of	Shamash-upahhir, governor of Habruri	Kummuhi conquered and a governor was appointed
707	In the year of	Sha-Assur-dubbu, governor of Tushan	the king returned from Babylon, the vizier and nobles, the booty of Dur-Jakin was carried off, Dur-Jakin was destroyed, on the 22nd of Teshrit, the gods of Dur-Sharrukin entered the temples
706	In the year of	Mutakkil-Assur, governor of Guzana	the king stayed in the land, the nobles [ ], on the 6th of Ayar, Dur-Sharrukin was completed
705	In the year of	Nashur-Bel, governor of Amidu	the king [ ] against Qurdi the Kullumean, the king was killed, the camp of the king of Assyria [ ], on the 12th of Ab, Sennacherib [became] king

Translation after Millard 1994: 46–8, 60.

its Middle Assyrian conditions. This reconquest included a resettlement of the region. For example, Assur-dan II (ruled 934–912) stated in his annals:

> I brought back the exhausted people of Assyria who had abandoned their cities and houses in the face of want, hunger, and famine, and had gone up to other lands. I settled them in cities and houses that were suitable and they dwelt in peace. I constructed palaces in the various districts of my land. I hitched up plows in the various districts of my land and thereby piled up more grain than ever before.[5]

Through the construction of palaces and official buildings the Assyrians turned the cities they controlled into centers from which the region could be ruled permanently. There was a conscious policy of developing the north Syrian territory: canals were built along the Habur River, for instance, in order to facilitate the transport of heavy goods, and the Middle Assyrian road system was repaired to maintain direct contacts with the heartland of Assyria.

This policy culminated in the reign of two kings who laid the basis for the Neo-Assyrian empire over a period of some sixty years: Assurnasirpal II (ruled 883–859) and Shalmaneser III (ruled 858–824). They consolidated control over the region from the Zagros Mountains to the Euphrates and from the foothills of the Taurus Mountains to the Babylonian border. This area then became the platform from which to campaign in more distant parts. The first ruler carried out a systematic conquest of the zone that immediately surrounded Assyria, relying on the positions that his predecessors had secured. His troops never covered the same area twice unless a rebellion forced them to do so. Assurnasirpal campaigned in the upper valleys of the Diyala and Lesser Zab, which controlled access to the Zagros Mountains and Babylonia, in the northeast up to the Taurus Mountains, in the north along the Tigris, where he built a fortress at the point where that river enters Mesopotamia, and in the west. From there he marched first on the Middle Euphrates, then turned against the powerful state of Bit-Adini, farther northwest. He secured the areas by building Assyrian centers in strategic locations, such as river crossings. At the end of his reign, Assurnasirpal had conquered all of the regions that had been considered part of Assyria in Middle Assyrian times. He had only once crossed the Euphrates in the west to obtain booty there.

His son and successor, Shalmaneser III, filled his thirty-five year reign with military campaigns, especially in the west and the north. In the west, he regularly crossed the Euphrates in order to gain access to the Mediterranean Sea and to the wealth of the small states there. Political fragmentation made Syria militarily weak and thus an easy target, but under the leadership of Damascus it formed a major coalition against Shalmaneser's forces. In 853, according to Assyrian sources, it fielded an army of 40,000 infantry, 2,000 cavalry, and 4,000 chariots. The troops came from Damascus, Hamath, Israel, and the Phoenician cities, with support from Arabs and Egyptians, and they seem to have been able to push the Assyrians back in a battle near Qarqar. In the next few years, Shalmaneser had to reassert control closer to home. But the Damascus coalition fell apart on the death of the king of Damascus, Hadad-ezer, and by 841 Shalmaneser III seems to have

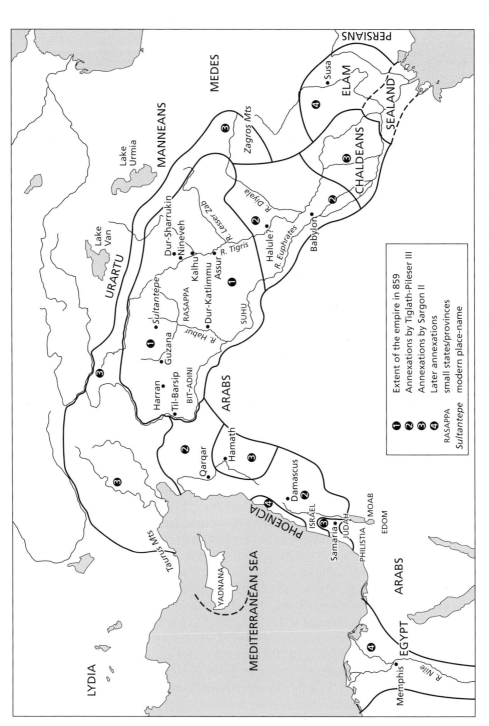

Map 12.1 Phases in the expansion of the Assyrian empire. After Mario Liverani, *Antico Oriente* (Rome and Bari: Laterza, 1988), p. 793.

removed all southern Syrian opposition. This enabled him to turn his attention to the north, where he subdued the Neo-Hittite states and gained access to southern Anatolian mines. The aim of these military actions was not the incorporation of Syria into Assyria. The states there remained independent, keeping their original rulers, and only had to provide tribute. There was thus no attempt at this time to expand the boundaries of the Assyrian state.

To the north of Assyria the state of Urartu had developed as a formidable opponent, as we saw in the previous chapter. From the beginning of his reign Shalmaneser III had probed its resistance, but only after he had subdued the west did he give it his full attention, organizing five campaigns in quick succession between 832 and 827. Shalmaneser stopped leading the army himself, leaving that role to his highest military official, the commander-in-chief (Akkadian *turtanu*) Dayyan-Assur. The expeditions aimed primarily at obtaining spoils and reducing the military threat of Urartu. They led Assyria into distant lands in the Zagros, where it first encountered peoples who would later become important opponents, such as the Medes and Manneans. Similarly, there was no attempt to control the southern neighbor of Babylonia. Shalmaneser campaigned there only twice, in order to intervene in a civil war that had erupted between the king and his brother.

Despite the high level of military activity, Shalmaneser III's Assyria was not an expansionist state. He maintained the borders Assurnasirpal had established, and campaigned beyond them only to protect them and to obtain booty and tribute (figure 12.4). But the area east of the Euphrates River became fully Assyrianized: the Aramaic city of Til-Barsip was renamed Kar-Shalmaneser after the king, and guarded the river crossing. Thirty kilometers (18 miles) upstream and across the river a new center called Pitru became the launching pad for Syrian campaigns. The border was well defended and clearly delineated: on the east bank of the Euphrates and on some small islands in the river stood a string of military fortresses to protect it.

The Assyrians maintained a clear distinction between two types of territories, those of "the land of Assur" and those under "the yoke of Assur," a system they inherited from Middle Assyrian times. Assyria proper, the region stretching from the Zagros to the Euphrates, was the land of Assur and by Shalmaneser III's time it was again under full Assyrian control. That land was uniformly organized under a provincial administration: to govern it the king appointed direct representatives, who resided in palaces constructed in Assyrian style, even if they were not as grand as those in the central capitals. The palace at Kar-Shalmaneser, for example, was decorated with frescoes representing the same type of scenes as were found in stone reliefs at Kalhu. The provinces were integrated into a system of maintenance of the god Assur, whose sole temple was in the city Assur, and who functioned as the god for the entire land of Assyria. Every province had to supply basic foodstuffs to support him. This was the ideological expression of the fact that the economies of the entire region were integrated into a single system in order to feed the central state bureaucracy. In political terms, the provinces were equivalent in status, although in practice Assyrian kings allowed some of them

Figure 12.4 Tribute bearers, detail on the Black Obelisk of Shalmaneser III. About
2 meters high, the obelisk contains an account of Shalmaneser's annual campaigns up to his
thirty-first year and shows five relief panels on each of its four sides. Those depict the
submission of rulers, some scenes from nature, and mostly foreigners who bring tribute. The
texts between the panels identify some of the tribute bearers and what they brought. The men
here are said to be from "Jehu of the house of Omri," that is, Israel, and to carry silver and
gold objects, as well as spears and "staffs of the king's hand." British Museum, London. Black
limestone. Credit: akg images/Erich Lessing.

a greater degree of autonomy. "Dynasties" of governors, with the office passing
from father to son, existed for example in the Middle Euphrates province of Suhu.
As long as they obeyed the Assyrian king, there was no need to reorganize them
to fit the provincial system.

Outside these boundaries, the Assyrians dominated states that remained nominally independent, but whose rulers were vassals. These were considered to be
under the yoke of Assur. Their duties included the delivery of annual tribute in
the form of valuable items, which was for the king, not the god Assur, and there is
no evidence that the deity's cult was imposed. As vassals, the tributary rulers had
to adhere to treaties, as was the case in the second millennium, and any breach
was considered a grave transgression that gave the Assyrians the right to impose
punishment. The clear distinction between Assyria proper and the outside shows
that, in the first phase of its empire, Assyria only wanted to recreate the state it
had in the Middle Assyrian period. Beyond the borders was a world that had to
obey, but did not need to become part of Assyria.

Even within these boundaries Assyria was a large entity, and the king, who was personally responsible for the proper functioning of the state, had to rely on an extensive bureaucracy to govern it. Higher administrators and military officers had considerable powers and they became more independent as Shalmaneser III grew old. The commander-in-chief, Dayyan-Assur, openly led military campaigns starting in 832, and in 827 a rebellion broke out involving the heartland of Assyria. Princes felt aggrieved at Dayyan-Assur's influence and also fought one another for the right of succession. The confusion lasted for seven years, including the first three of the reign of King Shamshi-Adad V, who had gained the throne in 823 with the help of Babylonia.

12.4   Internal Assyrian Decline

Because of the highly centralized structure of the Assyrian state, the dynastic struggles at the end of Shalmaneser III's reign had a disastrous impact on the entire system. Although Shamshi-Adad V ruled for thirteen years (823–811) and portrayed himself as a victorious warrior, Assyria's dominance over Syria had weakened and states there held back tribute. Early on in his reign the Babylonians forced him to accept a treaty on unfavorable terms, a situation he could reverse only years later. Within Assyria itself royal power also slipped. This became clearer after Shamshi-Adad's reign, but the process had already started under Shalmaneser III. Local governors and officials within Assyria became virtually independent. They commissioned inscriptions, some of them bilingual Assyrian and Aramaic, in which they portrayed themselves as kings, even if they continued to pay homage to the Assyrian ruler. These men included governors of provinces close to Assyria's heartland, such as Rasappa and Guzana. As we saw, Hadad-yith'i of Guzana depicted himself as a king and claimed that title in the Aramaic version of the inscription on his statue (see figure 11.5). The commander-in-chief, Shamshi-ilu, was perhaps the most powerful man of his time. He was active under four kings for most of the first half of the eighth century and, from Kar-Shalmaneser, campaigned west of the Euphrates on his own behalf. He used his status to arbitrate conflicts between local north Syrian rulers without reference to the king in Assyria. On the Middle Euphrates around ancient Mari, a dynasty of governors left royal-style inscriptions without acknowledging the Assyrian king. Instead, they claimed descent from Hammurabi of Babylon! Governors and officials from cities such as Kalhu and Assur arrogated royal powers to themselves. The king, who was nominally owner of all the land of Assyria, gave them large estates in order to keep them on his side. Even in the palace itself, competition for power was rife. In this context we have to see the importance of Queen Sammuramat, who was the inspiration for the legendary Semiramis. The widow of Shamshi-Adad V, she remained so influential in the reign of her son Adad-nirari III (ruled 810–783) that official inscriptions mentioned the two as acting together. Special emphasis on dynastic succession may have been needed to affirm the king's status. These internal problems put an end to the emergence of Assyria as the major Near Eastern power in the ninth century. The state's initial successes seem to have overwhelmed its administrative capacities and the center was insufficiently unified to function properly under a ruler who was not particularly forceful. The dynasty survived, with rule passing from father to son, but the kings had to buy officials' favors in order to remain in place.

What Assyria accomplished in the ninth century was a restoration and consolidation of the territorial state it had controlled in the late second millennium. It had started to use it as a platform for campaigns farther afield, especially in the west. There are no statements from the Assyrians themselves, or reports from their victims, that explain why they mounted such huge military operations annually, at great expense of manpower and resources. Assyrian kings only assert that they did so at the command of the god Assur. Scholars are mystified as to why the Assyrians behaved in this way, and have suggested mainly ideological, economic, and defensive reasons as an explanation (see debate 12.1). Most likely the reasons for the expansionism changed as the nature of the state evolved. The first phase was one of reconquest in order to control groups, such as the Arameans who had seized political power after 1100, and to gain access to agricultural lands. When Assyrian expansion reached the Euphrates, western Syria provided an appealing source of wealth for its elites, who had become used to living off the income from foreign conquests. Western Syria was also an easy target, as there was no unified territorial state to mount a strong opposition. There was no attempt to integrate these regions into Assyria, only a demand for goods, and Assyria's kings tolerated the existence of independent neighbors as long as these did not threaten their interests. The official records, both textual and pictorial, paint an image of the Assyrian king forcing all others into submission, through battle or the threat of it, and then being presented with their goods. The whole of the external world supplied his needs and enabled the king to display his enormous assets through acts such as large building projects. The system of extracting resources from the surrounding area may have functioned in the ninth century but, when central power weakened, it came to a halt. Assyria had to develop another approach, systematic expansion, which was to characterize the second phase of its empire.

Debate 12.1   *Why did the Assyrians create an empire?*

Despite the fact that the Assyrian empire dominates every published history of the ancient Near East in the first millennium BC, scholars have not paid much attention to the reasons for its imperialism. They have written numerous pages relating its military accomplishments with great detail and accuracy, but, when it comes to explaining why this empire was created, and what was accomplished in doing so, scholars have been less clear. Oftentimes they do not discuss the issue at all. The reason for this reticence may lie in the fact that an early explicit discussion was so ideologically inspired by Nazism that it made the question distasteful. In 1937, the very famous scholar of ancient Mesopotamia, Wolfram von Soden, identified an Aryan joy of battle among the Assyrians, which they gained from the "Nordic" blood in their veins, acquired through contact with the Indo-European Mittani (von Soden 1937). Such racial theories are now fully rejected.

When more recent scholars do try to explain why Assyria created its empire, they tend to focus on internal factors and within Assyrian society on the kings whose personalities dominate the evidence we have. Some scholars have accused Assurnasirpal II of megalomania and jealousy of the wealth he saw in the hands of the rulers of Syria and Phoenicia (Garelli et al. 2002: 218). Others stated that royal ideology demanded that the king campaign every year, and that as a result he brought order to a chaotic periphery (Grayson 1982: 280; Cancik-Kirschbaum 2003: 121–2; Liverani 2014: 509–11). Sometimes, religion is seen as a driving force: the god Assur was king and the mortal king had to follow the divine command to enlarge the state (Garelli 1980: 33–4; Saggs 1984: 265–6; Fales 2010). A study that was provoked by the Soviet invasion of Hungary in 1956 saw no rationale at all: the Assyrians had no mission, no ideology. They may have been inspired by self-preservation, but expansion was self-evident to them (Kraus 1957–8).

When the focus of attention shifts from the personality of the king to the entirety of Assyria, the question of security guides explanations. Empire building at first was a defensive reaction against the Arameans who threatened Assyria's western border (Garelli et al. 2002: 229; Joannès 2004: 25). The threat was not necessarily a military one, but economic concerns were at play as well. The newly arrived peoples jeopardized Assyria's access to sources of raw materials (Labat 1967: 16), and the Assyrians reacted by seizing the resources themselves (Yoffee 1988: 57). One scholar, examining economic reasons in detail, argued that commercial concerns presented a more encompassing explanation than defensive imperialism. Because Mesopotamia was devoid of many essential natural resources, both basic products such as wood, metals, and stone, and luxury products, and because of its location on major trade routes, Mesopotamians felt the need to control these lines of communication and seized them through empire building. He considered this to be a valid explanation for all moments of Mesopotamian expansionism, not only the Assyrian empire, but also the preceding Old Akkadian, Ur III, Old Babylonian, and Middle Assyrian empires, and the succeeding Neo-Babylonian one (Larsen 1979). This does detract from the special character of the Neo-Assyrian empire, however.

In recent years more nuanced explanations that rely on theories of empires formulated in other fields of study have started to emerge and scholars are urging that we take a comparative approach (Garfinkle 2007; Cline and Graham 2011: 42–52). We probably also have to historicize the question more and see various attitudes over time. There were adjustments both in the Assyrian core, where elites and the economy changed their needs as the empire developed, and in the periphery, which had to deal with an aggressor with evolving demands. No party in the interactions remained the same as time went by. Assyrian pressure caused discrete groups to join forces in reaction, its requests for tribute incited rebellions, and so on. Recalcitrance triggered an Assyrian response. At the same time in Assyria, elites came to rely on the empire for their careers, the economy needed foreign assets, and so on. The empire lasted some 250 years and it is inconceivable that its goals and the reasons for its actions remained the same for the entire period. We need to look for a dynamic explanation.

NOTES

1   Oded 1979: 20.
2   Grayson 1991b: 293.
3   Fales & Postgate 1995: 138.
4   Millard 1994: 41.
5   Grayson 1991b: 134–5.

13

Assyria's World Domination

3000	2500	2000	1500	1000	500

744	Tiglath-pileser III initiates structural changes in Assyria
722	Conquest of Samaria
689	Sennacherib sacks Babylon
671	Esarhaddon captures Egyptian capital Memphis
664–3	Assurbanipal captures Egyptian capital Thebes
652–648	Babylonian rebellion under Shamash-shuma-ukin
626	Independent dynasty in Babylonia
612	Sack of Nineveh by Medes and Babylonians

Between 745 and 612 Assyria became a true empire. It extended its military dominance over the entire Near East and briefly even incorporated the distant country of Egypt. It eliminated all its rivals and gradually incorporated more territories into a centrally controlled administrative system. In this late Assyrian period the empire brought together under one ruler a vast territory from western Iran to the Mediterranean and from southern Anatolia to Egypt. As before, the king played a crucial role in the activities of the empire and its military successes, and the six men who occupied the throne in succession were strong and able rulers (for a list, see Section 18 of the King Lists at the end of the book). The imperial project was flawed, however, and frictions and instabilities undermined the state. Although the rulers belonged to the same family, almost every succession

A History of the Ancient Near East ca. 3000–323 BC, Third Edition. Marc Van De Mieroop.
© 2016 John Wiley & Sons, Inc. Published 2016 by John Wiley & Sons, Inc.

was contested and the new kings had difficulties establishing full control. Assyria's internal weakness may explain why the kings after Assurbanipal lost their grip on the state, and why the collapse of the Assyrian empire was so sudden.

13.1 The Creation of an Imperial Structure

In the first half of the eighth century Assyria had lost its ability to campaign outside its borders, and internally officials had usurped many of the royal powers. Provincial governors were able to act with a great deal of independence, although they still had to acknowledge their subservience to the king. Scholars disagree about the extent of internal weakness: some see the regional officials as virtually autonomous, others consider them as fully integrated within the Assyrian state structure and their activities as coordinated with those of the king. Their proclaimed independence would then have been more a rhetorical device for local audiences than a lack of obedience to the king. Whatever the case, the early eighth-century Assyrian rulers were not strong military leaders and the impact of the state on its surroundings was much less significant than it had been in the mid-ninth century. Moreover, Urartu was able to extend its influence over northern Syria, thereby threatening Assyria's access to the Mediterranean. Finally, in the years 762 to 759, a number of cities, including the ancient capital of Assur, rebelled against the royal power. Assyria had reached a low point.

Powerful kings reversed this situation, starting with Tiglath-pileser III whose reign (744–727) represented a real turning point. He and his second successor, Sargon II (ruled 721–705; figure 13.1), restructured Assyria internally, campaigned almost annually outside its borders, and began to annex vast foreign territories. The internal reorganization focused on thwarting the powers of local officials. The kings divided the old provinces under strong governors into smaller ones, and increased their number from twelve to twenty-five. Similarly they made the most important military and administrative offices less powerful by assigning them to two persons rather than one. For example, instead of one commander-in-chief (*turtanu*), two men shared that post, one "of the left" and one "of the right." They often appointed eunuchs in high government positions so that there was no possibility that fathers could pass on their offices to their sons. The "land of Assur" was thus reformed in order to limit the powers of officials and increase the king's control.

Simultaneously, Tiglath-pileser III initiated a policy of territorial expansion far beyond the borders that had been maintained since Middle Assyrian times. He probably reorganized the army and replaced the annual levy of troops from the Assyrian population with a standing professional army, using conquered people for the infantry and Assyrians as the core of the cavalry and chariotry. Tiglath-pileser III crossed the Euphrates, as his ninth-century predecessors had done, but the policy toward the region changed fundamentally. Instead of merely forcing the states there to pay tribute, he and his successors gradually incorporated them into

Figure 13.1   Relief from Dur-Sharrukin depicting King Sargon II and an official. Relief sculpture in late Assyrian times became even more monumental than before. In particular, the works Sargon II commissioned at Dur-Sharrukin were massive in size, and can include elaborate scenes. Shown here is a sober depiction of the king, on the right, with one of his high officials. Louvre Museum, Paris, AO 19873-19874. Limestone, H. 330 cm. Credit: akg images/Album/Prism.

the empire as provinces. This policy actually may not have been Assyria's initial intention but was forced upon it by the resistance of the local populations.

Ideally, Assyria did not want to exert direct control over areas beyond its traditional borders. Its intention was to exact tribute and to enforce political obedience, and local rulers were left in place as long as they complied with Assyrian demands. But this policy no longer worked. We can distinguish three types of political arrangements with the states in the west, reflecting three stages toward their full incorporation into the empire: (1) vassal states where the ruler remained in charge but was to deliver annual tribute; (2) puppet states where a local man considered to be more faithful to the Assyrians was placed on the throne; and (3) provinces, where a governor directly under Assyria's control ruled. Acts of disobedience usually precipitated the progression from one stage to the next: only if the arrangement failed to produce the desired results did the Assyrians reduce autonomy further. They planned the creation of provinces strategically to maximize control and reduce direct confrontation with surrounding enemies.

For example, Tiglath-pileser III at first expanded the number of provinces along the Mediterranean coast and stopped at the Philistine city-states, which he left independent. He had thus guaranteed access to the sea and control of the north–south route running alongside it, but there was still a buffer with the powerful enemy state of Egypt. Only later, in reaction against their disobedience, did he turn inland Syro-Palestinian states into provinces, but the entire region was never fully incorporated within the empire's provincial system (see map 13.1).

The history of the kingdom of Israel provides a good example of how this policy operated and shows the various stages of Assyrian control as well as local reaction to it. The biblical account allows us to see the non-Assyrian point of view, while the Assyrian annals give the empire's version of events. Early in Tiglath-pileser's reign, the Israelite King Menahem provided tribute voluntarily and was left in peace. Soon after his death, the anti-Assyrian rebel Pekah assassinated Menahem's son and successor Pekahiah in 735, and seized the throne with the support of Damascus and of Israel's population that resented the heavy tribute payments. In 734, Tiglath-pileser III campaigned along the Syrian coast and turned the regions there into provinces. Only in 732 did he advance against Damascus, the focus of opposition to Assyria, which he annexed. At the same time, he turned the northern parts of Israel into Assyrian provinces. Tiglath-pileser III claims that the people of Israel overthrew Pekah and replaced him with a pro-Assyrian ruler, Hoshea, an act certainly prompted by his military presence nearby. When Tiglath-pileser died, Hoshea at first remained loyal to Assyria, but later on, possibly as part of a general rebellion, he stopped paying tribute. This triggered retaliation by Shalmaneser V (ruled 726–722), who laid siege to Israel's capital Samaria for three years and conquered it just before his death. His successor Sargon II claimed the victory for himself and turned the region into the province of Samaria.

The repercussions for Israel were great. The Assyrians deported a substantial number of people – 27,290 according to Sargon – and settled them in northeastern Syria and western Iran. People from other parts of the empire resettled the region of Samaria, creating a less homogeneous population that was more docile toward Assyria. While the northern parts of the original state, the provinces of Megiddo and Karnaim, were left almost depopulated, the Assyrians promoted Samaria's economy through the creation of villages and agricultural estates. They restructured the administration to fit Assyria's needs; legal transactions were now recorded in the Assyrian language and cuneiform script. They rebuilt the capital and, along with a few other cities, it came to be the seat of governors, who lived in residences constructed in the Assyrian style. They set up fortresses along the borders to protect the province against incursions from the south and east. Israel became an integral part of the empire.

Israel provides a good example of how Assyrian rule in the Syro-Palestinian area changed, and many other states were similarly affected. But the Assyrians' policy was flexible. They kept states outside the provincial system when this was better for the empire's interests. Local vassal or puppet rulers continued to govern Judah and all other states to the south and east of Israel, although their territories were

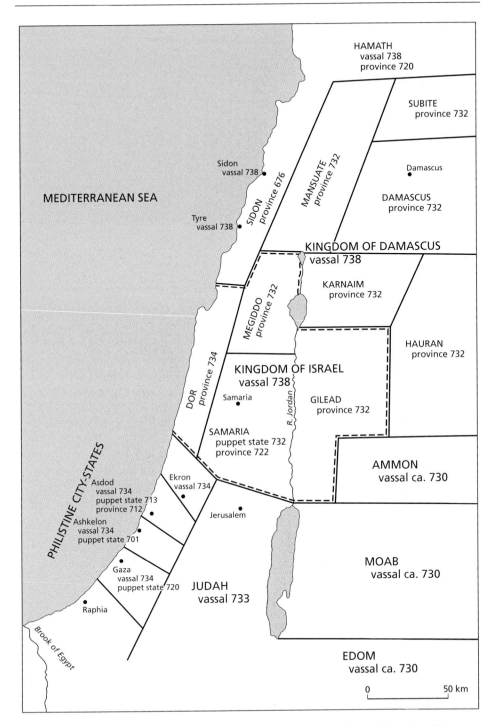

Map 13.1   Assyrian annexation of western states in the eighth century. After Benedikt Otzen, "Israel under the Assyrians," in M. T. Larsen, ed., *Power and Propaganda* (*Mesopotamia* 7, Copenhagen: Akademisk Forlag, 1979), p. 252.

often much reduced in size. The Assyrians adopted this policy to create a buffer between their empire and the Egyptians and Arabs, and probably also to enable trade with these peoples. They similarly preserved the political structures of the Phoenician cities, as their trade was important to Assyria. They fully exploited the economic assets of regions, even of those not turned into provinces. In the Philistine area, for example, Assyria's influence changed the production of olive oil from a cottage industry to a centralized system that guaranteed supply. Thus the empire cannot be considered as driven by a mere desire to acquire territory. It was a structure that aimed at maximizing resources for its core. The policies described here were ideal for interactions with smaller political units and were applied from southern Anatolia to Palestine, and in the mountain areas to Assyria's east. In its interactions with the great states Assyria used different approaches, however.

13.2   The Defeat of the Great Rivals

In 744, when Tiglath-pileser III came to the throne, Assyria shared control over the Near East with several great states at its borders: Babylonia in the south, Elam in the southeast, Urartu in the north, and, in the distance beyond the Syro-Palestinian region, Egypt. Whereas their predecessors had accepted these states' existence, even if military clashes had occurred, all kings from Tiglath-pileser III to Assurbanipal decided to confront and subdue them. Once again Assyria needed to adopt a flexible approach, however, as these opponents were too large and too powerful to be completely controlled, or, in the case of Babylonia, special considerations prevented full incorporation into the empire. The defeat of the great rivals preoccupied the Assyrian military for many decades.

The Assyrians never solved the question of how to control Babylonia. While they could not accept the existence of a disobedient neighbor at their southern border, they seem to have been reluctant to take over the country openly. Probably the knowledge that Babylonia had fundamentally influenced Assyria's culture and religion induced a sense of respect that prevented similar treatment to that meted out to other regions. Furthermore, Babylonia was not a homogeneous area: the ancient cities that preserved cultural and political traditions were like small islands in a countryside where tribal groups held sway. Even worse, the extreme south of the region was impossible to control through traditional military means as it was covered with marshes where the army could not deploy its usual tactics. These areas provided refuge to anti-Assyrian forces like the Chaldeans, who competed with the Assyrians for the throne of Babylon (figure 13.2).

During the reigns of the six major late Assyrian kings, some twenty transitions of power took place in Babylon (for a list of kings, see Section 15 of the King Lists at the end of the book). The kings there could belong to one of five groups:

1   the Assyrian king himself;
2   a family member of Assyria's king;

Figure 13.2   Assyrian representation from Nineveh showing refugees in the southern marshes. Assyrian palace reliefs can be very detailed in their depictions of the environment of foreign territories. The marshes of southern Babylonia were challenging to the Assyrian army because they made regular campaigns impossible. The representation here shows them as a place of hiding and unrealistically depicts the troops as fighting in small boats using the same tactics as on firm ground. British Museum, London 124774,b. Gypsum, H. ca. 120 cm; W. ca. 150 cm. Credit: Werner Forman Archive.

3   a native Babylonian, placed on the throne by Assyria;
4   a Babylonian independent from Assyria; or
5   a Chaldean who was anti-Assyrian.

The numerous changes show both Assyria's inability to find an effective way of controlling Babylonia and the strength of local opposition, which often could rely on support from Elam.

The relations between Assyria and Babylonia over the twelve decades from 745 to 627 are too intricate to discuss in detail here. As a good example of how frustrating the experience could be we will look at Sennacherib, who was king of Assyria from 704 to 681, and his various, well-documented initiatives to govern Babylonia. In those twenty-four years the rule of Babylon changed hands

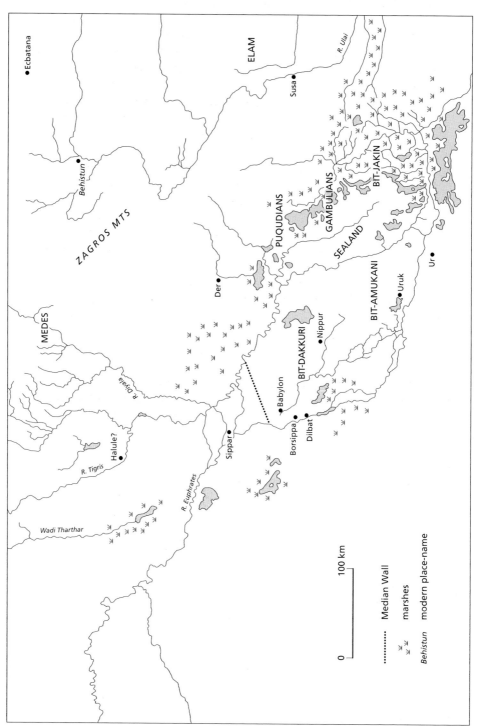

Map 13.2 Babylonia in the first millennium.

seven times, which in itself shows how volatile the situation there was. When Sennacherib came to the throne of Assyria, he did what his three most recent predecessors had done: he also became king of Babylonia, which remained a separate kingdom. After two years he lost that kingship to a native Babylonian, Marduk-zakir-shumi II, who a few weeks later was himself overthrown by the fiercely anti-Assyrian Chaldean Marduk-apla-iddina II (who in the Bible appears as Merodach-baladan). In reaction Sennacherib devoted his first formal campaign to the reconquest of the south in 703. He drove Marduk-apla-iddina into the marshes and this time placed a native Babylonian on the throne, probably in an effort to appease the local urban population. Sennacherib described the man, Bel-ibni, as having grown up in his palace "like a young puppy." He was thus a Babylonian groomed in Assyria and his loyalty was expected to be absolute. Babylonia was reduced to a puppet kingdom. But soon, Assyrian governors had to assist Bel-ibni to counter the Chaldean threat, and in 700 Sennacherib had to mount another campaign to deal once and for all with Marduk-apla-iddina, during which he replaced Bel-ibni with his own eldest son, Assur-nadin-shumi. Six years later, the Babylonians took advantage of an Elamite raid in the region to capture Sennacherib's son and hand him over to the Elamite king. He was taken off and disappeared for good. A new native Babylonian became king but Sennacherib quickly removed him, although he failed to take Babylon. Then a Chaldean leader, Mushezib-Marduk, seized the throne and formed another large anti-Assyria coalition, including Chaldeans, Arameans, Babylonians, and Elamites whose support he bought using the temple treasury. In 691, the coalition engaged Sennacherib in a major battle, which was probably indecisive, near Halule on Assyria's border. The next year Sennacherib started a fifteen month long siege of Babylon, and when he was finally successful on the first day of the month Kislimu (November–December) in 689, he took revenge for the problems it had caused him. His accounts describe in detail how he razed the temples and houses, looted the treasuries, and deported the population. He concludes: "So that in future days the site of that city and its temples would not be recognized, I totally dissolved it with water and made it like inundated land."[1] Having exhausted all other possibilities, Sennacherib left Babylonia in disarray. For the next eight years very little activity took place, and the handful of records preserved either name Sennacherib or his deceased son, Assur-nadin-shumi, as king.

Babylonia was too important to be left disarray for long, so Sennacherib's successor, Esarhaddon, immediately began its reconstruction. He rebuilt Babylon and made a concerted effort to portray himself in the official record as the king who unified the two states. The idea that Babylonia and Assyria were united does not seem to have been comfortable, however, and before he died Esarhaddon appointed two of his sons as future kings of the separate kingdoms. The younger, Assurbanipal, received Assyria, the older, Shamash-shuma-ukin, Babylonia. The dominance of the first was clear, and he treated his brother as a vassal, albeit a favored one. In protest Shamash-shuma-ukin rebelled in 652 and, joining forces with Chaldeans, Arameans, and Elamites, he essentially started a civil war that drained the resources of both states. The resistance to Assyria at first was successful and Assurbanipal had to campaign for four years before Babylon fell. Babylonia's next king was Kandalanu. As he died at the same time as Assurbanipal in 627, it is sometimes thought that Kandalanu was a Babylonian throne-name of the Assyrian king. But no solid evidence for this connection exists and it is probably best to see the Babylonian and Assyrian kings at this time as two men, the former being a puppet ruler under Assyria's control. Despite the proximity of Babylonia to Assyria and all the effort expended to dominate it, the region was never fully integrated into the empire. Assyria gave it special treatment because of the respect it deserved, but equally important was Babylonia's resilience and its ability to keep up its opposition.

The respect shown Babylonia did not exist in the cases of Urartu and Elam. They were detested enemies who continued to make Assyria's life difficult. Both were the targets of many extensive campaigns, described in chapter 11, which ended up reducing their strength, although Assyria did not annihilate them. Sargon II's raid on Musasir in 714 seems to have finished off the threat from Urartu, while Assurbanipal, exasperated by Elam's support for his brother's rebellion, sacked Susa in 647. The two weakened states survived, however, and only later lost their independence to the Persian empire.

The final important rival to Assyria was Egypt, which from the ninth century on had supported Syro-Palestinian rebels. Its distance and the weakness of Assyrian control over the regions in between had made an invasion impossible in the early phase of the empire. But Egypt's great wealth made it a very tempting target. Nubians from Sudan had conquered the country in the mid-eighth century and they controlled the gold mines that supplied the entire Near East. Their rule over Egypt was probably indirect and local Egyptians were mostly in charge of the administration. The idea of conquering Egypt must have attracted Esarhaddon and his court, and when the Assyrian king had sufficiently consolidated his hold over southern Palestine through a system of loyal vassals, he invaded. Already advanced in years, he organized three campaigns, defeated the Nubian King Taharqo, and conquered the northern capital of Memphis. The Assyrian captured an enormous quantity of spoils, which he used partly to fund Babylon's reconstruction. But he could not impose direct governance on Egypt, so Esarhaddon turned Nubia's Egyptian vassals in the Nile Delta area into his own.

Assyria's hold over Egypt was weak, however, and by the time Esarhaddon died, the Nubian Taharqo had reasserted his power over the entire country. Assurbanipal sent out an expedition that first had to confront the Delta vassals, who had changed sides back to Nubia. The Assyrian army defeated them with the assistance of an army recruited from the Syro-Palestinian vassals, such as Judah, Edom, and Moab, and with ships it obtained in Phoenicia and Cyprus in order to sail down the Nile. He punished the vassals but again, because he was unable to establish direct rule, he reinstated one of them, Nekau, who became his special representative (document 13.1). When Assyria's army departed, a new Nubian king, Tantamani, returned to Egypt, which triggered Assurbanipal's final attack in 664 and 663. This time he reached the capital of Thebes in central Egypt and collected huge spoils. He brought Nubian influence in the country finally to an

Document 13.1   *Assurbanipal and Egypt*

Excerpt from Assurbanipal's account written after 664

Egypt was the most distant target of Assyrian campaigns and it was only in reach at the end of the empire, at a time when the kingdom of Nubia to its south had control over the country. Assurbanipal reports here how the Nubian King Taharqo returned to Memphis after his father Esarhaddon had raided the country and how the Assyrian vassals had switched sides to Nubia. In 667 and 666, Assurbanipal sent troops – he did not lead them himself – to retake Memphis and then Thebes, the country's old and very wealthy religious capital. On the way the Assyrians captured the Egyptian vassals (Nikkû and Sharru-lu-dari), and sent them to Nineveh for punishment. But Assurbanipal had no choice but to return one of them, Nikkû, back to Egypt to govern in Assyria's name. Not much later Nikkû's son, Psamtek, would declare himself king of an independent Egypt.

Tarqû,[1] the godless, came out in order to take Egypt and [   ]. He forgot about the power of Assur, my lord, and trusted his own strength. The harsh things, which my father had done to him, did not occur to him, so he came and entered Memphis, and turned the citizens to his side. He sent an army to kill, destroy, and plunder against the people of Assyria who were in Egypt, my servants, whom Esarhaddon king of Assyria, my father, had entrusted with kingship there.

A fast messenger came to me in Nineveh and informed me of this. I became infuriated at these deeds and was enraged. I called the commander-in-chief and the governors with the men under them, my mighty force, and ordered them to hurry and go help the kings and governors, my servants. I ordered them to go to Egypt. They marched fast and came to the city of Kar-Banite. Tarqû, the king of Kush,[2] who heard of the coming of my army in Memphis, raised his army to do battle in the open field. Under the protection of Assur, Sin, and the great gods, my lords who go at my side, they defeated them in open battle. They cut down with the sword the troops in which he had trusted.

Fear and terror fell upon him, and he went insane. He left Memphis, his royal city, which he had trusted, and boarded a ship in order to save his life. He left his camp, fled alone, and entered the city Ni'.[3] All the warships that were with him and his battle troops they seized. A messenger described to me the happy events that he had witnessed. To my mighty troops (there) I added strength by sending the chief-cupbearers, the governors and the kings of the areas across the River, all of them my servants, and the kings of Egypt, my servants, together with their forces and ships, in order to chase Tarqû from Egypt and Kush. To Ni', the fortress of Tarqû, king of Kush, they went in a march of one month and ten days. When Tarqû heard of the approach of my army, he left Ni', his fortress, crossed the Nile, and set his camp up at the other side.

Nikkû,[4] Sharru-lu-dari and Paqruru, the kings whom my father had established in Egypt, violated the oath of Assur and the great gods, my lords, and broke their word. They forgot the good my father had done to them and planned evil in their hearts. They spoke false words, and they counseled each other in a counterproductive way. "If they chase Tarqû out of Egypt, where shall we stay?" They sent their emissaries to swear an oath of peace, saying: "We want to establish peace and be in agreement amongst ourselves. We want to divide the land amongst ourselves. Let there be no lord among us."

They repeatedly planned evil against the mass of the troops of Assyria, the strength of my rule. They plotted to take their lives, and endeavored to do unheard evils. My officials heard of these things and played a trick on them. They captured their messengers with their messages, and saw their treacherous doings. They captured Sharru-lu-dari and Nikkû, and shackled their hands and feet. The curse of Assur, king of the gods, came upon them, they who had sinned against their mighty oath. Those to whom I had done good deeds, I called to task. The people of the cities, all who had joined them and had plotted evil, great and small, they cut down with their weapons, and not a single person inside these cities was saved.

To him, whom they brought to me in [Nineveh], my royal city, I Assurbanipal, king of Assyria, the broad-minded, the well-doer who seeks goodness, to Nikkû, my servant, to whom had been entrusted the city Kar-Bel-Matati, I showed mercy, although he had sinned. I laid upon him a loyalty oath that was stricter than what existed before. I encouraged him, put bright garments on him, and gave him a golden hoe, the symbol of his kingship. I put golden rings on his fingers, and gave him an iron dagger with a sheath inlaid with gold on which I had written my name. Chariots, horses and mules I granted to him for his royal journeys. I sent to him my officials and governors to help him. I sent him back to Sais, which is now called Kar-Bel-Matati, where my father had made him king. I showed him kindness even greater than my father had done.

Translation after Onasch 1994: 104–15.

[1] Taharqo, king of Nubia, ruled Egypt 690–664.
[2] Nubia.
[3] Thebes.
[4] Nekau, ruler of Sais.

end, but his own system of vassals lasted a short time only. By 656 a son of Nekau, Psamtek, who had been educated in Assyria and installed on a local throne, proclaimed himself sole king of the whole of Egypt with full independence. Egypt in this era was thus at the mercy of two foreign powers that both had to rely on local vassals to govern: Assyria and Nubia. In the end these Egyptians gained enough strength to assert independence. In the last years of the Assyrian empire, Egypt started to help it against the threat from the east, and together they tried to prevent the Babylonian conquest of Syria. This was to no avail, however, and the conquest of Egypt became a goal of the Babylonian empire, albeit unfulfilled.

The resilience of the states surrounding Assyria shows that the empire was not invincible and that opposition to it could be successful. Beyond this world of well-established and ancient states, there were other people, often nomadic, who caused Assyria serious trouble. These included the Scythians and Cimmerians in Anatolia, who had to be kept at bay through military and diplomatic means. In the Arabian Desert east of Syria-Palestine, the Assyrians clashed repeatedly with Arabs, who could easily escape in the desert and were never fully controlled. There were also a number of states outside the reach of Assyria but in contact with it. In the Persian Gulf, a king of Dilmun ruled, but we do not know much about his state. In central Anatolia was the kingdom of Lydia, attested in Greek sources, which is known to have sent envoys to Assyria but also to have aided anti-Assyrian rebellions. The Assyrians portrayed such countries as being subservient to them, but the reality of that claim is doubtful.

13.3   The Administration and Ideology of the Empire

The vast empire the Assyrians had created required a large and well-oiled administration. With the expansion of the provincial system, the earlier distinction between the "land of Assur" and the "yoke of Assur" disappeared, and throughout the Near East Assyria exercised direct control. Beyond the provinces were located vassal and puppet states, which were administered indirectly through diplomacy and the threat of military action.

The structure of Assyria's administration is poorly known, although a large array of titles appear in the sources. One of its basic characteristics was that there was no separation of duties among officials: their positions were simultaneously administrative, military, and religious. Men with titles that we translate in a military sense were also governors of provinces, for instance. Assyrian society in general can be regarded as a pyramid-like structure with the king at its apex and the mass of the population at the bottom. A multitude of officials functioned in between them and regulated the interactions between the two. There is still a great deal of uncertainty about the hierarchy of offices. As in all other courts in history, men held titles that said little about their duties. Thus the cupbearer (*rab shaqe*), for instance, was a highly placed official who led diplomatic missions. A trio of officers assisted the king: the *turtanu*, *ummanu*, and *rab sha muhhi ekalli*. Our translations of commander-in-chief, chancellor, and majordomo respectively probably limit the range of their duties too much. Scholars often compare the Assyrian court to later Middle Eastern ones, especially the Ottoman court, but we have to be careful not to let such a comparison determine the details of how we see Assyria's administrative structure.

Personal loyalty was crucial in the interactions between king and officials. Duties were not formulated in legal terms, but officials were expected to serve the king faithfully and he trusted them in return. He requested tax payments and the like by letter as if this were a private arrangement and granted tax exemptions as if they were personal favors. Such a system led to the need for an army of scribes to maintain contacts. The large quantity of letters found at Nineveh and Kalhu, some 2,300 in number, certainly constitutes only a small part of what was originally written. As a reward for loyalty the subject remained in office, a position that was granted and withdrawn at the king's pleasure, not on the basis of hereditary rights. In any case, many officials seem to have been eunuchs, so offices reverted to the crown upon death or retirement. Officials also received estates that could be very extensive as recompense for their services, but these remained the king's property.

The idea that loyalty was owed to the king extended to all people of Assyria and to the subject rulers. At times the entire population was made to swear an oath before the gods that they accepted a royal decision – or at least the kings claimed that all had sworn the oath. This happened, for example, when Esarhaddon appointed his younger son Assurbanipal as his successor. According to a later inscription of Assurbanipal, "Esarhaddon convened the people of Assyria, great and small, from coast to coast, made them swear a loyalty oath by the gods and established a binding agreement to protect my crown-princeship and future kingship over Assyria."[2] If anyone opposed the new king, they would break their oath and set off divine retribution. Loyalty oaths were also at the basis of the interactions between the Assyrian king and his vassals. The latter had specific responsibilities to the person of the king, such as providing troops in case of war, and shirking them would mean the breach of an agreement that the gods supervised.

The empire's central administration was paralleled in the provincial system of government. One governor (Akkadian *shaknu*) headed each province and his residence was the equivalent of the royal palace in Assyria itself. The governors were high officials in the empire's administration, army commanders, cupbearers, and so on, and it is unclear how they divided their time between central and provincial duties. The provinces had to generate resources for the empire and provide laborers and soldiers. Sometimes the production of certain goods, such as olive oil in the Philistine area, was restructured in order to increase supply. Most often, however, it seems that the Assyrians relied on the structures in place and did not interfere much. The provincial administration was the only one with which the people came into contact. Similarly, an official, the mayor (Akkadian *hazannu*), headed cities in the heartland, such as Assur and Kalhu, and it was his duty to represent those people not directly dependent on the palace. Some larger cities had more than one mayor, probably to prevent their power from becoming too great, as we know that at times cities rebelled against the empire.

The complete focus on the person of the king in these interactions was a result of the ideological basis of rule. The king, as agent of the god Assur, represented order. Wherever he was in control, there was peace, tranquility, and justice, and where he did not rule there was chaos. The king's duty to bring order to the entire world was part of the justification for military expansion. All that was foreign was hostile, and all foreigners were like non-human creatures. Images of swamp-rats or bats, lonely, confused, and cowardly, were commonly applied to those outside the king's control. This message was communicated through a variety of means. Royal inscriptions are the most eloquent to us today, but in Assyrian times they were incomprehensible to the mostly illiterate population. Events such as victory parades informed the people of these ideas, and there is evidence that certain campaign accounts were read aloud in the cities. Moreover, the new cities themselves, with their planned layout and great walls and gates, instilled the idea of safety and order in their residents and visitors. When Sargon II described the building of his capital Dur-Sharrukin, he used language that resembled the description of the god Marduk's organization of the universe in the *Epic of Creation*. The royal palaces, inaccessible to most people but visited by foreign dignitaries, were decorated with wall-reliefs that portrayed the king as master of the world. Stelae and rock-reliefs representing the king stood on the empire's periphery to indicate the same idea. There was no doubt in the Assyrians' minds that military campaigning was justified and for the good of all.

The gods of Assyria benefited from the empire in that their cults were well provided for with tribute and booty. As main priest of the god Assur the king supported that cult, and other temples were probably also entirely dependent on the state for their maintenance. Provincial taxes were often collected as temple offerings. There is no evidence, however, that the Assyrians imposed their gods upon conquered populations, certainly not at the expense of existing religions. They sacked foreign temples for their treasuries and stole the divine statues as an act of domination. There was no religious intolerance and vassal treaties, for instance, were sworn in the names of the vassal's gods as well as those of Assyria.

13.4 Assyrian Culture

Many studies of Assyria focus on the military aspects of its history as a logical result of the dominance of that topic in the official accounts. But Assyrian remains also show a strong interest in literature and scholarship under the auspices of the palace. Most revealing in this respect is the library that Assurbanipal collected in his capital, Nineveh: some 5,000 literary and scholarly texts were found there with the letters and administrative documents that detail the daily affairs of state. Many of the texts appear in up to six manuscripts, and in total the library contained some 1,000 to 1,200 compositions. It is estimated that these represent an accurate reflection of all Mesopotamian learning and literature up to that time. Successive kings consciously brought the library together, but Assurbanipal was most active in this enterprise. A catalogue of texts that were acquired in the year 648 listed some 2,000 tablets and 300 writing boards, that is, wooden or ivory boards covered with wax and inscribed with a cuneiform text, which were confiscated mostly from private libraries of Babylonian priests and exorcists.[3] A letter written by an unnamed king to his representative in the Babylonian city Borsippa (perhaps a later literary fiction rather than an actual letter) states that he should take tablets from specialists' homes and temples:

> Nobody should withhold tablets from you, and if you come across any tablet or ritual, which I myself have not mentioned to you and that is good for my palace, take it too and send it to me.[4]

The manuscripts were not merely collected but were copied out according to a standard library format (see figure 13.3). The cuneiform script and tablet layout were uniform, and a statement at the end of each tablet identified it as part of Assurbanipal's library. These subscripts or colophons could be stamps with the brief text "belonging to the palace of Assurbanipal, king of the universe, king of Assyria," but often indicated at length that the scribe had copied the preceding text carefully from an older tablet, and that he had reviewed and checked the copy. Indeed, the scribes were careful in their work. They indicated when they found a break in the original tablet and, when they restored a lacuna, they

Figure 13.3   A manuscript from Assurbanipal's library. This tablet contains the poem of the *Descent of Ishtar into the Netherworld* and can serve as a typical example of the manuscripts preserved in Assurbanipal's library. The scribe copied out the text in neat handwriting and, after completing it, drew a horizontal line beneath which he wrote: "belonging to the palace of Assurbanipal, king of the universe, king of Assyria." British Museum, London, K.162. Clay; L. 16.82 cm; W. 8.57 cm; Th. 2.85 cm (6.6 × 3.4 × 1.1 in). Credit: © The Trustees of the British Museum.

corrected mistakes and, very rarely, indicated the variants they found in different older manuscripts.

The texts were kept in order to provide authorized versions that diviners and exorcists could use. Many of the manuscripts contained omens, and it was imperative that a correct version was on record. The library also held literary and scholarly texts, as the specialists whose duty it was to protect the king and the state sometimes needed to quote them in their reports, and the accuracy of these quotes was important. Assurbanipal took personal pride in his library; he made statements such as: "the wisdom of Ea, the art of the learned priests, the knowledge of the sages, and that which provides solace to the great gods, I (Assurbanipal) wrote on tablets according to texts from Assyria and Babylonia, and I reviewed and checked."[5] The king clearly wanted to distinguish himself by claiming knowledge of writing and of secret lore, and presented the library as something he compiled for his own interests (see debate 13.1).

The compositions preserved in Nineveh were of a very varied nature. About 300 tablets contain omens, 200 lexical lists, one hundred bilingual Sumerian–Akkadian texts of varied characters, sixty medical texts, and only some thirty-five to forty contain the epics and other purely literary compositions. The predominance of omens shows the importance these texts had in Assyria and in Mesopotamia in general. They were meant to predict the future based on the observation of everything in the surrounding world. Like earlier laws, the entries were all phrased according to the pattern, "if . . . , then . . ." The second part of the statement, the apodosis, indicated what the observation foretold. The first part, the protasis, could be anything in the world that was readily observable or realized through special procedures. Any occurrence in the natural world was ominous, such as the flight of birds or the physical aspects of animals. Unusual events were, of course, even more important. There were omens that interpreted malformed births, such as lambs with more than one head. In addition to observations of spontaneous events, specialist diviners would cut open sheep to examine their livers, and all discolorations and anomalies were considered significant. For example, "If the left lobe (of the liver) is covered by a membrane and it is abnormal – The king will die from illness."[6] They would interpret the patterns rising smoke made, the configurations of oil poured on water, and so on. The scribes created massive lists of omens by elaborating on a theme, exploring it in every possible way. For example, they spun out the appearance of a cat into a list of good and bad omens depending on its color:

If a white cat is seen in a man's house – hardship will seize the land.
If a black cat is seen in a man's house – that land will experience good fortune.
If a red cat is seen in a man's house – that land will be rich.
If a multicolored cat is seen in a man's house – that land will not prosper.
If a yellow cat is seen in a man's house – that land will have a year of good fortune.[7]

In the first millennium, astronomical omens became increasingly widespread and the series describing and interpreting planetary alignments, eclipses, the appearance of stars, and many other celestial events became extremely lengthy. One popular series, *Enuma Anu Enlil*, was copied out on seventy tablets and contained omens dealing with the moon, the sun, the weather, and the planets. For example: "If the moon makes an eclipse in Month VII on the twenty-first day and sets eclipsed – they will take the crowned prince from his palace in fetters."[8]

The observations were not simply made to determine whether the omens were propitious or not, but so that actions could be taken to change the gods' minds. Specialist priests would recite prayers to urge them to alter the future and courtiers took measures to guarantee that the king would not be hurt. A practice repeatedly attested in the Neo-Assyrian period was the appointment of a substitute king. When omens predicted that the king's life was in danger, a man was selected to replace him temporarily and the true king went into hiding, to reappear only once the danger had passed (and the substitute king probably was murdered). The idea was not that the future was unalterable, but that steps could be taken to avoid the evil it held or to change it into something positive. Omens were important for every level of society, and many people paid diviners to ascertain the future and exorcists to implore the gods to remove evil.

The lexical texts in Assurbanipal's library similarly had practical uses. They contained within them a full record of the Sumerian lexicon with Akkadian translations, and included lists of signs and sign combinations, and of words for animals, stones, woods, implements, city-names, and so on. Knowledge of the Sumerian terms was important to the scholars who needed to read cultic texts in Sumerian and had to understand difficult cuneiform signs for their interpretative work.

The third largest group of tablets in the library consisted of incantations and prayers in Sumerian, which had died out as a spoken language many centuries earlier. The texts received a line-by-line translation into Akkadian. Similarly, some Sumerian epics and myths were preserved with Akkadian translations, not necessarily the ones that had been the most popular in the early second millennium when most of Sumerian literature was recorded. Incantations, that is, lists of spells to ward off evil, and manuals for exorcists were also an important part of monolingual Akkadian texts.

Medical texts were very similar in format to the omen texts and were based on the same concept that any observation could determine the outcome of a disease. Even things that happened when the physician walked to the patient's house were indicative. For example, "If the *ashipu* (Akkadian term for diagnostician) sees a black dog or a black pig, the ill man will die. If he sees a white pig, the ill man will get well, or he will be seized by distress."[9] The diagnosis was also based on whether parts of the body were hot or cold, the color of the skin and urine, and other elements that we would consider medically relevant. But other signs that seem trivial to us – for example, whether the patient's chest hair curled upwards or downwards – were also important.

Finally, Akkadian literary texts made up the smallest group of compositions in Assurbanipal's library. Today the most famous composition from the library is the *Epic of Gilgamesh* (box 13.1), but this is only one of a group of narrative poems that revolved around the gods and heroes of Babylonia. Gods were the sole characters in myths such as the *Descent of Ishtar into the Netherworld*, a summary of a lengthy Sumerian text known from the early second millennium, where the goddess tries to extend her powers over the netherworld but is trapped there until a substitute can be found. Mortals played important roles in stories like that of *Adapa*, a primordial sage who visited the gods in heaven and failed to obtain immortality. A flood story was preserved in the story of *Atrahasis*, the man whom the god Ea saved so that humans could continue to provide offerings to the gods. These were compositions whose origins went back to the early second millennium, some with Sumerian antecedents. More recent were Akkadian compositions such as the *Creation myth*, describing the organization of the universe by the god Marduk, who in some Assyrian versions was replaced by the god Assur. Of first-millennium date was the *Erra Epic*, describing the violent destruction of Babylonia (see document 10.2).

Box 13.1   *The Epic of Gilgamesh*

The most famous literary composition from ancient Mesopotamia today is the *Epic of Gilgamesh*, a tale of the hero's search for immortality after the death of his friend Enkidu. The quest takes him to the edge of the world, where he meets the only survivor of the flood, Utnapishtim, who tells Gilgamesh that he will never obtain physical immortality. But the version found at Nineveh indicates that a king can be remembered for eternity through his deeds, including building. The epic begins and ends with praise of the walls of Uruk, through which Gilgamesh will be known forever:

> Go up, pace out the walls of Uruk,
> Study the foundation terrace and examine the brickwork.
> Is not its masonry of kiln-fired brick?
> And did not seven masters lay its foundation?[1]

At the library of Assurbanipal several copies of a version written on twelve tablets were found, and its author was said to be Sin-leqe-unninni. This name places him in the Kassite period and many Babylonian scribes of the first millennium regarded Sin-leqe-unninni as their ancestor. The Gilgamesh story underwent a long development before the version found at Nineveh. At its basis lay a number of Sumerian tales from the early second millennium, and in the Old Babylonian period the first Akkadian version is attested. It was one of the Babylonian literary works known in Syria-Palestine and Anatolia in the late second millennium. The version from Nineveh incorporated previously independent literary works such as the Flood story, also known from the Old Babylonian period on. After the sack of Nineveh, the epic remained popular in Babylonia, although the known manuscripts are all fragmentary. The figure of Gilgamesh survived in first-millennium AD classical Aramaic, and possibly Arabic sources, but he seems to have been confused with other heroic figures then.

[1] Translation from Foster 2001: 3.

The scholars in Assurbanipal's library also collected commentaries on literary and scholarly texts (document 13.2). They clarified antiquated and technical terms, listed attributes of the gods, or elaborated on their acts in mythological texts. The function of the library was practical. The scholarship undertaken was focused on understanding the signs of the gods that could be seen everywhere in the surrounding world and which had to be properly read. In order to further their knowledge, scholars all over the empire reported what they observed and interpreted events based on their understanding of the omens. The palace archives contain numerous letters written to the king in order to help him with problems such as illness, making a decision to go to war, and royal succession. The final goal of all this work was to protect the king and the state, and to ensure that he was not unaware of any impending danger.

> ## Document 13.2   *Scholarly commentaries*
>
> *By the seventh century, when the Library of Assurbanipal had its greatest growth, the literature of Mesopotamia was already very old and many literary and scholarly texts had a history of more than a thousand years. As happens with any language, the grammar and vocabulary of Akkadian had evolved, and certain words and expressions were no longer clear. In the Nineveh library, and elsewhere in Assyria and later Babylonia, appeared scholarly texts that provided help to clarify such difficulties. They mostly explained omen texts, whose understanding was especially important to scholars in the king's employ. Also for some literary texts, difficult words were explained with synonyms. The scholar wrote out a line with a difficult term and then gave an explanation of it. This example from Assurbanipal's library lists unconnected verses of a composition we call "The poem of the righteous sufferer," possibly created in the thirteenth century, and elucidates some words. The example here discusses lines 11, 21, 24, and 43 of the second tablet of the composition. I provide the difficult Akkadian words and their ancient explanations in parentheses.*
>
> I look behind: persecution, harassment (Akkadian *ip-pe-e-ri*)
> harassment (Akkadian *ip-pi-ri*) = weariness (Akkadian *ma-na-aḫ-tum*) = illness (Akkadian *mursu*)
> Like one possessed(?) (Akkadian *im-ḫu-ú*), who forgot his lord: possessed(?) (Akkadian *im-ḫu-ú*) = cumbersome (Akkadian *ka-ba-tum*)
> Prayer to me was the natural recourse, sacrifice my rule (Akkadian *sak-ku-ú-a*): rule (Akkadian *sak-ku-u*) = cultic rite (Akkadian *par-ṣi*)
> What (the gods) intend for people changes in a twinkling (Akkadian *ki-i pi-te-e ù ka-ta-me*) = day and night (Akkadian *u₄-mu ù mu-ši*)
>
> Translation based on Lambert 1960: pl. 15 and Foster 2005: 398–9.

While Assurbanipal's palace library was by far the most extensive in Assyria, it was not unique. In Nineveh itself there was another library in the Nabu-temple, and temples in other cities contained collections of literary and scholarly tablets. In addition, private houses could hold libraries. At Sultantepe in southern Turkey, one was found in the house of a priest called Qurdi-Nergal and his son Mushallim-Baba, which contained incantations, medical texts, prayers, epics, and wisdom literature. These libraries suggest the importance of literate culture in Assyria. There was a clear awareness that it derived from Babylonia, which probably led to that country's unique position in the Assyrian empire. In sharp contrast, the Assyrians made no attempt to incorporate the literature of any other region they occupied into their own culture.

13.5   Assyria's Fall

By 640, Assyria was at the height of its powers and controlled a vast landmass from western Iran to Egypt, having eliminated all potentially significant forces of opposition. Thirty years later the Assyrian empire no longer existed. What happened is unclear: we have to piece together events primarily from terse Babylonian sources, while the limited attestations of royal names in documents inform us which one of the pretenders to the throne had control over a specific city. Why the empire so easily collapsed is open to several interpretations; most likely we have to search for the reasons within its structure itself.

Assurbanipal was one of the longest reigning kings of Assyria, but we are uncertain about how and when exactly his rule ended and what happened afterwards. Different scenarios are possible. Assurbanipal's last dated royal inscription is from 639, and the last mention of the king in an administrative document is from 631. Some scholars think that he retired then and handed the throne to his son, but most now believe that he died in 631 or 630. The reach of the empire had already weakened at that time and some peripheral areas had become independent. There was no longer an Assyrian presence in the southern Levant, for example, and the Egyptians had filled the power vacuum there. Assurbanipal had designated his infant son Assur-etel-ilani as successor, but various other men challenged the decision. These included a eunuch and high official, Sin-shumu-lishir, who seems to have been the most powerful man at court, and Sin-shar-ishkun, another of Assurbanipal's sons. All three held kingship over Assyria at some point and ultimately Sin-shar-ishkun gained full control and ruled for another fifteen years or so. Succession problems were not unusual in the Neo-Assyrian empire; earlier in the century one of Sennacherib's sons had murdered him and the rightful heir Esarhaddon had to fight for months to gain the throne. But this time Assyria's cohesion was weaker and the wars lasted longer. During the troubles in Assyria, Assurbanipal's appointed ruler in Babylonia, Kandalanu, died in 627 and the conflict spread into that region. All the contenders to the throne in Assyria appear in Babylonian sources as king there. Moreover, in 626 a former Assyrian official from Uruk, Nabopolassar, proclaimed himself the founder of a new native, Chaldean, dynasty. Various Babylonian cities did not side with him, but pledged allegiance to the different Assyrian claimants to the throne, and the Chaldean had to conquer several of them, causing great hardship among the inhabitants. But by 616 Nabopolassar had consolidated his powers over Babylonia to such an extent that he was able to invade Assyria.

Simultaneously, in western Iran a mountain people called the Medes had strengthened its army, probably taking advantage of the power vacuum caused by Assurbanipal's defeat of Elam. In 615, they began to attack cities in Assyria's heartland and concluded an alliance with Nabopolassar, possibly selling their services as mercenaries to him. In 612, the combined forces, aided by other groups like the Scythians, attacked the capital Nineveh and sacked it. The Assyrian ruler at the time, Sin-shar-ishkun, died in battle, and his successor, Assur-uballit II, took a last stand in the north-Syrian city of Harran. The Assyrians put up strong resistance, relying on support from Egypt. For two more years they governed parts of western Syria and even after Harran fell in 610 they continued to do battle. Local rulers tried to influence the situation. In 609, for example, King Josiah of Judah lost his life at Megiddo in an attempt to stop an Egyptian army sent out in support of Assyria. In the same year Assur-uballit II died, but local defiance of the Babylonians continued until 605. It was only then that Babylonia essentially became Assyria's successor, taking control of most of its territories.

The conquerors set out to destroy the cities of Assyria, taking revenge for the humiliations they had suffered at Assyria's hands. On wall-reliefs of kings Sennacherib and Assurbanipal in Nineveh, for example, they identified the representations of the kings with the help of the inscriptions accompanying them, and ritually destroyed them by cutting out the eyes and ears. These were not random acts of mutilation. In the detailed depiction of Assurbanipal's defeat of the Elamites, for example, they only defaced the king and a soldier who was shown cutting off the head of the king of Elam (see figure 11.1). This was probably the work of Medes, who saw the Elamites as their ancestors. The attackers burned down the palaces only after the task of defacing images and destroying symbols of submission to Assyria had been completed, and the Babylonian king returned home with some of the ashes of Nineveh to avenge Sennacherib's destruction of Babylon. Assyria's heartland lost its urban characteristics and the remaining population resided in small settlements on top of the massive mounds.

The causes of Assyria's swift collapse were probably rooted in problems inherent in the empire's organization. The concentration of power in the hands of one man was effective when there was an able king, but the task of government could easily exceed an individual's capabilities. While we do not know how old Assurbanipal was when he ascended the throne, he must have been advanced in age late in his long reign. Moreover, the struggle between Assurbanipal and his brother Shamash-shuma-ukin that led to the devastating war in Babylonia must have been extremely disruptive to both states. The functioning of the empire was always disturbed when internal problems occurred.

Indeed, Assyria's rapacious attitude toward the territories it conquered, with deportations and heavy demands for tribute, made any opportunity to rebel appealing. Tributary states constantly revolted despite heavy-handed Assyrian responses, and in the last decades they may have been successful in withholding tribute. Cut off from the empire's supply base, the core could not maintain its massive cities and enormous army. Moreover, as many of the inhabitants of the heartland were deportees, their loyalty to the state was probably minimal and Assyrians by themselves could not continue to exercise the control needed to preserve their empire. In essence, that empire had always been built on a weak basis, and fissures could undermine the whole system. The combination of external pressure and internal conflict led to the sudden collapse of the entire structure.

As no Assyrian power was ever again to emerge, there are no native reflections on these events as there were, for example, after the Ur III state. Later traditions of people Assyria had conquered did examine the empire's fall, however, and attributed the destruction of Nineveh, for example, to divine retribution. Babylonians believed that Sennacherib's sack of Babylon was avenged in Nineveh. Biblical authors saw that city's devastation as a punishment for the attacks on Judah by successive Assyrian rulers. Assyria had been arrogant, and its victims reveled in its ruin. The fourth-century Greek historian Ktesias presented the downfall in the context of the perceived opposition between Greeks and easterners. Sardanapallos, the Greek name for Assurbanipal, was doomed to fall because of his effeminate life of luxury. That tradition inspired nineteenth-century European images of the ancient Near East, which judged Assyria as the paradigm of oriental decadence (figure 13.4). That was surely an inaccurate evaluation of this powerful empire, which had been highly successful for some three centuries.

Debate 13.1   *Was King Assurbanipal a scholar?*

Only a handful of the long list of Mesopotamian kings known to us claimed publicly that they knew how to read and write (Frahm 2011). One of them was the Ur III King Shulgi who described his education at the academy (see document 4.2), another the Assyrian Emperor Assurbanipal who more elaborately wrote about his time as crown prince:

> I learned the lore of the wise sage Adapa, the hidden secret, the whole of the scribal craft.
> I can discern celestial and terrestrial portents and deliberate in the assembly of the experts.
> I am able to discuss the series "If the liver is a mirror image of the sky" with capable scholars.
> I can solve convoluted reciprocals and calculations that do not come out evenly. I have read cunningly written text in Sumerian, dark Akkadian, the interpretation of which is difficult.
> I have examined stone inscriptions from before the flood, which are sealed, stopped up, mixed up. (Livingstone 2007: 100)

Was this true, however? In the same inscription Assurbanipal stated: "Ninurta and Nergal gave me physical fitness, manhood and unparalleled strength," while he also claimed that he already was a great war leader and fully knew how to behave as a king while his father was still in charge. He was perfectly fit to become a ruler from a young age, and advanced scholarship was part of his qualifications. Yet few rulers of premodern times are known to have been well educated and the apparent difficulty of cuneiform writing makes it conceivable that his claims were an idle boast.

Scholars used to think that literacy was a restricted expertise in ancient Mesopotamia (e.g., Beaulieu 2007: 473–4), but recently many have started to argue that this was not the case. Despite appearances cuneiform writing was not so difficult to learn – in many periods fewer than one hundred signs were in common use – and there are many indications that a large number of people wrote and read (Parpola 1997; Wilcke 2000; Charpin 2010: 53–67), including women (Lion 2011). There is indeed evidence that business people and the like wrote their own letters and contracts, but we have to keep in mind that there are different levels of literacy. Everywhere some people can only write simple texts, others have the ability to express subject-specific technical language, while a minority only has scholarly literacy (Veldhuis 2011). In his inscription Assurbanipal claimed to have the most advanced knowledge. He could read inscriptions from before the flood – also Gilgamesh was said to have mastered this (Pongratz-Leisten 1999: 312) – and he was able to interpret obscure Sumerian with difficult Akkadian translations. He also knew complicated mathematics. Even more impressive were his talents to "read" divinatory signs in heaven and on earth and to discuss liver omen texts. These were sciences that required many years of intensive training, which a crown prince did not necessarily have, but there are some indications that Assurbanipal did not lie. A letter from an astrologer to him suggests he could consult celestial omen lists (Parpola 1993: no. 101; cf. Villard 1997: 145), while some colophons on scholarly tablets in his library state that "I Assurbanipal" wrote them. Would a common scribe have dared to impersonate the king (Livingston 2007: 113–14)?

In the library some tablets with complicated texts stand out because they are inexpertly written and there is a letter from Assurbanipal to his father that is quite clumsy (Luukko & Van Buylaere 2002: no. 19), which suggests that they were the crown prince's own work (Livingstone 2007). He may thus not have been as experienced as he intimated, but Assurbanipal was able to read and write scholarly materials at an elementary level (Zamazalová 2011). It is then no surprise that he made the library at Nineveh his personal project, and we may conclude that he was an unusually learned king.

NOTES

1   After Luckenbill 1924: 834.
2   Parpola & Watanabe 1988: xxix.
3   Fales & Postgate 1992: no. 49.
4   After Frame & George 2005: 281.
5   After Hunger 1968: 102, no. 328.
6   After Koch-Westenholz 2000: 169.
7   After A. Guinan in Hallo 1997–2002, volume 1: 424.
8   Brown 2000: 135.
9   After Labat 1951, volume 1: 2–3.

14

The Medes and Babylonians

3000	2500	2000	1500	1000	500

670s	Esarhaddon of Assyria queries sun god about Median ruler Kashtaritu
626	Nabopolassar founds Neo-Babylonian dynasty
612	Medes and Babylonians sack Nineveh
605	Nebuchadnezzar II defeats Egyptians at Carchemish
587	Nebuchadnezzar II sacks Jerusalem
552	Nabonidus moves to Teima
539	Cyrus captures Babylon

The military defeat of Assyria was primarily the work of two peoples who were relative newcomers to the Near Eastern scene and represented two very different political organizations and livelihoods, the Medes and the Babylonians. The Medes were a pastoral mountain people from the central Zagros Mountains, where only in the eighth century did fortified cities appear in strategic locations. To our knowledge they had no native written tradition, and their history must be pieced together from references in external sources. The Babylonian dynasty rose to power in the late seventh century, and became heir to the urban traditions that had long existed in southern Mesopotamia. Its kings continued earlier political, cultural, and administrative practices and emphasized connections with their country's past. They left rich records of their accomplishments, but unlike the Assyrians they mostly ignored military achievements to focus on their work as

A History of the Ancient Near East ca. 3000–323 BC, Third Edition. Marc Van De Mieroop.
© 2016 John Wiley & Sons, Inc. Published 2016 by John Wiley & Sons, Inc.

Map 14.1   The Near East in the sixth century.

builders. The Babylonians ruled an empire as dominant in the Near East as the Assyrian empire had been, but they were not alone. They confronted a resurgent Egypt, various states in Anatolia, and the nascent Persia in southwest Iran. Moreover, marauding groups such as Scythians and Cimmerians entered the area from the north and often caused serious disturbances. All these various states and peoples determined the history of the sixth century until the Persians totally changed the political map of the region.

14.1   The Medes and the Anatolian States

Throughout their history the Assyrians had encountered various population groups in the Zagros Mountains to their east. We know of those people only from

Figure 14.1   Assyrian relief showing Medes. This relief from Sargon's palace at
Dur-Sharrukin depicts mountain people, probably Medes, bringing tribute to the Assyrian
king. Items of tribute often reflected the specialties of the subject region and in this case it is
made up of horses. Beside horses two of the men carry small models of cities, which were
given as symbols of subjection. Louvre, Paris. Gypseous alabaster, 165 × 370 cm. Credit: ©
RMN-Grand Palais/ Hervé Lewandowski.

Assyrian sources as there was no indigenous written tradition, and the information provided is confused. Often the Assyrians seem to have jumbled names and
they were unclear about what group resided exactly where. One of these peoples
was called the Medes, and because they would defeat the Assyrian empire they
gained special attention in the ancient historical tradition. They should be seen
as a typical example of a mountain people, however, who turned against their
wealthy lowland neighbors.

Rare references to the Medes appear in Assyrian records from the mid-ninth
century on and suggest that they inhabited the central Zagros region along the
Khorasan road, east of the sources of the Diyala River. This road provided the
main connection between lowland Mesopotamia and central Iran, and all overland traders in luxury goods such as metals and semi-precious stones had to
use it. The desire to control the route may explain why the Assyrians in the late
eighth century turned the region into three provinces, unlike other parts of the
Zagros where they kept vassals in place. They established a string of fortified cities
and collected taxes, mostly consisting of horses. Assyria's political control was
not complete, however. Many Medes remained independent, although in small
groups, and Sargon II mentions that he received tribute from some twenty-two of
their chiefs (figure 14.1).

The Assyrians and Medes interacted in the same way as other lowland and
mountain peoples throughout Near Eastern history. As settled farmers and city-
dwellers the Assyrians feared the Medes as unruly enemies, but they probably also
relied on them to gain access to resources. In the archives of King Esarhaddon

(ruled 680–669) at Nineveh appear about 150 queries directed to the sun god Shamash, asking advice on how to deal with perceived threats. He implored the god to answer through messages inscribed in the organs of slaughtered rams, a typical way in which omens were communicated. Among those queries, thirty-three deal with the Medes, especially their ruler Kashtaritu. They ask, for example:

> I ask you, Shamash, whether from this day, the 3rd day of this month, the month Iyyar (April–May), to the 11th day of the month Ab (July–August) of this year, either Kashtaritu and his troops, or the troops of the Cimmerians, or the troops of the Manneans, or the troops of the Medes, or of any other enemy, will capture that city, Kishassu, enter that city, Kishassu, conquer that city, Kishassu, and whether it will be delivered to them.[1]

Assurbanipal's defeat of the state of Elam in 646 most likely gave space to the Medes to expand their influence over the Zagros, and in 614 under the guidance of one Umakishtar they attacked Assyria and soon destroyed that empire with Babylonian help. Umakishtar may have been temporarily selected as the leader of the Medes, but there is no indication he was king of a unified state. With the end of the empire, the Assyrian fortifications were abandoned and the Medes and other Zagros people continued to raid neighboring areas. To counter them the Babylonians built a massive wall connecting the Tigris and Euphrates rivers just north of Babylon, which was later called the Median wall. The Persians, who lived in southern Iran, ended the situation of political fragmentation and instability. In 550, their king, Cyrus, took control over the entire Zagros and all territories of the Medes, using this as a base to create the Persian empire. The Medes had been important in the history of the ancient Near East, because of their role in Assyria's overthrow, but were not unusual among the people of the Zagros Mountains.

They did play a very prominent role, however, in later reflections on this period as they are preserved in classical sources, especially the Greek historian Herodotus (box 14.1). In the first book of his *Histories* he wrote a story of state formation, where disparate groups selected a king to judge and guide them and as a reward built him a capital. The new Median state grew into a great empire with the defeat of Assyria and the conquest of eastern Anatolia, where it faced the powerful Lydian state at the Kızıl Irmak River. Herodotus describes how a full solar eclipse, which we can date to May 28, 585, stopped their battle, and how they concluded a peace agreement negotiated under the auspices of the kings of Babylonia and of Cilicia. According to him, one of its vassals, the Persian Cyrus, finally overthrew Media and integrated it in his much larger empire. While elements of Herodotus' story agree with the bits of information we have on the Medes from Assyrian and Babylonian sources, the whole is a fictional account. No Median empire ever existed. Why was it concocted then? Herodotus imagined there had been a sequence of world empires in Asia before the Persian one that the Greeks confronted. He knew about Assyria and Persia, but in between them was a void. This he filled with the Medes, and thereby he created a phantom empire whose image is still widely accepted today.

Box 14.1   *Classical sources and the history of the ancient Near East*

With the development in Greece of a rich literary tradition, and especially that of narrative history, a whole new perspective on the Near East becomes available through the eyes of these outsiders. Most prominent is the fifth-century work of Herodotus, who sought to explain the origins of the Persian wars by studying the histories of the people involved, both Persians and Greeks. He wrote numerous stories about the Medes, Babylonians, and Egyptians as well as of other people with whom the Persians interacted, such as the Scythians and Ethiopians. Other Greek authors included Xenophon, a mercenary commander who fought on one side of the Persian civil war in 401, and Ktesias, a physician at the Persian court around the same time. Their focus was on Persian history. A third-century Babylonian priest, Berossus, wrote a history of Babylonia in Greek for his Greek ruler, but his text is only poorly preserved in later excerpts. Altogether the record remains small. The evidence is richest on the Persians, since their powerful empire and the threat it posed to Greece spurred the Greeks to write about them. References to earlier Near Eastern history are scanty. Herodotus paid attention to Babylonia mostly because he knew Babylon as a grand city of fabulous wealth and proportions, but he gave very little historical data. He failed to fulfill his promise to write a history of Assyria.

The stories provided in these works have great appeal to a modern audience as they are structured in the style of contemporary history writing and give a coherent narrative on such topics as the history of the Medes. The accounts can only be used with great caution, however, and have to be critically evaluated. A fundamental difficulty lies in the fact that the Persians were the archenemies of the Greeks, and thus the negative bias toward them was very strong. Often Greeks portrayed Persians and other people in the Near East as the incarnation of all that was evil. They became a mirror image displaying all the opposites of Greek virtues (sobriety–excess, masculinity–femininity, etc.). Thus in Ktesias' account, Sardanapallos, his name for Assurbanipal, was an effeminate ruler whose decadence explained the downfall of the Assyrian empire. Moreover, many of the Greek stories were based on hearsay and confused names and events. In the fifth century, Herodotus knew little about seventh-century Assyrians except that they had ruled the Near East and had been very wealthy. His history of the Medes reads like a smooth and detailed account, but seems to be mostly fictional and based on Persian tales about them. The classical authors are thus not a reliable source for Near Eastern history, which needs to be reconstructed from native evidence.

If we can believe Herodotus, the Medes raided central Anatolia and threatened regions farther west. The Assyrians had annexed only the southern part of the Anatolia and from there launched sporadic campaigns north and east. Assyria's main opponent there had been Phrygia, a central Anatolian state that was legendary in later Greek tradition for the enormous wealth of its king, Midas. Sargon II campaigned against a Mita of Mushku, who must be the same man. Together with the king of Urartu, Midas supported anti-Assyrian rebellions in northern

Syria and southern Anatolia, but finally he concluded a peace treaty with Sargon. His nemesis came from the north. In 695, nomadic Cimmerian warriors overran Phrygia and sacked the capital Gordion. Together with another northern nomadic group, the Scythians, they caused great disruption in many parts of the Near East. Urartu and Assyria repeatedly engaged in battle against them or tried to keep them at bay through diplomacy, while, according to Herodotus, the Scythians temporarily dominated the Medes. Both the Cimmerians and the Scythians participated in the final defeat of Assyria and remained in Anatolia, although they never formed a state. The homeland of the Scythians seems to have been the region north of the Black Sea, and it was there that the Persian king, Darius, would unsuccessfully campaign against them.

After the Cimmerians had severely reduced Phrygia in strength, its western neighbor, Lydia, became the main power in the west of Anatolia. Its King Gyges established contacts with the Assyrians (he appears in their sources under the name Guggu) and wanted to be included among the great kings of the time. Access to gold and silver mines made the state famous for its wealth. In the sixth century, Lydia under King Alyattes (ruled ca. 610–560) expanded in all directions, bringing it in direct contact with the Greek settlers on the west coast of Anatolia. The close interactions between the two peoples led to a dramatic expansion of the use of coinage, a Lydian invention originally minted in electrum (a naturally occurring alloy of gold and silver). Moreover, the Greeks became interested in Lydia, and Herodotus describes its history in detail, seeing the origin of the animosity between Greeks and easterners in the Greek cities' conflict with the Lydian state. Alyattes' successor Croesus (ruled 560–547) wanted to extend firm dominion from the Aegean Sea to the Kızıl Irmak River, and constantly put pressure on Greek cities in the west of Anatolia. His attack on Persia brought about his downfall. Crossing the Kızıl Irmak River with a vast army, he was held back by Cyrus of Persia, who chased him into his own territory and took the capital Sardis as well as the entire Lydian state.

Other states existed in Anatolia, such as Cilicia, Caria, and Lycia, whose histories can be similarly reconstructed from Near Eastern and classical sources. Their remains, textual and archaeological, demonstrate the survival of some of the second-millennium traditions in language and culture and the adoption of influences from the surrounding world, especially of the maritime Phoenicians and Greeks. There was a great diversity of cultures and intense interaction and cross-fertilization in western Anatolia. The fact that preclassical Greek culture was much influenced by the civilizations of the Near East should not, therefore, come as a surprise. The literature and arts of eighth- through sixth-century Greece were part of the cultural *koine* of the eastern Mediterranean world that was imbued by Near Eastern traditions.

14.2 The Neo-Babylonian Dynasty

Once Assyria's control over southern Mesopotamia had slipped following the death of Assurbanipal and the subsequent infighting over his succession, a

Chaldean called Nabopolassar took the throne of Babylon in 626. He founded a new dynasty (often called Neo-Babylonian in modern scholarship) that would reestablish Babylonia's political preeminence in the Near Eastern world for almost a century (for a king list, see Section 16 of the King Lists at the end of the book). In official writings he presented himself as "the son of nobody," but we know that his father and likely he himself had been high officials working for the Assyrians in the city of Uruk – probably he did not want to publicize that his family had collaborated with the enemy. By 616 Nabopolassar united all of Babylonia and, as we saw, his troops were of crucial importance in the overthrow of the Assyrian empire. Babylonia was the successor to that empire, taking over most of its territory, but it had to fight hard to accomplish this, especially in the west. Already in the last decade of Assurbanipal's reign, Assyria's grasp over the Syro-Palestinian area had disappeared and Egypt had filled the void there. Thus, even after Babylonia had eliminated the last Assyrian stronghold at Harran in 610, it faced Egypt for control over the region.

Nebuchadnezzar II led the Babylonian forces, first as crown prince, then as king. He would rule for forty-three years (605–562), and spent close to thirty of them conquering and pacifying Syria-Palestine. Unlike the Assyrians, the Babylonians did not advertise their military adventures in annals and wall reliefs, and we have to piece together information about them from terse chronicles, which only cover a small part of the period, and external sources. These do demonstrate, however, how difficult the challenge was. The chronicles cover the first twelve years of Nebuchadnezzar II's reign; in ten of them the Babylonian army campaigned in the west. In 605, just before his accession, Nebuchadnezzar inflicted a serious defeat on the Egyptians near the north Syrian city of Carchemish. In 601, the armies of the two countries faced each other in open battle close to the Egyptian border or even within that country. A Babylonian chronicle states that "both sides suffered severe losses" and that the next year Nebuchadnezzar had to stay home to refit his horses and chariotry.[2] The outcome was inconclusive.

Even if Egypt's influence was diminished, the western areas remained rebellious. Best known to us is what happened in Judah, whose final years as a kingdom the Hebrew Bible vividly portrays. Events there show how closely the Babylonians followed the patterns of behavior towards enemy states Assyria had established centuries before. Possibly misled by Babylonia's military losses in 601, Jerusalem refused to acknowledge its supremacy, so in 598–597 Nebuchadnezzar laid siege to the city and after ten months was able to capture it and its King Jehoiachin, who only three months earlier had succeeded his father Jehoiakim. Nebuchadnezzar deported him together with 3,000 leading citizens, and placed his uncle, Zedekiah, as puppet ruler on the throne. Around 590, however, anti-Babylonian sentiment ran high in Judah and other western states, and the newly installed king turned against his master, possibly asking Egypt for support. Nebuchadnezzar's army returned and needed an eighteen-month-long siege to take Jerusalem. The punishment in 587 was severe: the Babylonians sacked its temple and deported large parts of Judah's population, settling them in the Babylonian heartland. The Hebrew Bible laments the events as among the most traumatic the Judeans experienced in their history. Judah became a province under a governor, a local man called Gedaliah. When the latter was assassinated in 582, Nebuchadnezzar ordered a third deportation. While all this happened he had to engage other western enemies as well, some of whom put up enormous resistance. The Phoenician harbor city of Tyre withstood a siege that lasted thirteen years! It was only in 568 that Nebuchadnezzar's dominion over Syria-Palestine was secure and that the border with Egypt was firm.

Nebuchadnezzar stands out as the great military leader of the Neo-Babylonian dynasty, but that image is probably exaggerated by the nature of the documentation available. Although for later Neo-Babylonian kings only vague references to military successes exist, their accomplishments in that area were not minor. Neriglissar (ruled 559–556) annexed Cilicia, the leading state in southwest Anatolia, and Nabonidus (ruled 556–539) conquered several oases in the Arabian Desert. The Babylonians were thus able to expand beyond the borders of the territory they had inherited from the Assyrians.

In contrast to the Assyrian situation, we have virtually no idea how the Babylonians administered their empire. They appointed governors but these are mostly anonymous individuals. We do not know the extent of the provinces, the way in which taxes were collected, and so on, because the archives of the Babylonian state are not preserved. This lack of information should not lead to the conclusion that the Babylonian empire was fundamentally different from its predecessor. On the contrary, it is best regarded as the successor to Assyria. Scribes in the Syrian city of Dur-Katlimmu continued Assyrian administrative practices, now with an acknowledgment of the king in Babylon as supreme ruler. As the example of Judah shows, the Babylonians deported entire populations, and the fact that people continued to rebel shows that imperial rule must have been harsh. One could even say that the Babylonian attitude toward conquered territories was more oppressive. Unlike the Assyrians, they did not develop the southern Levant after they annexed it, but left the region uninhabited and the cities in ruin. This was probably due to the fact that the Babylonian heartland was so rich that it did not need supplies from the periphery.

The focus of royal inscriptions of the period is on building activity, and indeed in this area the Babylonian kings were extremely active, as archaeology confirms. Nebuchadnezzar wanted Babylon to express in its physical layout and monuments the idea that it was the center of the universe, bringing order in a world of chaos and constantly renewing the primordial act of creation. His rebuilding of the city caught the imagination of the ancient world (see debate 14.1). The awe in which Babylon was held is evidenced by Herodotus' description (Book I, 178–83). Scholars strongly disagree about whether the Greek historian visited the city, a question that will never be settled. The answer is not really that crucial; more important is the fact that he and his contemporaries saw Babylon as the epitome of wealth and majesty. Excavations there, which started in 1899, have substantiated that image. At 900 hectares (2,225 acres), the city was gigantic in size. The outer walls formed a triangle with a perimeter of 18 kilometers (11 miles), the inner city was a rectangle surrounded by a three rings of walls, two of them of

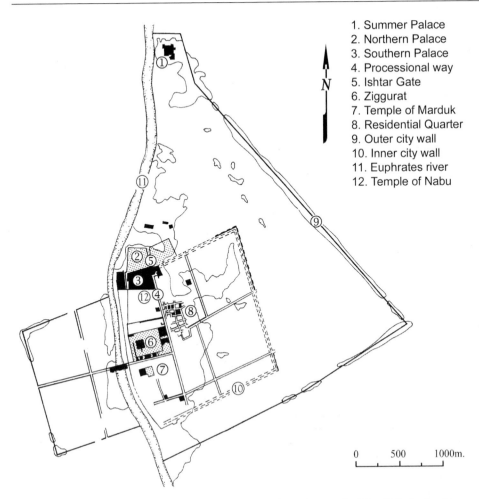

1. Summer Palace
2. Northern Palace
3. Southern Palace
4. Processional way
5. Ishtar Gate
6. Ziggurat
7. Temple of Marduk
8. Residential Quarter
9. Outer city wall
10. Inner city wall
11. Euphrates river
12. Temple of Nabu

0   500   1000m.

Figure 14.2   Plan of Babylon in the sixth century. In its layout the Neo-Babylonian kings who rebuilt Babylon wanted to express how the city was a place of order that protected its inhabitants against chaos. All the walls were massive, and the inner city in particular was designed as a fully protected rectangle that could only be entered through a limited number of massive gates. Credit: Van De Mieroop, 2003. Reproduced with permission from American Journal of Archaeology/Archaeological Institute of America.

baked bricks (figure 14.2). The gates were especially monumental. Most famous is the Ishtar gate, an entrance that was entirely decorated with glazed colored tiles forming images of bulls, lions, and dragons in low relief (figure 14.3). The ziggurat of Marduk was so massive that it inspired the biblical tale of the tower of Babel and, through it, western imagination until today. In the building inscription commemorating its restoration Nebuchadnezzar proclaimed that people from all over the empire contributed to the project: "The totality of the distant populations that Marduk had given to me, I set them to work on the Etemenanki (i.e., ziggurat) and made them carry the brick baskets."[3] While Nebuchadnezzar was not the only Babylonian king responsible for these construction projects, his extensive involvement is clear from the thousands of bricks and stone tiles inscribed with his name. Many other cities of Babylonia were similarly restored and their temples embellished. As in the case of Assyria, the spoils of empire financed a huge building program at home.

Nebuchadnezzar's succession was problematic; three kings ruled for a total of six years only, and two of them were assassinated. Finally, a man of non-royal descent, Nabonidus (ruled 555–539), rose to the throne. He is one of the most intriguing figures in Mesopotamian history and the subject of much ancient literature: he left behind a number of inscriptions that presented his ideas, others who opposed him wrote tracts that decried those same ideas, while later writings depicted him as a madman. It is rare for us to have such varied portrayals of the same character, and it is hard to disclose exactly what lay behind them. Unlike for most other individuals in Near Eastern history we know who Nabonidus' mother was: Adad-guppi, a devotee of the moon god Sin whose cult center was in the north Syrian city of Harran. An inscription that purports to be her autobiography was found there and she states in it that she was born in the twentieth year of King Assurbanipal, cared for the god for ninety-five years before her son became king, and lived to the age of 102 (document 14.1). She introduced her

---

Document 14.1   *Excerpts from Adad-guppi's autobiography*

The text was found in two copies on paving stones at the entrance to the mosque of Harran, the city commemorated here as the center of the moon god Sin's cult. It starts with a first-person account by Adad-guppi, who relates that she served the god for ninety-five years over the reigns of two Assyrian and three Babylonian kings before her son Nabonidus became king – he must have been in his sixties by then. The text ends with a description of her burial, and it is likely that the autobiographical part was a fiction Nabonidus created to justify his usurpation of the throne.

"I am Adad-guppi, mother of Nabonidus, king of Babylon, a servant of Sin, Ningal, Nusku, and Sadarnunna, my gods, for whose divinity I have cared since my youth. . . .

From the twentieth year of Assurbanipal, king of Assur, in which I was born, until the forty-second year of Assurbanipal, the third year of Assur-etel-ilani, his son, the twenty-first year of Nabopolassar, the forty-third year of Nebuchadnezzar, the second year of Evil-Merodach, the fourth year of Neriglissar – for ninety-five years I cared for Sin, the king of the gods of heaven and earth, and for the sanctuaries of his great divinity. He looked upon me and my good deeds with joy. Having heard my prayers and agreeing to my request, the wrath of his heart calmed. He was reconciled with Ehulhul, Sin's house, located in the midst of Harran, his favorite dwelling.

Sin, the king of the gods, looked upon me. He called Nabonidus, my only son, my offspring, to kingship. He personally delivered the kingship of Sumer and Akkad, from the border of Egypt and the upper sea, to the lower sea, all the land. . . .

When, in my dream, Sin, the king of the gods, had set his hands on me, he said thus: 'Through you I will bring about the return of the gods (to) the dwelling in Harran, by means of Nabonidus your son. He will construct Ehulhul; he will complete its work. He will complete the city Harran greater than it was before and restore it. He will bring Sin, Ningal, Nusku, and Sadarnunna, in procession back into the Ehulhul.'

I was attentive to the word of Sin and I saw it come true! Nabonidus, (my) only son, my offspring, completed the neglected rites of Sin, Ningal, Nusku, and Sadarnunna. He constructed the Ehulhul anew. He completed its work. He completed Harran better than before, he restored it; he brought Sin, Ningal, Nusku, and Sadarnunna from Babylon, the royal city, into the center of Harran, into Ehulhul their favorite dwelling. He made (them) dwell there in joy and in happiness.

What Sin, the king of the gods, had not done before and had not granted to anyone, for love of me who worshipped his divinity, (who) beseeched him, the king of the gods – he raised my head; he gave me a fine reputation in the land, long days and years of well-being he added to me. From the period of Assurbanipal, king of Assur, until the ninth year of Nabonidus, king of Babylon, my offspring, they established me for 104 years[1] in the worship of Sin, the king of the gods. He kept me alive and well. My eyesight is clear and my mind is excellent. My hands and my feet are healthy. Well chosen are my words; food and drink still agree with me. My flesh is vital; my heart is joyful. My little ones living four generations from me I have seen. I have reached a ripe old age."

In the ninth year of Nabonidus, king of Babylon, she [died]. Nabonidus, king of Babylon, her son, her offspring, buried her corpse, . . . , fine (clothing), a [bright] mantle, gold . . . [bright] beautiful stones, (choice) stones, precious stones . . . her corpse with fine oil they placed in a hidden location. He sl[aughtered] fattened sheep before her. He gathered together Babylon and Borsippa [with the people] dwelling in distant regions, [kings, princes], and governors, from the [border] of Egypt, the [upper] sea, to the lower sea he [caused to arise] . . . mourning and [ ]. They cried out [bitter]ly. They threw down their [ ] seven [days] and seven nights [ ]. They piped; they cast down [their] clothes. On the seventh day, the troops of the entire land cut [their] hair [ ] their garments [ ] their clothes chest [ ] in food [ ] he [colle]cted perfume [ ] fine oil on [their] heads he poured. He caused their hearts to rejoice. . . .

Translation by Longman 1991: 225–8, reproduced with the author's permission.

[1] She actually only lived 102 years (649–547), but reaches the number 104 by ignoring the overlap of several reigns.

son into court under Nebuchadnezzar, and when rebels overthrew the infant ruler Labashi-Marduk in 556 they offered Nabonidus, who was probably already in his sixties by then and a grandfather, the throne. Like his mother, Nabonidus expressed great devotion for the god Sin, an attitude that caused the enmity of the Marduk priesthood. He gave special attention to the temples of Sin in Harran and Ur and made his daughter high priestess in the latter city, reviving an office that had lapsed many years before. In his inscriptions he proclaimed Sin to be preeminent and portrayed other gods as mere aspects of him. Most disturbing to the Marduk priesthood probably was his decision in 552 to abandon the capital and move to the oasis of Teima in the Arabian Desert. He left his son Belshazzar in charge in Babylon, but the absence of the king resulted in the

cancellation of the New Year's festival in which he in person had to lead the ceremonies. The annual introduction of Marduk's statue into his temple, which indicated the beginning of the year and reaffirmed that god's status as the creator of
the universe, could not take place. Furthermore, when Nabonidus returned after
ten years from Teima, he turned several temples, including Marduk's at Babylon,
into sanctuaries for Sin.

Both the texts commissioned by Nabonidus and those written about him portray a man who sought to change Babylonian culture, looking at the ancient written traditions in order to put his personal mark on them. These acts made him
highly unpopular with the priests and traditional scholars of Babylon, and possibly
even during his reign they composed texts portraying his behavior as a crime that
Marduk would avenge. A text written when Cyrus of Persia was king of Babylon
states:

> He plotted against the worship of Marduk, the king of the gods and continually did
> evil against his city. Daily, [   ] he brought ruin upon its people unrelentingly by
> imposing corvée upon them.[4]

Scholars have suggested many reasons for Nabonidus' move to the desert, and
the true ones will probably never be known, but possibly it was informed by an
astute understanding of the international political situation rather than by purely
religious motives. The cult of the moon god was indeed prominent in Arabia,
but there is no clear indication in Nabonidus' inscriptions that he promoted it
there. More important in his decision to move the court to Teima may have been
the political changes that were taking place in Iran. By 559, Cyrus had become
the leader of the Persians and in 550 he had established full control over the
Zagros region. The expansionist aims of the new king may have been clear to
Nabonidus. Northern Mesopotamia and Syria were easy targets for armies coming from Anatolia, and the loss of these territories would have cut off Babylonia
from the Mediterranean Sea. Nabonidus may have explored new routes through
the desert from Babylon to the west to secure access to that sea. Moreover, north
Arabia was known for its wealth, which must have appealed to king and court.
The move to the desert was thus not frivolous, although it may have exacerbated
hostility toward him at home.

Possibly because of the Babylonian population's resentment of their king, the
Persian conquest of the region seems to have been straightforward. In 539, Cyrus
entered the country from the east. After a major battle near the confluence of
the Diyala and Tigris rivers, which the Persians won, he took over cities without resistance. He became king of Babylon and for many centuries afterwards no
native ruler would sit on its throne. With the capital, Persia received the entire
territory of the Babylonian empire and profited from Babylonia's earlier achievements in its unprecedented expansion. Cyrus used Nabonidus' negative image
in support of his claim to kingship in Babylonia and portrayed himself as the
savior Marduk had selected to restore order and justice. This representation of
Nabonidus survived in later Jewish tradition. In the first century BC, he appears

in the Dead Sea scrolls as having been struck by an evil disease while in Teima. In the biblical book of Daniel, written in the Hellenistic period, the negative aura shifted to Nebuchadnezzar, better known and more hated in Jewish tradition. It says about him: "He was driven from among men, and ate grass like an ox, and his body was wet with the dew of heaven till his hair grew as long as eagles' feathers, and his nails were like birds' claws" (Daniel 4:33).

The Neo-Babylonian period initiated twelve centuries of great economic prosperity for Babylonia, rooted in its agricultural resources. The often-devastating wars of the early first millennium had brought the economy to its lowest point in many centuries, but with the return of peace after the dynasty had established full control the situation changed drastically, aided by an increased humidity of the climate. Although no official texts report on it, archaeology shows that the state financed a massive expansion of the irrigation system and that a grid pattern of canals came to cover the entire countryside. Large tracts could now be cultivated and there was also an intensification of land use. In cereal agriculture seed-plows deposited much more seed into furrows that were closer together than before and there was a major development of date orchards, which provided even greater yields. The need for water in such agrarian practices was great and it remained an expensive and closely monitored resource. Labor was also difficult to obtain and the Neo-Babylonian rulers continued the Assyrian practice of deportations, settling many foreign people in Babylonia itself. This may reflect a policy of internal colonization, the organized development, with coerced labor, of territory within the state itself.

There was much exchange of goods, both within Babylonia and with other regions of the empire and abroad. Instrumental in making this possible was the widespread use of silver as a means of payment even for relatively cheap commodities. Although coinage was not yet in use, the state started to supervise the purity of silver, and it also introduced the metal into the economy by paying it out for labor, for example. The booty from its campaigns and subsequent tribute payments enabled it to do so. Moreover, the canals provided an easy way to transport agricultural produce by boat, and many documents record shipments of barley, dates, and other bulk items. Trading houses financed those ventures, most prominent among them the house of Egibi from Babylon. Its entrepreneurs accepted deposits, provided loans, paid off clients' debts, and provided credit to others so that they could acquire goods for trade. The family was so successful in its business in agricultural products that it could acquire large tracts of land and some of its members became leading officials in Babylon. In the cities, small-scale peddlers sold salt, beer, cooking wares, and so on. Long-distance trade was conducted between the regions of the empire and beyond: Egypt, Cyprus, Anatolia, Syria-Palestine, Babylonia, and western Iran made up a world where goods such as iron, copper, tin, lapis lazuli, textiles and the products needed for textile manufacture (natron, dyes, etc.), wine, honey, and spices were exchanged in great quantities. Merchants were attached to the palace and the temples, or could act independently. Political boundaries did not seem to affect their work. Pottery from Athens, for example, was shipped to Babylon. In addition, the change in political regimes did not negatively affect this activity, and the Egibi house continued its business without interruption when the Persians captured Babylonia.

The extensive economic activity required detailed record keeping, and the Neo-Babylonian and subsequent early Achaemenid eras provide us with the greatest abundance of documents from Babylonia after the Ur III period. From the period that has been coined the "long sixth century" between the fall of Assyria in 612 and the Babylonian revolts against Xerxes in 484 well over 16,000 tablets have been published and many more are known to exist in museums. They derive almost exclusively from temple and private archives. The palace's role in the economy is thus not directly documented, which certainly biases our view of affairs. Many temples owned large and self-contained agricultural estates with fields, orchards, and animal herds. A substantial part of their wealth derived from "tithes" paid by all who owned land or another source of income and lived nearby the temple estates. While the figure was not always exactly 10 percent, all people, including the king, had to give a share of the profits they made on fields, orchards, herds, and so on to the temple. Officials collected these in kind or in silver, and if people were unable to pay, they had to take out loans from private moneylenders or give their children to the temple as slaves. As hired labor was rare, slaves were very useful for performing menial tasks. Another source of slaves was prisoners of war, who the king gave to the temples. Yet non-slave laborers farmed the majority of temple land; they were assigned plots from which they were required to pay a share of the harvest as rent. The palace and private landowners used the same arrangement on their estates. They provided seed grain, tools, and plow animals when these were needed, so the tenant farmers had little invested in the land. Yet they were not allowed to leave without permission, and runaways were arrested and returned in shackles.

The collection of rents and the distribution of seed and tools, as well as marketing the harvests, required a complex organization. Landowners, both institutional and private, were reluctant to undertake this themselves so they relied on entrepreneurs, as was done in earlier Babylonian history from the early second millennium on. These middlemen were often organized in business houses that administered such affairs for various owners in the same region and continued to do so under different political regimes. Their access to silver allowed them to purchase in advance of the harvest, to finance transport to cities, and to issue loans to defaulting tenants. They also used their assets to finance trade. Private archives provide the second largest source of documentation from the Neo-Babylonian period, and contain records of many activities beyond the entrepreneurs' businesses. Anything that involved a transfer of property was recorded in a detailed contract witnessed by several people (document 14.2). Numerous private family archives are preserved today: they documented all assets, such as real estate, slaves, and animals, and outstanding debts. The records were often kept for several generations and they show that relatives such as cousins and in-laws regularly worked together and owned property in common.

Neo-Babylonian society was very much concentrated in cities. The level of urbanization was substantially higher than at any time in the preceding centuries,

Document 14.2   *Neo-Babylonian private contracts*

The Neo-Babylonian period has provided one of the richest textual records for the study of ancient Near Eastern society and economy, and thousands of cuneiform tablets with documents of daily life are preserved. Among them is a group of marriage contracts that stipulate agreements made between a husband and his wife's family. Contracts of this type often contain a direct speech, where one party asks the other to initiate a transaction.

Mr. Dagil-ili, son of Mr. Zambubu, spoke to Ms. Hamma, daughter of Mr. Nergal-iddin, descendant of Mr. Babutu, as follows: "Please give me Ms. La-tubashshinni, your daughter. Let her be my wife."

Ms. Hamma agreed with him and gave Ms. La-tubashshinni, her daughter, to him as wife. And Mr. Dagil-ili voluntarily gave to Ms. Hamma, in consideration of Ms. La-tubashshinni her daughter, Mr. Ana-muhhi-bel-amur, a slave who was bought for one-half pound of silver, and in addition another one and one-half pounds of silver.

Should Mr. Dagil-ili take another wife, Mr. Dagil-ili will give one pound of silver to Ms. La-tubashshinni, and she may go wherever she pleases.

(This agreement was concluded) in the presence of Mr. Shum-iddin, son of Mr. Ina-teshi-etir, descendant of Mr. Sin-damaqu. The witnesses (were): Mr. Bel-ahhe-iddin, son of Mr. Nabu-bel-shumati, descendant of the priest of Ishtar of Babylon; Mr. Marduk-sharrani, son of Mr. Balatu, descendant of the potter; Mr. Marduk-etir, son of Mr. Nergal-iddin, descendant of Mr. Babutu; and the scribe Mr. Nabu-mukin-zeri, son of Mr. Marduk-zer-ibni, descendant of the priest of Ishtar of Babylon.

(Written in) Babylon, month Marchesvan (October–November), day 9, year 13 of Nebuchadnezzar, king of Babylon.

Translation after Roth 1984: 42–3.

although it did not reach early second-millennium levels. Places such as Babylon became enormous in terms of their size and number of inhabitants and had to be fed by a large hinterland. Agricultural production was probably partly specialized by region to satisfy demand. The cities were self-governing organizations centered on the temple, which is the source of most of our documentary evidence. Cities had their own law courts and cases were often decided in assemblies. We do not know who was allowed to sit in them, however. The temples provided the social structure of these cities, as an individual's position in the temple hierarchy determined his social status and authority in the urban government. Free laborers, such as skilled craftsmen, could negotiate their rights as a group. Rural populations were not in such a privileged position. Tied to the land they worked, they were forced to provide labor and rent to the landowners. High state officials received estates, which changed hands repeatedly during political crises such as the succession problems following Nebuchadnezzar II. The owners were absentee landlords with little connection to their properties, who left the management to local entrepreneurs and were only interested in profits. Many of the farmers were deportees brought in from distant parts of the empire and housed together in villages. Another important part of the population remained the non-sedentary groups, who are much less visible in the documentation. The royal house was of Chaldean origin and had to maintain good contacts with the tribal communities, although its power was mainly located within the cities. The kings had thus to negotiate carefully between different constituencies: the old Babylonian urban elites, the state officials, and non-sedentary people. These tensions may have caused the troubled years after Nebuchadnezzar's death.

The policy of deportation to the heartland of the empire and extensive contacts with foreign states resulted in cities such as Babylon becoming multi-ethnic on an unprecedented scale. People from Syria-Palestine, Phoenicia, Elam, Persia, Media, Ionia, Cilicia, and Egypt lived in close proximity and mingled in the same urban spaces. Individuals from enemy states were welcome, too, possibly because they were political refugees. Egyptians, for example, are attested all over Babylonia, remarkably often as scribes of cuneiform tablets. One became a judge in Babylon in the reign of Nebuchadnezzar. Ration lists show that members of the deported upper classes were allowed to live at the royal court. Commoners were settled in the countryside to work on the agricultural projects the state initiated. They lived in communities in which they were allowed to uphold their original identities and which were often named after them: town of the Arabians, after the people; of Judah, after the country of origin; etcetera. They could give their children names in their native languages and refer to their own gods – Egyptian Isis, Judean Yahweh, Iranian Mithra, etcetera – but intermarriage between the various communities led to successive generations of the same family showing different linguistic and cultural affinities. There was no cultural isolation, it seems.

A great mixture of languages and customs must have been heard and seen on the streets of Babylon. However, the kings pursued a policy of maintaining, and even reviving, ancient Babylonian culture and traditions. Akkadian was probably no longer widely spoken and Aramaic had replaced it as the main vernacular, but it remained the language of culture and administration. As in the Neo-Assyrian period, highly educated scribes copied out and preserved ancient literature. But the interaction with the past went further. Royal inscriptions consciously used outdated Akkadian expressions and Sumerian words, entire inscriptions were composed in the Old Babylonian dialect, and sometimes the cuneiform script was made to look like that of the third millennium. Interest in the past was not limited to texts, but also ancient artworks were valued, safeguarded, and restored (figure 14.4). Nabonidus reports that he found a statue of Sargon of Akkad, set it up in a temple, and provided it with regular offerings. In the temple of Shamash at Sippar modern excavators discovered objects dating back as far as the Jemdet Nasr period, from Babylonia and from neighboring regions, including inscribed stone bowls, statues, boundary stones, and so on. Similar collections were kept in other cities as well. When temples were restored it was important that the earliest foundations were located, so something resembling modern archaeological research took place. According to Nabonidus, Nebuchadnezzar had failed to do so when he restored the Sippar temple and the work had been shoddy as a result. So he

Figure 14.4 Tablet of Shamash. This stone tablet shows the ninth-century Babylonian king Nabu-apla-iddina approaching the sun god Shamash in the company of two interceding deities and its text describes how Nabu-apla-iddina ordered a new statue of the god be made. King Nabopolassar found the tablet 250 years later and placed it in a ceramic box for safekeeping, placing clay impressions of the carved panel over the stone to protect it. British Museum, London (ME 91000). Babylonian, early ninth century, from Sippar. L. 29.210 cm; W. 17.780 cm. Credit: © The Trustees of the British Museum.

repeated the excavations until a foundation deposit from the time of Naram-Sin of Akkad was found, and only then was the temple properly rebuilt. Nabonidus even determined that Naram-Sin had ruled 3,200 years before him, a gross miscalculation but an indication that he saw himself as heir to a very old tradition. Such an attitude explains how he could revive the office of high priestess of the moon god at Ur, which had originally been created by Sargon. Notwithstanding the innovations Nabonidus attempted, the religious practices in the Neo-Babylonian period were traditional and continued to focus on the age-old gods of the region. As in the past, each city was considered to be the home of a particular deity and the main temple was that god's residence. Because of the central role of temples in the economy, many of them were very wealthy and cults flourished. Some of the oldest cults of Babylonia experienced a revival, for example those of gods Anu and Ishtar at Uruk. In the city of Babylon the god Marduk was preeminent, and his leading status in the pantheon was confirmed annually in the New Year's festival. At that time the statues of other gods visited the god and entered the city in a public procession leading to the main sanctuary where Marduk's kingship over them was renewed. His son, Nabu, the patron of nearby Borsippa, came close to equal to him in importance. Three of the kings of the dynasty honored him in their names (Nabopolassar, Nebuchadnezzar, and Nabonidus) and all of them devoted as much attention to his sanctuary as they did to Marduk's. Babylon and Borsippa were considered to be twin cities and Nabu's presence at the New Year's festival was as essential as Marduk's. When Nabonidus tried to elevate the god Sin above others, his moves were not unprecedented, but they certainly antagonized powerful lobbies.

The Neo-Babylonian dynasty was the last native Mesopotamian dynasty in ancient Near Eastern history and therefore we may regard its end as a momentous event, although the people at the time probably did not think so. The Neo-Babylonian kings saw themselves as very much part of an old tradition of Babylonian greatness going back to the third millennium, and promoted an awareness of that tradition. Babylonian culture was extremely strong by the time the dynasty was overthrown, and survived unscathed in the following historical era.

Debate 14.1   *Where were the Hanging Gardens of Babylon?*

Everyone knows of the Seven Wonders of the Ancient World, a list of monuments that have all disappeared, except for the great pyramids of Egypt. In antiquity the list at first varied in contents, but when fixed around the year 1, the Hanging Gardens of Babylon were included. They stood out even then, because, while a traveler from Rome could visit all the others easily, the wonder of Babylon was in the distant east outside the Roman empire (see map in Finkel & Seymour 2008: 106). There exist several ancient Greek and Latin accounts about the gardens, however, all of them dating to the first century BC and the first century AD, but quoting earlier authors. Among them Josephus (1st c. AD) cites the Babylonian historian Berossus (ca. 290 BC), who wrote that Nebuchadnezzar II built them for his homesick Median wife. Elsewhere Berossus calls Nebuchadnezzar's wife Amytis. Diodorus (1st c. BC), quoting Ktesias (4th c. BC), states that an unnamed Syrian king constructed the gardens for an unnamed Persian concubine, who longed for "the meadows of her mountains" and he gives technical details about their layout. The story has thus a romantic appeal and the gardens have become an integral part of our ideas about ancient Babylon (for the classical quotes, see Finkel & Seymour 2008: 104–11).

Early visitors to the site speculated whether solitary trees in the then barren countryside descended from those in the gardens. When large-scale excavations started in 1899, the German director Robert Koldewey wanted to uncover the city's entire plan, and naturally the question of where the gardens had been arose. He discovered a complex of vaulted rooms with very thick walls on the east side of the southern palace behind the Ishtar gate, and tentatively suggested they had supported the gardens (Koldewey 1914: 91–100). Later he became more assertive about this but there was an obvious difficulty with a location so distant from the Euphrates River which would have provided water. When later on tablets documenting oil rations, including to the exiled Judean King

Jehoiachin, were discovered in the building, its function as a storage area was clear. Scholars suggested alternative locations along the Euphrates (e.g., Wiseman 1985: 56–60), but none was founded on conclusive evidence.

Doubts about the gardens' existence became common (e.g., Finkel 1988). The lack of clear archaeological proof is reinforced by a silence in the most eloquent ancient written sources about Babylon. No Neo-Babylonian building inscription mentions gardens, nor does the cuneiform *Description of Babylon*, a set of five tablets that list Babylon's temples, gates, streets, and so on (George 1992). Herodotus, the Greek author whose account of Babylon is the most detailed ancient source available, does not speak of gardens, nor do they appear in the Hebrew Bible (Van der Spek 2008). Were they entirely fictional?

Not so, says the scholar who has devoted twenty years to the question and very recently published an entire book on it (Dalley 2013). She aims to prove that the hanging gardens were not in Babylon, but in its ideological counterpart, the earlier Assyrian capital Nineveh, alongside Sennacherib's "palace without a rival." The Assyrians had the technology to raise Tigris water up to the level needed to irrigate gardens at that height and there is visual evidence in the Assyrian reliefs for the existence of palace gardens. Moreover, a rereading of Sennacherib's building inscriptions in her opinion confirms that he planted the gardens. Colleagues have been skeptical of this suggestion in the past (e.g., Van der Spek 2008) and it is too early to tell whether the book-length study will convince more of them. In any case, mystery will always remain part of Babylon's appeal, which is why it has stirred the western imagination for so long (cf. Finkel & Seymour 2008; Wullen & Schauerte 2008).

NOTES

1   Translation by Starr 1990: no. 43.
2   Grayson 1975: 101.
3   Wetzel & Weissbach 1938: 47.
4   See document 15.1.

15

The Creation of a World Empire: Persia

3000	2500	2000	1500	1000	500

559	Cyrus rises to power in Persia
539	Cyrus conquers Babylonia
525	Cambyses conquers Egypt
521	Darius usurps the throne
490	Battle of Marathon in Greece
480	Battle of Salamis in Greece

In a few decades of the second half of the sixth century, the Persians of south-west Iran created an enormous empire covering the entire Near East and regions beyond from the Indus valley to northern Greece, from Central Asia to southern Egypt (for a king list, see Section 17 of the King Lists at the end of the book). It was to last more or less intact for two hundred years, a long time when compared to previous and subsequent empires in the region. It successfully brought together areas with different languages, cultures, economies, and sociopolitical organizations, and was the first in Near Eastern history to acknowledge the diversity of its subjects. Its swift expansion ended shortly before the wars between Persia and Greece that have dominated the reconstructions of Persia's history until recently. The enormous extent of the empire and its impact on so many peoples and places has left a great record for us to study and permits a nuanced approach to what can be called the first world empire in history.

A History of the Ancient Near East ca. 3000–323 BC, Third Edition. Marc Van De Mieroop.
© 2016 John Wiley & Sons, Inc. Published 2016 by John Wiley & Sons, Inc.

15.1   The Sources and Their Challenges

The sources on the Persian empire present the historian with a conundrum, not because they are so scarce but because they are so diverse and to fit them into a coherent whole is especially challenging. The empire was never forgotten and in the western tradition Classical Greek and Roman authors and the Hebrew Bible shaped its image and continue to have a strong impact on historical scholarship and popular imagination. The Greeks naturally focused on the two moments when interactions with Persia were the most intense: the Persian wars in 490 and 480–479 and Alexander of Macedon's conquest of the empire in the late 330s. Both were failures for Persia and the Greeks' defeat of this gigantic opponent inspired speculations about their moral superiority and the reasons for Persia's powerlessness. The idea that Persian rulers were doomed appeared in Greek writings such as Aeschylus' tragedy *The Persians*, which otherwise contains a very sympathetic representation of the Persian queen as a worried mother. The greatest historian of the Persian wars was Herodotus (late fifth century), who saw their roots in an age-old opposition between Asia and Europe, and provided the most detailed account of events. Alexander took writers with him to record his military feats, and although their reports are now lost, they inspired historians from the Roman empire to create what were essentially hagiographies.

Greeks customarily worked for the Persian court and some recorded their experiences. In the early fourth century Ktesias, who had been the king's physician, wrote a twenty-three volume *History of Persia*, only known from a ninth-century AD summary and sundry quotes. He loved to recount palace intrigues so much that modern historians often disparage his work. At the same time an Athenian mercenary leader, Xenophon, in 401 fought on the losing side of a Persian war of succession and described his voyage through the western empire. He also wrote a laudatory *The Education of Cyrus*, presenting the founder of the empire as a model ruler.

The Hebrew Bible too saw Cyrus in a very positive light, as the king who freed the Jews from exile and allowed them to rebuild the temple of Jerusalem. The books of *Ezra* and *Nehemiah* document events in the new Judah – though these books present numerous historical problems – while the prophet Isaiah in particular heralded Cyrus as a liberator. The positive image, which also influenced the historian Josephus (1st c. AD), was not absolute, however. The book of *Esther*, written when Judah was part of the Hellenistic world, portrays a Persian court riddled with intrigue and senseless killing. These ancient sources, as well as the ruins of Persepolis described in travel accounts, enabled the reconstruction of some sort of history of Persia before materials from the empire itself were understood. On balance, despite the positive elements, these ancient writings presented Persia as a failed civilization, gigantic in size and extremely wealthy but crippled by decadence and the whims of its elites. It was the antithesis of what Classical Greece stood for in western imagination, that is, creativity and the love of freedom. In this view, the battle of Marathon saved Europe from Oriental despotism.

The negative appraisal of Persia persisted even when exploration in the countries the empire ruled provided a mass of documentation. Unlike the previously available narratives these were primarily terse documents of governance and administration. Because of its vast extent and its interactions with so many cultures and peoples from the Nile to the Indus River, these records are extremely diverse. When written they involve a multitude of languages, scripts, and administrative practices: Demotic in Egypt; Babylonian in Mesopotamia; Elamite and Old Persian in Persia; Greek, Phrygian, and Lydian in Anatolia; and Aramaic all over the empire. When they are archaeological, they include cities, palaces, tombs, irrigation systems, canals, a mass of assorted objects, and much more. The bias of the written documentation lies heavily in the western part of the empire where it adopted well-established bureaucratic practices, but the isolated find in Afghanistan of fourth-century Aramaic documents written on wood and leather shows how the administration extended throughout its territory. The sources produced within the empire are huge in number, yet the narrative structure of its history is still grounded in Greek writings with their negative attitude. It is only in the last thirty years that scholars of ancient Persia have come to confront this bias and consciously tried to reverse the hellenocentric approach. They sought to undermine the "Orientalist" stereotypes, sometimes going too far, perhaps. Persia is no longer considered to have been an exhausted giant waiting to be revived by Alexander and his followers, but a complex organization that faced numerous challenges successfully over the two hundred years that it ruled the Near East.

15.2 The Rise of Persia and Its Expansion

The heartland of Persia was located in southwest Iran, in the region today called Fars, the eastern part of the earlier state of Elam and south of Media. It was home to a local dynasty that used the title "King of Anshan," thereby recalling the days of Elam, whose rulers were kings of Susa and Anshan. The population was not made up of Elamites, however, but of Persians, an Iranian people that spoke an Indo-European language and had migrated into the region at the start of the first millennium. Virtually nothing is known about the country until Cyrus, the second member of the dynasty with that name, came to power in 559. He would become the creator of the largest empire the world had seen up to that moment – that is why he is often labeled Cyrus the Great. In 550 he defeated the Median ruler Ishtumegu (Astyages in Greek sources). Herodotus claims that Cyrus was a vassal who overthrew his master, while Babylonian sources report that Ishtumegu set out to conquer Anshan and that his troops rebelled and surrendered their king to Cyrus. With this act the Persian took over the entire territory the Medes had controlled, and he and his immediate successors pursued rapid military expansion from this base. In 547 Cyrus defeated King Croesus of Lydia, thereby reaching the Aegean Sea and Greek cities on the Ionian coast. From 546 to 540 he probably campaigned in eastern Iran, but the details are unknown, and in 539 he marched against the Babylonian empire. In September 539 the armies led by both kings faced each other near Opis on the confluence of the Tigris and Diyala rivers at the east side of the Median Wall. Cyrus won the battle, ransacked the city, and massacred its inhabitants, which scared the people of Sippar on the western edge of the Median Wall so much that they surrendered to him without a fight. Cyrus then sent a general to Babylon, who took King Nabonidus prisoner and probably negotiated the city's capitulation. Only afterwards, on October 12, 539, did he enter Babylon as its new king. The capture of its throne made Cyrus ruler of the entire Neo-Babylonian empire, whose various populations seem to have accepted him without resistance. The smoothness of the transition is remarkable when we compare it to the difficulties the Babylonians had faced in the Levant half a century earlier.

Cyrus could now turn his attention to the northeast and took his troops into eastern Iran and Central Asia where he annexed vast territories. The previous political organization of those areas is unclear to us, but as nomads played a great role in them it was certainly very different from the centralized urban-based system in the west. How Cyrus managed to impose his rule is a mystery, as there are few reports on his conquests in the written sources with their western bias. According to Herodotus, Cyrus died in battle in 530 fighting the nomadic Massagetae in Central Asia. In twenty years he had turned a small royal house from southwestern Iran into the rulers of a vast territorial empire of unprecedented size. He benefited from prior centralizations of power under the Medes, Lydians, and Babylonians, but still must have had remarkable military and administrative skills to accomplish this.

His successor Cambyses (ruled 529–522) had already been active in campaigns in the west as crown prince and co-regent, and extended the empire farther in that direction. He captured Cyprus and in 525 invaded Egypt. This was not a raid, as it had been under the Assyrians, but a true incorporation of the country into the Persian empire. Cambyses became king of Egypt and seems to have stayed there for the remainder of his reign until 522. He ordered his troops south into Nubia and west into the Libyan Desert and along the North African coast. According to Herodotus these campaigns were failures that ended in disaster, but Nubia was part of the empire by 521. Expansion did not stop there, however. Darius (ruled 521–486) brought the empire to its greatest extent. He conquered Libya, Thrace in Europe, the Aegean island of Samos, and annexed Western India. He also made Macedonia and Nubia tributary. His invasion of Scythia across the Danube River was a failure, and may have been a sign that the empire had reached its limits.

Darius began the military engagements against Greece that preoccupy so much of the Classical literature on Persia and modern reconstructions of its history. Despite the wealth of information on the events, it is not so easy to determine how important these wars were to the Persians. To the Greeks they certainly were momentous, and however hard we try, it will always be impossible to disregard their interpretation of the Persian wars (see debate 15.1). Greece was not a unified country at the time, but a network of city-states with different political organizations. Leaders among them were Athens with its democracy of free male citizens,

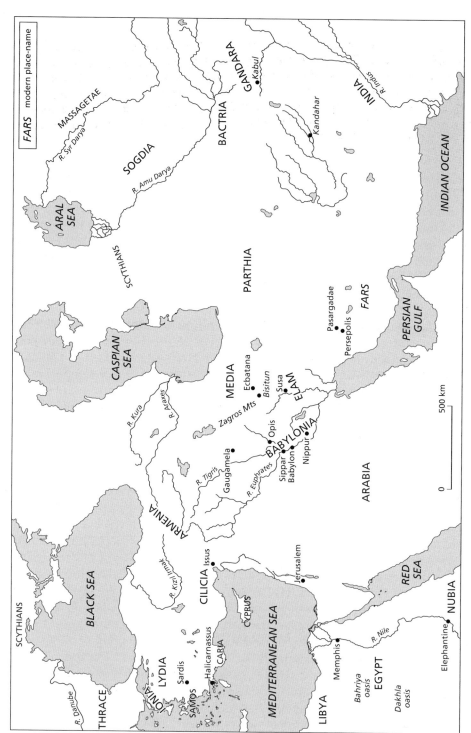

Map 15.1 The Persian empire.

and Sparta with its oligarchy under two kings. Both cities had extended their influence over the neighboring regions. So-called tyrants, that is, kings who had seized power illegitimately, ruled many of the cities. Athens itself had just overthrown a family of tyrants that held power from 545 to 510. The system of Greek city-states extended into coastal Anatolia, where they had been forced to accept first Lydian, and later Persian, domination. In 499 the Ionians there rebelled against the empire and Athens, despite its treaty with Persia, sent them military help. Those troops accidentally burned down a temple in the Lydian capital, Sardis, which, so Herodotus tells us, Darius vowed never to forget.

In 490 he sent his navy out into the Aegean, sacking various Greek cities, and Persian troops landed in the bay of Marathon, where a surprise attack by the Athenians caused them heavy losses. Athens' victory was a surprise and certain to trigger a Persian reaction. Darius was preoccupied elsewhere, however, and could not retaliate, but his son and successor Xerxes (ruled 485–465) did so as soon as he had dealt with problems in the core of the empire. In 481 he sent delegations demanding submission, which many Greek cities agreed to, but others rallied around Athens and Sparta, the leading military power in the region. Xerxes assembled a massive army – Herodotus gives the unbelievable number of 2,617,610 men (Book VII, 185) – and navy. The Greeks set up land and sea defenses to protect central Greece, but in 480 the Persians broke through the pass at Thermopylae despite the now mythical resistance of Leonidas and his 300 Spartans. The Persian army ransacked Athens, which had been evacuated in a tactical move to fight at sea. The Athenians crushed the Persian navy at Salamis. Xerxes withdrew and left behind an elite contingent of 10,000 men in northern Greece. The Greeks routed it at Plataea in 479, while they mopped up the remainder of the Persian fleet soon afterwards. This put an end to Persia's plans for the occupation of Greece, although it continued to meddle into Greek politics later on. After the Greek adventure Persia added little territory elsewhere, although its army was kept busy dealing with rebellious subjects and in internal fights for power.

Regardless of the setbacks in Greece, the Persian army had been extremely effective in bringing together numerous earlier states and empires under one rule, and had done so quite swiftly. It must have been very well organized and there was a system in place to muster forces fast whenever and wherever they were needed. Because of the vast extent of the empire they could not be stationed near the capital and marched to battle in the fighting season, as had been the case with the Assyrian army, for example. According to Herodotus (Book V, 54) a single traveler needed three months to reach the Aegean coast from Susa and an army was much slower. When Xerxes invaded Greece he assembled the troops at Sardis in western Anatolia and must have relied to a great extent on local manpower. The main Persian fighting force was the infantry made up of lancers and archers. The elite was the king's personal bodyguard, a corps of 10,000 lancers, also called "Immortals." Recruited from native Persians, their number remained exactly the same as each fallen man was immediately replaced. Bows and spears were the primary weapons of the army's core (figure 15.1). Mobile light infantry first showered the enemy with arrows and then attacked with spears. As we saw, Medes were famous for their horses and they assisted the infantry with cavalry attacks. The Persians used the special skills of the people they conquered very effectively: Arabian camel drivers fought next to Libyan charioteers; Phoenicians manned the navy with Egyptians, Cypriots, and Ionians. The Persians employed the same tactics as their predecessors in the region, such as the Assyrians, although they did not detail them in royal inscriptions. When needed they massacred civilians and they regularly deported populations from one part of the empire to another, although seemingly in smaller numbers than the Assyrians. Greek sources indicate that they moved peoples from the Mediterranean coast to Bactria, Babylonia, Elam, and islands in the Persian Gulf. As did the Assyrians, the Persians habitually sent delegates in advance of the army to demand submission and the threat of military action was often enough to obtain surrender. Cyrus could claim that the Babylonians welcomed him with open arms as a liberator, but he gave them little choice.

The Persian army's main strength seems to have been its size, an aspect that Greek authors exaggerated. Herodotus' figure of more than two and a half million men invading Greece was truly fantastic, but there is no doubt that the numbers the Persians could field were very large. Their reliance on size may explain why the Greeks were successful in defeating them. The Greeks chose battlegrounds where the full forces could not be deployed: Leonidas held a narrow passage at Thermopylae – and the Persians only broke through because they had discovered an alternative route – and during the naval battle in the bay of Salamis the Persian ships had no space to maneuver.

The system of Persian military recruitment is known from Babylonian sources. The state had confiscated vast areas of land after the conquest and assigned fields to groups of men who, in return, had to provide military service, as charioteers, cavalrymen, or, most often, archers. The records identify the tracts explicitly as "chariot land," "horse land," and "bow land," given in use to units of soldiers under the control of a superintendent who was part of the royal administration. When the soldiers passed the use of the fields on to several sons the parcels became too small to support a family and the system became an administrative fiction. On the one hand, cash payments became a crucial part of a soldier's reward and on the other hand the soldiers no longer worked the fields themselves but engaged others to do so. But by then the empire's expansion had ended and there was less need for men serving in the army.

Babylonia's system need not have been universally applied throughout the empire, but it is clear that the vast manpower available, as well as the resources to pay for the soldiers, gave the king access to an immense army. Classical sources depict a situation in which the use of mercenaries, especially Greeks and Anatolians, increased over time, and suggest that by the fourth century they alone made up the army's true strength. It is undeniable that Persia employed mercenaries. The Greek author Xenophon, for example, was one of 10,000 Greek mercenaries who in 401 fought for Cyrus the Younger in an unsuccessful bid to seize the throne, and we know of colonies of Jewish and other mercenaries at Egypt's borders. The growing importance of mercenary forces is overstated, however, and forms part of the Greek portrayal of Persia as a decadent society after Xerxes.

Mercenaries had served armies throughout the Near East for centuries and when Cambyses invaded Egypt both sides used them – Herodotus blames Egypt's defeat to a great extent on the fact that a mercenary leader defected to Cambyses and revealed Egypt's weak points. The assertion that mercenaries became the mainstay of the Persian army should not be taken at face value. It did indeed collapse between 334 and 330 under Macedonian attacks, but this seems to have been the result of Alexander's skillful use of the phalanx rather than of a gradual decline in Persian military might.

15.3   Governance of the Subject States

Conquest is the first step toward creating an empire, pacification the second and more difficult one. The small population of Persia took charge of an enormous conglomerate of states and peoples with different political and administrative practices and needs. Unlike the Assyrians before them they could not extend their own system of governance over the newly acquired territories. We know nothing concrete about Persia's pre-imperial organization but it must have been unequipped to deal with the complexities of empire. The Persians were highly innovative in this respect in that they inserted themselves within existing political structures and acknowledged the heterogeneity of their empire.

At the top of government the king of Persia took over existing thrones, a practice that is the clearest to us in Babylonia and Egypt. After Cyrus had conquered Babylon he commissioned official statements written in traditional Babylonian cuneiform that explained his rise to kingship there (figure 15.2). The famous *Cyrus Cylinder* described how the god Marduk turned against the last Babylonian

Figure 15.2   Cyrus Cylinder. In the text on this very traditional Babylonian object the Persian Cyrus explains how he came to be king of Babylon and liberator of the city's inhabitants. The clay cylinder was to be placed in the foundations of the Imgur-Bel wall at Babylon, the reconstruction of which it commemorates. In the broken passage he refers to an inscription of the Assyrian King Assurbanipal, which he discovered during the works. British Museum, London, ME 90920. Clay, L. 22.5 cm. Credit: akg images/Album/Prisma.

ruler Nabonidus because of that king's disregard for his cult, and that he searched all over the world for a replacement. Marduk ordered Cyrus to seize Babylon and helped the Persian army to do so. Cyrus became "king of the world, great king, strong king, king of Babylon, king of the land of Sumer and Akkad, king of the four quarters of the universe," adopting all the traditional titles of Babylonian kingship (see document 15.1). Soon afterwards he made his son Cambyses king of Babylon, but he continued to participate in important festivals, such as the New Year's celebration. He acknowledged that he was a foreigner but understood the importance of ancient rituals. The behavior of his son Cambyses in Egypt was the same. He took on all the trappings of local kingship and even adopted an Egyptian name, Mesutira, "Offspring of the god Ra." We do not know the details of how the Persians made their rule elsewhere official but when Darius asserted his dominance over the empire he did so as king of twenty-three countries (see document 16.1).

Document 15.1   *The Cyrus Cylinder*

Perhaps the most famous cuneiform text after the Code of Hammurabi or even on a par with it, is the so-called Cyrus Cylinder, *a typical Babylonian object but written on behalf of the Persian conqueror of Babylon and detailing the reasons for his victory. The cylinder is damaged and just over a third of the text is missing. Very recently two fragments of a large tablet that contained a copy of it were identified in the British Museum in London. The cylinder has become celebrated as the earliest declaration of human rights and a modern facsimile of it is on display at the United Nations in New York. Its actual content is less exciting, however, but it is of special interest as it presents Cyrus as the savior of the Babylonians from oppression by King Nabonidus. It says of that Babylonian king:*

He plotted against the worship of Marduk, the king of the gods and continually did evil against his city. Daily, [   ] he brought ruin upon its people unrelentingly by imposing corvée upon them. (lines 7–8)

Marduk felt pity for the people and sought a replacement for their king:

He searched and looked in all the countries, seeking for the upright king of his choice. He took the hand of Cyrus, king of Anshan, and called him by his name, proclaiming him for kingship over everything. (lines 11–12)

The god then ordered the troops of Persia and Media to march on Babylon and made them enter the city without a fight, delivering Nabonidus into Cyrus' hands. The Babylonians welcomed his rule and Cyrus could adopt all the traditional titles of their country's kingship. He set about restoring peace for the people of Babylon:

I sought the welfare of the city Babylon and all its sanctuaries. The people of Babylon who had bore a yoke not decreed for them, as if they were without a god, I relieved from their weariness and freed from their burdens. (lines 25–6)

Cyrus then returned the gods, whose statues Nabonidus had moved to Babylon, to their homes:

From [Babylon] to Assur and Susa, Akkad, Eshnunna, Zamban, Meturnu, Der, up to the land of the Guti – sanctuaries across the Tigris River that had been abandoned for a long time – I returned the gods and let them dwell in permanent places. All their people I gathered together and returned to their homes. The gods of Sumer and Akkad, whom Nabonidus had settled in Babylon, thereby angering the lord of the gods, at the command of Marduk, I made reside in peace in their sanctuaries and I made them happy. (lines 30–4)

He asked for the gods' constant blessings and listed the restoration works he did on the wall of Babylon – the cylinder is a building inscription. The critical passage of the inscription is where Cyrus states that he returned the gods and people who had been displaced to their homes. All the places he mentions are located to the east of the Tigris and he used an image of royal benevolence that earlier Mesopotamian kings, including Hammurabi, had invoked. After the disturbances of war the people needed to go back to their homes. The passage actually casts suspicion on Cyrus' claim that Babylon's conquest was unopposed. It seems that the war involved did harm the population and that he had to take action to return the situation to normal.

Translation after Schaudig 2001: 551–4.

The same approach was used with existing bureaucracies. When they were well established, the Persians did not meddle with them but allowed them to continue as before. Archives such as that of the Egibi family in Babylon show no changes except for in the names of the kings who were acknowledged the same way as their Babylonian predecessors. Similarly in Egypt record-keeping on papyri in the Demotic language and script continued as before. Developments did happen over time, naturally, which we will discuss in the next chapter, but to an average inhabitant of these countries the change from a native to a foreign dynasty must have made no difference.

The arrival of the Persians did not cause disruption in religious and cultural life either. As we saw, in Babylonia Cyrus presented himself as the champion of the god Marduk who reinstated the cult practices Nabonidus had disrupted. Temples continued their traditional role in society, including in the intellectual sphere. Throughout the earlier first millennium temples had been sponsors of scholarship and supported scribes, diviners, astronomers, and others who preserved and elaborated on the literate culture of the region. This continued uninterrupted under Persian rule. Marduk's temple at Babylon employed more than a dozen astronomers simultaneously in the fourth century. At Sippar in the temple of Shamash archaeologists excavated a scholarly library of the early Persian period, which contained some 800 tablets stacked in rows two or three deep in fifty-six niches. They included all genres of Babylonian literate scholarship: omens, medical texts, lexical lists, cultic material, hymns and prayers, epics, wisdom literature, and copies of ancient inscriptions – including the prologue of Hammurabi's code (see document 15.2). In Egypt we see the same attitude. Persian rulers supported

Document 15.2   *The Persian library at Sippar*

The tolerance of the Persians toward the traditions of the regions they conquered is visible in many ways, and Babylonian culture continued to flourish under them. Because the empire brought together an enormous landmass that had previously been divided, it enabled activities impossible before. This is vividly demonstrated in the remains of a library excavated in the Babylonian city of Sippar. It was located in the temple of the sun god Shamash, and contained many manuscripts of earlier Babylonian literature and scholarship. Those were mostly copied from locally available exemplars, but not all. In its collection was a copy of the prologue to the code of Hammurabi carved on the famous stele now in the Louvre Museum (see figure 6.2). This stele had been carried off to Susa in Elam in the twelfth century (cf. chapter 9) and had thus been inaccessible to people from Babylonia for many centuries. With the unification of Elam and Babylonia under the Persian empire, this was no longer a problem, and someone had gone there to copy the inscription from the original stele. He identified the inscription by its first words (When the august god Anu), as was the common practice in ancient Mesopotamia, and declared at the end of his tablet:

First tablet of the composition called "When the august god Anu," not complete. Written in accordance with the wording of the original old stele that Hammurabi, king of Babylon, set up in Susa. A clay tablet of Marduk-shumu-usur, son of Mushallim of the city Akkad.

Translation after Fadhil 1998: 726.

existing temples and cults and appeared as traditional pharaohs in representations and inscriptions. The most quoted example of Persian respect for local religions is the case of Jerusalem and its temple. According to the biblical book of *Ezra* Cyrus issued an edict that ordered the temple's rebuilding and promised funding for it. He also allowed the Jews in Babylonian exile to return home. In the first century AD the historian Josephus devoted a whole book in his *Jewish Antiquities* (Book 11) to the project and stated that reading the prophet Isaiah had inspired Cyrus. And indeed that biblical book (*Isaiah* chapters 44–55) presents Cyrus as chosen by the God of Israel to lead its people from exile.

The Persians' general respect and support for existing traditions and the biblical and Babylonian portrayals of Cyrus as a liberator have inspired the idea that the empire was extremely tolerant or at least so in the early decades of its existence. It is true that Persia did not impose cultural or religious practices upon its subjects, but scholars have become more hesitant in accepting this glowing image. In particular, the idea that Cyrus was an enlightened promoter of human rights, which remains strong in popular imagination, is contested. Pragmatism guided the Persians' attitude toward their subjects' traditions. They knew how to insert themselves into existing ideologies in order to make their rule acceptable.

15.4   The Creation of an Imperial Structure

The official rhetoric stated clearly that the Persian empire was a heterogeneous entity made up of numerous peoples and states. But it was also a unified state and the king in person provided the bond that kept the various parts together. He was "king of kings" and the founders of the empire had to create an infrastructure to buttress his special status. As a small country Persia did not have the trappings of imperial rule, so the first rulers developed those borrowing heavily from earlier empires. First, there was the need for a capital city and the early Persians set up several of these in the core of the empire (see box 15.1). Cyrus founded Pasargadae in the late 540s, allegedly on the site where he had defeated the Mede Ishtumegu. Darius started to construct Persepolis in 518 and he and his successors turned it into the most grandiose expression of imperial rule. Its treasury was so rich that according to Roman sources it took 10,000 pairs of mules and 5,000 camels to remove its contents after Alexander seized it. Nearby these two capitals were the tombs of most Persian kings – a freestanding building for Cyrus near Pasargadae and rock cut tombs near Persepolis – which indicate that these were considered their primary residences. Darius also rebuilt the old city of Susa to house a summer palace and other capitals of former kingdoms served the Persian rulers as well.

In the building inscriptions of the palace at Susa Darius stressed how all people of the empire worked on it and that they used resources from all over to do so. Babylonians molded bricks, Ionians carved stone columns, and so on. Timber came from Lebanon in the west and Gandara in the east, silver and ebony from Egypt, ivory from Nubia, Sind, and Arachosia, other materials from elsewhere. This was a clear expression of how the building was an imperial project. Likewise the decorative program at Persepolis showed that it was the center of an empire with varied peoples and resources. The reliefs represented emissaries from all the provinces bearing gifts to the king. Bactrians from Central Asia brought camels, Ionians from the Aegean Sea coast cups, bowls and folded fabrics, Nubians from the region south of Egypt ivory tusks, and so on (figure 15.3). Central in these scenes were images of the king surrounded by courtiers and soldiers, either seated on a throne or standing beneath a parasol, oftentimes receiving the emissaries. Many representations showed Persia's subject peoples holding up the platforms beneath the king's throne (see figure 16.2). The capital cities showed the king's control over all his people. Unlike the Assyrians, however, who showed how their power was based on military strength, the Persians portrayed images of peace and order: all subjects benefited from being part of the empire and voluntarily contributed to its projects.

The empire required an art style that expressed this concept as well. The Persians used many artists from subject territories who had been trained to create in very diverse local traditions and asked them to produce works in an imperial style that incorporated the multiple influences into something entirely new. A freestanding statue of Darius found at Susa shows the wish to synthesize clearly

Box 15.1 *Persian capital cities*

Before the defeat of Babylonia the Persians did not have major cities or a tradition of monumental architecture. One of the necessities of the empire was a capital city, and the Persians constructed several of them in succession. Cyrus built the earliest capital at Pasargadae in central Fars, the homeland of the dynasty. It was a large walled area in which were placed at considerable distance from one another a number of palaces and audience halls, with extensive gardens in between them irrigated with special channels. The Greeks called those gardens *paradeisos*, the basis for our word paradise. Gardens were especially popular among the Persians who laid them out throughout the empire as part of agricultural estates. At Pasargadae there was also a fortified citadel and a cultic area including a fire altar, while Cyrus' tomb stood nearby as a separate building. All the structures were of stone.

Darius moved the capital to Persepolis some 40 kilometers (25 miles) to the south. Construction of the city started in 518 and continued under his two immediate successors. At its center was an enormous platform, 450 by 300 meters, partly carved into the natural rock, partly constructed with layers of cyclopean stones in places 12 meters above the plain. On it stood placed several palaces, audience halls, and a treasury. These buildings were of stone, and prominent in them were tall columns with capitals carved in the shape of griffins and bulls carrying the wooden roof-beams. The columns of the largest building, the *apadana* or reception hall, were almost 20 meters high. Another building contained a hall of one hundred columns. On the sides of the platform was carved a large procession of royal servants, soldiers, and representatives from all satrapies bearing gifts for the king, who was shown seated on his throne. Oftentimes the winged sun disk, probably depicting the god Ahuramazda, was carved above the king. Persepolis extended far beyond the monumental stone buildings that have been excavated. It was one of the main administrative centers of the empire and contained its greatest treasury. It lay at the heart of a fully developed agricultural area with numerous settlements. The tablets found at Persepolis derive from two locations. In the fortifications were found thousands of records of food disbursements to people of widely differing social status, from royal family members to laborers. In the treasury a smaller group records payments to workers. We do not have the imperial archives, however. Alexander of Macedon burned down the city, either deliberately or by accident when he was drunk.

Together with Persepolis, Darius also redeveloped the old city of Susa as a capital, because it had direct access to the western parts of the empire and was cooler in the summer. The work involved a full remodeling of the city's layout with an 18 meter high wall encircling an area of 100 hectares (250 acres) that contained a high citadel, an *apadana* and palace, and a royal town. The constructions were in mud brick and the palace was decorated with glazed brick representations of Persian soldiers and servants (figure 15.1). All of these constructions reveal a mixture of architectural and artistic influences, Assyrian, Babylonian, Greek, Egyptian, and local. The Persians used materials from different parts of the empire and employed specialist workmen from the various regions, not to work in their local styles but to contribute to an imperial form of expression that showed Persia as a multicultural unit.

Figure 15.3   Tribute bearers from Persepolis. Several of the buildings at Persepolis were extensively decorated with stone reliefs. They showed Persian soldiers in full ceremonial dress, as well as long processions of emissaries from the twenty-three provinces of the Persian empire bearing gifts to the king. These can oftentimes be identified because of the gifts they bear. The men shown here bringing a water buffalo to the king were probably Babylonians. Credit: © 2014 De Agostini Picture Library/Scala, Florence.

(figure 15.4). According to the inscription it was sculpted in Egypt and its overall form follows Egyptian principles: the posture with one foot forward and the way the king holds his hands as well as the base with its symbol of the unification of upper and lower Egypt. But the king wears a Persian robe and boots, has an Elamite dagger, and alongside the hieroglyphic inscription are texts in three other languages and two scripts (which we will discuss in detail next). More common in Persian monumental art were relief sculptures, which brought together elements from the traditions of Egypt, Babylonia, Assyria, Elam, Urartu, Ionia, and other parts of Anatolia in a unique whole. Many of these reliefs were on the outside of buildings and tombs, and thus visible to a wide audience. In subject territories the Persians also commissioned hybrid monuments that combined two different styles. In Egypt, for example, Darius set up carved stelae along a canal he had

Figure 15.4 Statue of Darius found at Susa. This statue shows how the Persians mixed artistic styles together in the works produced for their kings. Carved by Egyptians, it shows Darius following Egyptian sculptural practices but wearing Persian clothing and boots. The statue must have been shipped in finished form to Susa for display in Darius' palace unless sculptors worked on it in Iran with stone imported from quarries in the south of Egypt. H. 2.46 m; base height 51 cm, L. 104 cm, W. 64 cm. Greywacke stone. Museum of Tehran. Credit: Perrot, *Le palais de Darius à Suse: une résidence royale sur la route de Persépolis à Babylone* (Paris: Presses de l'Université Paris-Sorbonne, 2010), p. 259.

dug from the Nile to the Red Sea. One side contained a fully Egyptian representation with the traditional symbol of unification and a hieroglyphic text; the other showed the Persian king in imperial style, albeit with Egyptian details, and a trilingual cuneiform inscription.

Monumental writing was very important for the development of an imperial image as well. Before their conquests the Persians did not use script as far as we know and even in the early decades of the empire they had no means to record Old Persian, the Indo-European language they spoke. It was only under Darius in the late sixth century that they developed an entirely new script specific to Old Persian. Almost all the texts preserved in this script are monumental inscriptions and it seems that the language reproduced was not really spoken but of an artificial character. The script was a highly simplified form of cuneiform with only thirty-six basic signs that mostly rendered consonants to be read with any vowel, similar to the practice with Semitic alphabets. Unlike the latter there were also signs to write out the vowels a, i, and u, while five terms were rendered with separate signs (king, country, earth, god, and Ahuramazda). The Old Persian script was not a development from an earlier cuneiform system, although it included elements particular to Urartian. It was almost never used by itself but appeared most often with parallel texts in two other languages written in syllabic cuneiform: Elamite and Babylonian. Sometimes a fourth version in Egyptian hieroglyphs was added. Most scholars believe that it was an invention from the reign of Darius who in the Bisitun inscription wrote that he "made a new form of writing." If this statement indeed refers to Old Persian, the few earlier inscriptions of Cyrus (there are none preserved of Cambyses) would be later fakes. The script went out of use in the reign of Artaxerxes III (ruled 358–338) and was never widespread. By far most texts written in it were monumental royal inscriptions, almost all from the Persian heartland, or brief texts on vases and seals. One administrative document found in Persepolis used it to write out what usually would have been done in Elamite. This may have been a scribal fancy, however. By all indications Darius felt that the emperor needed a special script for the carving of royal statements in the Old Persian language and he introduced the script for that purpose.

Although, as we saw, the Persians maintained local administrative practices, the empire also needed a system that it could use for official business everywhere. For that purpose it selected Aramaic, which had established itself as a common language and script in the western parts earlier on. Mostly written on perishable materials like parchment and papyrus it was widespread in Syria, Anatolia, and Mesopotamia before these regions were integrated into Persia. Aramaic became the language of administration and official correspondence throughout the empire. When the high official Arshama wrote from Babylonia to the steward of his estates in Egypt, for example, he did so in Aramaic: two bags full of his letters have been preserved. Until very recently Aramaic materials were only known from the western part of the empire. A group of thirty parchments and eighteen strips of wood with letters, debt-notes, and administrative records dated to the period from 353 to 324 (that is, after Alexander's conquest of Persia) and written in Aramaic was very recently published (figure 15.5). They were found in northern Afghanistan, the ancient province of Bactria, and deal with local matters involving the Persian governor. The language and expressions used in these texts are exactly the same as in those found in Egypt, which indicates that the scribes and bureaucrats were trained in the same way all over the empire.

An empire needs a ruling class to represent its interests in all its territories. In the Persian empire that elite was made up of true Persians, men who belonged to

Figure 15.5 Tally with an Aramaic text, from Bactria. The spread of Aramaic as the administrative language throughout the Persian empire is clear from parchments and wooden strips that were recently discovered in modern Afghanistan. On this piece of wood an accountant carved sixty-one notches and wrote that unidentified objects were "with Taitaka, from Gauza" in the third year of King Darius. Bactria Khalili collection, London. Credit: The Khalili Collection of Aramaic Documents, T 1; copyright The Khalili Family Trust.

families of the original home country. Babylonians, Egyptians, and others could have high positions, but Persians held the highest ones in government and the army. They formed thus a type of aristocracy that was stationed throughout the empire. The king strengthened personal ties with them by granting special privileges – they ate at the king's table – and large estates. To be a Persian was a mark of distinction that opened up opportunities denied to other subjects of the empire.

A final element that was specific to the empire was in the area of religion and the cult. As we saw, the Persians tolerated and even promoted local gods, but the emperor had a special connection to one god only: Ahuramazda. Old Persian inscriptions constantly invoked the deity as the one who selected the king to rule and supported him. Ahuramazda was the ruler's personal god and the king was the god's representative on earth. In many visual representations the image of the king is beneath a winged disk from which an anthropomorphic figure emerges; scholars most often identify this as a symbol of Ahuramazda. That god was not the only one the Persians recognized but he had a special connection to the dynasty. He inspired truth and correct behavior against what official inscriptions called "the Lie." The cult involved outdoor fire altars rather than closed temples. Because these elements also appear in the later well-attested Zoroastrian religion of Iran, it is possible, yet uncertain, that the Old Persian rulers already adhered to that faith. Zoroastrianism represents the teachings of Zarathustra (Zoroaster in Greek), which are first documented in written form in the ninth century AD, but certainly derive from an earlier time. Suggestions for when exactly Zarathustra lived range throughout the first millennium BC and rely on an analysis of the language used in the *Avesta*, which records his words. Because the dating is uncertain and we do not know the details of the earliest forms of Zoroastrianism it is probably best to conclude that the Persians were followers of the god Ahuramazda whom they saw as the protector of the dynasty, and that several of their ideas and practices became central to later Zoroastrian religion.

All these elements, which were established while the empire was being created, provided a practical and ideological foundation that presented unity within a great diversity. The Persians were remarkably successful in this. Although there were attempts by subject territories to gain independence and violent struggles over succession to the throne, as we will see in the next chapter, the empire never split up into parts ruled by different members of the same family or elite. This happened regularly in later empires, starting with the division of Alexander's empire among his generals. Although they too belonged to the same small ruling class, they broke up the unified territory that the Persians had held together for some two hundred years. That the Persians managed to maintain this unity by itself is a significant fact.

Debate 15.1   *How important were the Greek defeats of Persia to world history?*

In 1846, the English political economist John Stuart Mill remarked: "the battle of Marathon, even as an event in English history, is more important than the battle of Hastings" (which led to the Norman conquest of England). The Greeks' victory at Marathon in 490 over the army of Darius and their subsequent success in resisting a Persian occupation is a David and Goliath story that any student of ancient history knows. This military feat happened at the start of the Classical Greek fifth century when Athens was home to democracy and had made giant strides forward in the fields of philosophy and the arts that had a fundamental impact on later history. Would it have been different if the Greeks had lost?

Counterfactual history is a dangerous business, but not uncommon and recently – because of the 2,500th anniversary of Marathon – several scholars have speculated how disastrous a Greek loss would have been for world history. A book entitled *Marathon: How One Battle Changed Western Civilization* (Billows 2010) ends with the statement that there would have been no democracy, no tragedy, comedy, philosophy, and visual arts as we know them, because the men who shaped these disciplines or their teachers would have been deported to the east. Others have asserted the same for the entire Persian wars, without explaining why (e.g., Pagden 2008: 31), and find evidence for this claim in comparing the vitality of pre-Persian Ionia with its (presumably moribund) intellectual life under Persian rule (Hanson 2007: 3). Also students of Persia have seen Xerxes' defeat as the start of a long decline: Xerxes became intolerant and self-absorbed and his assassination thirteen years later was the start of a long chain of palace intrigues that made the empire an easy prey for Alexander (e.g., Frye 1963: 117–23).

The source material on the Persian wars is extremely biased: we only know of them from testimonies of the Greeks to whom they were of enormous importance. They inspired some of the greatest works of Classical antiquity, including Herodotus' *Histories*. Evidence from Persia is essentially absent. One administrative document from Persepolis dating to 494 may report on the Ionian revolt that triggered the events (Briant 2002a: 148–9), but Persian royal inscriptions did not discuss wars. Darius' defeat at Marathon may have inspired unsuccessful rebellions in Egypt (486) and Babylonia (484), but more likely other reasons lie behind them. These troubles were of much greater concern to the Persians than the events on the periphery and Xerxes dealt with them before taking revenge on Greece. To many scholars his losses there were inconsequential and unimportant (Briant 2002a: 542) and life went on as usual in Persepolis (Kuhrt 2007a: 239). To the Persians it was not a big deal. The Greeks, however, saw their victory as the result of their political and cultural superiority and started a long tradition of contrasting the west to the east, a process of self-definition often called Orientalism (cf. Bridges, Hall & Rhodes 2007).

Can we say for certain that the Persians would have irreparably disrupted the political and intellectual developments in Greece? In politics they sometimes replaced tyrants with democratic regimes in Asia Minor and they did not cause noticeable changes in the intellectual life of Babylonia and Egypt. Their domination could have prevented the devastating Peloponnesian wars that raged through Greece when Athenian artists and thinkers produced their great works. Would they have benefited from the peace? Moreover, while philosophers like Socrates had to survive on payments they received from their students, Babylonian scholars under the Persians received full support from temples that themselves relied on royal munificence. Life could have been more comfortable for intellectuals.

It is clear that modern ideologies determine how we see the past and the historiography of ancient Persia in general is a prime example of this (Harrison 2011). It is hard not to admire the accomplishments of fifth- and fourth-century Greeks and if they had lived in the Persian empire things would have been different. How much so is hard to say, however.

16

Governing a World Empire: Persia

3000	2500	2000	1500	1000	500

521	Darius seizes the throne of Persia
484	Rebellion in Babylonia
404	Egypt secedes from the empire
401	Artaxerxes II and Cyrus the Younger battle at Cunaxa
343	Artaxerxes III recaptures Egypt
334	Alexander marches into Anatolia
331	End of the empire

16.1 Political Developments

All the information about Persia's political history available to us involves the royal house. Political power in Persia, as in all the other states we have discussed, was in the hands of a single ruler who based his legitimacy on descent: he belonged to a dynasty that usually traced its ancestry back to distant times. Royal families tended to become large, and we have seen many cases where competition over the succession to the throne caused major upheavals. This too was the case in the royal house of Persia and led to the best-documented event in the early history of the empire: Darius' usurpation of kingship. Cyrus the Great had become king as the son of Cambyses, grandson of Cyrus, and descendant of Teispes, all of them kings of Anshan. Quite early on in his reign he selected his son Cambyses as crown prince and gave him important military and political tasks. Thus the succession

A History of the Ancient Near East ca. 3000–323 BC, Third Edition. Marc Van De Mieroop.
© 2016 John Wiley & Sons, Inc. Published 2016 by John Wiley & Sons, Inc.

upon Cyrus' death in battle in 530 went smoothly and as a well-prepared adult Cambyses asserted power immediately.

Cambyses did not take similar precautions, however, and in addition spent the last five years of his reign in Egypt, far from the center of the empire. He set the scene for a major power struggle, the details of which have to be extracted from the obviously biased description by the final victor, Darius. We can safely conclude that he was not a legitimate successor to the throne and he took great pains to justify his ascent, commissioning a long apologetic account of it. The most famous version today was carved in three languages (Old Persian, Elamite, and Akkadian) on the rock facade at Bisitun in the main Zagros Mountain valley connecting Babylonia to Iran (see document 16.1 and figure 16.1). The text was

---

Document 16.1 *The Bisitun inscription of Darius*

This inscription, carved in three languages (Old Persian, Elamite, and Akkadian) on the cliff at Bisitun in the Zagros Mountains on the road from Babylon to Ecbatana, is the longest preserved Old Persian text and the only one that comments on specific events. It seems that the Elamite version was carved first and that the Old Persian one was added only later on. The text explains how Darius came to be king of Persia and justifies his seizure of the throne as a return of kingship to the legitimate Achaemenid dynasty. The battles he recounts against many rivals in different parts of the empire show how confused the situation was after the death of Cambyses. There are divergences between the three versions of the text, and the translation of excerpts here is based on the Babylonian version. Whenever the Old Persian text refers to the god Ahuramazda, the Babylonian text uses Bel-Marduk.

I am Darius the king, the son of Hystaspes, the Achaemenid, the King of Kings, the Persian, the king of Persia. . . .

Thus says Darius, the king: These are the countries that listen to me – it is under the protection of the god Ahuramazda that I am their king: Persia, Elam, Babylonia, Assyria, Arabia, Egypt, the Sealand, Sardis, Ionia, Media, Urartu, Cappadocia, Parthia, Drangiana, Aria, Choresmia, Bactria, Sogdiana, Gandhara, Scythia, Sattagydia, Arachosia, and Maka, in total twenty-three countries. . . .

Thus says Darius, the king: This is what I have done in one year under the protection of the god Ahuramazda. After becoming king, I have fought nineteen battles in one year, and under the protection of Ahuramazda I have won them. I have captured nine kings: The Magian named Gaumata, who lied saying: "I am Bardiya, son of Cyrus, king of Persia," and who caused the lands of Persia and Media to rebel; an Elamite called Atrina, who lied saying: "I am the king of Elam," and who caused Elam to rebel; a Babylonian called Nidintu-Bel, who lied saying: "I am Nebuchadnezzar, son of Nabonidus, the king of Babylon," and who caused Babylonia to rebel; a Persian called Martiya, who lied saying: "I am Immanieshu, the king of Elam," and who caused the Elamites to rebel; a Mede called Parmartish, who lied saying: "I am Hashatritu, descendant of Umakishtar," and who caused Media to rebel; a Sagartian called Shitirantahmu, who lied saying: "I am the king of the Sagartians, descendant of Umakishtar," and who caused the Sagartians to rebel; a Margian called Parada, who lied saying: "I am the king of Margia," and caused Margia to rebel; a Persian called Umizdatu, who lied saying:

"I am the son of Cyrus, king of Persia," and who caused Persia to rebel; an Urartian called Arahu, who lied saying: "I am Nebuchadnezzar, son of Nabonidus," and who caused Babylonia to rebel.

Translation after Malbran-Labat 1994: 93–103.

also translated into various languages to be distributed throughout the empire: we know a monumental version from Babylon, written in a local form of Akkadian different from what was used in Bisitun, and an Aramaic one from southern Egypt written on papyrus. Probably Herodotus used one of these translations as the basis for the story he told in his *Histories*. We have thus a very detailed narrative of the events but need a careful reading to unravel what really happened.

Cambyses seems not to have had an heir and when he stayed in Egypt after its conquest his younger brother Bardiya claimed kingship at home. Cambyses rushed back but, according to Herodotus, died on the way. Bardiya abolished

Figure 16.1 Detail of the Bisitun relief. Carved high up the side of a cliff in the Zagros Mountains the relief shows the victorious King Darius with his left foot on top of the "false Bardiya" lying on the ground and faced by nine bound men, who are identified in the epigrams as rebel kings. The last king with the pointed hat, for example, is the Sacian Skunxa. Above the row of captives hovers the figure of the god Ahuramazda. Beneath and on either side of the relief are carved the three versions of the text. Credit: akg images/De Agostini Picture Library/W. Buss.

taxes and military levies for three years in order to gain popular support, yet failed to turn the Persian elite to his side. They killed him, and one of them, Darius, seized the throne for himself. He had no legitimate claim to it and made up an elaborate tale to explain what happened. Cambyses had killed Bardiya before going to Egypt without people knowing it, and during his long absence a priest called Gaumata incited rebellion claiming to be the son of Cyrus. Because Darius knew the truth, he killed the false Bardiya and restored order. Since neither Cambyses nor Bardiya had a son, Darius claimed the throne and he explained why he could do so legitimately. The god Ahuramazda bestowed kingship upon him, but more importantly his lineage gave him the right. The Bisitun inscription starts with the genealogy of Darius, tracing his ancestry back to Achaemenes, the father of Teispes. Darius states: "Eight of our family were kings before; I am the ninth; nine kings we are in succession."[1] He ignored the dynastic line of his predecessors Cyrus and Cambyses, who claimed to be descendants of Teispes, and replaced it with his own ancestors, all descendants of Teispes' father, Achaemenes. From then on the Persian dynasty continued that claim – that is why it is often called Achaemenid. Although Darius was not directly related to Cyrus, he was part of the original dynasty. It was very important that there was a proper succession of kings and afterwards each new king buried his predecessor with full honors to show a correct continuation of power. Even Alexander of Macedon did so when he took over the Persian empire. When the dead body of the last emperor Darius III was brought to him, he sent it to Persepolis for a royal burial near his ancestors.

The dynastic struggles after Cambyses' death had very serious consequences for the empire in that many countries rebelled, including those in its very core: Persia, Media, and Elam. Darius devoted most of his inscription to detailing how he overcame these problems. Throughout the empire rebels proclaimed themselves descendants of the last independent ruler of their states: in Persia a general claimed to be Bardiya, in Media a Fravartish said he was the descendant of Umakishtar, the Mede who had defeated Assyria. In Babylon two men in succession called themselves Nebuchadnezzar, son of Nabonidus, and claimed kingship. Darius said the local men were liars and not of royal blood, since he himself was the legitimate heir to these various thrones. The insurrections lasted several years, from 522 to 519, and Darius and his supporters were often forced to return to a region multiple times to deal with repeated uprisings. When they were preoccupied in one place, people elsewhere claimed independence and it is clear that some of the rebels had support in various countries. Several of them were Persian and Median noblemen and the troubles seem to have been a giant battle over the imperial throne. Darius' task was to make himself accepted as ruler by all the populations and elites. He managed to do so only after prolonged military action and the relief at Bisitun shows him as victorious over ten enemy kings.

These problems may have inspired Darius to consolidate the idea of empire using the tools described in the previous chapter. He developed an official script for royal proclamations (Old Persian), built capitals at Persepolis and Susa, established a firm genealogy of kingship descendant from Achaemenes, and instituted administrative changes, which we will discuss later on. Darius was the one who turned the empire into a well-organized structure.

To ensure that kingship passed on securely from father to son, later kings usually appointed an heir in an official ceremony, but tensions still arose. Greek authors, such as Ktesias who liked to portray Persia as a decadent and intrigue-ridden state, exaggerated the problems and suggested that successful claimants tried to execute all possible rivals. There is clear evidence of several serious struggles. For example, when Artaxerxes II succeeded his father in 404, his brother Cyrus the Younger rebelled and raised an army of 10,000 Greek mercenaries, among them the author Xenophon. In 401 they marched from Syria to Babylonia and engaged Artaxerxes' troops at Cunaxa, 80 kilometers (50 miles) north of Babylon. Cyrus died in the battle, although the Greeks supposedly caused massive losses to the Persian side. They offered to make another Persian king, but all refused because they were not of royal blood. Darius' line thus continued to rule.

The final Persian king was also not in direct line to the throne. Greek sources claim that the eunuch Bogoas assassinated Artaxerxes III in 338 and two years later assassinated his son and successor, Artaxerxes IV, and then raised a cousin of Artaxerxes III, Darius III Ochos, to power before being purged himself soon afterwards. This is probably a fabrication as Babylonian evidence suggests otherwise, but Darius III indeed was not the chosen heir. He suffered Alexander's invasion of the empire and, again according to Greek sources, is said to have died in a conspiracy by his own noblemen. One of them, Bessus, the governor of Bactria, declared himself King Artaxerxes IV, and Alexander could now present himself as the avenger of the betrayed king and his legitimate successor. By then, the Persian empire had ended, however.

16.2 Administration of the Empire

Herodotus tells us that Darius organized the empire into twenty provinces, to which he gave the label "satrapies," a term we still use today. The word has no Persian origin, but was based on the Greek rendering of the Old Persian term for "protector of the kingdom," a title we now see as the governor's and render as satrap. Herodotus probably knew only of the administrative system as it had developed over various reigns. It is likely, however, that Darius sought to diminish the autonomy of regional elites after the rebellions at the start of his reign by imposing a more centralized structure of government. The boundaries of the satrapies coincided more or less with pre-Persian entities, but they could be redrawn if the king wished to do so. Xerxes, for example, split the gigantic province of Babylonia into two and made the area west of the Euphrates into a separate "Beyond the River," with its capital probably at Damascus. He also reduced the size of Lydia. In the fourth century Caria and Lycia were combined into a single satrapy.

Satraps were almost always Persians or Iranians and they were appointed for indefinite periods of time. Their loyalty had to be absolute and the king kept himself informed through agents at the local courts whom the Greeks called his "Eyes and Ears," and whom they considered to be a kind of intelligence service. He also stationed military garrisons that would keep his local representatives in line at strategic locations. Although no correspondence between the imperial court and the satraps has survived, there are clear indications in various sources that contacts in writing were intense and the king must have dealt constantly with requests. One of the empire's major accomplishments was its system of royal roads with rest houses at regular intervals, where precedence was given to the king's emissaries. The most famous road was that from Sardis to Susa, a distance of some 2,500 kilometers (1,550 miles), which a man could cover in ninety days, according to Herodotus. Other roads connected Central Asia and Egypt to the Persian heartland. Travelers carried passports that ordered local officials to provide them with food and fodder for their horses.

The satrapal system was very flexible and the Persians often adapted preexisting situations to suit their purposes best. Certain regions were very difficult to control with a regular army, so the emperor made arrangements with their inhabitants that gave them privileges in return for loyalty. That was the case with Zagros Mountain people and Palestinian Arabs, for example, whose leaders received financial rewards for acknowledging Persian supremacy. Elsewhere, local dynasts became satraps of the Persian king. In Caria, on the southwest Anatolian coast, an indigenous dynasty still ruled in the fourth century, more than 150 years after the area had been incorporated into the empire. Its most famous member was Mausolus (ruled 377–353), who acknowledged in his inscriptions that he was a satrap although he behaved in many respects like a king. He moved his capital to Halicarnassus on the coast, where he created a court with many majestic monuments the architecture and style of which merged Greek, Anatolian, and Persian influences. His tomb – the Mausoleum of Halicarnassus – was one of the seven wonders of the ancient world. Greek sources claim that he joined a rebellion against Persia, but there is no proof for that. On the contrary, he promoted Persian interests by acting against neighboring rebels and fomenting strife between Athens and its allies. He did gain great wealth and territorial influence, probably benefiting from his association with the empire.

Beyond its borders as well, Persia maintained a pragmatic approach to its diplomatic relations. As we saw it had a treaty with Athens before the Persian wars, which it felt the Athenians broke when they assisted the Ionian revolt. Before Xerxes invaded Greece he offered the city-states the option to submit, which several of them did. Also, after the Persians had withdrawn from Europe, they kept up strong diplomatic influence. They readily gave refuge to Greek politicians who had fallen into disgrace at home – Alcibiades of Athens, for example. Late in the empire's existence there is evidence both of treaties of friendship and alliance between Persia and Macedon and of Greeks, such as Demosthenes, looking for Persian help in averting a Macedonian take-over. Diplomatic missions went back and forth. At other borders too the Persians made arrangements with their neighbors, as archaeological evidence indicates. Scythian tombs as far away as the Altai Mountains near China contained carpets that may have originated in Persia and were donated as diplomatic gifts, and local dynasts in Georgia and Armenia imitated Persian palaces for their residences, which demonstrates contacts between the empire and these regions.

Figure 16.2   Façade of a royal tomb, probably of Xerxes, at Naqsh-i-Rustam. The façades of the rock-cut tombs of Persian kings showed the emperor worshipping the god Ahuramazda while standing on top of a platform held aloft by figures representing the various peoples of the empire. Thirty men are shown here, each one with specific physical features and local dress. The identification of the tomb is not certain, but since it imitates that of Darius closely, scholars assume it belonged to his son Xerxes. Credit: The Art Archive/Collection Dagli Orti.

With this flexible attitude it is no surprise that the territories and people included in the empire were not invariable. There exists no straight inventory of Persia's subjects, only a set of lists that enumerate peoples under the king's control – regularly they are represented as supporting his throne (figure 16.2). From Darius' reign there are at least five such lists and he also recorded who contributed to the building of his palace at Susa (cf. chapter 15). The latter text included sixteen peoples, while those enumerated in the lists range from twenty-three to twenty-nine. A list from the time of Xerxes gives thirty-one names. The core regions remain constant – Persia, Media, Elam, Babylonia, etcetera – but those on the periphery vary: Libya, Ethiopia (that is, Nubia), and Caria for example do not always appear. In addition, the Persepolis procession of tributaries presents this idea: twenty-three groups of delegates are represented each in their national dress and bringing animals and gifts typical of their homeland. No text accompanies the images and modern identifications are based on the nature of their dress and gifts and parallels with the images of throne bearers. These are idealized visions and not certain indicators of administrative control.

The closest we get to a systematic account of the empire's provinces is a list Herodotus provides as the outcome of Darius' reforms. It identifies twenty provinces, each of which had to pay tribute in amounts of silver, sometimes with additional gifts in the form of a local specialty: for example, 360 white horses from Cilicia, one for each day of the year. Herodotus states that the Indians were the most numerous and had to pay the highest tribute, exceptionally in gold dust. The total amount gathered from the entire empire was 14,560 talents silver, that is, 376,522 kilograms. In addition, Herodotus writes, other people provided gifts; for example, Ethiopians gave gold, ebony, elephant tusks, and boys, while Arabs gave frankincense (see document 16.2). There are certainly errors in Herodotus' account – Persia was not tax-exempt as he claimed, for instance – but it is hard to doubt that the empire extracted an enormous wealth from its subjects. It also collected duties from ships that anchored in its harbors and on riverine trade, and sales of slaves and probably other commodities carried a tax. A major asset was its control over irrigation water, which was essential for most farmers in its territories. Records from Babylonia show that people had to pay fees for it. Herodotus (Book III, 117) claims that the Persian king blocked off tributaries from flowing into a river in Central Asia and only opened the gates after he had received huge payments from the farmers. This was a folktale but suggests how he regulated this resource.

Document 16.2   *Taxes of the Persian provinces according to Herodotus*

The Persian empire certainly had to raise taxes for it to function, and although the amounts extracted must have been enormous none of the documents preserved from it gives us details. Only the Greek historian Herodotus provides a comprehensive list, which he states reflects the situation as Darius created it when he reorganized the empire into twenty satrapies. Even if certain elements are clearly wrong, the list gives an idea about the extent of the empire and its numerous subjects. What follows are extracts from Book III of Herodotus' Histories.

(89) Having done these things in Persia, Darius set up twenty provinces, which they call satrapies. He set up the provinces and appointed governors, and set the tribute they should pay according to the peoples. He included with each people the ones living nearby, and those living far away he allotted to this or that group. (...)

(90) From the Ionians, the Magnesians in Asia, Aeolians, Carians, Lycians, Milyans, and Pamphylians (who paid their tribute as one), there came 400 talents of silver. This formed the first district. (...)

(91) From the city of Posideium, founded by Amphilochus, the son of Amphiareus, on the frontier between the Cilicians and Syrians, up to Egypt, with the exception of the Arabs (who were not subject to tax), the tribute was 350 talents. In this district was the whole of Phoenicia, the so-called Palestinian Syria and Cyprus – the fifth district. (...)

(92) From Babylon and the rest of Assyria came 1,000 talents of silver and 500 boys for castration; this being the ninth district. (…)

(94) The number of Indians is greater than any other people we know of and they brought in more tribute than the others – 360 talents of gold dust; this being the twentieth district.

(95) Converting the Babylonian silver into the Euboean talent, it comes to 9,880 talents; reckoning the gold as thirteen times worth the silver, the gold dust is worth 4,680 Euboean talents. Adding it all up, the total yearly tribute in Euboean talents for Darius was 14,560. I omit the bits less than a talent.

(97) Now these were the provinces and the settings of the tribute rates. Persis is the only region I have not listed as paying tribute, for the Persians held the land free of tax. The following do not pay a set tribute, but bring gifts: the Ethiopians next to Egypt, subjected by Cambyses when he campaigned against the long-lived Ethiopians (…) These two together bring every second year (and they were still doing so in my day) four pounds of unrefined gold, two hundred logs of ebony, five Ethiopian boys and twenty large elephant tusks. (…) The Arabs brought a thousand talents of frankincense every year. These were the gifts they brought to the king over and above the tribute.

Translation from Kuhrt 2007a: 673–5.

16.3   Local Forms of Persian Administration

It is no surprise that the concrete impact of the empire on its many territories varied enormously. It incorporated lands with very different environments and the practices that existed prior to the empire continued to play a great role under Persian rule. All provinces and the regions within them had their peculiarities and could be analyzed separately. The nature of the evidence varies greatly: from some places there are abundant textual data (e.g., Babylonia and Egypt), while for others archaeology provides most of the information (especially the eastern satrapies). We will concentrate here on three regions in the Near Eastern part of the empire where the documentation is relatively rich and it is possible to reconstruct at least some of the administrative and economic practices in detail: Persia, the political center of the empire; Babylonia, with its well-known age-old traditions; and Judah as a subdivision of the "Beyond the River" satrapy. The documentation in each focuses on a limited set of activities that rarely overlap, so it is hard to determine whether the practices attested were purely regional or in use elsewhere as well.

Persia was the heartland of the empire and the homeland of its dynasty and the political elite. As we saw, by far the majority of the highest functions in government and the military were in the hands of Persians, who must have kept contacts with the region even if they were stationed far away. This part of southwest Iran was mountainous and had lush valleys and plains, and when the Persians migrated into it in the early first millennium they found it virtually uninhabited, it seems. They did not become sedentary farmers at first but lived as pastoralists,

moving seasonally and leaving few archaeological remains. That changed drastically when kings Cyrus and Darius constructed capitals at Pasargadae and Persepolis, both of them large cities with monumental buildings and substantial residential areas. Development did not stop there, however. State initiative turned the
land of Persia into a lush countryside with a large sedentary population and rich
agricultural estates. Those were for the benefit of Persian nobles and included
fields, orchards, gardens, and hunting grounds. They were *paradeisoi* in Greek
eyes, worked by local and imported farmers, foresters, and other laborers, and
the state actively promoted their development. It dug and maintained irrigation canals and provided, for example, seedlings of fruit trees for planting. One
record from Persepolis accounts for 6,166 trees in five estates nearby, primarily
apple, pear, and an unidentified fruit tree. These estates were the envy of Greek
travelers.

We know how the state managed the region from two archives excavated at
Persepolis: one of about 100 records was found in the Treasury, the other – massive in size – in the Fortifications. The exact number of preserved documents is
uncertain. Estimates range between 15,000 and 18,000. These are all clay tablets
inscribed primarily with Elamite texts written in cuneiform. A large number has
Aramaic notes impressed in the clay or written in ink, and other languages are
attested as well: one tablet each in Greek, Phrygian, and Old Persian, and two in
Babylonian. There are also several hundred tablets without any writing but with
one to four seals impressed on them, which must have served as some kind of
receipt. Although the preserved numbers are large, the actual archives at Persepolis must have been vastly larger. The Fortification archive, as we know it, only
covers the years 509 to 494 and half of it comes from 500 and 499. The Treasury
texts are from 490 to 459, two-thirds of them from the year 466 alone. Entire
sectors of the economy, such as textile production, are not documented in them.
Thus large quantities of other clay tablets must have existed, as well as numerous
parchments and papyri.

As was the case in earlier Near Eastern states, such as under the Ur III dynasty,
the accounting was extremely detailed and included small individual transactions
as well as comprehensive annual summaries. The purview of the Fortification
tablets was almost entirely local and dealt with the collection and distribution of
agricultural produce: cereals, fruit, wine, beer, large and small cattle, and poul-
try. That the state saw this as important is clear from the fact that Darius' uncle
was in charge between 506 and 497. The state used a type of ration system and
many tablets record the distribution of food to workers of all levels as well as to
royal messengers. The Fortification archive held many tablets written in regional
centers and sent to Persepolis. The Treasury tablets dealt with precious materials
and included authorizations for payments of silver to craftsmen, including foreigners from Egypt, Babylonia, Bactria, Ionia, etcetera. Both the archaeological
and textual evidence shows thus that the empire had a radical impact on its heartland. Using a centralized administration that borrowed earlier Elamite practices it
turned a region of pastoralists into a prosperous district with agricultural estates
that fed the inhabitants of villages, towns, and small and large cities.

The conditions in Babylonia were very different from those in Persia before the empire. The region had known peace and economic development for almost a century under Neo-Babylonian rule and the inhabitants of its great ancient cities satisfied their needs from rich agricultural areas nearby. Moreover, Babylonia had age-old bureaucratic practices and a massive number of cuneiform tablets are preserved from the Neo-Babylonian period. When Cyrus annexed the region he took over a well-organized and flourishing economy, and we do not see any break in the administration until fifty-five years later. The empire did interfere, however, and confiscated huge tracts of land for its own purposes. It awarded some of it as estates to its nobles, not only officials stationed in the region but also many active elsewhere. Arshama, the satrap of Egypt in the late fifth century, for example, had several estates in Babylonia, as did Queen Parysatis. They were thus absentee landlords.

The crown spread the use of the land far beyond the nobility, however. Numerous men were given the rights to fields and in return had to provide service to the state, especially in the military. These fields were grouped into corporations mostly defined by what the holders did for the state, and a royal official supervised each one of these units. There were bow-lands for archers, chariot-lands for charioteers, horse-lands for cavalry, and also units for artisans, and agricultural and administrative occupations. Some were named after the institutions to which people were attached or after their original homeland. The holders could divide the land among heirs, make it part of a dowry, or use it as collateral for loans, but they could not sell it. They only had the right to its use and many of them did not work the fields in person but engaged tenant farmers to do so.

The organization of all this was complex and, unlike in Persia where the crown kept track of everything, in Babylonia this was the work of private entrepreneurs often active in family firms. One such family was called Murashu and its archive of some 700 tablets dating from 440 to 416 was excavated at Nippur (figure 16.3). The Murashu managed the estates both of prominent men like Arshama and of small landowners. They found farmers, collected fees, provided loans when needed, and converted agricultural produce into silver. In many ways they acted like the entrepreneurs of Old Babylonian times (cf. chapter 5). Because they also provided credit, farmers were regularly indebted to them and, unlike their Old Babylonian predecessors, the Persian kings may not have abolished these debts. Scholars debate the issue, however, as Herodotus claims that Bardiya did so to win popular support for his claim to the throne at the end of Cambyses' reign. Some believe that this was pure rhetoric while others think that debt remission was not an unusual occurrence in the Persian era. In any case, the private businessmen were crucial to the management of the Babylonian economy and mostly thrived as a result.

The Murashu archive dates to the second half of the fifth century and shows a family of Babylonians working hand-in-hand with the Persians. Cooperation had not always been that smooth, however. Even if the Persians had adopted Babylonian practices and administrators early in the empire, they had to assert their authority and break the power of long-established families. A serious

Figure 16.3 Tablet from the Murashu archive. Babylonian scribal skills continued unabated in the Persian era. This tablet dated to the thirty-ninth year of King Artaxerxes is part of the Murashu family archive and contains a carefully written cuneiform text as well as a short note in Aramaic written on an area left blank by the cuneiform scribe. Clay, 6.3 × 7.5 × 2.6 cm, from Nippur. Credit: Courtesy of Penn Museum, image number B5304.

crisis occurred in the second year of King Xerxes' rule (484): in that summer two Babylonian men started rebellions in different parts of northern Babylonia. Bel-shimanni and Shamash-eriba gained support in several cities where scribes called them "king of Babylon" in the date formulae of the tablets they wrote. The first rebel survived perhaps only two weeks, the second three months, and either they ended up fighting each other or joined forces before Xerxes crushed them. At this time a large number of archives from north Babylonian cities ceased to function, which indicates that the families to whom they belonged lost their economic power. All were old families that had strong ties with the temples and gained income from them, except for the Egibi family mentioned before, which was closely associated with the provincial governor of Babylon, an office that disappeared around this time. Some families of northern Babylonia continued their businesses, however, as did those from the south. The survivors in the north were relative newcomers who had benefited from the Persians by serving them as managers in the same way as the Murashu did later on. They and the families from the south had not joined the rebellion, but those who had, Xerxes brought to ruin. The revolt thus probably produced a firmer Persian control over Babylonia than before, which lasted uninterrupted until Alexander's victory at Gaugamela in 331.

Possibly in reaction to the rebellion, Xerxes split the satrapy of Babylonia in two, making the area from the Euphrates to the Egyptian border into the new province "Beyond the River." This was still a vast territory that included many different political entities and economic conditions: Syrian agricultural areas, Phoenician harbors for maritime trade, hill countries and desert zones. Within this mix was the land of Judah around the city Jerusalem, which Nebuchadnezzar II had sacked in 587 and whose population he had deported to Babylonia. As we saw, one reason for Cyrus' reputation as a liberator was the permission he gave the Judeans to return home and rebuild their temple. To reconstruct Judah's history we rely on very heterogeneous sources that are unevenly spread over time. They include two short biblical books, *Ezra* and *Nehemiah*, as well as brief administrative accounts written in ink on potsherds – we give them the Greek name ostraca – mostly in Aramaic. Stamps with short inscriptions impressed on jar handles and coins also give some idea of administrative practices. The archaeology of the region provides important information too.

Judah was a small area located in the highlands and surrounded by other administrative subdivisions of the satrapy. To its west the Mediterranean coast was of great importance to the Persians because of its harbors, and Phoenician leaders had been given authority over the entire zone. The harbors gave access to overseas trade and were crucial for Persia's military actions in Greece, the Mediterranean islands, and Egypt. The inland areas were of much less interest to the Persians, however, because economic assets there were limited and the land had been neglected in Neo-Babylonian times. The province of Samaria, which the Assyrians had subdued in the distant past, still had a substantial population and its capital Samaria was a fortified city. Judah on the other hand only had a small population and its capital Jerusalem had been sacked in the early sixth century. The Bible suggests that three substantial waves of exiles returned to Judah from Babylonia: one immediately after Cyrus created the empire, the second early in Darius' reign, and the third in the mid-fifth century when Ezra and Nehemiah led the community and turned Jerusalem into a great city once again. Archaeology shows this not to be true. The population of Judah remained limited, with exiles returning as individual families, and Jerusalem stayed small even when its walls were rebuilt around 445. No rich tombs or other finds show great wealth, and most people lived in villages and farmsteads. Politically Judah may have been under the authority of the governor of Samaria until the mid-fifth century and only with Nehemiah's mission did it become the capital. According to the biblical book of *Nehemiah* he was a Persian courtier at Susa who asked King Artaxerxes for permission to rebuild the city, still in ruins, and as governor he implemented strict adherence to Jewish law. The centralization of power in Jerusalem may have been a method to strengthen the ties between the community and the temple hierarchy.

Little concrete evidence of administrative practices exists until the fourth century, when there is a substantial number of ostraca, some from Judah itself, but primarily from the region to its immediate south. A large group published as the Idumea ostraca and of unknown provenance, as they appeared on the antiquities market, contains the detailed records of payments mostly in cereals and of the hire of day laborers. There is no evidence that the government required such accounting but it is possible that the fact that Egypt was independent at this time triggered a firmer grasp of the empire over this region. Archaeology shows that the Persians fortified the region south of Judah then.

Some of the accounts mention the names of governors of Judah and of high priests of Jerusalem. That Jews throughout the empire felt a special relationship with these authorities is clear from a set of papyri excavated at Elephantine on the southern border of Egypt. A colony of Jewish mercenaries had existed there from before the Persian conquest and its members left behind a rich collection of letters, contracts, accounts, and even literary texts (such as the Ahiqar story, cf. chapter 10), written on papyri in the Aramaic language. A small group of these document a quarrel between this community and its Egyptian neighbors, which festered for at least three years. Most informative is a long letter from the priests of Elephantine to a governor of Judah called Bagohi. This is a Persian name but most likely he was a Judean. The writers recall that three years earlier, in the summer of 410, priests of the Egyptian god Khnum with the support of the local Persian official had destroyed the temple of Yahweh. They did so when the Persian satrap Arshama, known to us otherwise from his correspondence, was out of the county. This, they claimed, was an old sanctuary, which Cambyses had respected when he conquered Egypt. Its existence seems to have been against official Jewish law, but it was not the only such temple at the time. The Elephantine priests had written to the high priest of Jerusalem and notables of Judah before for help in its rebuilding but no one had replied. Now they implored Bagohi to use his connections in Egypt and obtain assistance for a new temple, and they ended the letter by mentioning that they had also contacted the sons of Sanballat, the governor of Samaria. What exactly happened is unclear. Many scholars now reject an old idea that Egyptian priests wanted to eradicate a foreign cult and they imagine that a more mundane property dispute was the source of contention. The case illustrates how Jewish communities outside Judah saw Jerusalem and its political and religious leaders as authorities that were relevant to them. Other documents in the dossier show that the Persian satrap Arshama ultimately settled things by ordering the temple to be rebuilt. He was thus drawn into such local matters.

The three cases discussed here show that the Persians adapted their administration to local circumstances. In Persia the new regime kept close track of everything itself, in Babylonia it continued the use of private intermediaries but also made sure to assert its authority, and perhaps only belatedly it organized a centralization of power in Judah through local officials. This flexibility is not a sign of laissez-faire, however. The Persians were very eager to develop the economic potential of its various territories and financed large infrastructural works to do so. They constructed irrigation systems to enable agriculture on the Iranian plateau and in the Egyptian desert oases. The empire's mere existence must have facilitated trade, as the world from the Nile to the Indus was under one political regime. But public works encouraged it further. Darius dug a canal from the Nile to the Red Sea to make it possible to ship bulk goods from Egypt to Persia. The empire developed the harbors on the Mediterranean, which gave it access to resources from the west, and also linked up the entire coastal area from Anatolia to Egypt. Ships from Ionia and the Levant imported oil, wine, metals, wood, wool, and other products into Egypt, for instance, and exported natron, a chemical needed for textile manufacture, and other Egyptian goods in return. Clearly, overseas trade crossed political boundaries. Greek merchants were active in Egypt under Persian rule and Syro-Palestinian traders traveled all over the Mediterranean. In the eastern territories sea trade must also have existed across the Arabian and Indian seas, but the available evidence is extremely slim.

Over time Persian rule started to influence local cultures and Persian customs spread. Local coinage and seals show Persian motifs, while high officials may have changed their clothing and habits to reflect Persian practice (see box 16.1). While respect for local traditions was a Persian characteristic, this did not prevent local people from trying to imitate imperial styles. We see that the two poles, local and central, interacted in various ways with each other throughout the empire. There was no eradication of local traditions, religious or otherwise, but rather a respect for them. On the other hand, the longevity of Persian control over the region had its unifying effects over time.

Box 16.1   *Coinage in the Persian empire*

A question historians have not been able to resolve is the importance of coinage in the Persian empire. Coins are small, portable disks of precious metal, stamped with an official mint that guarantees their value, and around 650 people from Lydia in western Anatolia had started to produce them. The earliest coins were made of electrum, a locally available mixture of silver and gold. Sometime later, others minted coins of pure gold and silver: each region or city could produce its own coins with distinctive stamps. They facilitated trade, as they provided an easily portable, guaranteed means of exchange. When Cyrus conquered Anatolia he encountered the use of gold and silver coins there, but it seems that only under Darius did the Persians start to mint them. Greek sources refer to gold darics – most probably named after King Darius – and silver *sigloi*, a word derived from the Semitic term shekel (although they did not weigh one shekel while a gold daric did). A substantial number of coins have been preserved from the Persian era, but it is clear that the empire did not consider them a tool to be applied systematically. The production of coins certainly was not an imperial prerogative. Many different types were in use: royal coins, which often seem to represent the king as a warrior (figure 16.4), coins issued by satraps and other officials, and Greek coins, either minted in Greek cities under Persian rule or in independent ones, such as Athens. All the mints were in the westernmost part of the empire, which is also where coins were mostly used. In regions such as Babylonia coins did not function as measures of value, and in Persepolis they were accounted for by their weight. Greek texts state that the salary of a non-officer mercenary was one daric per month and the empire seems to have paid out coins regularly, but it never turned them into the exclusive or even preferred form of payment. The imagery on royal coins suggests that they functioned as symbols of power, but this did not lead to a prohibition for others to issue coins.

Figure 16.4   Gold daric coin. Persian imperial coinage often showed the king as a warrior, an image rare in the official reliefs that focus on peace. Only the obverse of the coin has a representation, the reverse contains a rectangular punch. This coin was minted in Asia Minor where all royal mints were located. British Museum, London (CM 1919-05-16-16 (BMC Persia 60)). Late fifth or early fourth century. Diameter 17 mm, weight 9.440 g. Credit: © The Trustees of the British Museum.

16.4   The End of the Empire

After 479, when Xerxes abandoned his attempts to conquer Greece, the sources for a political history of Persia become slim. Although the writings of the Greek physician Ktesias, who resided at the court in the early fourth century, have only survived in brief later excerpts, they have been very influential in modern considerations of the era. Ktesias placed great focus on intrigues, especially when they involved royal women, and created an impression of decadence within the court, from which historians have extrapolated that the entire empire was in trouble. Xenophon's account of the bloody war for succession between Artaxerxes II and his brother Cyrus the Younger, which ended with the latter's death in 401, seemed to confirm the image that instability characterized Persia's history from Xerxes' reign until the conquest by Alexander in the 330s. This view is now very much contested, however (see debate 16.1), and scholars instead stress the signs of continuity in governmental practices until the end of the empire. The still relatively rich evidence from Babylonia shows that cultural and scholarly activity continued there unabated and archives such as that of the Murashu family illustrate how the state successfully worked together with locals to develop agriculture.

Debate 16.1   *Were the Persians decadent?*

In 1975 a leading scholar of ancient Iran concluded an article studying a tri-lingual inscription from Anatolia in the Persian era with these remarks:

This is just a small event in the spotlight when compared to the tragedy of Shakespearean proportions that at the same time was shown on the bigger stage of the Persian empire in the final years of the aged Artaxerxes II, which were filled with family murders, intrigues and assaults, and in the beginning of the reign of Artaxerxes III who only knew how to secure his power as ruler by assassinating all princes. Our inscription, so delightful for linguists and historians of religion, takes the historian into a dark dying world in which the brilliance of Alexander's charismatic emergence had not yet penetrated. Nevertheless we cannot turn away from it: or to say it in the words of one of the deepest historical thinkers: " ... also the periods of decline and failure have the sacred right to our sympathy." (Mayrhofer 1975: 282, my translation)

These words of doom reflect a sentiment that was far from unusual until recently. Scholars and popular opinion customarily saw the ancient Persians as a decadent people, spoiled by excessive luxuries, cruel, and inflicting what Mayrhofer called agony upon their subjects, who could only wait for the "springtime" that Alexander would bring. They found abundant inspiration for these ideas in Greek sources. The philosopher Plato, for example, saw the roots of the Persian problems in the imbalance between "servitude and freedom" and blamed the lack of strictness in education. They were no longer raised in the open fields but in harems under the supervision of women and eunuchs (cf. Briant 2002b). Because many Greeks admired the founder of the empire Cyrus, they saw this weakness as a historical development connected to their own engagement with the Persians. After Xerxes had failed to conquer Greece he became increasingly eccentric and his reign started a cycle of senseless violence and palace intrigues. Especially malicious in this respect were women, whose prominent role in Persian society was in direct opposition to that of Greek women. Ammunition for these views was easily found in the writings of Ktesias, whose alleged eyewitness account of Persian court life reveled in sordid details (cf. Sancisi-Weerdenburg 1987).

Because moral decrepitude is not the most convincing historical explanation, scholars tried to find more concrete elements in Persian behavior that led to the empire's weakness. Foremost in their minds was the despotism of rulers, "receptive of the flattery of courtiers and officials who would say only what they thought the King would wish to hear" (Cook 1983: 132). Persia crushed the population with heavy taxes (Ghirshman 1954: 200), on top of which it demanded humiliating gifts, such as the five hundred Babylonian boys for castration (Olmstead 1948: 289–99). The subjects rebelled and were unwilling to defend the empire. In response the Persians had to rely more heavily on Greek mercenaries, but they were too stingy to pay them well (Cook 1983: 220). Still, the empire had too much wealth and wasted it on a lavish lifestyle. Greek writings always provided sufficient evidence for such statements and we cannot discount them as pure fantasy. There were many Persian customs whose full meaning the Greeks did not grasp and they could turn these differences with their own habits into signs of decadence. Banquets were an important aspect of court ceremony that tied the king to his nobles, for example, but it was easy to see them as extravagances (Harrison 2011: 57–72).

When historians of ancient Persia started to focus more on materials from the empire itself, and, when they became more sensitive to the biases contained in the Greek narratives, they were able to deconstruct many of these negative elements. The perceived structural weaknesses of the state were either chosen policies – such as the careful balancing between local autonomies and central control – or the natural outcome of the underlying system – in any monarchy the death of a king is disruptive (Wiesehöfer 2007).

But the Persian empire was not a failure at all: it survived for two hundred years, resisted Alexander for more than a decade, and its Seleucid successors adopted many of its governmental practices (Kuhrt 1995: 701). One of the great, unanswered questions does remain, however: why did it succumb to the minor kingdom of Macedon to its west (Kuhrt 1995: 675, Briant 2002b: 210 note 20)?

The empire was never fully pacified and rebellions did occur, especially when a king died and his successor had to assert his authority. Much of the instability this caused seems to have been the result of fights among the Persian elites, however. The most restive province was Egypt, which rebelled repeatedly, for example late in Darius' reign (486). Possibly taking advantage of the war between Artaxerxes II and Cyrus the Younger after Darius II's death in 405, the country managed to secede for sixty years (404–343). Interestingly, Egypt's kingship in that period changed hands many more times than in Persia (seven times versus once), with various families competing for it, and not all Egyptians seem to have preferred the native dynasts over the Persians. In the year 400 inhabitants of Elephantine still acknowledged Artaxerxes II as their king. Egypt's wealth must have enabled the various contenders to acquire Greek mercenary services and kings also used them to raid the Syro-Palestinian coast, possibly to prevent a Persian naval build-up there. Yet in 343 Artaxerxes III managed to recapture the country, which shows that the empire was still able to assert itself.

Perhaps the existence of the Persian empire encouraged people at its borders to join together into more centralized territorial states, and late in its history the foundations of the Mauryan empire developed in northern India, while the Kingdom of Macedon united the entirety of Greece. The latter state brought about Persia's downfall. In origin a small kingdom remote from the political and cultural developments in Greece, it became the dominant power in the area under King Philip, who reigned from 359 to 336. He imposed Macedonian rule over the Greek city-states in 338 and the next year declared war on Persia. His assassination prevented him from starting an invasion, but his son Alexander did not wait long to do so. In 334 he marched his army into Anatolia with a great deal of nerve. At first his situation was quite precarious as he did not control the sea and had to rely on local supplies for rearming his troops. But his hard won victories over the harbors of Tyre and Gaza eliminated Persia's naval capabilities and guaranteed contacts with the home front. A continuous ten year campaign followed in which he led his troops throughout the Persian empire, annexing all its satrapies. King Darius III offered fierce resistance in the battles of Issus in northwest Syria (333) and Gaugamela in northern Iraq (331), but was finally defeated. Classical sources portray Alexander's conquest as a deliverance from oppressive Persian rule, and the people of Egypt and Babylonia, for example, are supposed to have welcomed him eagerly. This is to a great extent Macedonian propaganda, however, and most people probably saw little difference between the old and new regimes. Alexander did appeal successfully to the political and religious elites in order to be accepted as the local king, just as the Persian Cyrus had done. He promoted cults, as an earlier ruler would have. At Babylon, for example, he initiated extensive reconstruction of the Marduk temple, including the (unfinished) rebuilding of the ziggurat. He also wanted to be considered the legitimate king of Persia, and buried Darius III with full ceremony after the latter had been assassinated by his own courtiers. Alexander married a local princess, Roxane, and urged his generals to find local wives as well. When in 324 his soldiers refused to campaign further, he returned to Babylon, where he set up his capital. He seems to have adopted the ceremonial habits of the Persians, including their duty to prostrate themselves in front of him. He was certainly much impressed by Near Eastern customs and traditions and, for instance, saw himself as the son of the Egyptian god Amun. This behavior may have led to the disenchantment of his Macedonian men, and it is possible, though not widely accepted among historians, that his death in Babylon in 323 was an assassination.

Soon afterwards his generals carved up the enormous empire Alexander had created. The Near East, Iran, and parts of Central Asia came to be ruled by the dynasty of Seleucus, which used northern Babylonia as its political and administrative center. The extent of the Seleucid empire, which was to last for two hundred years, was originally similar to that of the Persians, except for Egypt. Until recently, scholars subscribed to the classical image of the Near East as tired and decadent by the fourth century, and that Alexander and his successors brought new life to it. This image of revitalization provided an example of, and justification for, nineteenth-century European colonial enterprise in regions that had known a glorious past but had not modernized. Although Hellenism was seen as the merging of European and Asian traditions, its vitality was thought to derive from Greek cultural and political practices (e.g., philosophy, literature, the city-state, etc.), introduced into regions that had stagnated despite having huge resources. Today, closer examination of the documentary evidence from the Near East has started to change this opinion. The Persian system, itself an amalgam of earlier traditions, persisted in many respects. Satrapies and political arrangements with local populations endured; kings used the local cults and their rituals to further their political interests; administrative practices survived. In Babylonia and Bactria, for example, the only change we see in documents is the name of the kings. One of the few Aramaic texts from Bactria dates to the seventh year of Alexander, 324. New political offices did indeed develop, new administrative languages replaced older ones such as Babylonian, Greek buildings appeared in old cities and new cities were founded that followed a Greek layout, but these changes were gradual. Alexander has been called "the last of the Achaemenids,"[2] but his death in 323 did not present a clear end or a new beginning in the long history of the Near East.

NOTES

1 Kuhrt 2007a: 141.
2 Briant 2002a: 876.

Epilogue

On February 15, 187 BC, the Seleucid King Antiochus III the Great (r. 222–187) visited the city of Babylon. He prostrated himself at the gate of Marduk's temple, received a golden crown weighing 1,000 shekels, and put on the purple robe of Nebuchadnezzar II, still kept in the treasury 370 years after that king's death. He stayed eight days in the city, making offerings in various temples and then moved on to Borsippa where he made more donations. Finally he went to Seleucia-on-the-Tigris, which his predecessor Seleucus I had founded around 305 as a Greek royal city, but that too was no longer the empire's capital – Antiochus ruled from Antioch on the Mediterranean coast. We know of Antiochus' visit because a Babylonian scholar recorded it in an astronomical diary, written in cuneiform on a clay tablet alongside observations of the planets and other celestial objects. The scholar was involved in a seven-century-long research project that has no parallel in world history and lasted from the mid-eighth century to 61 BC. He was part of an intellectual tradition that had survived many changes in political regimes, none of which had been in the hands of native Babylonians since 539. The Greek Antiochus felt it necessary to don the robes of his long-dead predecessor, although he probably did not know a word of Babylonian and understood little of the local cults. He saw himself as part of a long chain of Babylonian rulers and was willing to put on what must have been a musty outfit to show this to a group of local officials and priests. This illustrates how difficult it is to establish endpoints in history. Ancient Near Eastern culture did not stop when Alexander, educated by the great Greek philosopher Aristotle, conquered the area. Intellectual life and political traditions survived. They merged with new inspirations and took on different forms and meanings, but their influence remained. It would take until 74–75 AD

A History of the Ancient Near East ca. 3000–323 BC, Third Edition. Marc Van De Mieroop.
© 2016 John Wiley & Sons, Inc. Published 2016 by John Wiley & Sons, Inc.

before the cuneiform script vanished as a writing system and long afterwards people would look to Babylonian gods like Sin and Ishtar for guidance. Today we too still take for granted aspects of life that the people of the ancient Near East first developed: we live in cities, obey laws, read and write, and much more. Many centuries may separate us from that past world, but its accomplishments remain with us.

King Lists

All dates indicate period of rule and are to be taken as approximate as they are often uncertain, especially in the earlier centuries. They are based for rulers of Mesopotamia (Sumerian, Babylonian, Assyrian) on Regine Pruzsinsky's list in Gonzalo Rubio, ed. *A Handbook of Ancient Mesopotamia* (Boston and Berlin: de Gruyter, in press). Descent is not always clear: when it is certain, successive kings are connected with |; when possible, by ?; when no direct family connection existed, successive rulers are separated by a blank space.

1 Akkad Dynasty

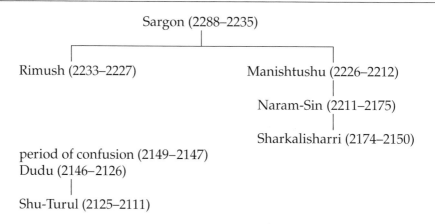

Sargon (2288–2235)

Rimush (2233–2227) Manishtushu (2226–2212)

Naram-Sin (2211–2175)

Sharkalisharri (2174–2150)

period of confusion (2149–2147)
Dudu (2146–2126)

Shu-Turul (2125–2111)

A History of the Ancient Near East ca. 3000–323 BC, Third Edition. Marc Van De Mieroop.
© 2016 John Wiley & Sons, Inc. Published 2016 by John Wiley & Sons, Inc.

2 Third Dynasty of Ur

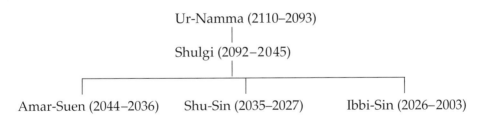

Ur-Namma (2110–2093)

Shulgi (2092–2045)

Amar-Suen (2044–2036)   Shu-Sin (2035–2027)   Ibbi-Sin (2026–2003)

3 First Dynasty of Isin

Ishbi-Erra (2019–1987)

Shu-ilishu (1986–1977)

Iddin-Dagan (1976–1956)

Ishme-Dagan (1955–1937)

Lipit-Ishtar (1936–1926)

Ur-Ninurta (1925–1898)

Bur-Sin (1897–1876)

Lipit-Enlil (1875–1871)

Erra-imitti (1870–1863)

Enlil-bani (1862–1839)

Zambija (1838–1836)

Iter-pisha (1835–1832)

Ur-dukuga (1831–1828)

Sin-magir (1827–1817)

Damiq-ilishu (1816–1794)

1793: Larsa conquers Isin

4   Larsa Dynasty

Naplanum (2025–2005)

?

Emisum (2004–1977)

?

Samium (1976–1942)

|

Zabaja (1941–1933)

?

Gungunum (1932–1906)

?

Abi-sare (1905–1895)

?

Sumu-el (1894–1866)

Nur-Adad (1865–1850)

|

Sin-iddinam (1849–1843)

?

Sin-eribam (1842–1841)

|

Sin-iqisham (1840–1836)

?

Silli-Adad (1835)

Warad-Sin (1834–1823)   Rim-Sin I (1822–1763)
                          1763: Babylon conquers Larsa

Rim-Sin II (1741–1740)

5 Eshnunna

The absolute dates for most rulers are unknown.

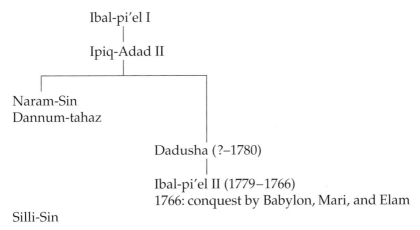

Ibal-pi'el I
   |
Ipiq-Adad II
   |

Naram-Sin
Dannum-tahaz

Dadusha (?–1780)
   |
Ibal-pi'el II (1779–1766)
1766: conquest by Babylon, Mari, and Elam

Silli-Sin

6 Mari

Yahdun-Lim
   |
Sumu-Yaman

Yasmah-Addu (ca. 1795–1776)

Zimri-Lim (ca. 1775–1762)

1761: Babylon conquers Mari

7   Yamkhad

All dates are approximate.

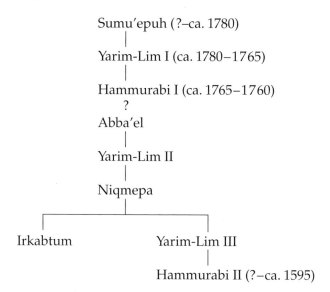

Sumu'epuh (?–ca. 1780)
|
Yarim-Lim I (ca. 1780–1765)
|
Hammurabi I (ca. 1765–1760)
?
Abba'el
|
Yarim-Lim II
|
Niqmepa
|
Irkabtum   Yarim-Lim III
|
Hammurabi II (?–ca. 1595)

8   First Dynasty of Babylon

Sumulael (1880–1845)
?
Sabium (1844–1831)
?
Apil-Sin (1830–1813)
?
Sin-muballit (1812–1793)
|
Hammurabi (1792–1750)
|
Samsuiluna (1749–1712)
|
Abi-eshuh (1711–1684)
|
Ammiditana (1683–1647)
|
Ammisaduqa (1646–1626)
?
Samsuditana (1625–1595)

9 Old Hittite Kingdom

All dates are approximate.

Hattusili I (1650–1620)

Mursili I (1620–1590)

Hantili I (1590–1560)

Zidanta I (1559–)

Ammuna

Huzziya I (–1526)

Telipinu (1525–1500)

10 Mittani

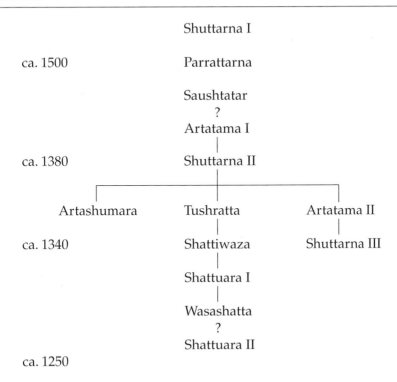

	Shuttarna I
ca. 1500	Parrattarna
	Saushtatar
	?
	Artatama I
ca. 1380	Shuttarna II

Artashumara   Tushratta   Artatama II

ca. 1340   Shattiwaza   Shuttarna III

Shattuara I

Wasashatta

?

Shattuara II

ca. 1250

11   Hittite New Kingdom

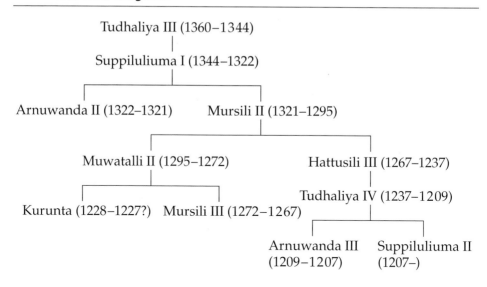

Tudhaliya III (1360–1344)

Suppiluliuma I (1344–1322)

Arnuwanda II (1322–1321)   Mursili II (1321–1295)

Muwatalli II (1295–1272)   Hattusili III (1267–1237)

Tudhaliya IV (1237–1209)

Kurunta (1228–1227?)   Mursili III (1272–1267)

Arnuwanda III   Suppiluliuma II
(1209–1207)   (1207–)

12   List of Selected Kings of the Syro-Palestinian Area

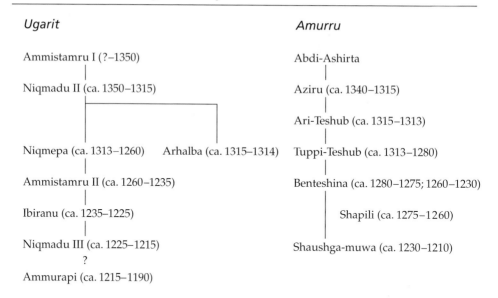

Ugarit	Amurru
Ammistamru I (?–1350)	Abdi-Ashirta
Niqmadu II (ca. 1350–1315)	Aziru (ca. 1340–1315)
	Ari-Teshub (ca. 1315–1313)
Niqmepa (ca. 1313–1260) Arhalba (ca. 1315–1314)	Tuppi-Teshub (ca. 1313–1280)
Ammistamru II (ca. 1260–1235)	Benteshina (ca. 1280–1275; 1260–1230)
Ibiranu (ca. 1235–1225)	Shapili (ca. 1275–1260)
Niqmadu III (ca. 1225–1215)	Shaushga-muwa (ca. 1230–1210)
?	
Ammurapi (ca. 1215–1190)	

13   Babylonia in Late Second Millennium

Kassite Dynasty

Kadashman-Enlil I (1374?–1360)

Burnaburiash II (1359–1333)

Kara-hardash (1333)
Nazi-Bugash (1333)

Kurigalzu II (1332–1308)

Nazi-Maruttash (1307–1282)

Kadashman-Turgu (1281–1264)

Kadashman-Enlil II (1263–1255)
?
Kudur-Enlil (1254–1246)
?
Shagarakti-Shuriash (1245–1233)

Kashtiliashu IV (1232–1225)

Enlil-nadin-shumi (1224)
Kadashman-Harbe II (1223)
Adad-shuma-iddina (1222–1217)

Adad-shuma-usur (1216–1187)

Meli-Shipak (1186–1172)

Zababa-shuma-iddina (1158)
Enlil-nadin-ahi (1157–1155)

Marduk-apla-iddina I (1171–1159)

Second dynasty of Isin

Marduk-kabit-ahheshu (1157–1140)

Itti-Marduk-balatu (1139–1132)

Ninurta-nadin-shumi (1131–1126)

Nebuchadnezzar I (1125–1104)   Marduk-nadin-ahhe (1099–1082)

Enlil-nadin-apil (1103–1100)

Marduk-shapik-zeri (1081–1069)

Adad-apla-iddina (1068–1047)
Marduk-ahhe-eriba (1046)
Marduk-zer-x (1045–1034)
Nabu-shumu-libur (1033–1026)

14 Middle Elamite Rulers

(a) Between 1500–1400 with uncertain affiliation

Kidinu
Tan-Ruhurater II
Shalla
Tepti-ahar
Inshushinak-sunkir-nappipir

(b)   Between 1400–1200

All dates are uncertain.

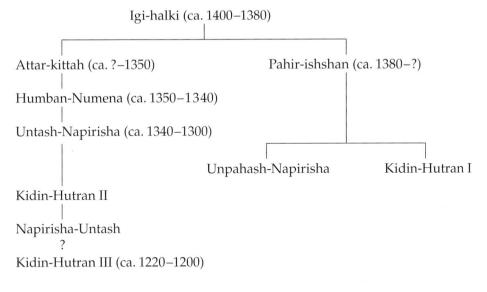

(c)   Between 1200–1100

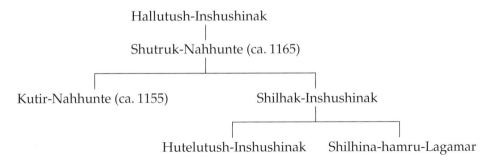

15 Babylonia in the Early First Millennium

Second Sealand Dynasty

Simbar-Shipak (1025–1008)
?   Ea-mukin-zeri (1008)
Kashshu-nadin-ahhe (1007–1005)

Bazi Dynasty

Eulmash-shakin-shumi (1004–988)
┌──────────────?──────────────┐
Ninurta-kudurri-usur I (987–985)   Shirikti-Shuqamuna (985)

Elamite Dynasty

Mar-biti-apla-usur (984–979)

Mixed Dynasties

Nabu-mukin-apli (978–943)
├──────────────────────────────────────┐
Ninurta-kudurri-usur II (943)   Mar-biti-ahhe-iddina (942–?)

Shamash-mudammiq (?–?)
?
Nabu-shuma-ukin I (?–?)
|
Nabu-apla-iddina (?–?)
|
Marduk-zakir-shumi I (?–?)
|
Marduk-balassu-iqbi (?–ca. 813)

Baba-aha-iddina (812)
Ninurta-apla-[ ] (?–?)
Marduk-bel-zeri (?–?)
Marduk-apla-usur (?–?)
Eriba-Marduk (?–?)
Nabu-shuma-ishkun (760?–748)

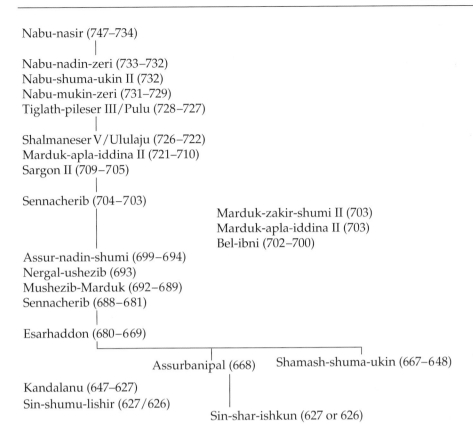

Nabu-nasir (747–734)

Nabu-nadin-zeri (733–732)
Nabu-shuma-ukin II (732)
Nabu-mukin-zeri (731–729)
Tiglath-pileser III/Pulu (728–727)

Shalmaneser V/Ululaju (726–722)
Marduk-apla-iddina II (721–710)
Sargon II (709–705)

Sennacherib (704–703)

Marduk-zakir-shumi II (703)
Marduk-apla-iddina II (703)
Bel-ibni (702–700)

Assur-nadin-shumi (699–694)
Nergal-ushezib (693)
Mushezib-Marduk (692–689)
Sennacherib (688–681)

Esarhaddon (680–669)

Assurbanipal (668)   Shamash-shuma-ukin (667–648)

Kandalanu (647–627)
Sin-shumu-lishir (627/626)

Sin-shar-ishkun (627 or 626)

16 Neo-Babylonian Dynasty

Nabopolassar (626–605)

Nebuchadnezzar II (604–562)

Evil-Merodach (561–560)

Neriglissar (559–556)

Labashi-Marduk (556)

Nabonidus (555–539)

17   Achaemenid Dynasty

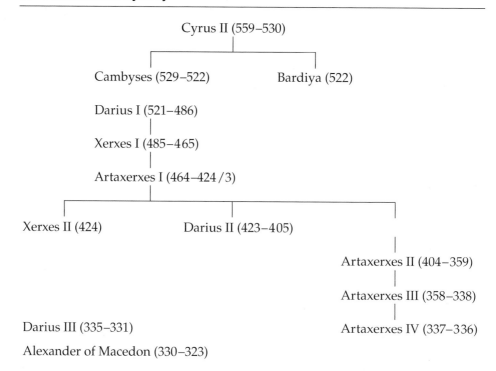

Cyrus II (559–530)

Cambyses (529–522)   Bardiya (522)

Darius I (521–486)

Xerxes I (485–465)

Artaxerxes I (464–424/3)

Xerxes II (424)   Darius II (423–405)

Artaxerxes II (404–359)

Artaxerxes III (358–338)

Darius III (335–331)   Artaxerxes IV (337–336)

Alexander of Macedon (330–323)

18 Assyria

Aminu
|
Sulili

Kikkija

Akija

Puzur-Assur I

Shalim-ahum

Ilushuma
|
Erishum I (1973–1934)
|
Ikunum (1933–1920)
|
Sargon I (1919–1880)
|
Puzur-Assur II (1879–1872)
|
Naram-Sin (1871–1828/18)
|
Erishum (1827/17–1808)

Shamshi-Adad I (1807–1775)
|
Ishme-Dagan (1774–?)

Assur-uballit I (1353–1318)
|
Enlil-nirari (1317–1308)
|
Arik-den-ili (1307–1296)
|
Adad-nirari I (1295–1264)
|
Shalmaneser I (1263–1234)
|
Tukulti-Ninurta I (1233–1197)

Assur-nadin-apli (1196–1193)   Enlil-kudurri-usur (1186–1182)
|
Assur-nirari III (1192–1177)

Assyria (*continued*)

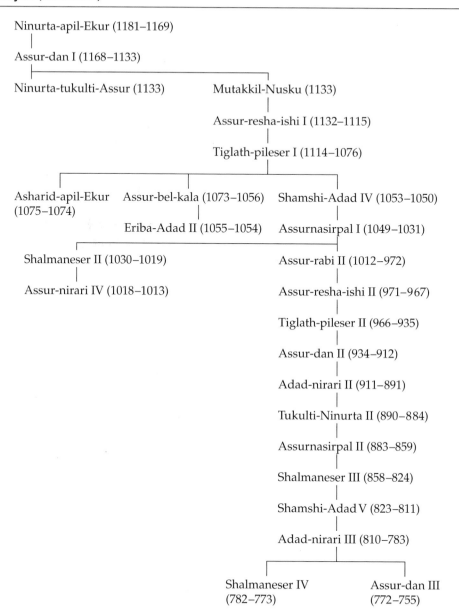

Ninurta-apil-Ekur (1181–1169)

Assur-dan I (1168–1133)

Ninurta-tukulti-Assur (1133)　　　　Mutakkil-Nusku (1133)

Assur-resha-ishi I (1132–1115)

Tiglath-pileser I (1114–1076)

Asharid-apil-Ekur　　Assur-bel-kala (1073–1056)　　Shamshi-Adad IV (1053–1050)
(1075–1074)

Eriba-Adad II (1055–1054)　　Assurnasirpal I (1049–1031)

Shalmaneser II (1030–1019)　　　　　Assur-rabi II (1012–972)

Assur-nirari IV (1018–1013)　　　　Assur-resha-ishi II (971–967)

Tiglath-pileser II (966–935)

Assur-dan II (934–912)

Adad-nirari II (911–891)

Tukulti-Ninurta II (890–884)

Assurnasirpal II (883–859)

Shalmaneser III (858–824)

Shamshi-Adad V (823–811)

Adad-nirari III (810–783)

Shalmaneser IV　　　　Assur-dan III
(782–773)　　　　　　(772–755)

Assyria (*continued*)

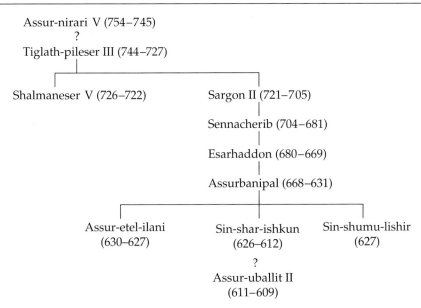

Assur-nirari V (754–745)
?
Tiglath-pileser III (744–727)

Shalmaneser V (726–722)   Sargon II (721–705)

Sennacherib (704–681)

Esarhaddon (680–669)

Assurbanipal (668–631)

Assur-etel-ilani   Sin-shar-ishkun   Sin-shumu-lishir
(630–627)   (626–612)   (627)

?
Assur-uballit II
(611–609)

Guide to Further Reading

The scholarly literature on the histories and cultures of the Near East is very substantial in size, and ranges from paragraph-long notes to multi-volume books. They are mostly written in English, French, and German, while some very important work has been published in other languages. A small selection of works, mostly in English, is provided here. I have given special attention to recent publications, where further up-to-date bibliography is available.

In recent years various publishers have commissioned reference works in which multiple authors discuss aspects of Near Eastern history and culture throughout ancient times. These include Oxford University Press's *Handbooks* on *Anatolia* (Steadman & McMahon, eds. 2011), *Iran* (Potts, ed. 2013), and *Cuneiform Culture* (Radner & Robson, eds. 2011), Blackwell's *Companion to the Ancient Near East* (Snell, ed. 2005), and *Companion to the Archaeology of the Ancient Near East* (Potts, ed. 2012), and Routledge's *Babylonian World* (Leick, ed. 2007) and *Sumerian World* (Crawford, ed. 2013). Most encompassing still is the four-volume *Civilizations of the Ancient Near East* (Sasson, ed. 1995). All these contain numerous contributions that deal with a wide array of subjects on history, archaeology, art, language, literature, etcetera, and range from general surveys to specialized discussions. Their up-to-date bibliographies provide students with the information needed to research most topics. Systematic discussions of subject matters arranged alphabetically range from the brief *Dictionary of the Ancient Near East* (Bienkowski & Millard, eds. 2000) to the comprehensive *Reallexikon der Assyriologie* (Ebeling et al., eds. 1932–), which has only reached the letter U so far. Its in-depth articles are written in German, French, and English.

English surveys of history include Kuhrt 1995, and the much shorter Hallo & Simpson 1998, Foster & Foster 2009, and the very short Podany 2014. Liverani 2014 is an English translation and update of the excellent Italian history (1988a). An authoritative multi-authored account is provided in *The Cambridge Ancient History* (Boardman et al., eds. 1971–88). The contributions were written from the 1960s to the 1980s, and some of them are outdated. They do provide the most detailed factual account available, however. In German recently appeared Frahm 2013, in Italian Milano, ed. 2012, while the most recent survey in French is the two-volume Garelli et al., 1997 and 2002.

A History of the Ancient Near East ca. 3000–323 BC, Third Edition. Marc Van De Mieroop.
© 2016 John Wiley & Sons, Inc. Published 2016 by John Wiley & Sons, Inc.

There exist some detailed long-term studies of specific regions of the Near East. For Syria: Klengel 1992 and Akkermans & Schwartz 2003; for Anatolia: Bryce 2005 and Sagona & Zimansky 2009; for western Iran: Carter & Stolper 1984 and Potts 1999; and for the Persian Gulf: Potts 1990.

Roaf 1990 contains very informative maps for the various periods of ancient history, and a good summary discussion of ancient Near Eastern history. The book also has numerous illustrations. Potts 1997 is a good discussion of the material world of the Mesopotamians, organized by topics. Oppenheim 1977 is the only true intellectual history of the region, also organized around different topics. Jacobsen 1976 provides a history of Mesopotamian religion.

Some illustrated websites with general information are: http://www.mesopotamia. co.uk from the British Museum in London; and http://www.metmuseum.org/toah/hi/te_ index.asp?i=7 from the Metropolitan Museum of Art, New York. http://www.archatlas. dept.shef.ac.uk/Home.php contains interesting satellite maps and discussions of issues such as the origins of agriculture and trade routes.

In addition to the books mentioned above which contain important information on almost all periods of Near Eastern history, the reader can consult the works below for more information on topics discussed in specific chapters here. The list is far from complete and provides only a summary guide.

Chapter 1: Introductory Concerns

What Is the Ancient Near East?: Van De Mieroop 1997.
Sources: Van De Mieroop 1999a, Matthews 2003, Glassner 2004, and Zimansky 2005.
Prehistoric developments: Nissen 1988 and various contributions in Potts, ed. 2012.
    For new research developments, Watkins 2010 and Pournelle 2013. On Göbekli Tepe:
    Schmidt 2011.

Part I: City-States

For prehistory and the early periods of Near Eastern history, see Nissen 1988 and Pollock 1999. Many aspects of society and culture are discussed in Postgate 1992a and Crawford 2004. The art of the third millennium is extensively illustrated in Aruz, ed. 2003.

Chapter 2: Origins: The Uruk Phenomenon

Sources: Bauer, Englund & Krebenik 1998: 13–233.
Uruk developments: Liverani 2006 and Algaze 2008.
Origins of cities: Van De Mieroop 1999b: chapter 2.
Texts and administrative tools: Nissen, Damerow & Englund 1993 (texts) and Collon
    1987 (seals). For lexical texts, see http://oracc.museum.upenn.edu/dcclt and Veldhuis
    2014.
Origins of writing: Walker 1987, Schmandt-Besserat 1992, Glassner 2003, and Cooper
    2004.
The Uruk expansion: Moorey 1995, Rothman, ed. 2001, Algaze 2005, and Jennings 2011:
    57–76.

Chapter 3: Competing City-States: The Early Dynastic Period

Sources: Cooper 1983 and 1986, Matthews 1993, Bauer, Englund & Krebenik 1998: 237–585, and Frayne 2008.

Political organization: Steinkeller 2002. On primitive democracy, see Jacobsen 1943.

The wider Near East: For Ebla, see Pettinato 1991, Matthiae 2010, and Milano 1995.

Early dynastic society: Maekawa 1973–4, Visicato 1995, and Zettler & Horne, eds. 1998.

Later literary reflections: Wilcke 1989, George 1999: chapter 5, Foster 2001: 99–154, Glassner 2004, and Vanstiphout 2004.

Chapter 4: Political Centralization in the Late Third Millennium

Sources: Frayne 1993 and 1997, Edzard 1997, Michalowski 1993 and 2011, and Sallaberger & Westenholz 1999. On the Iri-Sagrig texts: Owen 2013.

The Akkad dynasty: Liverani, ed. 1993b. On Puzur-Inshushinak: Steinkeller 2013.

The Ur III state: Steinkeller 1987 and 2003; Sharlach 2004. On labor in the Garshana archive: Adams 2010.

Syria and northern Mesopotamia in the late third millennium: Sallaberger 2007.

Later literary reflections: Westenholz 1997, Van De Mieroop 1999c and 2000, and Potts 2001.

Chapter 5: The Near East in the Early Second Millennium

Sources: Frayne 1990; Charpin, Edzard & Stol 2004; Veenhof & Eidem 2008.

Nomads and sedentary people: Schwartz 1995 and Fleming 2004.

Babylonian society in the Isin-Larsa period: Van De Mieroop 1992, Renger 2002, and Goddeeris 2007.

Old Assyrian history and trade: Veenhof 2003 and Barjamovic, Hertel & Larsen 2012. Michel 2001 contains a rich selection of Old Assyrian letters translated into French.

Mari: Durand 1997–2000 contains a vast number of Mari letters translated into French with very up-to-date general introductions to many topics. Heimpel 2003 translates many letters into English. Charpin & Ziegler 2003 is a detailed history.

Chapter 6: The Growth of Territorial States in the Early Second Millennium

Sources: see chapter 5.

Kingdom of Upper Mesopotamia: see Mari in chapter 5.

Old Babylonian dynasty: Charpin 2012 and Van De Mieroop 2005. For the rebellion against Samsuiluna, see Seri 2013: 20–54, 238–42. Roth 1997 provides translations of the Code of Hammurabi, as well as all other law codes from Mesopotamia and the Hittites. For aspects of the economy and society, Stol 2004. Extensive translations of Sumerian literature can be found in Black et al. 2004 and http://www-etcsl.orient.ox.ac.uk. For the school curriculum, see Tinney 1998.

Old Hittite state: Bryce 2005: 1–107.

Aftermath: Van Lerberghe 1995 and Sassmannshausen 2004 (Kassites), Salvini 1998 (Hurrians), and Podany 2002 (Kingdom of Hana).

PART II: TERRITORIAL STATES

Chapter 7: The Club of the Great Powers

Sources: Moran 1992 translates all Amarna letters into English, and Beckman 1999 contains translations of a large selection of treaties and other diplomatic material from the Hittites.

The international system: Liverani 1990 and 2001a, Cohen & Westbrook, eds. 2000, Bryce 2003, Feldman 2005, Van De Mieroop 2007, and Podany 2010. Aruz, Benzel & Evans, eds. 2008 contains a wealth of images of objects and archaeological sites of the period, as well as excellent introductions to many subjects. Aruz, Graff & Rakic, eds. 2013 provides further scholarly analyses of these subjects.

Chapter 8: The Western States of the Late Second Millennium

Sources: Hoffner 1980 and Liverani 2004 for surveys and analyses. For translations, see Moran 1992 (Amarna letters), Beckman 1999 (Hittite treaties and diplomatic correspondence), Hoffner 2009 (Hittite letters), and Beckman, Bryce & Cline 2011 (texts regarding Ahhiyawa).

Mittani state: Wilhelm 1989, von Dassow 2008 (Alalakh), Maidman 2010 and Postgate 2013: chapter 7 (Nuzi), and Cancik-Kirschbaum, Brisch & Eidem, eds. 2014.

Hittites: General surveys: Gurney 1990, Klengel 1999, Bryce 2005, Collins 2007, Genz & Mielke eds. 2011, and Beal 2011. On Hattusa: http://www.hattuscha.de/English/english1.htm.

Levant: Singer 1991 (history of Amurru) and Watson & Wyatt, eds. 1999 (Ugarit).

Chapter 9: Kassites, Assyrians, and Elamites

Sources: König 1965, Brinkman 1976, and Grayson 1987.

Kassites: Brinkman 1976–80, Balkan 1986, and Sassmannshausen 2001.

Middle Assyria: Machinist 1982 and Postgate 2013.

Elam: Potts 1990: 188–258.

Chapter 10: The Collapse of the Regional System and Its Aftermath

Numerous books treat the end of the Late Bronze Age. Most recent is Cline 2014, which contains most of the relevant bibliography. See Liverani 1997 and Van De Mieroop 2007: chapter 10 for the approach used here.

Aftermath: Brinkman 1984a, Healy 1990, and Sherratt 2003.

PART III: EMPIRES

Several contributions in Larsen, ed. 1979 are important for the Assyrian empire. Cancik-Kirschbaum 2003 is a brief German introduction to it. Joannès 2004 surveys all the Mesopotamian empires of the first millennium.

Chapter 11: The Near East at the Start of the First Millennium

Sources: Frame 1995 (Babylonia), Hawkins 2000 (Neo-Hittite), and Salvini 2008–12 (Urartu).
Babylonia: Brinkman 1984b.
Elam: Waters 2000.
Urartu: Salvini 1995, Radner 2011, Zimansky 2011, and Kroll et al., eds. 2012.
Phoenicia: Markoe 2000 and Woolmer 2011.
Arameans: Niehr, ed. 2014
Israel and Judah: Finkelstein 1999 and 2013, and Liverani 2005a, 2005b.

Chapter 12: The Rise of Assyria

Sources: Grayson 1991b and 1996. The letters, administrative records, legal documents and sundry other texts found in the Nineveh archives are being fully re-edited by a team in Helsinki. Thus far nineteen volumes have appeared in a series called *State Archives of Assyria* under the general editorship of Simo Parpola. Fales 2001 contains an analysis of these sources.
The army and warfare: Bahrani 2008 (ideological aspects) and Fales 2010.
Expansion of the empire: Liverani 1988b and Postgate 1992b.
The capital Kalhu: J. and D. Oates 2001.

Chapter 13: Assyria's World Domination

Many contributions in Parpola & Whiting, eds. 1997 are important for the study of this period.
Sources: Tadmor & Yamada 2011 (Tiglath-pileser III and Shalmaneser V), Fuchs 1993 (Sargon II), Grayson & Novotny 2012 and 2014 (Sennacherib), Leichty 2011 (Esarhaddon), and Borger 1996 (Assurbanipal). See also http://oracc.museum.upenn.edu/rinap/. For letters and other texts, see *State Archives of Assyria*.
The western areas: Stern 2001: 1–300.
Babylonia: Frame 1992 and Porter 1993.
Ideology: Bahrani 1995 and 2008.
For the contents of Assurbanipal's library, see Oppenheim 1977: 14–23. For the literature of the first millennium in general, Foster 2007. English translations of numerous Akkadian literary texts can be found in Foster 2005, with a concise version published in 1995. The same author translated *The Epic of Gilgamesh* (2001). Another recent translation of that epic is George 1999, who also published an authoritative edition, George 2003. For astronomy, see Brown 2000 and Rochberg 2004.
Assyria's fall: Liverani 2001b.

Chapter 14: The Medes and Babylonians

Sources: Da Riva 2013 (Nabopolassar, Evil-Merodach, and Neriglissar) and Schaudig 2001 (Nabonidus and Cyrus). Da Riva 2008 surveys all royal inscriptions, and Jursa 2005 all administrative archives.

Medes: Lanfranchi et al., eds. 2003 and Radner 2013. Phrygia: http://sites.museum. upenn.edu/gordion/.

The Neo-Babylonian empire: Vanderhooft 1999 and Stern 2001: 301–50.

Individual rulers: Wiseman 1985 and Sack 2004 (Nebuchadnezzar II), Sack 1972 (Amel-Marduk), and Beaulieu 1989 and Michalowski 2003 (Nabonidus).

The Babylonian economy: Jursa 2010, conveniently summarized in Jursa 2013. On the Egibi family: Wunsch 2007.

For deportees in Babylonia: Dandamayev 2004 and Wunsch 2013.

The city of Babylon: Van De Mieroop 2003.

Interest in the past: Winter 2000.

Chapter 15: The Creation of a World Empire: Persia

The *Encyclopædia Iranica* (http://www.iranicaonline.org) contains many up-to-date entries that deal with ancient Persia.

Sources: Old Persian inscriptions: Schmitt 2009; http://www.avesta.org/op/op.htm. English translations of all types of sources organized by topic appear in Kuhrt 2007a. For their interpretation, see Harrison 2011. Aramaic documents from Bactria: Naveh & Shaked 2012.

General surveys: Wiesehöfer 1996, Kuhrt 2001, Briant 2002a, Allen 2005, and Brosius 2006.

For Cyrus: See Kuhrt 2007b.

Chapter 16: Governing a World Empire: Persia

Administrative structure: Wiesehöfer 2009.

The Persian heartland: Briant, Henkelman & Stolper, eds. 2008; Babylonia: Stolper 1985; Judah: Grabbe 2004.

Bibliography

Abusch, Tzvi et al., eds. (2001) *Proceedings of the XLV Rencontre Assyriologique Interna-tionale*, Vol. 1: *Historiography in the Cuneiform World*, Bethesda, MD.

Adams, Robert McC. (1966) *The Evolution of Urban Society*, Chicago.

Adams, Robert McC. (2010) "Slavery and Freedom in the Third Dynasty of Ur: Implications of the Garshana Archives," *Cuneiform Digital Library Journal* 2010/2 http://cdli.ucla.edu/pubs/cdlj/2010/cdlj2010_002.html.

Akkermans, Peter M. M. G. and Glenn M. Schwartz (2003) *The Archaeology of Syria. From Complex Hunter-Gatherer to Early Urban Societies (ca. 16,000–300 BC)*, Cambridge.

Algaze, Guillermo (2005) *The Uruk World System*, 2nd ed., Chicago.

Algaze, Guillermo (2008) *Early Mesopotamia at the Dawn of Civilization*, Chicago.

Algaze, Guillermo (2013) "The End of Prehistory and the Uruk Period," in Crawford 2013: 68–94.

Allen, Lindsay (2005) *The Persian Empire: A History*, London.

Aruz, Joan ed. (2003) *Art of the First Cities. The Third Millennium BC from the Mediterranean to the Indus*, New York.

Aruz, Joan, Kim Benzel, and Jean M. Evans, eds. (2008) *Beyond Babylon. Art, Trade, and Diplomacy in the Second Millennium BC*, New York.

Aruz, Joan, Sarah Graff, and Yelena Rakic, eds. (2013) *Cultures in Contact: From Mesopotamia to the Mediterranean in the Second Millennium BC*, New York.

Baadsgaard, Aubrey, Janet Monge, Samantha Cox, and Richard L. Zettler (2011) "Human Sacrifice and Intentional Corpse Preservation in the Royal Cemetery of Ur," *Antiquity* **85**: 27–42.

Bahrani, Zainab (1995) "Assault and Abduction: The Fate of the Royal Image in the Ancient Near East," *Art History* **18**: 363–82.

Bahrani, Zainab (2007) "The Babylonian Visual Image," in Leick 2007: 155–70.

Bahrani, Zainab (2008) *Rituals of War: The Body and Violence in Mesopotamia*, New York.

Balkan, Kemal (1986) *Studies in Babylonian Feudalism of the Kassite Period*, Malibu.

Barjamovic, Gojko, Thomas Hertel, and Mogens Trolle Larsen (2012) *Ups and Downs at Kanesh. Chronology, History and Society in the Old Assyrian Period*, Leiden.

A History of the Ancient Near East ca. 3000–323 BC, Third Edition. Marc Van De Mieroop.
© 2016 John Wiley & Sons, Inc. Published 2016 by John Wiley & Sons, Inc.

Bauer, Josef, Robert K. Englund, and Manfred Krebenik (1998) *Mesopotamien. Späturuk-Zeit und Frühdynastische Zeit*, Fribourg and Göttingen.

Beal, Richard A. (2011) "Hittite Anatolia: A Political History," in Steadman and McMahon 2011: 917–33.

Beaulieu, Paul-Alain (1989) *The Reign of Nabonidus, King of Babylon 556–539 BC*, New Haven.

Beaulieu, Paul-Alain (2007) "Late Babylonian Intellectual Life," in Leick 2007: 473–84.

Beckman, Gary (1999) *Hittite Diplomatic Texts*, 2nd ed., Atlanta.

Beckman, Gary (2005) "The Limits of Credulity," *Journal of the American Oriental Society* **125**: 343–52.

Beckman, Gary, Trevor Bryce, and Eric Cline (2011) *The Ahhiyawa Texts*, Atlanta.

Bienkowski, Piotr and Alan Millard, eds. (2000) *Dictionary of the Ancient Near East*, London.

Bietak, Manfred (2003) "Science versus Archaeology: Problems and Consequences of High Aegean Chronology," in Bietak 2000–7, Vol. II: 23–34, Vienna.

Bietak, Manfred, ed. (2000–7) *The Synchronisation of Civilisations in the Eastern Mediterranean in the Second Millennium BC*, 3 vols., Vienna.

Billows, Richard (2010) *Marathon: How One Battle Changed Western Civilization*, New York and London.

Bittel, Kurt (1976) "Das Ende des Hethiterreiches aufgrund archäologischer Zeugnisse," *Jahresbericht des Instituts für Vorgeschichte, Universität Frankfurt a.M.*: 36–56.

Black, Jeremy et al. (2004) *The Literature of Ancient Sumer*, Oxford.

Boardman, John et al., eds. (1971–88) *The Cambridge Ancient History*, Vols. 1–4, Cambridge.

Borger, Riekele (1996) *Beiträge zum Inschriftenwerk Assurbanipals*, Wiesbaden.

Bottéro, Jean, ed. (1954) *Le problème des Habiru à la 4e Rencontre assyriologique internationale*, Paris.

Bottéro, Jean (1972–5) "Habiru," *Reallexikon der Assyriologie* 4, Berlin and New York: 14–27.

Bottéro, Jean (1981) "Les Habiru, les nomades et les sédentaires," in *Nomads and Sedentary Peoples*, ed. J. S. Castillo, Mexico: 89–107.

Bottéro, Jean (1992) *Mesopotamia: Writing, Reasoning, and the Gods*, trans. Z. Bahrani and M. Van De Mieroop, Chicago.

Bottéro, Jean and Samuel Noah Kramer (1989) *Lorsque les dieux faisaient l'homme*, Paris.

Briant, Pierre (1982) *État et pasteurs au Moyen-Orient ancien*, London.

Briant, Pierre (2002a) *From Cyrus to Alexander: A History of the Persian Empire*, Winona Lake, IN.

Briant, Pierre (2002b) "The Greeks and 'Persian Decadence,'" in *Greeks and Barbarians*, ed. Thomas Harrison, Edinburgh: 193–210.

Briant, Pierre, Wouter Henkelman, and Matthew W. Stolper, eds. (2008) *L'Archive des Fortifications de Persépolis*, Paris.

Bridges, Emma, Edith Hall, and P. J. Rhodes, eds. (2007) *Cultural Responses to the Persian Wars: Antiquity to the Third Millennium*, Oxford.

Bright, John (1959) *A History of Israel*, Philadelphia (2nd ed. 1972; 3rd ed. 1981; 4th ed. 2000).

Brinkman, J. A. (1976) *Materials and Studies for Kassite History*, Vol. I: *A Catalogue of Cuneiform Sources Pertaining to Specific Monarchs of the Kassite Dynasty*, Chicago.

Brinkman, J. A. (1976–80) "Kassiten," in *Reallexikon der Assyriologie* 5, Berlin and New York: 464–73.

Brinkman, J. A. (1984a) "Settlement Survey and Documentary Evidence: Regional Variation and Secular Trend in Mesopotamian Demography," *Journal of Near Eastern Studies* **43**: 169–80.

Brinkman, J. A. (1984b) *Prelude to Empire*, Philadelphia.

Brosius, Maria (2006) *The Persians*, London.

Brown, David (2000) *Mesopotamian Planetary Astronomy – Astrology*, Groningen.

Bryce, Trevor (2003) *Letters of the Great Kings of the Ancient Near East. The Royal Correspondence of the Late Bronze Age*, London and New York.

Bryce, Trevor (2005) *The Kingdom of the Hittites*, new ed., Oxford.

Bryce, Trevor (2012) *The World of the Neo-Hittite Kingdoms: A Political and Military History*, Oxford.

Cancik-Kirschbaum, Eva (2003) *Die Assyrer. Geschichte, Gesellschaft, Kultur*, Munich.

Cancik-Kirschbaum, Eva, Nicole Brisch, and Jesper Eidem, eds. (2014) *Constituent, Confederate, and Conquered Space. The Emergence of the Mittani State*, Berlin.

Carter, Elizabeth (1992) "The Middle Elamite Period," in Harper, Aruz, and Tallon 1992: 121–2.

Carter, Elizabeth and Matthew W. Stolper (1984) *Elam: Surveys of Political History and Archaeology*, Berkeley.

Charpin, Dominique (1988) *Archives épistolaires de Mari*, Paris.

Charpin, Dominique (2004) "Histoire politique du Proche-Orient Amorrite (2002–1595)," in Charpin, Edzard, and Stol 2004: 23–480.

Charpin, Dominique (2010) *Reading and Writing in Babylon*, Cambridge, MA.

Charpin, Dominique (2012) *Hammurabi of Babylon*, London and New York.

Charpin, Dominique, Dietz O. Edzard, and Marten Stol (2004) *Mesopotamien. Die altbabylonische Zeit*, Fribourg and Göttingen.

Charpin, Dominique and Nele Ziegler (2003) *Florilegium marianum V. Mari et le Proche-Orient à l'époque amorrite. Essai d'histoire politique*, Paris.

Charvát, Petr (2002) *Mesopotamia Before History*, rev. and updated ed., London and New York.

Cline, Eric (2014) *1177 BC. The Year Civilization Collapsed*, Princeton.

Cline, Eric and Mark Graham (2011) *Ancient Empires. From Mesopotamia to the Rise of Islam*, Cambridge and New York.

Cogan, Mordechai and Hayim Tadmor (1988) *II Kings*, New York.

Cohen, Andrew C. (2005) *Death Rituals, Ideology, and the Development of Early Mesopotamian Kingship: Toward a New Understanding of Iraq's Royal Cemetery of Ur*, Leiden.

Cohen, Raymond and Raymond Westbrook, eds. (2000) *Amarna Diplomacy. The Beginnings of International Relations*, Baltimore and London.

Collins, Billie Jean (2007) *The Hittites and Their World*, Atlanta.

Collon, Dominique (1987) *First Impressions. Cylinder Seals in the Ancient Near East*, London.

Coogan, Michael D., ed. (2001) *The Oxford History of the Biblical World*, Oxford.

Cook, J. M. (1983) *The Persian Empire*, London.

Cooper, Jerrold S. (1983) *Reconstructing History from Ancient Inscriptions: The Lagash-Umma Border Conflict*, Malibu.

Cooper, Jerrold S. (1986) *Sumerian and Akkadian Royal Inscriptions, I. Presargonic Inscriptions*, New Haven.

Cooper, Jerrold (2001) "Literature and History. The Historical and Political Referents of Sumerian Literary Texts," in Abusch et al. 2001: 131–47.

Cooper, Jerrold (2004) "Babylonian Beginnings: The Origin of the Cuneiform Writing System in Comparative Perspective," in *The First Writing. Script Invention as History and Process*, ed. S. D. Houston, Cambridge: 71–99.

Crawford, Harriet (2004) *Sumer and Sumerians*, 2nd ed., Cambridge.

Crawford, Harriet, ed. (2013) *The Sumerian World*, London and New York.

Cryer, Frederick H. (1995) "Chronology: Issues and Problems," in Sasson 1995: 651–64.

Da Riva, Rocio (2008) *The Neo-Babylonian Royal Inscriptions. An Introduction*, Munster.

Da Riva, Rocio (2013) *The Inscriptions of Nabopolassar, Amēl-Marduk and Neriglissar*, Berlin.

Dalley, Stephanie (2013) *The Mystery of the Hanging Garden of Babylon*, Oxford.

Dandamayev, Muhammad (2004) "Twin Towns and Ethnic Minorities in First-Millennium Babylonia," in *Commerce and Monetary Systems in the Ancient World: Means of Transmission and Cultural Interaction*, ed. R. Rollinger and C. Ulf, Munich: 54–64.

Dercksen, J. G. (2005) "Adad Is King! The Sargon Text from Kültepe," *Jaarbericht van het vooraziatisch-egyptisch Genootschap "Ex Oriente Lux"* **39**: 107–29.

Dickson, D. Bruce (2006) "Public Transcripts Expressed in Theatres of Cruelty: The Royal Graves at Ur in Mesopotamia," *Cambridge Archaeological Journal* **16**: 123–44.

Driver, G. R. and John C. Miles (1952–5) *The Babylonian Laws. Edited with Translation and Commentary*, Oxford.

Durand, Jean-Marie (1997–2000) *Les documents épistolaires du palais de Mari* I–III, Paris.

Ebeling, Erich et al., eds. (1932–) *Reallexikon der Assyriologie*, Berlin.

Eder, Walter and Johannes Renger, eds. (2007) *Chronologies of the Ancient World: Names, Dates and Dynasties* (Brill's New Pauly, Supplement), Leiden and Boston.

Edzard, Dietz O. (1970) "Die Keilschriftbriefe der Grabungskampagne 1969," *Kamid el-Loz – Kumidu. Schriftdokumente aus Kamid el-Loz*, Bonn: 55–62.

Edzard, Dietz O. (1997) *Gudea and His Dynasty*, Toronto.

Fadhil, Abdulillah (1998) "Der Prolog des Codex Hammurapi in einer Abschrift aus Sippar," *XXXIV. International Assyriology Congress*, Ankara: 717–29.

Fales, F. Mario (2001) *L'impero Assiro: storia e amministrazione, 9.–7. secolo a.C.*, Rome and Bari.

Fales, F. Mario (2010) *Guerre et paix en Assyrie: religion et impérialisme*, Paris.

Fales, F. Mario and J. N. Postgate (1992) *Imperial Administrative Records*, part 1 (State Archives of Assyria 7), Helsinki.

Fales, F. Mario and J. N. Postgate (1995) *Imperial Administrative Records*, part 2 (State Archives of Assyria 11), Helsinki.

Farber, Walter (1983) "Die Vergöttlichung Naram-Sins," *Orientalia* **52**: 67–72.

Feldman, Marian H. (2005) *Diplomacy by Design: Luxury Arts and an "International Style" in the Ancient Near East, 1400–1200 BCE*, Chicago.

Finkel, Irving L. (1988) "The Hanging Gardens of Babylon," in *The Seven Wonders of the Ancient World*, ed. Peter A. Clayton and Martin J. Price, London and New York: 38–59.

Finkel, I. L. and M. J. Seymour, eds. (2008) *Babylon*, Oxford.

Finkelstein, Israel (1999) "State Formation in Israel and Judah," *Near Eastern Archaeology* **62**: 35–62.

Finkelstein, Israel (2013) *The Forgotten Kingdom: The Archaeology and History of Northern Israel*, Atlanta.

Finkelstein, J. J. (1963) "Mesopotamian Historiography," *Proceedings of the American Philosophical Society* **107**: 461–72.

Fleming, Daniel E. (2004) *Democracy's Ancient Ancestors: Mari and Early Collective Governance*, Cambridge.

Foster, Benjamin R. (1995) *From Distant Days: Myths, Tales, and Poetry of Ancient Mesopotamia*, Bethesda, MD.

Foster, Benjamin R. (2001) *The Epic of Gilgamesh*, New York and London.

Foster, Benjamin R. (2005) *Before the Muses. An Anthology of Akkadian Literature*, 3rd ed., Bethesda, MD.

Foster, Benjamin R. (2007) *Akkadian Literature of the Late Period*, Munster.

Foster, Benjamin R. and Karen Polinger Foster (2009) *Civilizations of Ancient Iraq*, Princeton.

Frahm, Eckart (2011) "Keeping Company with Men of Learning: The King as Scholar," in Radner and Robson 2011: 508–32.

Frahm, Eckart (2013) *Geschichte des alten Mesopotamien*, Ditzingen.

Frame, Grant (1992) *Babylonia 689–627 BC. A Political History*, Istanbul.

Frame, Grant (1995) *Rulers of Babylonia. From the Second Dynasty of Isin to the End of Assyrian Domination (1157–612 BC)*, Toronto.

Frame, Grant and Andrew George (2005) "The Royal Libraries of Nineveh: New Evidence for King Ashurbanipal's Tablet Collecting," *Iraq* **67**: 265–84.

Frayne, Douglas R. (1990) *Old Babylonian Period (2003–1595 BC)*, Toronto.

Frayne, Douglas R. (1993) *Sargonic and Gutian Period (2334–2113 BC)*, Toronto.

Frayne, Douglas R. (1997) *Ur III Period (2112–2004 BC)*, Toronto.

Frayne, Douglas R. (2008) *Presargonic Period (2700–2350 BC)*, Toronto.

Frye, Richard N. (1963) *The Heritage of Persia*, Cleveland and New York.

Fuchs, Andreas (1993) *Die Inschriften Sargons II. aus Khorsabad*, Göttingen.

Garbini, Giovanni (1988) *History and Ideology in Ancient Israel*, trans. J. Bowden, New York.

Garelli, Paul (1980) "Les empires mésopotamiens," in *Le concept d'empire*, ed. M. Duverger, Paris: 25–47

Garelli, Paul et al. (1997) *Le Proche-Orient asiatique. Volume I: Des origines aux invasions des peuples de la mer*, Paris.

Garelli, Paul et al. (2002) *Le Proche-Orient asiatique. Volume II: Les empires mésopotamiens, Israël*, Paris.

Garfinkle, Steven J. (2007) "The Assyrians: A New Look at an Ancient Power," in *Current Issues and the Study of the Ancient Near East*, ed. M. Chavalas, Claremont: 53–96.

Gasche, H. et al. (1998) *Dating the Fall of Babylon: A Reappraisal of Second-Millennium Chronology*, Chicago.

Genz, Hermann (2013) "No Land Could Stand Before Their Arms, from Hatti … on …? New Light on the End of the Hittite Empire and the Early Iron Age in Central Anatolia," in *The Philistines and Other "Sea Peoples" in Text and Archaeology*, ed. A. E. Killebrew and G. Lehmann, Atlanta: 469–77.

Genz, Hermann and Dirk Paul Mielke, eds. (2011) *Insights into Hittite History and Archaeology*, Louvain.

George, A. R. (1992) *Babylonian Topographical Texts*, Louvain.

George, Andrew (1999) *The Epic of Gilgamesh*, London.

George, Andrew (2003) *The Babylonian Gilgamesh Epic: Introduction, Critical Edition and Cuneiform Texts*, Oxford and New York.

Ghirshman, Roman (1954) *Iran. From the Earliest Times to the Islamic Conquest*, Harmondsworth.

Glassner, Jean-Jacques (2003) *Writing in Sumer. The Invention of Cuneiform*, ed. and trans. Z. Bahrani and M. Van De Mieroop, Baltimore.

Glassner, Jean-Jacques (2004) *Mesopotamian Chronicles*, Atlanta.

Goddeeris, Anne (2007) "The Old Babylonian Economy," in Leick 2007: 198–209.

Grabbe, Lester L. (2004) *A History of the Jews and Judaism in the Second Temple Period. Volume I. Yehud: A History of the Persian Province of Judah*, London and New York.

Grabbe, Lester L., ed. (2011) *Enquire of the Former Age: Ancient Historiography and Writing the History of Israel*, New York.

Grayson, A. Kirk (1975) *Assyrian and Babylonian Chronicles*, Locust Valley, NY.

Grayson, A. Kirk (1982) "Assyria: Ashur-dan II to Ashur-Nirari V (934–745 BC)," *The Cambridge Ancient History*, 2nd ed., Vol. III/1: 238–81.

Grayson, A. Kirk (1987) *Assyrian Rulers of the Third and Second Millennia BC (to 1115 BC)*, Toronto.

Grayson, A. Kirk (1991a) "Assyria: Sennacherib and Esarhaddon (704–669 BC)," *The Cambridge Ancient History*, 2nd ed., Vol. III/2, Cambridge: 103–41.

Grayson, A. Kirk (1991b) *Assyrian Rulers of the Early First Millennium BC I (1114–859 BC)*, Toronto.

Grayson, A. Kirk (1996) *Assyrian Rulers of the Early First Millennium BC II (858–745 BC)*, Toronto.

Grayson, A. Kirk and Jamie Novotny (2012) *The Royal Inscriptions of Sennacherib, King of Assyria (704–681 BC)*, part 1, Winona Lake, IN.

Grayson, A. Kirk and Jamie Novotny (2014) *The Royal Inscriptions of Sennacherib, King of Assyria (704–681 BC)*, part 2, Winona Lake, IN.

Greenberg, Moshe (1955) *The Hab/piru*, New Haven.

Greenfield, Jonas and Aaron Shaffer (1983) "Notes on the Akkadian-Aramaic Bilingual Statue from Tell Fekherye," *Iraq* **45**: 109–16.

Günbatti, Cahit (1997) "Kültepe'den Akadlı Sargon'a âit bir tablet," *Archivum Anatolicum* **3**: 131–55.

Gurney, Oliver (1990) *The Hittites*, London.

Hallo, William W. (1998) "New Directions in Historiography," in *Dubsar anta-men: Studien zur Altorientalistik: Festschrift für Willem H. Ph. Römer*, ed. M. Dietrich and O. Loretz, Munster: 109–28.

Hallo, William W. (2001) "Polymnia and Clio," in Abusch et al. 2001: 195–209.

Hallo, William W., ed. (1997–2002) *The Context of Scripture*, 3 vols., Leiden.

Hallo, William W. and William K. Simpson (1998) *The Ancient Near East: A History*, 2nd ed., Forth Worth.

Hanson, Victor Davis (2007) "Persian Versions. Myth and Reality in Wars Between West and East," *The Times Literary Supplement*, May 18: 3–4.

Harper, Prudence O. (1992) "Mesopotamian Monuments Found at Susa," in Harper, Aruz, and Tallon 1992: 159–82.

Harper, Prudence O., Joan Aruz, and Francoise Tallon, eds. (1992) *The Royal City of Susa: Ancient Near Eastern Treasures in the Louvre*, New York.

Harrison, Thomas (2011) *Writing Ancient Persia*, London.

Hawkins, John David (2000) *Corpus of Hieroglyphic Luwian Inscriptions: Inscriptions of the Iron Age*, Berlin.

Healy, John F. (1990) *The Early Alphabet*, London.

Heimpel, Wolfgang (2003) *Letters to the King of Mari. A New Translation with Historical Introduction, Notes, and Commentary*, Winona Lake, IN.

Heinz, Marlies and Marian H. Feldman, eds. (2007) *Representations of Political Power: Case Histories in Times of Change and Dissolving Order in the Ancient Near East*, Winona Lake, IN.

Hoffner, Harry A. Jr. (1980) "Histories and Historians of the Ancient Near East: The Hittites," *Orientalia* **49**: 283–332.

Hoffner, Harry A. Jr. (1992) "The Last Days of Khattusha," in *The Crisis Years. The 12th century BC*, ed. William A. Ward and Martha S. Joukowsky, Dubuque, Iowa: 46–52.

Hoffner, Harry A. Jr. (2009) *Letters from the Hittite Kingdom*, Atlanta.

Hunger, H. (1968) *Babylonische und assyrische Kolophone*, Kevelaer.

Jacobsen, Thorkild (1943) "Primitive Democracy in Ancient Mesopotamia," *Journal of Near Eastern Studies* **2**: 159–72.

Jacobsen, Thorkild (1976) *The Treasure of Darkness*, New Haven and London.

Jahn, Brit (2007) "The Migration and Sedentarization of the Amorites from the Point of View of the Settled Babylonian Population," in Heinz and Feldman 2007: 193–209.

Jennings, Justin (2011) *Globalizations and the Ancient World*, Cambridge and New York.

Joannès, Francis (2004) *The Age of Empires: Mesopotamia in the First Millennium BC*, trans. Antonia Nevill, Edinburgh.

Jursa, Michael (2005) *Neo-Babylonian Legal and Administrative Documents. Typology, Contents and Archives*, Munster.

Jursa, Michael (2010) *Aspects of the Economic History of Babylonia in the First Millennium BC*, Munster.

Jursa, Michael (2013) "The Babylonian Economy in the Sixth and Early Fifth Centuries BC: Monetization, Agrarian Expansion and Economic Growth," in *L'economia dell'antica Mesopotamia (III–I millennio a.C.) Per un dialogo interdisciplinare*, ed. Franco D'Agostino, Rome: 67–89.

Kitchen, K. A. (2007) "Egyptian and Related Chronologies – Look, no Sciences, no Pots!," in Bietak 2000–7, Vol. III: 163–72.

Klengel, Horst (1992) *Syria: 3000 to 300 BC*, Berlin.

Klengel, Horst (1999) *Geschichte des hethitischen Reiches*, Leiden.

Knapp, A. B., ed. (1996) *Sources for the History of Cyprus. Volume 2: Near Eastern and Aegean Texts from the Third to the First Millennia BC*, Albany, NY.

Koch-Westenholz, Ulla (2000) *Babylonian Liver Omens*, Copenhagen.

Kohler, J. and F. E. Peiser (1904–23) *Hammurabi's Gesetz*, Leipzig.

Koldewey, Robert (1914) *The Excavations at Babylon*, London.

König, Friedrich W. (1965) *Die elamischen Königsinschriften*, Graz.

Kraus, F. R. (1957–8) "Assyrisch imperialisme," *Jaarbericht van het Vooraziatisch-Egyptisch Gezelschap "Ex Oriente Lux"* **15**: 232–39.

Kraus, F. R. (1960) "Ein zentrales Problem des altmesopotamischen Rechts: Was ist der Codex Hammu-rabi?" *Genava* **8**: 383–96.

Kraus, F. R. (1968) *Briefe aus dem Archiv des Shamash-hazir*, Leiden.

Kroll, S. et al., eds. (2012) *Biainili-Urartu*, Louvain.

Kuhrt, Amélie (1995) *The Ancient Near East c. 3000–330 BC*, 2 vols., London and New York.

Kuhrt, Amélie (2001) "The Achaemenid Persian Empire (c. 550–c. 330 BCE): continuities, adaptations, transformations," in *Empires: Perspectives from Archaeology and History*, ed. S. Alcock et al., Cambridge: 93–123.

Kuhrt, Amélie (2007a) *The Persian Empire. A Corpus of Sources from the Achaemenid Period*, 2 vols., London and New York.

Kuhrt, Amélie (2007b) "Cyrus the Great of Persia: Images and Realities," in Heinz and Feldman 2007: 169–91.

Kupper, Jean-Robert (1957) *Les nomades en Mésopotamie au temps des rois de Mari*, Paris.

Labat, René (1951) *Traité akkadien de diagnostics et prognostics médicaux*, Paris.

Labat, René (1967) "Assyrien und seine Nachbarländer (Babylonien, Elam, Iran) von 1000 bis 617 v. Chr.," in *Fischer Weltgeschichte* Bd. 4: *Die Altorientalischen Reiche* III, ed. J. Bottéro, E. Cassin and J. Vercouter: 9–111.

Lambert, W. G. (1960) *Babylonian Wisdom Literature*, Oxford.

Lanfranchi, Giovanni B. and Simo Parpola (1990) *The Correspondence of Sargon II, Part II. Letters from the Northern and Northeastern Provinces* (State Archives of Assyria 5), Helsinki.

Lanfranchi, Giovanni B. et al., eds. (2003) *Continuity of Empire(?) Assyria, Media, Persia*, Padua.

Larsen, Mogens Trolle (1979) "The Tradition of Empire in Mesopotamia," in *Power and Propaganda*, ed. Mogens Trolle Larsen, Copenhagen: 75–103.

Leichty, Erle (2011) *The Royal Inscriptions of Esarhaddon, King of Assyria (680–669 BC)*, Winona Lake, IN.

Leick, Gwendolyn, ed. (2007) *The Babylonian World*, London and New York.

Lion, Brigitte (2011) "Literacy and Gender," in Radner and Robson 2011: 90–112.

Liverani, Mario (1965) "Il fuoruscitismo in Siria nella tarda età del bronzo," *Rivista Storica Italiana* 77: 315–36.

Liverani, Mario (1988a) *Antico Oriente. Storia, società, economia*, Rome and Bari.

Liverani, Mario (1988b) "The Growth of the Assyrian Empire in the Habur/Middle Euphrates Area: A New Paradigm," *State Archives of Assyria Bulletin* 2: 81–98.

Liverani, Mario (1990) *Prestige and Interest*, Padua.

Liverani, Mario (1993a) "Model and Actualization. The Kings of Akkad in the Historical Tradition," in Liverani 1993b: 41–67.

Liverani, Mario, ed. (1993b) *Akkad, the First World Empire*, Padua.

Liverani, Mario (1997) "Ramesside Egypt in a Changing World. An Institutional Approach," in *L'impero ramesside*, Rome: 101–15.

Liverani, Mario (2001a) *International Relations in the Ancient Near East, 1600–1100 BC*, New York.

Liverani, Mario (2001b) "The Fall of the Assyrian Empire: Ancient and Modern Interpretations," in *Empires: Perspectives from Archaeology and History*, ed. S. Alcock et al., Cambridge: 374–91.

Liverani, Mario (2004) *Myth and Politics in Ancient Near Eastern Historiography*, London.

Liverani, Mario (2005a) *Israel's History and the History of Israel*, trans. C. Peri and P. R. Davies, London.

Liverani, Mario, ed. (2005b) *Recenti tendenze nella ricostruzione della storia antica d'Israele: convegno internazionale: Roma, 6–7 marzo 2003*, Rome.

Liverani, Mario (2006) *Uruk: The First City*, trans. Z. Bahrani and M. Van De Mieroop, London.

Liverani, Mario (2014) *The Ancient Near East: History, Society and Economy*, London.

Livingstone, Alasdair (2007) "Ashurbanipal: Literate or Not?," *Zeitschrift für Assyriologie* 97: 98–118.

Longman, Tremper III (1991) *Fictional Akkadian Autobiography*, Winona Lake, IN.

Loretz, Oswald (1984) *Habiru-Hebräer*, Berlin and New York.

Luckenbill, Daniel David (1924) *The Annals of Sennacherib*, Chicago.

Luukko, Mikko and Greta Van Buylaere (2002) *The Political Correspondence of Esarhaddon* (State Archives of Assyria 16), Helsinki.

Machinist, Peter (1982) "Provincial Governance in Middle Assyria," *Assur* **3/2**: 1–37.

Maekawa, Kazuya (1973–4) "The Development of the é-mí in Lagash during Early Dynastic III," *Mesopotamia* **8–9**: 77–144.

Maidman, Maynard Paul (2010) *Nuzi Texts and Their Uses as Historical Evidence*, Leiden and Boston.

Malbran-Labat, Florence (1994) *La Version akkadienne de l'inscription trilingue de Darius à Behistun*, Rome.

Manning, S. W. (1999) *A Test of Time: The Volcano of Thera and the Chronology and History of the Aegean and East Mediterranean in the Mid Second Millennium BC*, Oxford.

Manning, S. W., et al. (2006) "Chronology for the Aegean Late Bronze Age 1700–1400 BC," *Science* **312**: 565–9.

Marchesi, Gianni (2004) "Who Was Buried in the Royal Tombs of Ur? The Epigraphic and Textual Data," *Orientalia* **73**: 153–97.

Markoe, Glenn E. (2000) *Phoenicians*, Berkeley and Los Angeles.

Matthews, Roger (1993) *Cities, Seals and Writing: Archaic Seal Impressions from Jemdet Nasr and Ur*, Berlin.

Matthews, Roger (2003) *The Archaeology of Mesopotamia. Theories and Approaches*, London.

Matthiae, Paolo (2010) *Ebla. La città del trono*, Turin.

Mayrhofer, Manfred (1975) "Kleinasien zwischen Agonie des Perserreiches und hellenistischen Frühling," *Anzeiger der österreichischen Akademie der Wissenschaften. Philosophisch-Historische Klasse* **112**: 274–82.

Mebert, Joachim (2010) *Die Venustafeln des Ammī-ṣaduqa und ihre Bedeutung für die astronomische Datierung der altbabylonischen Zeit*, Vienna.

Michalowski, Piotr (1993) *Letters from Early Mesopotamia*, Atlanta.

Michalowski, Piotr (2003) "The Doors of the Past," *Eretz Israel* **27**: 136–52.

Michalowski, Piotr (2011) *The Correspondence of the Kings of Ur*, Winona Lake, IN.

Michel, Cécile (2001) *Correspondance des marchands de Kanish*, Paris.

Milano, Lucio (1995) "Ebla: A Third Millennium City-State in Ancient Syria," in Sasson 1995: 1219–30.

Milano, Lucio, ed. (2012) *Il Vicino Oriente antico dalle origini ad Alessandro Magno*, Milan.

Millard, Alan (1994) *The Eponyms of the Assyrian Empire, 910–612*, Helsinki.

Molleson, Theya (1994) "The Eloquent Bones of Abu Hureyra," *Scientific American* **271/2** (August): 70–5.

Moorey, P. R. S. (1977) "What Do We Know about the People Buried in the Royal Cemetery?" *Expedition* **20**(1): 24–40.

Moorey, P. R. S. (1995) *From Gulf to Delta and Beyond*, Beer-Sheva.

Moran, William L. (1992) *The Amarna Letters*, Baltimore and London.

Moscati, Sabatino (1960) *The Face of the Ancient Orient: A Panorama of Near Eastern Civilizations in Pre-Classical Times*, Garden City, NY.

Naveh, Joseph and Shaul Shaked (2012) *Aramaic Documents from Ancient Bactria (Fourth Century BCE)*, London.

Niehr, Herbert, ed. (2014) *The Arameans in Ancient Syria*, Leiden and Boston.

Nissen, Hans J. (1988) *The Early History of the Ancient Near East. 9000–2000 BC*, trans. E. Lutzeier and K. Northcutt, Chicago and London.

Nissen, Hans J., Peter Damerow, and Robert K. Englund (1993) *Archaic Bookkeeping. Early Writing and Techniques of Economic Administration in the Ancient Near East*, Chicago and London.

Oates, Joan and David (2001) *Nimrud. An Assyrian Imperial City Revealed,* London.

Oded, Bustenay (1979) *Mass Deportations and Deportees in the Neo-Assyrian Empire,* Wiesbaden.

Olmstead, A. T. (1948) *History of the Persian Empire,* Chicago.

Onasch, Hans-Ulrich (1994) *Die assyrischen Eroberungen Ägyptens,* Wiesbaden.

Oppenheim, A. Leo (1977) *Ancient Mesopotamia,* 2nd ed., Chicago.

Owen, David I. (2013) "The Archive of Iri-Sagrig/Āl-Šarrākī: A Brief Survey," in *From the 21st Century BC to the 21st Century AD: The Present and Future of Neo-Sumerian Studies,* ed. Manuel Molina and Steven Garfinkle, Winona Lake, IN: 89–102.

Pagden, Anthony (2008) *Worlds at War. The 2,500-Year Struggle between East and West,* New York.

Parker, Barbara (1961) "Administrative Tablets from the North-West Palace, Nimrud," *Iraq* **23**: 15–67.

Parpola, Simo (1987) *The Correspondence of Sargon II, Part I. Letters from Assyria and the West* (State Archives of Assyria 1), Helsinki.

Parpola, Simo (1993) *Letters from Assyrian and Babylonian Scholars* (State Archives of Assyria 10), Helsinki.

Parpola, Simo (1997) "The Man without a Scribe and the Question of Literacy in the Assyrian Empire," in *Ana šadî Labnaāni lū allik: Beiträge zu altorientalischen und mittelmeerischen Kulturen Festschrift für Wolfgang Röllig,* ed. Beate Pongratz-Leisten et al., Kevelaer and Neukirchen-Vluyn: 315–24.

Parpola, Simo and Kazuko Watanabe (1988) *Neo-Assyrian Treaties and Loyalty Oaths* (State Archives of Assyria 2), Helsinki.

Parpola, Simo and R. M. Whiting, eds. (1997) *Assyria 1995,* Helsinki.

Pettinato, Giovanni (1991) *Ebla. A New Look at History,* Baltimore.

Podany, Amanda (2002) *The Land of Hana,* Bethesda, MD.

Podany, Amanda (2010) *Brotherhood of Kings,* Oxford.

Podany, Amanda (2014) *The Ancient Near East: A Very Short Introduction,* Oxford.

Pollock, Susan (1999) *Ancient Mesopotamia. The Eden that Never Was,* Cambridge.

Pollock, Susan (2007) "The Royal Cemetery of Ur: Ritual, Tradition, and the Creation of Subjects," in Heinz and Feldman 2007: 89–110.

Pongratz-Leisten, Beate (1999) *Herrschaftswissen in Mesopotamien,* Helsinki.

Porter, Barbara N. (1993) *Images, Power, and Politics. Figurative Aspects of Esarhaddon's Babylonian Policy,* Philadelphia.

Postgate, J. N. (1992a) *Early Mesopotamia: Society and Economy at the Dawn of History,* London.

Postgate, J. N. (1992b) "The Land of Assur and the Yoke of Assur," *World Archaeology* **23**: 247–63.

Postgate, J. N. (2013) *Bronze Age Bureaucracy. Writing and the Practice of Government in Assyria,* Cambridge.

Potts, D. T. (1990) *The Arabian Gulf in Antiquity,* Oxford.

Potts, D. T. (1997) *Mesopotamian Civilization. The Material Foundations,* Ithaca.

Potts, D. T. (1999) *The Archaeology of Elam,* Cambridge.

Potts, Dan, ed. (2012) *A Companion to the Archaeology of the Ancient Near East,* Oxford.

Potts, Dan, ed. (2013) *The Oxford Handbook of Ancient Iran,* Oxford and New York.

Potts, Timothy (2001) "Reading the Sargonic 'Historical-Literary' Tradition. Is There a Middle Course?," in Abusch et al. 2001: 391–408.

Pournelle, Jennifer R. (2013) "Physical Geography," in Crawford 2013: 13–32.

Pritchard, James B., ed. (1969) *Ancient Near Eastern Texts Relating to the Old Testament*, 3rd ed., Princeton.

Pruzsinszky, Regine (2009) *Mesopotamian Chronology of the 2nd millennium BC: An Introduction to the Textual Evidence and Related Chronological Issues*, Vienna.

Radner, Karen (2011) "Assyrians and Urartians," in Steadman and McMahon 2011: 734–51.

Radner, Karen (2013) "Assyria and the Medes," in Potts 2013: 442–56.

Radner, Karen and Eleanor Robson, eds. (2011) *The Oxford Handbook of Cuneiform Culture*, Oxford and New York.

Reiner, Erica and David Pingree (1975) *Babylonian Planetary Omens*, Malibu.

Renger, Johannes (2002) "Royal Edicts of the Old Babylonian Period – Structural Background," in *Debt and Economic Renewal in the Ancient Near East*, ed. M. Hudson and M. Van De Mieroop, Bethesda, MD: 139–62.

Roaf, Michael (1990) *Cultural Atlas of Mesopotamia and the Ancient Near East*, Oxford.

Roaf, Michael (2012) "The Fall of Babylon in 1499 NC or 1595 MC," *Akkadica* **133**: 147–74.

Robson, Eleanor (1999) *Mesopotamian Mathematics, 2100–1600 BC*, Oxford.

Rochberg, Francesca (2004) *The Heavenly Writing. Divination, Horoscopy, and Astronomy in Mesopotamian Culture*, Cambridge.

Roth, Martha T. (1984) *Babylonian Marriage Agreements 7th–3rd Centuries BC*, Kevelaer.

Roth, Martha T. (1997) *Law Collections from Mesopotamia and Asia Minor*, 2nd ed., Atlanta.

Rothman, Mitchell S., ed. (2001) *Uruk Mesopotamia & Its Neighbors*, Santa Fe.

Rothman, Mitchell S. (2004) "Studying the Development of Complex Society: Mesopotamia in the Late Fifth and Fourth Millennia BC," *Journal of Archaeological Research* **12**: 75–119.

Rowton, Michael B. (1965) "The Topological Factor in the Hapiru Problem," *Studies in Honor of Benno Landsberger*, Chicago: 375–87.

Sack, Ronald H. (1972) *Amel-Marduk 562–560 BC*, Kevelaer.

Sack, Ronald H. (2004) *Images of Nebuchadnezzar*, 2nd ed., Selingsgrove.

Saggs, H. W. F. (1984) *The Might that Was Assyria*, London.

Sagona, Antonio and Paul Zimansky (2009) *Ancient Turkey*, London and New York.

Sallaberger, Walther (2007) "From Urban Culture to Nomadism: A History of Upper Mesopotamia in the Late Third Millennium," in *Sociétés humaines et changement climatique à la fin du troisième millénaire: une crise a-t-elle eu lieu en Haute Mésopotamie?*, ed. C. Kuzuzuoglu and C. Marro, Paris: 417–56.

Sallaberger, Walther and Aage Westenholz (1999) *Mesopotamien. Akkade-Zeit und Ur III Zeit*, Fribourg and Göttingen.

Salvini, Mirjo (1995) *Geschichte und Kultur der Urartäer*, Darmstadt.

Salvini, Mirjo (1998) "The Earliest Evidences of the Hurrians before the Formation of the Reign of Mittanni," in *Urkesh and the Hurrians. Studies in Honor of Lloyd Cotsen*, ed. G. Buccellati and M. Kelly-Buccellati, Malibu: 99–115.

Salvini, Mirjo (2008–12) *Corpus dei testi urartei*, 4 vols., Rome.

Salvini, Mirjo and Ilse Wegner (1986) *Die Rituale des AZU-Priesters*, Rome.

Sancisi-Weerdenburg, Heleen (1987) "Decadence in the Empire or Decadence in the Sources?," in *Achaemenid History I. Sources, Structures and Synthesis*, ed. H. Sancisi-Weerdenburg, Leiden: 33–45.

Sassmannshausen, Leonard (2001) *Beiträge zur Verwaltung und Gesellschaft Babyloniens in der Kassitenzeit*, Mainz.

Sassmannshausen, Leonard (2004) "Kassite Nomads. Fact or Fiction?" in *Nomades et sédentaires dans le proche-orient ancien*, ed. C. Nicolle, Paris: 287–305.

Sasson, Jack M., ed. (1995) *Civilizations of the Ancient Near East*, 4 vols., New York.

Schaudig, Hanspeter (2001) *Die Inschriften Nabonids von Babylon und Kyros' des Großen*, Munster.

Schmandt-Besserat, Denise (1992) *Before Writing*, Austin.

Schmidt, Klaus (2011) "Göbekli Tepe: A Neolithic Site in Southeastern Anatolia," in Steadman and McMahon 2011: 917–33.

Schmitt, Rüdiger (2009) *Die altpersischen Inschriften der Achaemeniden*, Wiesbaden.

Schwartz, Glenn (1995) "Pastoral Nomadism in Ancient Western Asia," in Sasson 1995: 249–58.

Seeher, Jürgen (2001) "Die Zerstörung der Stadt Ḫattuša," in *Akten des IV. Internationalen Kongresses für Hethitologie Würzburg, 4.–8. Oktober 1999*, ed. G. Wilhelm, Wiesbaden: 623–34.

Selz, Gebhard J. (1989) *Die altsumerischen Wirtschaftsurkunden der Ermitage zu Leningrad*, Wiesbaden.

Seri, Andrea (2013) *The House of Prisoners. Slavery and State in Uruk during the Revolt against Samsu-iluna*, Boston and Berlin.

Sharlach, Tonia M. (2004) *Provincial Taxation and the Ur III State*, Leiden.

Sherratt, Susan (2003) "The Mediterranean Economy: 'Globalization' at the End of the Second Millennium BCE," in *Symbiosis, Symbolism, and the Power of the Past: Canaan, Ancient Israel, and Their Neighbors from the Late Bronze Age through Roman Palaestina*, ed. W. G. Dever and S. Gitin, Winona Lake, IN: 37–54.

Singer, Itamar (1991) "A Concise History of Amurru," in Shlomo Izre'el, *Amurru Akkadian*, Vol. II, Atlanta: 134–95.

Snell, Daniel C., ed. (2005) *A Companion to the Ancient Near East*, Oxford.

Starr, Ivan (1990) *Queries to the Sungod* (State Archives of Assyria 4), Helsinki.

Steadman, Sharon R. and Gregory McMahon, eds. (2011) *The Oxford Handbook of Ancient Anatolia, 10,000–323 BCE*, Oxford and New York.

Steinkeller, Piotr (1987) "The Administrative and Economic Organization of the Ur III State: The Core and the Periphery," in *The Organization of Power. Aspects of Bureaucracy in the Ancient Near East*, ed. McGuire Gibson and R. D. Biggs, Chicago: 19–41.

Steinkeller, Piotr (2002) "Archaic City Seals and the Question of Early Babylonian Unity," in *Riches Hidden in Secret Places. Ancient Near Eastern Studies in Memory of Thorkild Jacobsen*, ed. Tzvi Abusch, Winona Lake, IN: 249–57.

Steinkeller, Piotr (2003) "Archival Practices at Babylonia in the Third Millennium," in *Ancient Archives and Archival Traditions*, ed. M. Brosius, Oxford: 37–58.

Steinkeller, Piotr (2013) "Puzur-Inshushinak at Susa: A Pivotal Episode in Early Elamite History Reconsidered," in *Susa and Elam: Archaeological, Philological, Historical and Geographical Perspectives*, ed. Katrien de Graef and Jan Tavernier, Leiden: 293–317.

Stern, Ephraim (2001) *Archaeology of the Land of the Bible. II: The Assyrian, Babylonian, and Persian Periods, 732–322 BCE*, New York.

Stol, Marten (2004) "Wirtschaft und Gesellschaft in altbabylonischer Zeit," in Charpin, Edzard and Stol 2004: 643–975.

Stolper, Matthew W. (1985) *Entrepreneurs and Empire*, Istanbul.

Tadmor, Hayim and Shigeo Yamada (2011) *The Royal Inscriptions of Tiglath-pileser III (744–727 BC) and Shalmaneser V (726–722 BC), Kings of Assyria*, Winona Lake, IN.

Thureau-Dangin, François (1912) *Une relation de la huitième campagne de Sargon*, Paris.

Tinney, Steve (1998) "Texts, Tablets, and Teaching. Scribal Education in Nippur and Ur," *Expedition* **40/2**: 40–50.

Ur, Jason (2014) "Households and the Emergence of Cities in Ancient Mesopotamia," *Cambridge Archaeological Journal* **24**: 249–68.

Van De Mieroop, Marc (1992) *Society and Enterprise in Old Babylonian Ur*, Berlin.

Van De Mieroop, Marc (1997) "On Writing a History of the Ancient Near East," *Bibliotheca Orientalis* **54**: 285–306.

Van De Mieroop, Marc (1999a) *Cuneiform Texts and the Writing of History*, London.

Van De Mieroop, Marc (1999b) *The Ancient Mesopotamian City*, Oxford.

Van De Mieroop, Marc (1999c) "Literature and Political Discourse in Ancient Mesopotamia. Sargon II of Assyria and Sargon of Agade," in *Munuscula Mesopotamica. Festschrift für Johannes Renger*, ed. B. Böck et al., Munster: 327–39.

Van De Mieroop, Marc (2000) "Sargon of Agade and his Successors in Anatolia," *Studi Micenei ed Egeo-Anatolici* **42**: 133–59.

Van De Mieroop, Marc (2003) "Reading Babylon," *American Journal of Archaeology* **107**: 257–75.

Van De Mieroop, Marc (2005) *King Hammurabi of Babylon: A Biography*, Oxford.

Van De Mieroop, Marc (2007) *The Eastern Mediterranean in the Age of Ramesses II*, Oxford.

Vanderhooft, David S. (1999) *The Neo-Babylonian Empire and Babylon in the Latter Prophets*, Atlanta.

Van der Spek, R. J. (2008) "Berossus as a Babylonian Chronicler and Greek Historian," in *Studies in Ancient Near Eastern World View and Society: Presented to Marten Stol on the Occasion of his 65th Birthday*, ed. R. J. van der Spek, Bethesda, MD: 277–317.

Van Lerberghe, Karel (1995) "Kassites and Old Babylonian Society. A Reappraisal," in *Immigration and Emigration within the Ancient Near East. Festschrift E. Lipinski*, ed. K. Van Lerberghe and A. Schoors, Louvain: 381–93.

Vanstiphout, H. L. J. (2004) *Epics of Sumerian kings: The Matter of Aratta*, Atlanta.

Veenhof, Klaas R. (1997–2000) "The Relation between Royal Decrees and Law Collections in the Old Babylonian Period," *Jaarbericht van het Vooraziatisch-Egyptisch Genootschap Ex Oriente Lux* **35/36**: 49–83.

Veenhof, Klaas R. (2003) "Archives of Old Assyrian Traders," in *Ancient Archives and Archival Traditions*, ed. M. Brosius, Oxford: 78–123.

Veenhof, Klaas R. and Jesper Eidem (2008) *Mesopotamia. The Old Assyrian Period*, Fribourg and Göttingen.

Veldhuis, Niek (2011) "Levels of Literacy," in Radner and Robson 2011: 68–89.

Veldhuis, Niek (2014) *History of the Cuneiform Lexical Tradition*, Munster.

Vidale, Massimo (2011) "PG 1237, Royal Cemetery of Ur: Patterns in Death," *Cambridge Archaeological Journal* **21**: 427–51.

Villard, Pierre (1997) "L'éducation d'Assurbanipal," *Ktema* **22**: 135–49.

Visicato, Giuseppe (1995) *The Bureaucracy of Shuruppak*, Munster.

Von Dassow, Eva (2008) *State and Society in the Late Bronze Age. Alalah under the Mittani Empire*, Bethesda, MD.

Von Soden, Wolfram (1937) *Der Aufstieg des Assyrerreichs als geschichtliches Problem* (Der alte Orient 37 1/2), Leipzig.

Walker, C. B. F. (1987) *Cuneiform*, London.

Waters, Matthew W. (2000) *A Survey of Neo-Elamite History*, Helsinki.

Watkins, Trevor (2010) "New Light on Neolithic Revolution in South-West Asia," *Antiquity* **84**: 621–34.

Watson, Wilfred G. E. and Nicolas Wyatt, eds. (1999) *Handbook of Ugaritic Studies*, Leiden.

Wells, Bruce (2005) "Law and Practice" in Snell 2005: 199–211.

Westbrook, Raymond (1989) "Cuneiform Law Codes and the Origins of Legislation," *Zeitschrift für Assyriologie* **79**: 201–22.

Westenholz, Joan (1997) *Legends of the Kings of Akkade*, Winona Lake, IN.

Wetzel, Friedrich and F. H. Weissbach (1938) *Das Hauptheiligtum des Marduk in Babylon, Esagila und Etemenanki*, Leipzig.

Whiting, Robert (1995) "Amorite Tribes and Nations of Second-Millennium Western Asia," in Sasson 1995: 1231–42.

Wiener, M. H. (2003) "Time Out: The Current Impasse in Bronze Age Archaeological Dating," in *Metron: Measuring the Aegean Bronze Age*, ed. K. Polinger Foster and R. Laffineur, Liege: 363–99.

Wiener, M. H. (2007) "Times Change: The Current State of the Debate in Old World Chronology," in Bietak 2000–7, Vol. III: 25–64.

Wiesehöfer, Josef (1996) *Ancient Persia from 550 BC to 650 AD*, London and New York.

Wiesehöfer, Josef (2007) "The Achaemenid Empire in the Fourth Century BCE: A Period of Decline?" in *Judah and the Judeans in the Fourth Century BCE*, ed. Oded Lipschits et al., Winona Lake, IN: 11–30.

Wiesehöfer, Josef (2009) "The Achaemenid Empire," in *The Dynamics of Ancient Empires*, ed. Ian Morris and Walter Scheidel, Oxford: 66–98.

Wilcke, Claus (1989) "Genealogical and Geographical Thought in the Sumerian King List," in *DUMU-E₂-DUB-BA-A: Studies in Honor of Åke W. Sjöberg*, ed. H. Behrens et al., Philadelphia: 557–71.

Wilcke, Claus (2000) *Wer las und schrieb in Babylonien und Assyrien. Überlegungen zur Literalität im Alten Zweistromland*. Bayerische Akademie der Wissenschaften. Philologisch-Historische Klasse. Sitzungsberichte. Jahrgang 2000, Heft 6. Munich.

Wilhelm, Gernot (1989) *The Hurrians*, Warminster.

Williamson, H. G. M., ed. (2007) *Understanding the History of Ancient Israel*, Oxford and New York.

Winter, Irene J. (2000) "Babylonian Archaeologists of The(ir) Mesopotamian Past," in *Proceedings of the First International Congress on the Archaeology of the Ancient Near East*, ed. P. Matthiae et al., Rome: 1785–800.

Wiseman, D. J. (1985) *Nebuchadrezzar and Babylon*, Oxford.

Woolley, Leonard (1982) *Ur "of the Chaldees,"* rev. and updated by P. R. S. Moorey, London.

Woolmer, Mark (2011) *Ancient Phoenicia: An Introduction*, London.

Wright, Henry T. and Gregory A. Johnson (1975) "Population, Exchange, and Early State Formation in Southwestern Iran," *American Anthropologist* **77**: 267–89.

Wullen, Moritz and Günther Schauerte, eds. (2008) *Babylon: Mythos*, Berlin.

Wunsch, Cornelia (2007) "The Egibi Family," in Leick 2007: 236–47.

Wunsch, Cornelia (2013) "Glimpses on the Lives of Deportees in Rural Babylonia," in *Arameans, Chaldeans, and Arabs in Babylonia and Palestine in the First Millennium BC*, ed. Angelika Berlejung and Michael P. Streck, Wiesbaden: 247–60.

Yoffee, Norman (1988) "The Collapse of Ancient Mesopotamian States and Civilization," in *The Collapse of Ancient States and Civilizations*, ed. N. Yoffee and G. Cowgill, Tuscon: 44–68.

Yoffee, Norman (2005) *Myths of the Archaic State: Evolution of the Earliest Cities, States and Civilization*, Cambridge.

Zamazalová, Silvie (2011) "The Education of Neo-Assyrian Princes," in Radner and Robson 2011: 313–30.

Zettler Richard L. and Lee Horne, eds. (1998) *Treasures from the Royal Tombs at Ur*, Philadelphia.

Zimansky, Paul (2005) "Archaeology and Texts in the Ancient Near East," in *Archaeologies of the Middle East. Critical Perspectives*, ed. S. Pollock and R. Bernbeck, Oxford: 308–26.

Zimansky, Paul (2011) "Urartian and the Urartians," in Steadman and McMahon 2011: 548–59.

Comprehensive Time Line

Political and military events	Cultural and technological developments
	11,000–7,000: development of agriculture
	ca. 6500: introduction of pottery
	ca. 5500: irrigation agriculture introduced in Babylonia
ca. 3400: appearance of the first city: Uruk	ca. 3400: invention of writing and tools of bureaucracy in Babylonia; start of use of bronze
ca. 3100: rise of city-state system in Babylonia	
2900–2288: Early Dynastic Babylonia	
ca. 2500–2350: Lagash–Umma border conflict in Babylonia	ca. 2500: earliest royal inscriptions from Babylonia
ca. 2400 Uru'inimgina of Lagash	ca. 2350: bilingual lexical lists at Ebla
2288–2111: Old Akkadian period	
2288: accession of Sargon of Akkad	
2288–2175: Akkadian military actions throughout Near East	ca. 2200: Naram-Sin declares himself a god; lost wax technique used in copper casting
ca. 2150: unraveling of Akkad's hegemony	
2110–2003: Ur III period in Babylonia	
ca. 2100: Puzur-Inshushinak of Awan unifies southwest Iran	

A History of the Ancient Near East ca. 3000–323 BC, Third Edition. Marc Van De Mieroop.
© 2016 John Wiley & Sons, Inc. Published 2016 by John Wiley & Sons, Inc.

Political and military events	Cultural and technological developments
ca. 2070: Shulgi creates Ur III state organization; unification of Babylonia	21st century: creation of royal celebratory literature in Sumerian
2003: Elamites capture Ur and its king Ibbi-Sin	
2003–1792: Isin–Larsa period in Babylonia	
2000–1775: Old Assyrian period in northern Mesopotamia	
1898: start of open warfare between the city-states of Babylonia	
ca. 1850: Eshnunna establishes hegemony over Diyala region, Mari over Middle Euphrates valley	19th–18th centuries: southern Babylonian students copy out Sumerian literary tablets
1793: Rim-Sin of Larsa unifies southern Babylonia	
ca. 1792: Shamshi-Adad creates the Kingdom of Upper Mesopotamia	
1792–1595: Old Babylonian period in Babylonia	
ca. 1775: Zimri-Lim gains kingship at Mari	
1766–1761: Hammurabi of Babylon eliminates his competitors	1755: Hammurabi sets up his law code
1712: southern Babylonia enters a Dark Age	18th–17th centuries: development of Akkadian-language literature
Early or mid-17th century: Hattusili I creates Old Hittite state	
1595: Hittite King Mursili I sacks Babylon	
16th century: Dark Age throughout the Near East. Creation of the Kassite state in Babylonia	16th century: introduction of the horse and chariot in the Near East
1500–1100: Middle Babylonian period in Babylonia; Middle Elamite period in southwest Iran	
ca. 1500: first evidence of Mittani state in northern Syria	
early 15th century: Egyptian raids in northern Syria	ca. 1450–1200: Babylonia's literate culture dominates the Near East
1400–1200: New Kingdom in Hittite history	
1400–1100: Middle Assyrian period in Assyria	
1365–1335: Mittani state dissolves into two parts subject to outsiders	

Political and military events	Cultural and technological developments
1353–1318: Assyria emerges as major power under Assur-uballit I	
1344–1322: Suppiluliuma I extends Hittite control over Syria	
13th century: sustained Assyrian expansion	
1274: battle of Qadesh between Ramesses II and Muwatalli II	
1259: peace treaty between Ramesses II and Hattusili III	1225: Tukulti-Ninurta I of Assyria brings Babylonian literature home as booty
1200–1177: collapse of the Late Bronze Age system	
1155: fall of the Kassite dynasty in Babylonia	1158: Shutruk-Nahhunte of Elam brings Babylonian monuments to Susa
ca. 1110: Nebuchadnezzar I sacks Susa	ca. 1110: creation of literature in honor of the god Marduk
Between 1200–900: Arameans gain political power in Syria	Between 1200–900: spread of the linear alphabet; increased use of iron; domestication of the camel; improvements in ship-building technology
900–612: Neo-Assyrian period 9th century. Assyria regains its Middle Assyrian territories	Early 1st millennium: development of local literate traditions in western Near East: Neo-Hittite, Aramaic, Phoenician, Hebrew
ca. 885–874: Omri initiates new dynasty in Israel	
mid-9th century: Sarduri I unifies state of Urartu	
853: Shalmaneser III of Assyria and coalition of western states clash at Qarqar	
823–745: Assyria's power declines	Early 8th century: earliest preserved alphabetic texts in Greece
745: Tiglath-pileser III initiates restructuring of Assyria as an empire	
740–646: Neo-Elamite period in southwest Iran	
722: Shalmaneser V captures Samaria	
714: Sargon II raids Urartu	
695: Cimmerians sack Gordion, capital of Phrygia	
689: Sennacherib sacks Babylon	
671: Esarhaddon invades Egypt	

(continued)

Political and military events	Cultural and technological developments
664–663: Assurbanipal invades Egypt	
652–648: civil war between Assurbanipal and his brother Shamash-shuma-ukin in Babylonia	7th century: Assurbanipal's library at Nineveh
647: Assurbanipal sacks Susa	
626–539: Neo-Babylonian period	
612: sack of Nineveh and Assyrian retreat to the west	
605: Nebuchadnezzar II wins battle of Carchemish	
587: Nebuchadnezzar II sacks Jerusalem	Early 6th century: Nebuchadnezzar rebuilds Babylon
559–331: Persian empire	
539: Cyrus ends Babylonia's independence	555–539: Nabonidus promotes cult of Sin over other Babylonian deities
521: Darius usurps Persia's throne	Late 6th century: Darius commissions the development of the Persian cuneiform alphabet
490 and 480–479: Persia fails to conquer Greece	
484: Xerxes crushes Babylonian rebellions	
401: Cyrus the Younger loses battle of Cunaxa	
331: Alexander enters Babylon	
323: death of Alexander	

Index

References to the terms on maps are in italics.

A History of the Ancient Near East ca. 3000–323 BC, Third Edition. Marc Van De Mieroop.
© 2016 John Wiley & Sons, Inc. Published 2016 by John Wiley & Sons, Inc.